MW00789627

Dear Uncle Sav,,,

Thank you so much for the
support (and presents) all
these years. I still hope
to see the tigers in India.

Love

Hilary

[signature]

TEACHERS AS STATE-BUILDERS

Teachers as State-Builders

EDUCATION AND THE MAKING OF THE MODERN MIDDLE EAST

HILARY FALB KALISMAN

PRINCETON UNIVERSITY PRESS

PRINCETON & OXFORD

Copyright © 2022 by Princeton University Press

Princeton University Press is committed to the protection of copyright and the intellectual property our authors entrust to us. Copyright promotes the progress and integrity of knowledge. Thank you for supporting free speech and the global exchange of ideas by purchasing an authorized edition of this book. If you wish to reproduce or distribute any part of it in any form, please obtain permission.

Requests for permission to reproduce material from this work should be sent to permissions@press.princeton.edu

Published by Princeton University Press
41 William Street, Princeton, New Jersey 08540
99 Banbury Road, Oxford OX2 6JX

press.princeton.edu

All Rights Reserved

ISBN 978-0-691-20433-8
ISBN (pbk.) 978-0-691-23425-0
ISBN (e-book) 978-0-691-20432-1

British Library Cataloging-in-Publication Data is available

Editorial: Fred Appel and James Collier
Production Editorial: Jill Harris
Cover Design: Chris Ferrante
Production: Erin Suydam
Publicity: Kate Hensley and Charlotte Coyne
Copyeditor: Anita O'Brien

Cover image: *Palestine Bursary Students, 1926–1927*. Photograph shows L–R: Mahfuz Ajluni, Ibrahim Matar, Ali R. Sha'th, Husayn Ghunaym, Dimitri Baramki (center), and Olga Wahbeh. American University of Beirut, University Libraries, Archives and Special Collections.

This book has been composed in Arno Pro

10 9 8 7 6 5 4 3 2 1

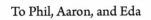

To Phil, Aaron, and Eda

CONTENTS

ILLUSTRATIONS

ACKNOWLEDGMENTS

THE RESEARCH and writing for this book lasted over a decade. It took place in Amman, Beirut, Boulder, Cambridge (Massachusetts), Greenville (South Carolina), Haifa, Jerusalem, London, New York City, Oxford, Palm Beach, al-Salt, Tel Aviv, Wainscott (New York), and Yuvalim.

I could not have completed this book without the financial support and time the following organizations gave me: the Sultan Program of the Center for Middle Eastern Studies at the University of California, Berkeley, the Institute of International Education with funding from the Andrew W. Mellon Foundation, the American Academic Research Institute in Iraq, the National Academy of Education/Spencer Foundation, the John Block Fund at Furman University, and the American Council of Learned Societies.

I would also like to thank the kind staff at the archives I visited, particularly those at the American University of Beirut archive, Beirut's Institute for Palestine Studies, the Middle East Centre at St. Antony's College Oxford, the Israel State Archive, and, in Jordan, the Human Resources Department Archive Section at the Ministry of Education and the Textbook Museum.

The following individuals helped make researching this book not only possible but pleasant: Professors Benjamin C. Fortna, Zainab Saleh, and Sami Zubaida and Emile Cohen, Professors Helene Sader, Louay Bazzi, Nadiya Slobodenyuk, and Lisa Arnold at AUB, especially Louay for his incredible hospitality, as well as Professor Sanjoy Mitter, for his continuing influence on his advisees, Professor Michael Fishbach, Hani Hourani, Dr. Sami Salaita, Lucine Taminian, Professors Yahya Jaber, Elie Podeh, Noga Efrati, the late Shmuel Moreh, and Sasson Somekh, and Dr. Zvi Yehuda.

Thank you to Professor Motti Golani and the Mandate Forum, Professors Graham Allison and Tarek Masoud, as well as the Middle East Initiative at the Belfer Center for Science and International Affairs at the Harvard Kennedy School.

Thank you to Professors Ilana Feldman and Orit Bashkin for their thoughtful reading of my manuscript, and to Orit for her continuing support.

I have benefited from the advice and mentorship of Professors Raka Ray, Stephan Astourian, Susan Pedersen, Salim Tamari, and James Vernon, and particularly from the help of the wonderful Tom Laqueur and of course my invaluable doctoral advisor, Beshara Doumani.

I would like to thank my colleagues at the institutions I have been privileged to be a part of: the history department at Furman University, especially Carolyn Day, Lane Harris, and Savita Nair, as well as Alfonse Teipen. At CU Boulder, my colleagues in both history and Jewish studies have been wonderful, but I give particular thanks to Elias Sacks, Paul Sutter, Beverly Weber, Marcia Yonemoto, Lucy Chester, Natalie Mendoza, John Willis, Samira Mehta, the History Department writing group, and David Shneer. May his memory be for a blessing.

For their advice, assistance, criticism, encouragement, and support, I offer my thanks to Professors Leena Dallasheh, Hannah Farber, Yoni Furas, Callie Maidhof, Maha Nassar, Mezna Qato, Talal al-Rashoud, Tehila Sasson, Julia Shatz, Elizabeth Terry-Roisin, Steven Wagner, Shayna Weiss, and Elizabeth Williams as well as Drs. Nimrod Ben Ze'ev, Doug O'Reagan, and Eli Osheroff.

Liora Halperin has been particularly insightful over the past several years, for which I am very grateful.

My thanks to Nora Barakat, *il miglior fabbro*.

I would also like to thank my friends and family: the late A. Alfred Taubman, Billy Taubman, and especially Bobby Taubman for his continuing support. Thank you to the Kalismans, who have given me several homes away from home, particularly Gayle and Michael, Jason and Josephine, Charles and Rose, Amir and Raya, Nir, Yael, Tamar, Hadas, Uri Sabach and Moran, Oren, Gali, Doron and Yael Maor, and all the wonderful cousins. I thank Anne, Steve, Justin, Ruth, and Greta Ouimette for their sweetness and for being so welcoming. Thank you to Ellie Browne and Yael Elmatad for combining friendship and exercise, and Alexis May for encouraging me. Abigail Cohen gave me her unwavering support, whether or not she knew or cared what I was studying. I thank my sister Alison for her commiseration, help, and understanding. I thank my parents, Peter and Karen Falb, for their love and patience, and for putting up with the difficulties of life, travel, the pandemic, and writing, usually at their dining room table.

Finally, I would like to thank my husband, Phil, and my children, Aaron and Eda. It is to you that I dedicate this book.

TEACHERS AS STATE-BUILDERS

Introduction

IN THE WINTER of 1933, two Palestinian educators wrote to each other across Iraq. Addressing their letters to "my national brother," Akram Zuʾaytir and Darwish al-Miqdadi spoke of Arab unity. They discussed Iraq's demand for teachers, which had brought them, alongside a plethora of educators "from outside," to work in Iraq's education system. Then principal of the secondary school for boys in Mosul, al-Miqdadi asserted that Iraq required "frank" young Arab men who "believed in the Arab cause." Seeking to convince Zuʾaytir, working at the Teachers College in Baghdad, to remain in Iraq rather than return to Palestine, al-Miqdadi added that these ideal young men would also be idealistic, "not greedy for the world, its funds, its government positions, and its leadership."[1]

Despite al-Miqdadi's appeal to the idealism of his "national brother," the interwar era's transnational world of government positions, leadership, and politics was one to which both he and Zuʾaytir were intimately connected. The polities educators crossed were subject to European hegemony, generally in the form of mandates. The League of Nations granted France and Britain authority over areas carved from the defeated Ottoman Empire, allegedly to ease the transition from Ottoman subjects to citizens of modern nation-states. In reality, the mandates also facilitated European colonial norms and influence. By the mid-1930s, Iraq possessed, on paper, a semi-independent status, while Transjordan and Palestine were still under British Mandatory regimes, and Lebanon and Syria were under that of the French. Nevertheless, all were subject to European control.

On his way to Iraq, Zuʾaytir passed through Palestine, Transjordan, and Syria. He met not only with "national brothers" but also with higher officials

1. Zuʾaytir, *Min Mudhakkirat Akram Zuʾaytir* [From the memoirs of Akram Zuʿaytir], 595.

in order to drum up support for Arab nationalism and against Zionism and imperialism.[2] According to Zuʾaytir, whenever he submitted his resignations, the most powerful administrators and ministers in Iraq's education system wrote imploring letters and set up in-person meetings to prevent his defection. When Zuʾaytir returned from Palestine to Iraq to teach in 1935, he and al-Miqdadi joined officials, politicians, various professionals, and other teachers in founding Nadi al-Muthanna. This pan-Arab political club sought "sovereignty for the Arabs, their independence, unity and awakening" while battling "imperialism and the Zionists especially."[3] Its different committees aimed to strengthen the links between Arabs across urban and rural areas, to foster a love of arts and poetry, to improve the bodily health of the Arab youth through exercise, and of course to develop education.[4]

Al-Miqdadi's and Zuʾaytir's entanglement in government service, intersecting Palestinian and pan-Arab politics, and travel continued after the mandates' end. Forced from Palestine due to the creation of the state of Israel and Palestinians' *Nakba* (catastrophe) in 1948, they moved through Turkey, Syria, Lebanon, and elsewhere. In later years, al-Miqdadi and Zuʾaytir would work as government ministers in Kuwait and Jordan, respectively.

Darwish al-Miqdadi and Akram Zuʾaytir are two of the most well-known examples of roving teacher-politicians. The correspondence between himself and al-Miqdadi that Zuʾaytir reproduced in his memoirs demonstrates three key, interrelated aspects of educators in the interwar era: a regional demand for teachers that led them to travel, links between teaching and governance, and a fluid notion of Arab unity, which educators both embodied and promoted. Al-Miqdadi's and Zuʾaytir's transnational stories encapsulate the experiences of roughly two generations of educators, the last of the Ottomans and the first of the mandates, who possessed an intimate and ambivalent relationship with multiple governments. Becoming a teacher in a government school meant joining the region's largest and lowest-ranking group of civil servants, the first step of a government career. Those careers presupposed movement, both in and out of various types of government work, and for various governments. As they traveled, educators goaded the interwar Middle East

2. Zuʾaytir, 581.

3. Zuʾaytir, 693.

4. "Wajib al-shabab: Thawra ʾala al-ghinaʾ al-marid juhud nadi al-Muthanna Ibn Haritha" [Youth's duty: The revolution of the worthy patient, the efforts of the Muthanna Ibn Haritha Club], *Al-Difa*, September 12, 1935, 6, NLIJ.

toward regional and national affiliations. Zuʾaytir and al-Miqdadi, extraordinary in the volume of materials left behind and fame as Palestinian, pan-Arab rabble rousers, were typical in their mobility and rise to power. Altogether, approximately one-third of the prime ministers who served in Iraq from the 1950s through the 1960s and in Jordan from the end of the British mandate through the early 1970s were former teachers in the public schools of Iraq, Transjordan/Jordan, and Palestine. Essentially all had studied or worked abroad.[5]

This book argues that the transnationalism of public school teachers was both crucial to state- and nation-building in the modern Middle East and disruptive of links between state and nation. Drawing from a collective biography of thousands of government teachers, principals, inspectors, and education officials who worked in Britain's Middle Eastern mandates, the book demonstrates the importance of transnationalism to public education, to anti-imperial movements, to nationalism, and to the nation-state. The growth of nationally bounded infrastructures, even those as integral to the construction of the nation-state as public education, was dependent on actors whose bodies and writings transcended these borders. I use the term *transnational* to describe educators and their politics, rather than regional, imperial, or international. This emphasizes the importance of educators' physical and textual movement through states, but also how that movement contributed to states' formation. Paradoxically, educators' travels helped create affiliations beyond the mandates while simultaneously crystallizing the mandate government bureaucracies as national units.

Under colonial rule, public education, a national institution, necessarily promoted regional and transnational notions of affiliation, shaping how individuals situated themselves in relation to separate spheres of nation and state. Educators were petty elites, carrying politics with them from one portion of the region to another. As states became larger, more powerful, and more independent, they became better at and more interested in aligning national ideologies with national borders, and in expanding national education systems in order to do so. The stronger a state, and the more control it had over

5. Suleiman al-Nabulsi, Fawzi al-Mulqi, Wasfi al-Tall, ʿAbd al-Munim al-Rifai, Ahmad Touqan, and Ahmad Lowzi were all teachers in the government schools in Jordan. In Iraq, Mustafa Mahmud al-ʿUmari, Fadhil al-Jamali, Ahmad Mukhtar Baban, Tahir Yahya, and Ahmed Hassan al-Bakr all worked as government school teachers before their turns as prime minister.

government schooling and politics, the less that schooling functioned as a means of becoming part of each government. Educators lost their privileged access to the upper echelons of governance. The easy slippage between regional and national affiliations would collapse into the hardened borders and alliances of nation-states.

In the particular case of Britain's Middle Eastern mandates, British colonial policies purposefully exacerbated a regionwide scarcity of educational institutions and of educators. The lack of even literate individuals forced the growing governments of Iraq, Transjordan, and Palestine to hire teachers where they could. These states drew from Ottoman-era educational hubs, which had become international rather than provincial centers. The circulation of educators, for schooling or for employment during the interwar era, encouraged transnational ideologies that comfortably overlapped with national ones. Public education under British colonial control therefore did not easily link each state solely to a nation encapsulated within each mandate's jurisdiction, even as British control created those jurisdictions in the first place. Moreover, the lack of adequate replacements, and the elite status secondary or even several years of elementary schooling imparted, allowed educators possessing these credentials to criticize the policies and colonial nature of the states that employed them, in print and in demonstrations, without fear of permanent dismissal. Public education not only incorporated a small but increasing segment of the Middle East's population into government service, it also became a key arena of antigovernment activities.

This book follows the arc of educators' changing status across the transition from colonial and elite to national and mass education. As teaching became a profession, educational practices developed increasing consistency within national borders while educators' sociopolitical, and regional role changed. The teachers who simultaneously protested and expanded the mandate governments were a diverse group. Teaching generally represented a means of advancement rather than a career in and of itself. Some teachers came from affluent families, with educations to match that status, attending the region's top public or private institutions. They and their relatives understood teaching to be a temporary and acceptable, if not ideal, stop on the road to work in the administration. Others used public schooling as a means of improving their social and economic status. Managing to obtain a secondary education allowed a select few to break into governance, alongside their more upper-class schoolfellows, as well as the landowning, legally or militarily trained career politicians and military officers who dominated Iraq's and Jordan's parliaments.

Teachers were a promotion or two away from the upper echelons of the civil service and, from there, governance. Zu'aytir's and al-Miqdadi's hobnobbing (and constant correspondence) with Iraq's political elite becomes more understandable if we view public school teachers as part of each mandate state's apparatus. Government educators frequently moved in and out of the civil service at various levels, calling into question the point at which these sometime employees were part of their government or not. Their mobility between states rendered their stories, their ideologies, and necessarily this book transnational.

Educators' integration into their states affected the ways and extent to which they participated in the region's political spheres. Whether or not the Ottoman, mandate, or, in the case of Iraq, postmandate governments were representative, educators benefited from the status quo. Their willingness to draw a government paycheck bolstered those governments' authority. Segments of the population other than public school teachers took up arms and sought their states' overthrow. While educators criticized their governments in writing and in speeches, they tended to avoid joining armed uprisings against those states, in which their students often participated. Educators' textually and verbally audacious yet physically circumspect rebellions point to the ways in which public education, as a state institution, can at once support and undermine the authority of the government.

As Britain's influence receded, postmandate states gained greater capacity to control schooling and educators. These governments also had more of a desire to do so. Freed from restrictive British colonial policies, an often new group of leaders in Iraq, Israel, and Jordan worked to make mass education a reality while improving education standards and professionalizing teaching. Increasing the number of schools and teachers represented a way of extending government authority, improving economies and global standing, while heightening domestic approval.[6]

Expanding schooling in the postcolonial era played a key role in state- and nation-building efforts. I argue that, in the process, mass education severed educators from their governments. The more power governments had over public schooling, the less it functioned as a means of entering the civil service, politics, and the state itself. Increasing access to education gradually rendered educators' formerly rare and valuable qualifications common. By eroding their

---

6. The United Nations Relief and Works Agency for Palestine Refugees in the Near East (UNRWA) also shunted funds and interest toward Palestinian education.

elite status, mass education pushed educators toward collective action: unionization, mass protests and other revolutionary activities. Public school teachers no longer possessed their formerly tangled role, which had combined being a respected civil servant, a member of a growing, transnational middle class, a nationalist rebel, and a potential politician. As they became professionalized and limited to advancement as teachers, their social and economic standing worsened. Simultaneously, educators' mobility over borders changed character, becoming more dependent on the educators' nationality and citizenship (or, in the case of Arab Palestinians, the lack thereof).[7]

The Transnational Civil Servant: State Building and State Boundaries

Governments are meant to possess authority over people within a particular area, or jurisdiction, which is, in the ideal case, separate from the territory belonging to other governments. State building involves consolidating institutions, including government education, that define the territory belonging to the state. Educators in Britain's Middle Eastern mandates were crucial to building state infrastructure as well as bureaucracy. As civil servants, they represented the mandate governments, connecting those states to their subjects, particularly young ones. Yet the movement of educators among various territories while working for multiple governments fashioned new, overlapping relationships between states, on the one hand, and education as a state- and nation-building institution, on the other.

I take modern state building as the processes of creating, re-creating, and strengthening governments. In this definition of state building, diverse processes associated with governments project an image of state coherence, even though the workings of the state may not agree with or may even be at cross purposes with one another. This image includes a state that is separate from non-state actors, society, and other states. As Timothy Mitchell and Joel Migdal have described, states appear coherent and unified but are in fact created through a myriad of practices and "mundane processes" that can overlap with the activities

---

7. Palestinians would often have a Palestinian nationality but therefore no citizenship. For a discussion of the differences between citizenship and nationality in the Palestinian case, see Banko, *The Invention of Palestinian Citizenship*.

of groups "inside and outside the official state borders and often promoting conflicting sets of rules with one another and with "official Law.'"[8]

Analyzing public school teachers across Britain's mandates unearths the difficulty in pinning down states' limits, in terms of where the state ends and society begins, but also where one state becomes separate from another. During the interwar era, though teachers were part of various governments, they acted, and were often viewed by the mandate populations, as separate and frequently antagonistic to their states and employers. Because states are formed of disaggregate institutions that project an image of coherence, the mandate populations could view government schooling less as a means of top-down, colonial control and more as an opportunity for social mobility through state service.

Concurrently, both mandate states and their teachers had to modulate their actions to accommodate each other. Educators rebelled against their governments' imperial goals. Yet states, societies, and educators themselves had little desire for the few literate individuals in the region to be forbidden from teaching. Therefore educators' rebellions not only were relatively nonviolent but also resulted in the teachers remaining in or only temporarily out of state employment. As educators could be fired and rehired within days, they crossed the limits of their states' porous boundaries. When they moved from one government to another, they disrupted correspondence between states, the territory those states purported to govern, and their citizens. The ability of these transnational civil servants both to represent state authority and to leave that state's jurisdiction when they chose to tended to hamper the consolidation of the state's territorial control, even as public education expanded within that territory.

Those states and territories, however, were also in flux. As Cyrus Schayegh argues in the case of Greater Syria, after World War I the mandate states were a particularly fraught set of spatial divisions: their boundaries as well as "British and French imperial infrastructures and policies were superimposed on, cut across, and hence transnationalized Bilad al-Sham, its interurban ties, and its cities' hinterlands."[9] Likewise, the borders of Iraq resulted in transnationalization, cutting links between Baghdad and Istanbul, to say nothing of those between Mosul and Syria or Turkey. Iraq, Palestine, and Transjordan were part

8. Mitchell, "Society, Economy and the State Effect," 185; Migdal, *State in Society*, 22.
9. Schayegh, *The Middle East and the Making of the Modern World*, 137.

of a newly British colonial space, but they had their own governments and infrastructures—most importantly, in our case, that of government education.

The mandate states' infrastructures could not exist without transnational personnel, who moved initially along Ottoman-era pathways between mandates but increasingly took different trajectories within the new map of the region: from Jerusalem to Beirut to Baghdad, rather than to Istanbul and then to other Ottoman provincial cities. Educators therefore extended their states' authority while both working against those states' programs and disrupting their territoriality, creating an uneasy relationship between governments and mobile populations.

Analyses of the relationships between governments and transnational populations nearly always presume that those groups are not only separate from but fundamentally opposed to state control. Nomads have been the transnational subject of choice for scholars of the Middle East, who describe a primordial antagonism between mobile populations and the modern or modernizing state.[10] Newer works have underscored the fallacy of this division: for example, Nora Barakat has shown late-Ottoman Jordan's Bedouin population to be busily involved in the consolidation of governmental authority.[11] This book pushes the discussion forward in time, focusing on actors who are explicitly and inescapably part of states and yet traverse national, rather than provincial, borders. In their banal interactions with children, inspectors, principals, and government officials, public school teachers in Britain's Middle Eastern mandates helped to consolidate new state boundaries while crossing them.

In addition to analyses of transnational individuals, a wave of scholarship since the 1990s has recovered the stories of international organizations, concepts, and networks, as well as their movement between polities. These have focused on the United States or Britain and the world, cross-border movements, the League of Nations, as well as individual mandate governments' interventions due to the problems migrations raised, particularly in terms of disease and taxation.[12] During an era of globalization, with its questions as to the continuing viability and relevance of the nation-state, scholars looked for

10. Deringil, "They Live in a State of Nomadism and Savagery"; Dodge, *Inventing Iraq*; Gibb and Bowen, *Islamic Society and the West*; Massad, *Colonial Effects*; Rogan, *Frontiers of the State in the Late Ottoman Empire*.

11. Barakat, "Marginal Actors?"

12. Kozma, *Global Women, Colonial Ports*.

international or global subjects to study, which did not fit an analytic lens limited to one country or another.

In researching the breakdown of nation-states, however, we must also consider how they were set up in the first place, particularly in light of today's resurgent populist nationalism. Most scholarly narratives presume the nation-state developed after World War I, when links between sovereignty, territorial control, and the nation-state formed and consolidated.[13] This was also the period when scholars began to develop nationalism as a theoretical concept and analytical framework.[14]

During the interwar era, the League of Nations defined an international politics predicated on the idea that nation-states were to be the main actors and that national-self-determination would align the category of nation with its territory. The mandates purported to make new nation-states, but British policy makers (like their French counterparts) hoped to suppress nationalism, which they viewed as naturally subversive to British rule.[15] Iraq, Palestine, and Transjordan, all three conglomerations of smaller Ottoman territorial divisions, were class A mandates, requiring a finite but undefined period of foreign "advice and assistance." This form of governance would prevent other powers from gaining a foothold in the region, satisfy American wishes, and, it was hoped, mollify the local population.

The outcomes of the mandates differed due to a variety of factors, not least of which was the way British officials chose to control each mandate. Palestine remained under direct British control through the end of the mandate in 1948. Unlike Iraq and Jordan, no Arab state of Palestine would succeed to fill its mandate-era borders. The Balfour Declaration, first published on November 2, 1917, and incorporated into the charter of the mandate for Palestine, required the British to "favor the development of a Jewish national home in Palestine," without any actions that would "prejudice" the civil or religious rights of its other inhabitants.[16] The wars at the end of the mandate resulted in the Jewish State of Israel and, for Palestinians, expulsion and exile.

13. Mazower, *Governing the World*, 187–88.

14. Breuilly, "Introduction," in Gellner and Breuilly, *Nations and Nationalism*, xvii.

15. In the case of schooling, British officials attempted to make public education apolitical. See Schneider, *Mandatory Separation*.

16. Council of the League of Nations, *Mandate for Palestine*, July 24, 1922, C. 529. M. 314. 1922. VI.

In Iraq, the British moved to indirect control, including the management of schools and education.[17] While certain British officials had hoped to annex parts of Iraq, by the waning days of 1917 it became clear that the United States and Wilson's principles of self-determination and antipathy toward annexation as peace conditions would restrict British aims in the region, preventing them from turning Iraq into a crown colony.[18] The extremely costly revolts of 1920 led British policy makers to conclude that Iraq was too expensive to govern directly. They made plans to leave Iraq as a constitutional Hashemite monarchy, but one amenable to British interests. By 1932 Iraq was nominally independent, although still subject to British influence, reinforced in 1941 after Iraq's defeat in the brief Anglo-Iraqi War. The Hashemite monarchy's end, and with it Britain's hegemony, came in 1958, in a series of coups and dictatorships.

During the Ottoman period, the area that would become Transjordan was variously part of Palestine, the Northern Hijaz, and Southern Syria.[19] The Hashemite leader Faysal Ibn Hussein Ibn Ali al-Hashimi held brief sway, from March through July 1920, as king in an Arab kingdom centered in Damascus that loosely included Transjordan. British officials planned to rule Transjordan in a more indirect form than either Iraq or Palestine, relying on a very limited British presence (in order to curb French influence) while setting up local institutions of governance.[20] This strategy failed, as certain tribes refused to recognize government authority, forcing the British to increase their military force and leading the French to threaten an invasion to maintain stability.[21] The British granted Amir Abdullah, older brother to Faysal, a trial period as ruler, with a cabinet of elected officials, as the region not only had proved difficult to govern directly but also offered little incentive to do so. Despite various threats, Jordan's Hashemite monarchy endured past the end of the Mandate in 1946 through the present day.

Susan Pedersen argues that Britain and the other colonial powers who were part of the League of Nations had hoped the mandates would demonstrate the value of imperial rule and therefore prolong it. Instead, the league's

17. For example, one official asserted that "the people of Erbil are suddenly showing great enthusiasm for education, but there is no bread with which to feed the multitude." Captain W. H. Hay, assistant political officer, Erbil, "Mesopotamia Administration Report, Erbil Division 1919, August, 1919," IOR L/PS/10/612, India Office Records 3, BL.

18. Renton, "Changing Languages of Empire and the Orient," 650.

19. Massad, *Colonial Effects*, 27.

20. Fischbach, *State, Society, and Land in Jordan*, 65.

21. Alon, *The Making of Jordan*, 35.

involvement, and the "internationalization inherent in League oversight" had the opposite effect, contributing to the emergence of a new world order, of states rather than empires.[22] The process of linking nations with states not only was nonlinear, it was also necessarily incomplete. Modern states required institutions of various types, regardless of whether those institutions and infrastructure aligned precisely with the nation the state was meant to support. In Britain's mandates, governments began to enact laws and to create bureaucracies that were meant to buttress state and British authority over specific mandate territories. The mandate governments relied on existing Ottoman institutions and infrastructure, which preceded these national borders. The suddenly transnational milieu of educators meant that schooling, where state and nation building ought to have combined, in fact tended to separate the two.

The National and the Transnational: Narratives and Infrastructures of Government Education

The great role scholarly works ascribe to public education is as a conduit of nationalism: public schools constitute the main site where modernizing and often expanding states indoctrinate their target populations. From Ernest Gellner's seminal analysis through works inspired by Benedict Anderson, state school systems and mass education function as necessary conditions for the spread of nationalism, from elites to the rest of the population.[23] Government schools in these accounts are organized conveyors of official nationalism, from each government to its budding citizenry. For example, Anderson's later monograph *The Spectre of Comparisons* states that official nationalism (juxtaposed against popular, spontaneous nationalism first seen through print capitalism) "manifests itself, not merely in official ceremonies of commemoration, but in a systematic programme, directed primarily, if not exclusively, through the state's school system, to create and disseminate an official nationalist history, an official nationalist pantheon of heroes, and an official nationalist culture, through the ranks of its younger, incipient citizens—naturally in the state's own interest."[24] For Anderson, as for many other scholars, official nationalism requires public education to spread. This means studies of public schooling

---

22. Pedersen, *The Guardians*, 13.

23. Gellner and Breuilly, *Nations and Nationalism*; Anderson, *Imagined Communities*; Hobsbawm, *Nations and Nationalism since 1780*.

24. Anderson, *The Spectre of Comparisons*, 253.

are naturally circumscribed by a national, imperial-to-national, or at best comparative lens.

It is perhaps unsurprising that schools are not the efficient factories of nationalism that Anderson describes, particularly during the transitional period of expanding state-sponsored education. Certainly, across the interwar Middle East, educators and students had other concerns, and other ideologies than nationalism. Nationalism was seldom exclusively connected to the mandate territories. Moreover, colonial governments sought explicitly to suppress nationalism because of its potential for expensive, destabilizing rebellions. Educators in Britain's Middle Eastern mandates also raise certain questions for Anderson's more general argument that nationalism sprang organically from disgruntled creole elites in the colonies of North and South America, traveling a colonial, bureaucratically delineated territory, who then used mass education to connect their newly discovered countrymen to their national project. For Anderson, nationalism originates and develops outside the state, until its ideologues control rather than staff the state apparatus.

Educators across Britain's Middle Eastern mandates show how, at a local and regional level, it is difficult to make this distinction between state functionaries and society and to separate state employees from the state. Educators moved in and out of governments, from the lowest to the highest ranks of the civil service, shaping each state at its edges. They traveled between bureaucratically delineated territories, within newly British as well as French imperial spaces, but nevertheless worked for those territories' governments. Educators contributed to what they explicitly defined as nationalism, but regionally, across different territorial configurations. Anderson's assertion that official nationalism must be disseminated through the school system ignores teachers as actors and would be hard pressed to encompass their agency, transnationalism, and propagation of ideologies that failed to correspond to their states' borders.

Nationalism, as both a lens and an object of study, has defined scholarship on schooling in the Middle East. From the mid-twentieth century, nationalism has been the overwhelming concern of scholars analyzing education in the region. For example, Albert Hourani's groundbreaking *Arabic Thought in the Liberal Age* linked European-based schooling to the growth of nationalism, specifically of a secular Arab type.[25] Nearly all works on education in Britain's mandates in the Middle East judge nationalism to be the most significant and

---

25. Hourani, *Arabic Thought in the Liberal Age*, 284–85.

interesting outcome of the growth of public schooling. They search for the origins of particular political ideologies: most frequently territorial nationalisms, namely, Palestinian, Iraqi, and Jordanian nationalisms, but also communism and pan-Arabism.[26]

As Keith Watenpaugh notes, this focus on nationalism as the locus and "culmination" of change tends to hide political and social organizations and beliefs that poorly matched a nationalist framework.[27] The Muslim Brotherhood, the irredentism of Kurdistan, which straddles parts of Iraq, Syria, Turkey, and Iran, as well as more militant organizations like al-Qaeda and al-Dawla al-Islamiyya fi al- 'Iraq wa al-Sham (ISIS) constitute prominent examples of movements occluded by a nationalist focus. Even the British Empire can be minimized by concentrating on education within the states that emerged in its wake.

Transnational ideologies had a competitive but also a constitutive relationship to nationalism as the intersections between pan-Arab (*qawmi*), territorial nationalist (*watani*), Islamism, and even communism and existentialism demonstrate.[28] In this book, by studying public education, a clearly national institution, transnationally, we gain new insight into which ideological platforms permeated the region, and how these intellectual and political stances spread. Educators lived in an age where national and supranational configurations could exist side by side. Their travels for schooling and work with the civil service rendered these combinations inescapable. For example, at the American University of Beirut (AUB) in the early 1920s, Ahmed Sousa, an Iraqi Jew from Hilla, would urge his "brothers" at the Iraqi student club to bring their fatherland to the level of advanced nations. Juggling religious, national, and transnational considerations, the other members of the group, who by and

26. Abu-Ghazaleh, *Arab Cultural Nationalism*; Anderson, *Nationalist Voices in Jordan*; Antonius, *The Arab Awakening*; Cleveland, *The Making of an Arab Nationalist*; Dawisha, *Arab Nationalism in the Twentieth Century*; Dawn, *From Ottomanism to Arabism*; Eppel, "The Elite"; Fleischmann, *The Nation and Its "New" Women 1920–1948*; Kahati, "The Role of Some Leading Arab Educators"; Lukitz, *Iraq*; Massad, *Colonial Effects*; Matthews, *Confronting an Empire*; Wien, *Iraqi Arab Nationalism*.

27. Watenpaugh, *Being Modern in the Middle East*, 7; Hourani, *Arabic Thought in the Liberal Age*.

28. Yoav Di-Capua, in *No Exit*, brings to light the fluctuating relations between pan-Arabism and existentialism across the Arab world in the wake of decolonization.

large became educators, incorporated Iraqi and Arab identities alongside one another.[29]

As Sherene Seikaly articulates, "Moving beyond nationalism as both the means and ends of politics is long overdue. Certainly, nationalism was one aspect of subjectivity formation, but it was not the only way to make politics."[30] In this case, moving beyond nationalism as the means and ends of public education allows for a ground-level view of the intersection between elite and vernacular political engagement. Maha Nassar's work shows how Palestinians, even within Israeli territory, remained within a pan-Arab transnational intellectual and political framework. Following her example, I place not only Palestinians but also Iraqis, Jordanians, and the myriad other shifting nationalities of mandate-era teachers back into the transnational milieu, which circumscribed their careers and politics in many ways more than any specific nation-state.[31] Instead of asking whether educators were nationalists, I ask: What did nationalism actually signify to its proponents? How and in what modes did politics manifest through education? What did the restricted political arena mean for the types of political engagement educators could attempt? And finally, what is the legacy of educators' involvement in politics, as both key articulators and practitioners of political stances?

For educators, nationalism meant not merely attachment to one specific territory or even to a people. Regionalism, nationalism, religious affiliation, and class necessarily overlapped with one another. Claiming the status of nationalist formed part of the habitus achieved through mandate-era schooling.[32] It demonstrated erudition, maturity, cultural capital, and a privileged status that cut across genders: the ability to engage with the ideologies of the modern world.[33] Educators did not perform this nationalism merely by transmitting an official curriculum, which in any case was frequently designed to denationalize pupils and educators.[34] Instead, they manifested nationalism in their dress, the books they chose to read, their friends and colleagues, their extracurricular activities, and indeed their off-script remarks within the

---

29. Sousa, *Hayati fi Nisf Qarn* [My life in half a century], 130–31.

30. Seikaly, *Men of Capital*, 13.

31. Nassar, *Brothers Apart*.

32. Harker, "On Reproduction, Habitus and Education," 118.

33. I seek to use gender in this work as Liat Kozma advocates, not as the "main category of analysis" but to add greater "insight" into the frameworks educators navigated, and their self-perception. Kozma, "Going Transnational," 574.

34. Schneider, *Mandatory Separation*.

classroom. This method of political engagement, which tended to span political borders, took place in conversations, journal articles, secret or semisecret societies, as well as negotiations with governments. It was also circumscribed by the narrow character of official politics. Educators could write and even lead protests against their governments while remaining in the civil service. They could become high-ranking government officials and ministers, often because they were from elite families. Yet their ability to affect sweeping political change was limited. With the advent of mass education, educators' tactics changed, from individual negotiations with their governments from within to collective bargaining. The transformation of teachers' social and economic status, from elite to everyday, altered their political tactics and relationship with their states as well.

Era Crossing: Teachers and Governments

The generations of teachers discussed in this book passed through temporal as well as territorial boundaries. They lived during transitions between multiple regimes, from Ottoman to mandate to postmandate states. Their biographies force a different periodization from one circumscribed by any of the three eras they experienced. Focusing on military education, Michael Provence underscores how schooling, war, and politics trained a regional, if not empire-wide, generation of leaders. They brought Ottoman-honed networks and understandings of government to bear on the mandates that divided the region.[35] As Ilana Feldman has demonstrated with her work on Gaza, the role of civil servants, and how their societies (and they themselves) perceived that role, persisted despite radical changes in governments.[36] The individuals discussed in this book, educators and civil servants both, were entwined in the stories and construction of multiple regimes and states. The travels, worldview, and impact of mandate educators passed through administrations, as well as the disparate governments that educators staffed and fought.

To trace the arc of educators' professionalization and concurrent changes in their relationships to their governments, this book begins with the final years of the Ottoman Empire and ends with the 1960s. The first chapter demonstrates how connections between government schooling and government service, and the need to travel for both, incorporated educators into the

---

35. Provence, *The Last Ottoman Generation*.
36. Feldman, *Governing Gaza*.

Ottoman state through wide-ranging geographic networks that persisted into the mandate era. Chapters 2 and 3 concentrate on the interwar years, particularly how educators capitalized on their rarity to push the limits of what the profession of teaching entailed, while shaping the authority of their governments overall. The mobility of government educators across the mandates' political borders caused states to both accept and at times support transnational civil servants; transnationalism formed an important yet contradictory part of state building. As government educators extended government bureaucracies, they necessarily traveled beyond those governments' purview, bringing back ideas that failed to correspond to the borders that education systems might seem to circumscribe.

In these chapters, I deploy Pierre Bourdieu's concept of *habitus* in two ways. The first is as "a system of dispositions common to all products of the same conditionings" here, a summation of repeated, common practices and experiences that shaped the outlook of elite, well-traveled educators.[37] The combination of higher education and movement within or between countries socialized educators into a habitus that stretched across the mandates. A graduate of the American University of Beirut or the Arab College of Jerusalem would recognize (and often seek to hire) a fellow alumnus or alumna hundreds or even thousands of miles from each alma mater. They would share language and a set of learned practices relating to education, politics, and governance. Travel, particularly that of cultured, well-dressed educators for schooling and for work, created networks of belonging and conscious understandings of individual and group habitus.[38] The social space educators came to occupy was conditioned by a particularly expansive physical space, a "distributional arrangement of agents and properties" in which economic and cultural capital was linked to movement rather than to a particular location.[39]

The second way I use habitus is to underscore the irregularity of mandate-era educational rules and the practical strategies educators used to navigate these patchwork regulations. As Jacques Bouveresse argues, habitus is important for explaining "regularities which have as part of their essence a certain amount of variability, plasticity, indetermination, and imply all sorts of adaptations, innovations and exceptions of many different varieties, the sort of regularity in short which characterizes the domain of the practical, of practical

37. Bourdieu, *The Logic of Practice*, 58–59.
38. Shusterman, "Introduction: Bourdieu as Philosopher," in *Bourdieu: A Critical Reader*, 5.
39. Bourdieu, "Physical Space, Social Space and Habitus," 10.

reason and the logic of practice."[40] The clash between the "regularities" prescribed by mandate governments in syllabi, gendered ideals, and education policies and the practical, idiosyncratic ways educators capitalized on the gaps between policies and practice was productive, both creating uneven education systems and offering educators themselves individual opportunities. Rather than viewing mandate-era schooling as a failure of standardization, I use Bouveresse's understanding of habitus to bring to light the fruitful and dynamic space created by rules' haphazard implementation, on the one hand, and educators' agency and power, on the other. By strategically manipulating overlapping and contradictory rules, educators solidified their place as anti-imperial, petty elite civil servants, fleshing out the empty corners of unenforced syllabuses with multiple ideologies.

This book does not focus on the Yishuv (the Jewish community in Palestine). The Yishuv's teachers were not part of the same circulation of educators or, with rare exceptions, such as Palestine's Law Classes or the American University of Beirut, of the same education systems.[41] As Yoni Furas argues, rising Arab/Jewish conflict and segregation, textual encounters, and the growing absence of the other shaped history teaching and education in Palestine.[42] Yet the transnational worlds that Arab and Jewish Palestinian educators inhabited seldom overlapped, even when their journeys took place in parallel with one another.

With the end of British hegemony came radical shifts in educators' socioeconomic status and methods of political engagement, as well as in the relationships among state, nation, and public schooling. Chapter 4 concentrates on educators' politics between the interwar era and the first decades of independence. Educators participated in the rebellions of the 1930s, but generally from within rather than outside of government service, tempering the nature of their protests. Educators' privileged position shaped a particular type of politics: fluid, anti-imperial ideologies encompassing pan-Arabism, territorial nationalisms, fascism, and communism, without requiring teachers to stop working for their governments. As governments gained independence in the 1940s and 1950s, new, more codified ideologies and new political actors eclipsed the teachers, politicians, and beliefs of the interwar era. Palestinian

40. Bouveresse, "Rules, Dispositions and the *Habitus*," 62.
41. Likhovski, *Law and Identity in Mandate Palestine*; Kahlenberg, "The Star of David in a Cedar Tree."
42. Furas, *Educating Palestine*, 12–13.

educators disrupted Israel's Zionist project in Israel proper and represented the limits of pan-Arabism in the diaspora. As pan-Arabism itself changed from an anti-imperial, revolutionary movement to a state ideology, it became more inflexible, excluding its former proponents: the educators and politicians who had risen to power during the mandates.[43]

Chapter 5 explores the seismic changes in the teaching profession wrought by independence for Iraq, Jordan, and Israel and diaspora and occupation for Palestinians. From the 1940s through the 1960s, mass education came to function as a crucial institution of postcolonial states but ended the automatic links between government education and government employment that had previously benefited teachers. Educators' qualifications increased, but they lost their role as political elites, forced to band together in often-repressed unions to press their case. The epilogue traces the legacy of mandate-era education into the present day, as teachers' unions call for strikes across the region. The loss of educators' individual power and collective status caused by mass education endures.

Following the Teacher: Collective Biography in Comparative and Transnational Frameworks

Unearthing the stories of public school educators in the interwar Middle East leads to two methodological challenges: how to account for the importance of different states to transnational actors (and vice versa), and how to balance the vastly different amounts of information available on educators themselves. In answer to the first challenge, this book uses a two-level analytic, deploying a comparative and a transnational approach.[44] Clearly, looking at public school teachers within only one polity would create blind spots, erasing segments of teachers' life stories, regional ideologies, and the changing relationships between governments and government education. Studying the travels of government educators in the interwar era demands a transnational framework. As we have seen, trying to account for Akram Zu'aytir's career and travels from within the bounds of Palestine or Jordan would be impossible. It is equally impossible, however, to ignore the states through which educators moved, and

43. Kevin Jones has shown this to be the case for Iraq's poets as well, in *The Dangers of Poetry*, 185.

44. A transnational lens has become increasingly popular as an approach to the history of education. See Fuchs and Roldán Vera, *The Transnational in the History of Education*.

the differences between those governments. Educators were a necessary part of government bureaucracies, which were nationally bounded by the mandates' legal and territorial borders. Their transnationalism was a basic component of the formation of nation-states in the region. In addition, comparing Britain's mandates underscores the importance of local individuals to the outcomes of colonial policies. The mandates themselves were run differently, although British policy makers sought to use the same educational methods throughout the areas under their control. Nevertheless, the scope for local initiative inherent in these policies varied. Ottoman legacies, British strategies of rule, and the power of educators themselves altered policies' results.

Differences regarding the amount of material available on educators are stark. Source levels range from the well-known Akram Zu'aytir's speeches, newspapers articles, voluminous autobiographies, and textbooks to the brief statistical information on the less than two-year career of Jureis 'Auweis in Jordan, whose record includes only his birthdate (1933), that he became a classified teacher at the lowest rank in 1951, and that he resigned from the teaching profession in 1953.[45] This book therefore combines microhistories of individual educators with a collective biography of educators as a social group. To the greatest extent possible, it zooms into the everyday and extraordinary experiences of teachers, as well as their agency in shaping their own careers, while altering the governments they served. Collective biography, also termed *prosopography*, is particularly useful when there are varying amounts of information on a large number of individual historical actors who share certain characteristics.[46] Combining scraps of data relating to ordinary individuals, including their biographical information, as well as the writings of more extraordinary ones enables investigations as to the political and social impact of these actors as a group, and how their incorporation and subsequent separation from their governments shaped state building in the region. The regional professionalization of teachers and its consequences for their political activity and place in society becomes clear only when we take a bird's-eye view of their role across multiple polities.

Telling teachers' stories also requires research across borders. I followed educators' life and career paths, traveling from Israel/Palestine to Lebanon, to Jordan, to the United Kingdom and the United States. This book also uses oral histories of twenty individuals, ranging from a satirical Iraqi author now living

45. "Jureis Isbitan 'Auweis" employee number 0001355, HRD.
46. Stone, "Prosopography."

in London to one of Jordan's erstwhile ministers of antiquities. Through archives and interviews, this social and cultural history exposes regionwide trends in schooling as well as political and ideological currents, shaped by a growing class of educated men and women.

Their stories underscore how government schooling supported the expansion of states, on the one hand, while undermining those states' territorial authority and creating overlapping notions of affiliation, on the other. As education changed from a privilege to a right, teachers became more professional but more marginalized. Expanding public schooling, particularly in the Middle East, changed public school teachers from an elite, intellectual, and individually politically influential population to a nonelite, unionized, and collectively important professional group. Mass education functioned as a crucial institution of postcolonial states but ended educators' intimate connections with governance. Likewise the anti-imperial, idealistic form of Arab nationalism that characterized the interwar era was rapidly supplanted by a more codified, more restricted, and harsher variety in the 1950s. To understand this transition, the fraught relationship between transnational and national ideologies, and the necessity of framing state building and public education in a transnational milieu, we must recover the period before mass education in the region, when networks of state schooling and state service were first being formed, during the final years of the Ottoman Empire.

1

From *Kuttab* to College

IMPERIAL LEGACIES

IN 1907, accompanied by the manager of Beirut's official gazette, a young man stood before the principal of the Sultaniye school in Beirut. The youth had taken time to rest before this important meeting, after his journey from Jerusalem. The Sultaniye, a high school–level institution, was one of approximately fifty in the entire Ottoman Empire.[1] Speaking in Ottoman Turkish, the manager (as instructed by the young man's father) explained to the principal that the young man had fled from foreign schools, happily, to government ones.

The youth, a Muslim notable named Omar Saleh al-Barghouti, had, in fact, attended a rather astonishing number of Jerusalem's foreign-sponsored institutions, from the Jewish Alliance School to the Anglican St. George's. The principal of the Sultaniye, well accustomed to students with mixed credentials, although less religiously varied than al-Barghouti's, sent for a proctor to examine the new entrant and place him in the appropriate class. As the proctor and the school's teachers interrogated the young man, he spoke confidently about his education, stating that his final exam had been official, up to government standard. It became apparent to his examiners, however, that his Turkish was not commensurate with his knowledge of other subjects, including his native Arabic, French, and English. They recommended that he take private lessons in Turkish and enroll in a class two years behind until his Turkish improved (angering al-Barghouti, who was proud of his scholastic achievements). Nevertheless, as he brought his things from the respectable hotel paid for by his wealthy parents, the new Sultaniye student was impressed by the size of the

---

1. Ágoston and Masters, *Encyclopedia of the Ottoman Empire*, 203.

school, its multiple floors, cafeteria, and grand mosque where he would pray five times a day.[2]

From the mid-nineteenth century through World War I, the Ottoman government strove to train students, like al-Barghouti, to form part of a cadre of civil servants: loyal graduates, sporting modern clothing and an enlightened outlook, receiving their training in new, well-controlled institutions. These institutions, like Beirut's Sultaniye, or Baghdad's Higher Teachers' Training College, were concentrated in urban areas, often provincial capitals. Yet educators and students would have come not just from Istanbul but from the empire's far-flung provinces as well. Ottoman policy makers hoped government-trained teachers, a subset of the civil servants produced in these new institutions, would then return to their communities, or other Ottoman peripheries, imbued with the knowledge and ability to modernize, and to inspire loyalty to the Ottoman government. As al-Barghouti's aristocratic background illustrates, government students' and likewise government teachers' credentials were widely varied. Al-Barghouti's travels—from his family's village to Jerusalem, from Jerusalem to Beirut, and, as his father hoped, to Istanbul's law school and a comfortable government career—illustrate the movement required to pursue higher education and, subsequently, state employment.

Ottoman officials, well aware of their empire's diversity of institutions and personnel, hoped to regulate ever-proliferating nongovernment schools in order to maintain stability and prevent rebellion. They feared foreign educational institutions might be conduits for the type of revolt, such as the Greek war of independence, that was exacerbated so often during the nineteenth century by external interference. Policy makers also intended educational reforms to promote devotion to the Ottoman state and its dwindling empire. However, the Ottoman government lacked the resources to see these desires to fruition, applying new educational regulations unevenly. Government and nongovernment schools often bore little resemblance to one another in terms of curriculum, pedagogical style, size, or even language. Students experienced older forms of schooling, usually religious, but also newer, more secular institutions, pointing to a messy rather than linear process of modernization and secularization. In the Arab provinces, students who received any kind of formal education faced a wide assortment of teachers, ranging from religious scholars ('Ulama) and military officers, to foreign and missionary-educated

2. Al-Barghouti, Al-Marahil [The phases], 119–20.

FIGURE 1.1. *Courtyard, Imperial High School, Baghdad,* between
1880 and 1893. (Reprinted from the Library of Congress,
Abdulhamid II Collection.)

intellectuals and translators.[3] Moreover, the students came from different
areas of the Arab provinces and the empire itself. Despite the government's
best efforts, the unintended consequences of the late Ottoman educational
landscape included a profound lack of systemization, both on an institutional
level and in terms of individual teachers.

The imperial high school in Baghdad, as seen in figure 1.1, represented one
of these efforts on the part of the Ottoman state, as it sought to use the school
to improve its citizenry and to incorporate them into the Ottoman
government.

Yet schools beyond the ʿidadi or preparatory level, like this imperial high
school and Beirut's Sultaniye, were concentrated in Istanbul and major cities
and hence difficult to access for the vast majority of would-be students in the
region. To become part of the Ottoman state's modernizing initiatives, as demonstrated in uniforms and drills, students would need to travel. Students

3. Evered, *Empire and Education under the Ottomans,* 31. Mandate-period educators had
widely varied backgrounds. For example, Sati al-Husri was educated by tutors before attending
the Mülkiye Mektebi, Khalil Totah attended Quaker schools, and Hussein Ruhi learned English
in Chicago as part of the Bahai delegation in 1899. Cleveland, *The Making of an Arab Nationalist;*
Ricks and Totah, *Turbulent Times in Palestine; The Baháí World: An International Record,* 13: 938.

sought out those schools that they (or their parents) believed could give them the best chance of securing a prosperous career. Higher state schools guaranteed employment in the bureaucracy; civil schools exempted their students from military service. Prospective civil servants, however, had to travel beyond their local, and even regional, purview in order to attend these rare institutions. The overwhelmingly rural area that would become Transjordan provides an extreme example, even within the context of the territories that would form Britain's mandates. By 1914 there were only nineteen government elementary schools, twenty-nine teachers, and no preparatory or secondary schools in a territory that covered more than thirty-five thousand square miles and possessed a population of about seventy-four thousand.[4] This lack of postelementary schools suggests both the assumption of travel and how disruptive post-Ottoman territorial divisions would be to the education networks of the Ottoman Empire. Inhabitants of the Arab provinces who sought further education and a government job had to travel at least to the closest major city, if not to Istanbul. In the case of students from northern Transjordan, the more plentiful schools of Damascus offered a solution to the lack of more local preparatory and secondary schooling.

This was not what the Ottoman government preferred. It was expensive to send teachers either to train in Istanbul and return to their provinces or to go from Istanbul to new frontiers. Local teachers, trained locally, would have been the cheaper solution. Had there been more institutions at the secondary level or above in the provinces, more Ottomans would have been willing and able to attend.[5] Missionary institutions as well as local schools inspired by the *Nahda*, a nineteenth-century intellectual and cultural movement across the Arabic-speaking world but mainly based in Beirut and Cairo, also granted Ottoman subjects educational options, albeit ones that taught in different styles, languages, and locations.

I argue that the demographically varied student population and the wildly different institutions they attended during the final years of the Ottoman Empire were key elements in the forging of networks of people and information linking the Arab provinces with one another and with the imperial capital. State schooling promised state employment. Both education and careers in the civil service required travel across the empire to rare, urban institutes of

4. Al-Tall, *Education in Jordan*, 51; Karpat, *Ottoman Population, 1830–1914*.
5. Evered, *Empire and Education under the Ottomans*, 90–91.

higher learning, and from one educational or administrative post to another.[6] Although travel and migration within the Ottoman Empire were not unheard of, including for education and government work, the number of individuals making these journeys—and the number of institutions available for them to travel to—greatly increased in the nineteenth century. The travels of these students, later educators, formed systems of schooling, affiliation, and employment that persisted after the imposition of mandate borders, and after the substitution of Arabism or other ideologies for Ottoman loyalties. In short, the geographic and personnel networks of late Ottoman education underlay the foundation of the type of state that would arise in the mandate era, as well as that era's transnational and regional ideologies.

Ottoman education policies allowed educated individuals, especially teachers, a certain degree of leeway with respect to their governments. Educators, and even students, petitioned, argued, and promoted their own interests within first an Ottoman and then a British system of proclaimed, but not imposed, and frequently experimental legislation. No system of education or of governance necessarily functions the way its architects imagine it will. Foucault's precise models of disciplinary spaces are also aggregate, cumulative ideals rather than clear descriptions of actual prisons, military barracks, or schools.[7] There is always slippage between policy, disciplinary ideals, practices, and their consequences. However, that slippage is also productive in specific ways, particularly in terms of the unintended outcomes of government policies. Unanticipated but still radical transformations in governance and subjectivity can take place due to government intervention.

In the case of Ottoman- and mandate-era schooling, governments reluctantly adopted education's lack of systemization, to the extent of making variability the rule. Teachers' qualifications and practices remained widely inconsistent for decades. Therefore each teacher defined the profession of teaching as an idiosyncratic individual rather than a standardized bureaucrat. These haphazard modes of governance and schooling often granted educated individuals enviable careers, enabling them to move through state education and the civil service. Simultaneously, Ottoman and later mandate educators' notion of government as accommodating to its qualified, sometime employees

6. In *The Last Ottoman Generation*, Michael Provence shows military education to be an even more extreme case of individuals traveling and being incorporated into state service and politics.

7. Foucault and Rabinow, *The Foucault Reader*, 262–63.

pushed the educated population of the region toward participation in the state, creating a culture of petitions that leaned toward individual rather than collective bargaining.

The educators employed in the first years of the British military and then mandate administrations studied at a wide variety of national, missionary, and Ottoman government elementary schools (frequently the first government schools founded in the Arab provinces). Khalil al-Sakakini (1880–1953), Muhammad ʿIzzat Darwazeh (1887–1984), Gertrude Nassar (1888–1976), and Omar Saleh al-Barghouti (1894–1965) from Palestine; Mustafa al-Tall (1899–1949) from Transjordan; and Talib Mushtaq (1900–1977) from Iraq all attended school during the final years of the Ottoman Empire and made their mark on education during the mandate period.[8] All six individuals are extraordinary in terms of the amount of written materials they left behind. For example, Nassar wrote an incomplete memoir, commissioned by friends in Beirut, in which she described vignettes of her schooling and teaching. The bombastic and incredibly prolific Darwazeh was one of Palestine's most politically active individuals, writing of his schooldays and role in politics. Historians have written extensively about these educators (with the exception of Nassar), focusing on their changing place in society, and on their views of Arab and/or Palestinian, Iraqi, or Jordanian nationalism.[9] Al-Sakakini's invaluable diary is a key source for many scholarly works on the region.[10] Taken together, however, their biographies show the political possibilities that education and government service afforded, and the consequences of travel for schooling and careers in state employ. Nassar worked as a teacher (including, rather radically, in a government boys' school), Mushtaq and al-Tall were teachers as well as government officials, while Darwazeh and al-Sakakini headed schools (al-Sakakini was also an inspector) and, along with al-Barghouti, who taught in the Jerusalem Law classes, authored textbooks in history and Arabic grammar that were read by generations of schoolchildren.

Their memoirs and diaries recall the diverse educational climate of the turn of the century, networks of empire-crossing texts and individuals, as well as

8. Kahati, "The Role of Education," 30.

9. Matthews, *Confronting an Empire*; Schneider, *Mandatory Separation*; Anderson, *Nationalist Voices in Jordan*; Simon, *Iraq between the Two World Wars*.

10. Salim Tamari is the leading expert, but scholars such as Elie Kedourie, Tom Segev, Michelle Campos, Abigail Jacobson, Noah Haiduc-Dale, Nadim Bawalsa, Murat C. Yıldız, and others have made intensive use of al-Sakakini's diaries.

the fluctuating relationships between the Ottoman government and its constituents. Meanwhile, education, and government involvement in it, became steadily more pervasive. These factors contributed to the rise of teachers' political and social personas based on a flexible interpretation of government, shifting notions of modernization and modern schooling, and a conception of political affiliation that encompassed multiple layers of territory and identity.

In analyzing the Ottoman territories that would become Britain's Middle Eastern mandates, I build on the work of Michael Provence and Cyrus Schayegh. Both of these authors reject other scholars' almost ubiquitous mandate to nation-state lens, which has privileged nationalism, attached to individual mandates, as the focus of inquiry. As Provence notes, "The durable tendency to view the history of the region through the lens of national histories of Turkey, Syria, Lebanon, Palestine, etc. obscures commonalities that were clear to all until at least the 1940s."[11] Instead, Provence, Schayegh, and I locate key historical shifts from the late Ottoman period through, as Schayegh puts it, the "Ottoman Twilight" of the 1920s and beyond.[12] To understand mandate-era education, we need to take into account the fact that the first generation of educators in this period necessarily went to school during the last years of the Ottoman Empire. They formed part of a multilayered late Ottoman landscape of schooling through which British colonial officials would impose the education policies and borders of the mandates. The late Ottoman era defined the world of overlapping policies and practices that mandate-era educators would navigate.

A Patchwork of Tradition and Modernity: Schooling in the Late Ottoman Empire

Globally, the late nineteenth and early twentieth centuries marked a watershed in the history of education. Expanding states promulgated ambitious plans for systemized governance. These included measures geared at modernizing, improving, and expanding education, while increasing the role of each state in the rearing of its subjects. Meanwhile, religious institutions and local individuals increasingly founded their own schools to educate their communities for

---

11. Provence, *The Last Ottoman Generation*, 6.
12. Schayegh, *The Middle East and the Making of the Modern World*.

a changing world. The battles over the hearts and minds of that world's children increased in frequency and intensity as governments and subjects came to associate formal schooling with both societal improvement and political strife.

For the Ottomans, the geopolitics of the nineteenth century granted education an even more urgent purpose than many of their imperial counterparts, including the British. From the late eighteenth century, the Ottoman Empire had suffered increasing military and territorial losses, as well as internal rebellions. These included the disruptive centralization of Mehmed Ali Pasha's government in Egypt, as well as foreign-supported victorious secessionist movements in Greece and the Balkans. The Eastern Question, namely, how to prevent the Ottoman Empire's disintegration from causing a world war, increased Ottoman involvement in European affairs but also encouraged European meddling in Ottoman separatist groups. The very real fear that the empire could end drove the Ottoman government to push schooling as a means of unifying Ottoman subjects while increasing the empire's chances of survival.

Begun during the Tanzimat era of government reforms (1839–1876), new, more sweeping educational initiatives would, Ottoman policy makers hoped, create dedicated and well-trained experts, soldiers, and civil servants. Under Sultan Abdulhamid II (1878–1909) and the Committee of Union and Progress (1908–1918), Ottoman government policies endeavored to link an Ottoman, albeit increasingly Muslim and Turkish, nation with the growing state. The reforms of the early years focused on secondary institutions designed to produce government employees located in Istanbul, the capital.[13] However, government officials during the Hamidian era worried over class mixing in secondary schools, voicing fears that lower-class graduates might, if not provided with upper-class jobs, unite in opposition to the Ottoman state.[14]

The solution the Ottoman government proposed in the mid-1890s was to provide preparatory schools "in every village" that would focus on literacy and moral instruction, while fees restricted higher levels of education, creating a small and eminently employable cadre of potential bureaucrats. For inhabitants of the Arab provinces, however, be they upper-class or not, the first steps toward a government post were frequently at schools that differed widely from upper-level state institutions, such as the Sultaniye al-Barghouti attended.

13. For example, the Civil Service School (Mülkiye Mektebi) was created in 1859. Evered, "The Politics of the Late Ottoman Education," 43.

14. Somel, *The Modernization of Public Education in the Ottoman Empire*, 119.

If they were Muslim, Ottomans generally began their education at a *kuttab* (plural *katatib*), a local elementary school frequently attached to a mosque wherein a sheikh taught the rudiments of reading, writing, and arithmetic and students memorized the Qur'an. Students of varied ages, nearly always boys but occasionally a few girls, would sit in circles around the sheikh, shouting out answers to the teacher's questions and presumably learning the skills necessary to practice their faith.[15]

The "traditional" kuttab existed simultaneously with institutions that employed cutting-edge methods and taught sciences and foreign languages, highlighting a muddled transition between what both present-day academics and our memoirists defined as premodern and modern forms of schooling. Timothy Mitchell compares premodern religious education, from the kuttab up through al-Azhar (the world's top institution of Sunni Islamic learning), to the Lancaster model of schooling, deployed in a scant number of model schools in colonial Egypt. For Mitchell, disciplinary practices such as attendance, the precise ordering of time, and the lack of spectacular punishment clearly separated modern schooling from premodern, even to the extent that "model schools offered the model of a modern system of power."[16] Suzanne Schneider, in her study of education, religion, and politics in mandate Palestine, counters Mitchell, showing how notions of the kuttab as traditional were in fact invented in the nineteenth century. While she disrupts narratives of a linear progression from traditional to modern schooling by uncovering their construction, individuals attended both supposedly modernizing schools as well as katatib.[17] The mandate governments would often take over katatib and retain some of their teachers (and buildings) as government elementary schools. Moreover, for most students, attending a kuttab, even if they tended to denigrate it in hindsight, represented a necessary step on their way to gaining an education. Rather than arguing for a hard-and-fast distinction between traditional and modern schooling, it makes more sense to explore their cluttered overlap in the late nineteenth-century Ottoman Empire and the effects of that intersection on students and teachers.

---

15. Ayalon, *Reading Palestine*, 26–30.

16. Mitchell, *Colonising Egypt*, 81. Gregory Starrett notes that local elites who attended and also observed *katatib* tended to emphasize differences between traditional and modern education; Starrett, *Putting Islam to Work*, 24.

17. Schneider, *Mandatory Separation*.

Omar Saleh al-Barghouti and Muhammad ʿIzzat Darwazeh remembered their earliest schooldays in Palestinian katatib as frightening and exasperating. Both authors emphasized the old-fashioned nature of their earliest education and the scant resources available to their teachers. They point out the pedagogical (and in their view detrimental) differences between these schools and the newer institutions they would attend, as well as differing levels of government involvement. The educational landscape of the late Ottoman era was shifting rapidly, as government involvement in schooling increased in fits and starts. These memoirs, it must be emphasized, were written well after their school days, when their concepts of modernity, particularly in terms of education, had been well honed. Like most recollections of nineteenth-century katatib, their stories emphasize the corporal punishments students experienced.[18] Darwazeh complained that Sheikh Masoud, who ran and taught at the kuttab Darwazeh attended in Nablus, treated his students cruelly, insulting and beating them. He noted that over one hundred students between six and fifteen years of age attended the school, and that these students "mostly learned from each other," repeating in chorus the sheikh's shouted lessons. Sheikh Masoud kept wooden sticks of various lengths: longer ones to goad the students who sat in the back of the classroom, and shorter ones for those who sat in front.[19] Al-Barghouti's memoir similarly describes how the sheikh in his village would keep handy a large stick as well as a bastinado (falaqa) used for beating the soles of his students' feet. The sheikh would strike whichever student was unlucky enough to arrive last in the morning with both the stick and the bastinado until they screamed.[20] The emphasis on corporal punishment was also a reflection of the schools' "traditional" nature, one that poorly and painfully inducted Ottoman students into literacy.

In their katatib, like many other small boys across the Ottoman Empire, Darwazeh, al-Barghouti, and Talib Mushtaq learned to read and write a little. They internalized these experiences as essentially negative, but also as the only way of gaining the literacy required to matriculate at better institutions and eventually gain a foothold in the Ottoman state. They also describe the kuttab as a traditional institution. Growing up in Kadhimain, a predominantly Shiʿite area of Iraq close to Baghdad, six-year-old Mushtaq would go each morning at

18. Blake, "Training Arab-Ottoman Bureaucrats," 81.
19. Darwazeh, Mudhakkirat Muhammad ʿIzzat Darwazeh [Memoirs of Muhammad ʿIzzat Darwazeh], 146.
20. Al-Barghouti, Al-Marahil, 81–82.

dawn to a local shrine. There he would study the Qur'an under the tutelage of a sheikh.[21] Mushtaq, Darwazeh, and al-Barghouti were all required to memorize the Qur'an before moving on to the next stage of their studies. Darwazeh and al-Barghouti complained of the style of this education as well as its content, particularly the emphasis on rote memorization—a feature that, along with the unquestionable authority of sheikhly figures, characterized early schooling throughout the Arab provinces. Like certain contemporary scholars, Darwazeh and al-Barghouti connected memorization and rote learning to tradition, as well as modern educational tactics to rational critical thought.[22]

Across the Arab provinces, religious and foreign institutions catered to diverse populations, particularly non-Muslim minorities. At times, entire school systems, technically separate from government education, overlapped with state schooling and state service. Jewish communities had heders, Talmud Torahs, and yeshivot: religious schools that taught in Yiddish, Ladino, or Arabic. Christian and some Muslim students benefited from a plethora of missionary and foreign institutions.

The imperial and global agendas of these schools could directly conflict with the goals of the Ottoman state vis-à-vis its subjects. Nevertheless, the Ottoman government and its successor mandate states relied on these schools to fill gaps in state education. Foreign schools, including those explicitly funded by foreign governments, were often used as a way of gaining influence over the Ottoman state, for example, as an excuse to intercede on behalf of the Ottoman's minority populations.[23] The Ottoman government worked to regulate and to compete with these institutions, but the overall result was a patchwork of schooling. Educated Ottomans attended the growing but still limited number of government and nongovernment institutions, leading to diverse qualifications but also a continued premium on education of any kind.

These educated Ottomans included the leading figures of the *Nahda*. In the Arab provinces, the *Nahda* both fed on and inspired the desire for improved schooling and more widespread educational institutions. The *Nahda*'s proponents, or *Nahdawis*, were focused on the idea of modernity, expanding the

21. Mushtaq, *Awraq Ayyami* [Pages from my life], 10–11; Khoury, "Ambiguities of the Modern," 325.

22. Jardine and Rahat, "Learning Not to Speak in Tongues," 643. See, for example, "Madrassas Backdrop to London Tragedy: Religious Schools Spawn Terror," *National Post (Canada)*, July 18, 2005.

23. Evered, *Empire and Education under the Ottomans*, 143.

Arabic language to include technical terms and educating the population to be at home in the rapidly changing world. More generally, an increase in the production of newspapers created a reading public centered in Cairo, Alexandria, and Beirut.[24] Many of the *Nahda*'s leading figures were educated to some degree overseas or in local missionary schools. These educational experiences broadened their horizons, putting them in touch with a global community in print and in person. Overwhelmingly they, like the Ottoman state, sought to reform institutions, decreasing the influence of religious authorities, both foreign and domestic, over politics and education. Muslim *Nahdawis* often sought to adapt Islam to fit the current needs of the Muslim community and to improve the lives of Ottoman citizens through social and educational programs.[25] Questions of identity and civilization gave rise to a variety of ideas centered on the connections between nations and states.

Although the specific areas that would become the British mandates were not hubs of literary production (though they were by no means without newspapers), their inhabitants read journals from centers of the *Nahda*: Egypt, present-day Syria, and Lebanon. The availability of written materials and their authors' and patrons' intellectual efforts reflected and contributed to a rise in demand for formal, and in their view modern, education. *Nahdawis* debated concepts of progress, civilization, the place of Arabs and Muslims globally as well as within the Ottoman Empire, the rule of law, religion, secularism, science, and the place of women in relation to all these debates.[26]

For girls, early schooling was even more ad hoc than for their male peers. Gertrude Nassar, born in late nineteenth-century Safad in northern Ottoman Palestine, had no formal schools available to her, or at least none that were acceptable to her parents. Her mother was a German missionary, while her father was an Ottoman Lebanese Christian anesthetist and pharmacist. Safad was also a historically Jewish city: a hub of Jewish mystical study. Nassar, along with her four siblings, was tutored by her aunt, another missionary. Like al-Barghouti, Darwazeh, and many other Arab Ottomans, she would travel to Beirut for, as she put it, "the finishing touches to my education."[27]

A lack of state schools across the provinces meant parents who hoped to groom their children for work, particularly for the growing Ottoman state, or

24. Ayalon, *Reading Palestine*, 67–68.
25. Khuri-Makdisi, *The Eastern Mediterranean and the Making of Global Radicalism*, 40–41.
26. Kassab, *Contemporary Arab Thought*, 20–22.
27. Nassar, Wagner, and Nicgorski, *My Life in Palestine*, 11.

indeed to educate these children past literacy, had to rely on a diverse assortment of educational institutions available to them. The process of linking the Ottoman Empire's youngest subjects with the Ottoman government always involved not just local participation in government educational initiatives but also nongovernment schools at one stage or another. Students frequently had to travel for days to attend these institutions. Networks of students, teachers, soldiers, and bureaucrats extended from Ottoman villages to local hubs such as Baghdad and Jerusalem, regional centers like Beirut, the capital, or even abroad. The wide range of educational qualifications, the Ottoman state and its subjects' expectation of travel, and the social networks formed by that travel would define schooling and government service past the end of the empire that had set those parameters in place.

Diversity and Flux: Preparatory and Secondary Schooling in the Arab Provinces

After completing their (painful) stints in katatib, or in Gertrude Nassar's case enjoying her aunt's ministrations, Nassar, Darwazeh, al-Barghouti, and Mushtaq transitioned to schools that were planned along more modern lines. Regardless of the diverse pedagogies these individuals experienced and the disparate qualifications to which they led, all four saw education as a path to social mobility and eventually toward government employment, an assumption borne out by their future careers. To continue their educations at larger urban centers, they either had to commute, board at the school, or stay with relatives, even at a tender age. Through the mandate period, schooling required travel and separation from home and family and included interactions with peers and teachers from across the region and empire.

All our memoirists understood that higher education and government employment meant movement. For Mushtaq, there was no elementary school in Kadhimain until 1908, forcing him first to study at a library under his father's tutelage, then to journey the few kilometers to Baghdad and later to Istanbul and beyond for secondary education. Darwazeh completed the schools available in Nablus, but his father did not have sufficient funds to send him to Beirut or Istanbul to continue his schooling. Instead, Darwazeh got a job as a clerk in the posts and telegraphs department in Nablus and then was promoted, moving to Beirut not for study but for work. He was briefly the principal of the private al-Najah school in Nablus, where he emphasized its nationalist activities rather than its pedagogy. Nassar attended the German Deaconess school in Beirut after completing a three-day journey to the city with her aunt, an armed guard, and her tuition in gold in a wooden box.[28] When she arrived, her brother was attending the Syrian Protestant College (renamed the American University of Beirut in 1920),[29] presumably giving her the social protection necessary to allow her to live so far from her parents. Al-Barghouti, wealthy scion of a Palestinian notable family, enjoyed access to the variety of institutions Jerusalem possessed—for those who could afford the fees. After his elementary and preparatory schooling in Palestine at Jewish and Christian institutions, he continued his studies at the Sultaniye in Beirut in the hopes of becoming an Ottoman civil servant. With the end of the Ottoman Empire, al-Barghouti would become a lawyer, educator, and politician in the mandate for Palestine before transitioning to Jordanian politics, including, briefly, as a member of the Senate and of the Chamber of Deputies.[30]

In his description of elementary school, al-Barghouti was struck by the dissimilarities between the kuttab in his village of Deir Ghassaneh and the Jewish Alliance Israélite Universelle School in Jerusalem. In an account of education that Timothy Mitchell and other Foucauldian scholars would appreciate, al-Barghouti carefully lists the differences between the kuttab and the Alliance school in terms of order, discipline, cleanliness, and methods of teaching. He remembers the Alliance school as "hygienic," having "a wide field for recreation and playing, and around it a garden and flowers. . . . The students came to class at the appointed time, the bell would ring thrice, and the students would rush to line up, each in their class in complete order."[31] When the teacher entered the classroom, students would stand while the teacher took attendance. Students would eat, play, and study in carefully defined intervals marked by the ringing of the bell. Moreover, the teacher would take upon himself a somewhat parental or even surveillance-based role, monitoring the cleanliness of the students, "looking after their clothes, their hands, their heads and all of their aspects."[32] The plentiful teachers at the Alliance school, according to al-Barghouti, were also specialists, each required to teach only one subject. The children were divided into numerous classes and sat not on mats as in the *kuttab* but in wooden chairs. They had a school band and were friendly

28. Nassar, Wagner, and Nicgorski, 11–12.

29. Anderson, *The American University of Beirut*, 25.

30. Tamari, *Mountain against the Sea*, 134; Majlis al-A`yan al-Urduni, "Al-Majlis Al-Sabiqa."

31. Al-Barghouti, *Al-Marahil* [The stages], 93.

32. Al-Barghouti, 93.

with each other.[33] Al-Barghouti does not recall methods of punishment. Instead, he simply describes how children energetically adhered to the disciplinary policies of the Alliance school. Teachers exhibited professional specialization and engaged in regularizing practices of attendance and division into classes. For al-Barghouti, this school was the beginning of his modern education due to its subject matter and methods.

The fact that al-Barghouti's parents chose to send him to a school that functioned as an arm of the French Jews' *Mission Civilisatrice*, and that al-Barghouti praised the school highly, underscores the importance of an education that prepared individuals for a career in government, regardless of who ran the school and to which religion they belonged. The Alliance schools provided a strong background for al-Barghouti in both French and Turkish, which enabled him to further his career in the advanced Ottoman schools in Istanbul.[34] After studying at the Alliance school, al-Barghouti attended the French Catholic Frères School, graduated from the Anglican St. George's School, and only then matriculated at the Ottoman government high school (Sultaniye) in Beirut, designed to prepare students for higher study in Istanbul.

A cosmopolitan port city, Beirut was a center of foreign and local trade, printing, and schooling. Traveling to the urban areas of Jerusalem, then Beirut, offered the teenage al-Barghouti a host of worldly delights, increasing contact with the Ottoman state, and, by World War I, disenchantment with that state. After an accident cut short his education career, he moved home, where to occupy himself he created an Arab secret political society, one of many in the Arab provinces in the early twentieth century. As Johann Büssow argues, this political engagement was an extension of al-Barghouti's induction into the modern world, which took place through schooling. While the governor of Jerusalem closed down al-Barghouti's society after an armed march during the Nebi Musa religious festival,[35] other societies tended to seek more Arab representation within an Ottoman umbrella, not secession. As Salim Tamari observes, notable families, including al-Barghouti's, maintained their relationships with the Ottoman state while engaging with growing separatist, or proto-separatist, tendencies. This "persistence of the old political

33. Al-Barghouti, 94.
34. Tamari, *Mountain against the Sea*, 136–37.
35. Büssow, "Children of the Revolution," 65–66.

game under new names," or the "reformist autonomist option," continued into the mandate era.[36]

Whether the schools al-Barghouti attended were Jewish, Christian, or sponsored by the Muslim Ottoman state, his parents were most concerned with which type of education would prove most useful to his future career. Al-Barghouti therefore attended some of the most prestigious schools in the area, irrespective of the cost of tuition and the creed the school espoused. Although his experience was somewhat unique, it was not a complete anomaly: for example, the wealthy, learned, and influential al-Khalidi family also sent Ahmad Samih al-Khalidi (1896–1951), later the principal of the Arab College of Jerusalem, to St. George's and the Syrian Protestant College.

In contrast to al-Barghouti's multifaith educational trajectory and Nassar's experiences with private tutoring and missionary education, both Darwazeh and Mushtaq attended Ottoman government-run primary schools, the first of their kind in their hometowns of Nablus and Kadhimain, respectively. The *Maârif-i Umûmiye Nizamnâmesi* or Ottoman Regulation of Public Education (RPE), which defined official education policies across the empire and indeed well into the British mandate period, had articulated an ambitious plan for educational expansion, standardization, and improvement in 1869. Implemented only in the late 1880s,[37] the law prescribed four years of compulsory education for boys and girls, elementary schools in every village, a secondary school in every large town, and a preference for schools to incorporate the Ottoman Empire's varied religions.[38] This meant students beyond urban areas were meant to travel to scarcer secondary institutions. Universally accessible elementary schooling would hypothetically expose all the empire's inhabitants to the state's program and ideology. The scarcity of secondary schools was in part a function of economy, but also of the assumption that those who would become part of the Ottoman bureaucracy would have the desire and the means to travel. Elementary schools were geared toward Muslim Ottomans, while secondary schools would also help bring non-Muslims, who had often

36. Tamari, *Mountain against the Sea*, 146.

37. Certain rules concerning high school teachers were never implemented, although other aspects of the RPE were applied, particularly after 1888. Somel, *The Modernization of Public Education in the Ottoman Empire*, 113.

38. Baysan, "State Education Policy in the Ottoman Empire during the Tanzimat Period," 158; Tibawi, *Arab Education in Mandatory Palestine*, 219; Somel, *The Modernization of Public Education in the Ottoman Empire*, 87–89.

studied at missionary, foreign, or other nongovernment schools, into the Ottoman state.[39]

In Mushtaq's case, a new government school opened after his first year of elementary school; therefore he spent one year attending elementary school in Baghdad, then two years at the new school in Kadhimain.[40] Attending a more local school meant Mushtaq no longer needed to take a horse-drawn tram to Baghdad, an experience frequently interrupted by floods and one that caused him to complain in his memoir about the inconvenience of his commute. To attend secondary school, Mushtaq had to resume his travels and, as was to become a bit of a habit, in a tram behind one animal or another. Darwazeh, on the other hand, remained in Nablus. In his memoir, he referred to the new government school as the "official," "government," or "somewhat governmental school of Nablus" and the "school of Sheikh Mahmoud Zaitr."[41]

According to Darwazeh, the Nablus government school was founded at the beginning of Sultan Abdulhamid II's reign, in the late 1870s. During Darwazeh's student years, the school was managed by the local committee of education. The government chose the committee members from among "the most distinguished and educated" of the area. Local notables had to support government education for that education to function. The school was funded by taxes, including the empire-wide education tax, as well as "unclaimed *waqfs* (pious endowments)," which the government controlled.[42] The Ottoman government was not above using somewhat suspect methods of seizing *waqf* revenue for education.[43]

The government school in Nablus, particularly during its early years, combined state control and local tradition, as well as the gradual introduction of new pedagogies and technologies. For example, students initially wrote on tin boards with ink, then blackened boards that required "special pens," and finally a blackboard in the front of the class.[44] Students learned reading, writing, some arithmetic, the Qur'an, and elocution, as well as geography, history, and a smattering of chemistry and physics. Darwazeh noted that teachers, all of whom were sheikhs, specialized in different subjects. The headmaster of the

39. Cicek, "The Role of Mass Education in Nation-Building," 225.
40. Mushtaq, *Awraq Ayyami*, 13.
41. Darwazeh, *Mudhakkirat Muhammad 'Izzat Darwazeh*, 148.
42. Darwazeh, 148.
43. Barnes, *An Introduction to Religious Foundations in the Ottoman Empire*.
44. Darwazeh, *Mudhakkirat Muhammad 'Izzat Darwazeh*, 148.

school, Sheikh Mahmoud Zaitr, did not teach classes; rather, he observed and punished students. Punishments ranged from verbal criticisms to hitting the students on their hands, to the use of the bastinado, which only Sheikh Mahmoud Zaitr could apply (although he had other students hold the offending boy's arms and legs). The school emphasized religious instruction: as in the katatib, the memorization of the Qur'an was required from all pupils before graduation.[45]

Political changes at the highest levels of the Ottoman state found their way into the schools of the Arab provinces. Their inhabitants, as Darwazeh observed, not only experienced but shaped the implementation of new education policies. During the Young Turk Revolution in 1908, the Committee for Union and Progress (CUP) succeeded in reducing the power of the Ottoman Sultan and reinstating, albeit briefly, the Ottoman Constitution. In the aftermath of the events of 1908, the Young Turk government articulated its education policy as part of a broad declaration of its political program. The government asserted that, as Turkish was the official language of the state, Turkish must be taught in elementary schools. In secondary and higher schools, "firm guidelines" were to "be adopted on the basis of the Turkish language."[46] The new government subsequently appointed a new committee of education in Nablus, drawn from members and supporters of the CUP. In the Arab provinces, these supporters generally consisted of younger, educated men.[47] The CUP therefore offered a chance for a new generation to engage with their state.

And engage they did, using the Ottoman Regulation for Public Education as a means of improving schooling by weeding out old, or old-fashioned, teachers. According to the RPE, teachers were required to possess a certificate of their qualifications issued by the government. This certificate could be achieved only by passing an examination, which few teachers, particularly in the provinces, had done. The "enlightened men" (in Darwazeh's opinion) of the new committee of education in Nablus were concerned that the teachers in the government school might not be sufficiently qualified or knowledgeable for their posts. Although the government did not impose an exam, locals seized the opportunity that Ottoman legislation permitted to improve the schools under their jurisdiction.

45. Darwazeh, 148–50.
46. Kayali, *Arabs and Young Turks*, 91.
47. Kayali, 79.

The education committee in Nablus used the legislation of the state to adapt their school as the committee saw fit. Specifically, it wanted to ensure that teachers themselves had been educated in the same way as committee members thought their own children and the children in their villages should be educated. Committee members demanded that the government school's teachers take an exam to prove their competence. The principal, Sheikh Mahmoud, refused to take the exam and was fired. Darwazeh noted approvingly that a young, educated man from Nazareth was appointed in his place. Several teachers did pass the exam, but many refused to take it or failed. Darwazeh asserted that "in Nablus and in some of its villages during the era of the new committee of education . . . and even in the remotest centers of Jenin and Tulkarem, new education committees were founded after the constitution, and the situation of elementary education in these centers and their surrounding villages improved."[48] These committees, as Darwazeh argued, incorporated various actors into the state while improving elementary education. He therefore tied local involvement not simply to the implementation of government policies but also to their beneficial effects.

Although Darwazeh appreciated local initiatives to remove "less" qualified elementary school teachers, he was not as sanguine about the persistence of underqualified instructors and the emphasis on the Turkish language at the expense of Arabic in the upper and preparatory levels of government schooling. He criticized Turkish in hindsight, after he had become essentially a professional Arab and Palestinian nationalist. His criticisms represent the nationalism of the mid- rather than early twentieth century. His opinion of "Turkification" was almost assuredly not fully formed during his earliest school days. Regardless, Darwazeh's recollections of his teachers show the diversity of individuals employed as educators during the final years of the Ottoman government. His teachers and principals at more advanced schools consisted of turbaned Turks, Arabs, and even an Afghan, of disparate qualifications. These instructors taught a variety of subjects, including French, Farsi, Arabic, mathematics, and the natural sciences. The only consistent requirement was that all teachers and students learn Turkish.[49]

Darwazeh assumed that the Ottoman policy of "Turkification" in government schools was intended to produce loyal teachers and government employees. Although Turkish was not legally mandated to be the language of

48. Darwazeh, *Mudhakkirat Muhammad ʾIzzat Darwazeh*, 151.
49. Darwazeh, 154–55.

instruction in *rüşdiye* (primary) or even *ʿidadi* (preparatory) schools, Darwazeh remembered that at the schools he attended in Nablus and throughout the empire, particularly in the capital, "the scientific subjects, such as history, geography, arithmetic, chemistry, physics and engineering and the natural sciences and civics were taught in Turkish from Turkish books even to the extent that the Arabic language and its grammar and its grammar rules were taught in the Turkish language from a book. . . . The students were taught (in Turkish) . . . irrespective of their nationalities and languages."[50] Students who spoke Arabic in the government schools of Nablus were punished with detention, having to write fifty or one hundred lines of Turkish literature or poetry after school.[51] Darwazeh argues (anachronistically) that the emphasis on the Turkish language, to the detriment of the languages and nationalisms of the minority groups of the empire, was partially due to the government's project of Turanianism.[52] He also blamed Turkification on the educational goals of the Ottoman regime: "to found schools . . . in Arab regions (like the government schools in Nablus) in order to train men to become educators, knowing the Turkish language, and to be employed by the government."[53] What is clear from his memoir, however, is the strong link between government schooling and government employment. His memories of local committee members' participation in shaping education standards indicates their willing incorporation into local governance. Similarly, attending a government school signified a chance at social mobility through employment. At every level, then, government education represented a site of incorporation into the civil service.

This incorporation of young Ottomans from the Arab provinces did not entail a meritocratic, equal-opportunity path to the highest ranks of Ottoman governance. Students from these areas had access to different types of institutions, based on religion and locale, as well as class and gender. Gertrude Nassar, who, as we have seen, was initially tutored at home, taught both girls and boys at German and English mission schools during World War I.[54] In his discussion of late Ottoman schools, Darwazeh mentions that wealthier

50. Darwazeh, 153–54.

51. Darwazeh, 155.

52. Darwazeh refers specifically to "Turaniyya."

53. Darwazeh, 152.

54. Nassar, Wagner, and Nicgorski. *My life in Palestine*, 21. These mainly catered to the children of English and German missionaries.

families would employ tutors. As Mushtaq noted in his memoirs, and as historians have pointed out, there was a class divide in Ottoman education.

Middle- and upper-class families sought to train their children to become civil servants, enrolling them in civilian schools in regional centers, such as the prestigious Maktab ʿAnbar in Damascus, which charged fees. Lower-class families viewed the army as a means of social mobility, hoping that their sons would gain admission to the military school in Istanbul and thereby obtain not only a scholarship but also a career.[55] Military schools were more numerous and had a clearer project of unity than civilian institutions, allowing them to leave their mark on mandate-era politics as well.[56] For example, Iraq's Sharifian officers attended military schools and served in the Ottoman Army. These experiences, along with their participation in the Arab Revolt and subsequent closeness to King Faysal, allowed them to become key players in Iraqi politics during the monarchical era. They were from Sunni backgrounds, born into middle- and lower-middle-class families.[57] While military schools would pay for themselves, according to Mushtaq, going to Istanbul to enroll in civilian schools required "expensive presents" and "gold liras." Along with bribes, however, this education would guarantee individuals a place in the Ottoman bureaucracy.[58]

Mushtaq actually tried repeatedly to gain admission to the military college in Baghdad, out of patriotism and the desire to "take revenge" on the "prostitute oppressors" of the Balkan states. He emphasized that learning about Ottoman defeats in the Balkan Wars of 1912 caused "an ember to ignite in his heart," such that one day these enemies "would feel the sword" when he became an Ottoman general.[59] A photograph of students at this college in figure 1.2 shows the dashing uniforms and military stance Mushtaq likely coveted.

However, Mushtaq was only thirteen years old, and although he was an extremely good student, he (sadly in his view) did not possess a strong physique. He was refused admission to the imperial military school and instead entered the Mülkiye, or civil service preparatory school, in Baghdad. When even his peers at the Mülkiye participated in military training, Mushtaq sent several petitions to the military and the head of local recruitment but was told

---

55. Simon, *Iraq between the Two World Wars*, 9; Provence, *The Great Syrian Revolt*, 39.
56. Provence, *The Last Ottoman Generation*, 26–29.
57. Batatu, *The Old Social Classes*, 319–20.
58. Quoted and translated in Pool, "From Elite to Class," 333, 335.
59. Mushtaq, *Awraq Ayyami*, 13.

FIGURE 1.2. *Students, Imperial Military Middle School, Baghdad,*
between 1880 and 1893. (Reprinted from the Library of
Congress, G. Eric and Edith Matson Photograph Collection.)

he could better serve his nation through study than military service. The Turkish general who led local recruitment applauded Mushtaq's patriotism while
steering him toward study, stating grandly that "the nation which begets sons
like you cannot ever perish. Indeed, you are still young my son, and your per-
severance in lessons to the extent that you have is patriotic (*watani*) work. . . .
As the soldier kills the enemy in the field, so you fight ignorance and back-
wardness in your journeys of study."[60]

To continue his educational career, and to become part of the Ottoman
state apparatus, Mushtaq traveled. Mushtaq's father moved to Kirkuk, where
Mushtaq sought admission to the local Sultaniye school. However, after an

60. Mushtaq, 14.

official intervened, the Ministry of Education agreed to admit Mushtaq to one of the Sultaniye schools in Istanbul, at government expense. The journey Mushtaq faced, from Kirkuk to Istanbul, in the midst of World War I was long and difficult, requiring varied means of transportation. Yet, there seems to be no question that Mushtaq would go.

Mushtaq, alongside his traveling companions, formed networks across the Ottoman Empire that would continue, albeit in truncated form, after the empire's end. In Kirkuk, Mushtaq met Sa'id Fihm (later the director of the Department of Culture of the Arab League) and they decided to travel together, as Fihm had been appointed principal in a government school in Anatolia. Their journey from Kirkuk began on a wooden cart, pulled by a team of oxen (set aside for Mushtaq and Fihm by the military and driven by a pious soldier): this cart could only go as far as Mosul. The travelers were then able to obtain a spot on a military car traveling to a rather out-of-the-way station, from which Mushtaq could take the train to Aleppo. There, Fihm and Mushtaq joined forces with the head of the courts in Baquba, as well as his wife and son.

In wartime there were few places available on the train for civilians, and nowhere to stay while waiting for a berth. Mushtaq, dressed as a scout (wishing to appear as much like a soldier as possible in order to gain sympathy), and with, as he put it, "his heart shaking in his chest," begged a military official to allow Mushtaq, and his companions passage on a train filled with German and Turkish soldiers. Mushtaq's petition was successful, and the travelers reached Aleppo by train, but again had to plead to be taken to Istanbul, fearing that if they did not reach their destinations shortly, Fihm might lose his appointment and Mushtaq a year of his "scholastic life."[61]

When he finally arrived in Istanbul, Mushtaq, like al-Barghouti in Beirut, was awed by the city, its modernity, and its connections to government service. He described Istanbul as the ultimate goal of young men's pilgrimages, "like the Kaaba for aspiring men of Iraq" who would take themselves to one of the state schools with the goal of joining the civil service or the army. He also admired Istanbul's electric lights, something he had never seen before. Mushtaq was not the only young Iraqi to make this journey: he immediately visited coffee shops known to be frequented by other Iraqis, mostly students at the war college, who promptly "welcomed" Mushtaq into the fold.[62] Mushtaq and his peers formed part of a wave of young provincials in Istanbul, planning

61. Mushtaq, 31.
62. Mushtaq, 38.

to make their fortunes in government service. However, Mushtaq's goal of studying in Istanbul would not be realized. He had arrived too late to obtain a place at one of Istanbul's Sultaniye schools and instead was to be sent to Izmit, where the next nearest school was located. After yet another journey by train, Mushtaq found himself the lone Arab in the town.

In Izmit, located along the Sea of Marmara, Mushtaq integrated himself into the school, community, and Ottoman government. According to his memoirs, he became the strongest student in Ottoman Turkish composition, writing petitions and complaints from his fellow students to the principal of the school, or even to the Ministry of Education. During the summer vacation, Mushtaq could not travel home to Iraq and instead sought to stay in the school, and to work as a daily laborer on a farm. Mushtaq, as he emphasized, was small. The principal of the school took notice and found Mushtaq a job more befitting his physical strength and status as a government school student and future civil servant. Instead of a farmworker, he became a tithe official in two nearby villages. After a few days of training, he traveled to each village (in an ox-drawn cart this time) and became part of the village communities, appreciated as an Arab, Muslim, and an educated man. As he described, he was not only "the tithe official, but also the scribe, the guide, the leader and the doctor."[63] His government education brought him, by tram, train, and ox-drawn cart across the Ottoman Empire, into the civil service. He met fellow Iraqis on his journey and defined Iraq, at least in hindsight, as his home and "homeland" but also found himself welcome in Anatolia. Even as a teenager, with less than a high school education, Mushtaq's schooling garnered him work as a low-level government official, prefiguring a lifetime of government service.

Having attended government schools and lived in Iraq and elsewhere in the Ottoman Empire rather than just in Palestine, Mushtaq reflected much more positively on his Ottoman loyalties than did Darwazeh. He asks rhetorically in his memoirs, "Were we really colonized when Iraq was under Ottoman rule? No, we were one community living under one flag and tied by the bonds of religion."[64] Yet this Ottoman nationalism, which in part inspired young Mushtaq's military hopes, would give way to a pan-Arabism of a strongly Islamic and anti-imperial character when the Ottoman Empire was defeated.

63. Mushtaq, 44.
64. Mushtaq, 30.

In contrast to Baghdad, Jerusalem, and Nablus, Irbid, now Jordan's second-largest city, lacked educational facilities, particularly beyond the elementary level. Irbid in the final years of the Ottoman Empire was not a bustling metropolis; its student population had to go elsewhere for postelementary education. Mustafa al-Tall, from one of the most prominent families in what would become Jordan, studied first in Irbid then Damascus, experiences that formed a key part of his troubled, lifelong career within and against his governments. Al-Tall became a poet, teacher, administrator, judge, alcoholic, frequent rabble-rouser, and prison inmate. The primary school Mustafa al-Tall attended in Irbid was founded due to the petitions of his grandfather; that school guaranteed government employment immediately, alleviating the local community's fears that graduates would be conscripted.[65] Mustafa al-Tall was then sent to Maktab ʿAnbar in Damascus in order to further his education.

Housed in a stately residence seized by the Ottoman government from a bankrupt merchant, the Maktab ʿAnbar preparatory school offered an elite education in the political currents of the day as well as training necessary to become an Ottoman bureaucrat.[66] Catering to the well-to-do boys of Greater Syria whose family could afford Maktab ʿAnbar's fees, the school combined a variety of ideological trends, traditions, and curricular innovations. Students learned Ottoman Turkish, the language of governance, with the goal of seeking further education and bureaucratic or professional careers in Istanbul.[67] They also studied laboratory sciences; local, European, and world history; and Islamic sciences taught by sheikhs.[68] As one enthusiastic graduate and author of a hagiographic text on the school, Zafir Qasimi, asserted, although the sheikhs did not know "the methods of modern education" and had not studied in teachers colleges, they were nonetheless "of the highest class of teachers of religion and language."[69] Teachers, like those at Maktab ʿAnbar, from the Ottoman through the Mandate period, even at elite levels, possessed very different types of training, from European institutions to al-Azhar.

At Maktab ʿAnbar, Mustafa al-Tall began to hone an Arabist, Ottoman identity as he sought employment with the state bureaucracy and studied with his

65. Rogan, "The Political Significance of an Ottoman Education," 82.

66. Provence, *The Great Syrian Revolt*, 39

67. Fortna, *Imperial Classroom*, 149.

68. Deguilhem, "State Civil Education in Late Ottoman Damascus," 245–47.

69. Qasimi, *Maktab ʿAnbar*, 39–40.

FIGURE 1.3. *East of the Jordan and Dead Sea, Village of Irbid,* ca. 1900–1920. Photo by American Colony, Photo Department. (Reprinted from the Library of Congress, G. Eric and Edith Matson Photograph Collection.)

peers from across the Levant. The experience of attending this elite state school was socially and culturally transformative for its students: they dressed differently (village boys were required to cut their long hair), sprinkled "their conversation with bits of French and Turkish and Persian," and perhaps became more at ease with their cosmopolitan fellow students than with their families.[70]

Students also began to test the limits of what was permissible, in terms of both ideology and conduct, frequently remaining at government schools even as they contributed to protests against policies of their schools (or government). Maktab ʿAnbar is better known for its nationalist students under the French mandate than for their late-Ottoman predecessors. Yet even in the early years of the twentieth century, Maktab ʿAnbar's students engaged in varying degrees of rebellion, while never quite giving up the valuable access to government posts that the school afforded them. Mustafa al-Tall's straitlaced father attended Maktab ʿAnbar, but his only potentially rebellious activity was smoking.[71] Mustafa, on the other hand, began to practice a type of activism that encompassed an understanding between the government, as represented by school administrators and officials, and its protégées: students' punishments for rebellious activities would be light and brief. For example, Mustafa al-Tall was suspended from Maktab ʿAnbar his first year for having shouted at a government official during a strike staged by the students.[72] Issues that permeated the school included divides between Arab students and Turkish students and teachers. Maktab ʿAnbar was the site of well-known student protests against the Turkish language and the formation of a clandestine group geared first toward promoting Arabic and later toward promoting Arab rights.[73] One of al-Tall's biographers argues that his youthful rebellions "against the ruling Turks" contributed to his pan-Arab nationalism, but it is by no means clear that this fledgling nationalism required him to cease supporting the Ottoman government.[74]

It is difficult to judge the degree of Pan-Arabism, or anti-Ottomanism, involved in these schoolboy protests, as memoirs or autobiographies written in hindsight, particularly in the mid-twentieth century, tend to overemphasize

---

70. Rogan, "The Political Significance of an Ottoman Education," 94.

71. Rogan, 87–88.

72. Al-Tall and Mutlaq, *Mustafa's Journey*, 3.

73. Tauber, *The Emergence of the Arab Movements*, 45.

74. Radwan et al., *Arar, the Poet and Lover of Jordan*, 18.

Arabism and the Ottoman yoke. For example, Qasimi describes students at Maktab 'Anbar as "pure Arab," asserting that the subjects they learned in school "naturally" lent themselves to inspiring a "nationalist spirit."[75] Qasimi assumes, likely anachronistically, that Arabism was a natural fit for Maktab 'Anbar's students, while Ottomanism, which Qasimi defines as pan-Turkish nationalism (Turanianism), was not.

For Mustafa al-Tall and others who attended the school, however, its approach to nationalism appear more nuanced. Arabism only gradually supplanted fealty to the Ottoman Empire. Al-Tall resumed his studies at the school after his suspension, and even wrote the following lines exalting the Ottoman Army in 1915, when German and Ottoman forces reached the Suez Canal: "May god bless our armies, for they / are the elite—the bravest of the brave. They surpass all the world in courage; no people can stand before them."[76] Like his peers, al-Tall evinced only a latent turn to Arabism. The poem includes no mention of antigovernment, pro-Arab, or anti-Turkish sentiment; in fact, quite the opposite. Through 1915, at any rate, al-Tall was ready to support Ottomanism.[77]

Al-Tall returned to Maktab 'Anbar in 1919, after having briefly worked as a teacher in the private school founded by his father back in Irbid, and as an assistant teacher in 'Arabkir ('Arapgir) in present-day Turkey. While at his father's school, al-Tall wrote and recited the following poem, to convince local notables to enroll their sons at his father's institution: "if you want o sons of my people, to achieve positions higher than others / And to fulfill all your ambitions, seek education until the time of your death. For the life of nations is in education. So, seek it on the highest summits."[78] In this poem, al-Tall promotes schooling (particularly his father's school) as a means of social mobility and national pride. He would continue to support these values throughout his career.

Subsequently, al-Tall participated in more student-led riots at Maktab 'Anbar and was forced to leave Damascus. He finally graduated from another

75. Qasimi, *Maktab 'Anbar*, 99.

76. Al-Tall and Mutlaq, *Mustafa's Journey*, 21.

77. For example, Fakhri al-Barudi attended the school in the early twentieth century and would go on to be a prominent Syrian nationalist, politician, and poet. As Rogan argues, al-Barudi's Arabism consolidated after the Ottoman state was no longer a viable option for employment, whether as a bureaucrat or a military officer. Rogan, "The Political Significance of an Ottoman Education," 81.

78. Al-Tall and Mutlaq, *Mustafa's Journey*, 24.

government school: the Sultaniye in Aleppo.[79] Al-Tall would move in and out of government service as he had with schooling, working as an educator and in various other posts, in between prison stints due to his politics.[80] As he shifted from governor to teacher and back again, he would travel to various places across the Ottoman Empire and, after its collapse, within Transjordan. Some of his brief and repeated dismissals, as well as punitive transfers, were due to his unabashed alcoholism. However, his continued participation in governance in multiple locations, while frequently rebelling against the state, indicates the flexibility afforded to educated persons, and the state's attempt to incorporate rather than alienate this limited cadre. The pattern set by intellectuals like Mustafa al-Tall persisted into the Mandate period. The Ottomans, and later the British, preferred to co-opt educated individuals rather than to exclude and risk radicalizing them.

The school founded by Mustafa al-Tall's father was one of many educational initiatives undertaken by local individuals, underscoring the diversity of educational institutions across the Ottoman Empire, but also the Ottoman population's desire for schooling on its own terms. For example, Khalil al-Sakakini, having successfully founded the unique Dusturiyya School in Jerusalem, sought to take advantage of potential expansion in education by petitioning local authorities as well as the director of education for a position at the same Sultaniye school in Beirut that Omar Saleh al-Barghouti had attended. Al-Sakakini had graduated from a similarly varied assortment of educational institutions, albeit all in Jerusalem: the Greek Orthodox School, the Christian Mission Society College, and the Zion English College.[81] As his daughter noted, however, he was mainly self-taught, with "no university degree" but with a penchant for knowledge, and an avid reader.[82] The Dusturiyya School, as exceptional as its founder, was meant to overcome sectarian divides and to offer a modern, national education. Named after the Ottoman Constitution, its students published their own newspaper and learned a variety of subjects. Free from written exams and corporal punishment, the curriculum embraced

79. Radwan et al., *Arar, the Poet and Lover of Jordan*, 19.

80. For example, his certificate of service during his first year of work for the government of Transjordan (1923) notes that he had already been a teacher, a judge, a teacher again, and a judge again in the years prior to the Mandate. Al-Tall, al-Zou'abi, and ʿAaish, *Watha'iq Mustafa Wahbi al-Tall (ʿArar)* [The documents of Mustafa Wahbi al-Tall (ʿArar)], docs. 1 and 2.

81. Matossian, "Administrating the Non-Muslims," 225.

82. Sakakini, *Jerusalem and I*, 78.

English, Turkish, and French as well as advanced Arabic grammar, literature, mathematics, Qur'anic studies for all pupils regardless of religion, and of course physical education.[83] Despite the school's clear commitment to Ottomanism, the language of instruction was Arabic rather than Ottoman Turkish, uniting *Nahdawi* values under an Ottomanist umbrella.[84]

Al-Sakakini's lobbying the government in writing, in person, and on his own behalf shows how educators could bargain with—and what they were likely to gain from—the Ottoman state. In the final months before the outbreak of World War I, al-Sakakini negotiated on an individual basis with representatives of the government to obtain a job as an educator and to help improve the schools in his region. Rather than wait for a position to be advertised, or for someone to take notice of him, he drafted a lengthy petition requesting employment with the Department of Education. He emphasized his patriotism, his passion for teaching, and the need for teachers (like him) who could apply modern methods and who had mastered the Arabic language and its literature. Al-Sakakini proclaimed his readiness to "enter the fray" to help produce "devoted teachers who [would] give their lives to the service of their nation."[85] The director of education spoke personally to him regarding his application, informing him there was no position available at the Sultaniye school that year, but that the following year enrollment would increase sufficiently for him to be appointed. The director mentioned that he hoped to found a teacher-training college, and that al-Sakakini would prove "indispensable" to that project. The interview process consisted of an informal meeting and discussion, without reference to exams or credentials. Instead, the flexibility of the Ottoman system of education allowed instructors like al-Sakakini to take initiatives on their own behalf, as he did with his petition. He viewed these prospects with optimism, writing in his diary that if he were able to take either post, it would be a "new role in his life."[86]

But al-Sakakini's dream would not be fulfilled under the Ottoman regime. During World War I, many schools were shut down, including al-Sakakini's Dusturiyya School.[87] The teachers college, which was founded during the war, did not employ him; instead, he worked for a brief period at the Salahiyya

83. Tamari, "Jerusalem's Ottoman Modernity," 17.
84. Tamari, *Year of the Locust*, 39–40.
85. Al-Sakakini, *Yawmiyyat Khalil al-Sakakini* [The diaries of Khalil al-Sakakini], 2:58.
86. Al-Sakakini, 2:58–59.
87. Tamari, "The Short Life of Private Ihsan: Jerusalem 1915," 17.

School in Jerusalem. This Ottoman government college was geared toward producing loyal Ottoman, Islamist elites but (due to one influential teacher, Rustum Haidar, later an Iraqi official) also pushed an idea of Arab solidarity under Ottoman sovereignty. When the school was moved to Damascus in 1918, both Haidar and al-Sakakini shifted their loyalties to Faysal's Arab Kingdom.[88] Al-Sakakini was briefly imprisoned for his association with a Jewish American spy.[89] By 1919, al-Sakakini returned to Palestine, resuming his career under British military occupation.

Selim Deringil has argued, in reference to the radical changes prescribed by the Tanzimat, that the Ottoman state suffered a "legitimation deficit." As the Ottoman government became ever more intrusive, it required new sources of legitimacy to normalize its rule in the lives of its subjects.[90] The changes in education wrought by the Ottoman and later British regimes in Ottoman and mandate Palestine, Transjordan, and Iraq required the acceptance of local intermediaries to function. These local employees provided legitimacy, normalizing and staffing the committees, schools, and bureaucratic posts each government prescribed. During the British mandate, government-employed educators and other civil servants acted according to Ottoman precedents, negotiating as they had with Ottoman officials, assuming, often correctly, they would obtain the same, positive results, including jobs, promotions, and beneficial transfers.

Under the British, al-Sakakini taught as he had under the Ottoman regime. His Dusturiyya School, founded in 1909, closed in World War I and reemerged as the Wataniyya College in 1925. While al-Sakakini could continue to teach as he wished, the ideal of Ottomanism that he and his contemporaries had believed in was no longer practicable. The transition from Ottoman to British administrations meant shifting ideologies and abbreviated educational journeys for students and teachers. They might go from Irbid to Jerusalem to Beirut rather than Istanbul, the former Ottoman capital. Yet the need to travel for schooling, diversity of educational institutions, pedagogical tactics, and educators' ability to bargain with their governments remained.

Ottoman educational endeavors created networks of people and information linking the provinces with one another and with imperial hubs, strong

---

88. Salim Tamari, *Year of the Locust*, 41.

89. This story is well documented by Tom Segev in *One Palestine, Complete: Jews and Arabs under the Mandate*.

90. Deringil, "Legitimacy Structures in the Ottoman State," 346.

connections between state schooling and state employment, and an emphasis on flexibility and negotiation. These journeys formed systems of schooling, affiliation, and employment that persisted even after the imposition of mandate borders, providing a basis for similar educational travels, and politics.

———

By the end of World War I, Arabs, even those who had been firmly committed to the idea of Ottomanism, realized there was little room for them in what would become Turkey. Mushtaq noted that, although he had been a strong proponent of Ottomanism, regarding it as a unification of Muslims under one banner, he turned to Arabism in part because could not find employment in occupied Turkey at the Ottoman Empire's end, whereas Faysal's short-lived Arab kingdom welcomed him with open arms.[91] Non-Turkish graduates of the Mülkiye school in Istanbul likewise did not attempt promotion in Turkey; rather, they returned to their homes, seeking whatever positions were open to them in the mandate bureaucracies and schools.[92] Journeys to Istanbul for schooling and state service ended. However, individuals like Mushtaq, al-Barghouti, Nassar, and al-Tall had experienced some schooling beyond their immediate geographic purview and had benefited from increasing educational connections between regions that were suddenly divided into mandates. Together with Darwazeh and al-Sakakini, they saw themselves as part of a wider world than that confined by the mandate boundaries. Moreover, although Nassar's leadership would take a different form, as headmistress of a government girls' school rather than as an intellectual or politician, she and her peers believed that they ought to play leading roles in the new, post-Ottoman world.

Corrine Blake, in her work on Syrian students who attended the Mülkiye Mektebi, argues that during the Young Turk period, despite charges of incompetence and other complaints, no Ottoman bureaucrats were severely punished for even antistate actions. Rather than being dismissed, they would be transferred to other jobs within the government bureaucracy. Even if they were tried criminally, they could safely assume they would be given their old posts back after the trial. Due to the scarcity of literate and qualified personnel, the Ottoman government was forced to "tolerate unethical and criminal behavior"

91. Mushtaq, *Awraq Ayyami*, 54–55, 57; Wien, *Iraqi Arab Nationalism*, 30.
92. Cleveland, *The Making of an Arab Nationalist*, 45.

in order to function.[93] Blake further notes that in the case of Syria, many Ottoman leaders and bureaucrats transitioned into being leaders during the mandate, continuing with the same political style, which she describes as "a secular western orientation, a belief in constitutional government, and a penchant for patronage." This political style also included a government career.[94] Co-opting rebellious individuals could perhaps even be traced to the sixteenth and seventeenth centuries, when, as Karen Barkey describes, rebellious bandits were pacified with official positions (and pensions).[95]

All the educators discussed became increasingly dissatisfied with the mandate system and with British rule. Seeking the nations promised by the mandate charter (if not necessarily within the charter's prescribed borders), collective representation, and, in the case of Palestine, an end to Zionist activities, educators became frustrated with their inability to control either their system of education or their government. Although they operated within restrictive educational and political frameworks, they could impede or facilitate their implementation. Ottoman traditions of education and political interactions framed an authority based on negotiations, from Mushtaq's lobbying to gain admittance to military activities or a space on a train, to al-Tall's more political student interests, to Nablus's inhabitants' selective interpretations of the RPE. Teachers, as intermediaries, possessed a privileged place within systems they navigated but could not control. During the mandate period, educators experienced tension between, on the one hand, relative freedom to express their political beliefs and, on the other, an inability or lack of desire to overthrow the governments that employed them.

The next chapter traces the consequences of overlapping Ottoman and British education policies, through an analysis of the educators employed in the first years of British control. The idiosyncrasies and regional and local variability of the late Ottoman period created an expansive notion of the teaching profession, including disparate qualifications, goals, and levels of interest in teaching. The mandate governments' imposed scarcity of teachers perpetuated educators' status as both rare and necessary, regardless of their hodgepodge training and qualifications. A lack of capable teachers only increased their ability to shape careers within and beyond the classroom during the 1920s.

93. Blake, "Training Arab-Ottoman Bureaucrats," 237.
94. Blake, 283–84.
95. Barkey, *Bandits and Bureaucrats*, 1997.

2

Policies and Practices

THE IDIOSYNCRASIES OF TEACHING
IN THE INTERWAR ERA

DURING THE early days of the mandate era, a wide range of individuals began
to teach in the overcrowded government school classrooms of Iraq, Palestine,
and Transjordan. Khalil al-Sakakini was one of them. When he took on a position with the British administration, this principled grammarian joined poor
village teachers who taught reading, writing, and some arithmetic in the dark
back room of a rented house, wealthy girls educated at expensive missionary
institutions or tutored by their fathers, elite Ottoman government professors,
and army officers fluent in Ottoman Turkish, French, German, and English.
In his diary, al-Sakakini averred, "Whether the British come or the land stays
under Ottoman control, I'll always remain a teacher, and I'll teach only what
my conscience dictates."[1]

Al-Sakakini's attitude toward shifting regimes paralleled that of many teachers employed in the government schools newly under British control in the
interwar period. Facing British occupation forces, former Ottoman educators
as well as petty civil servants tended to interact with their new regimes as they
had with the old. They adapted the nebulous boundaries of an already flexible
profession, refusing some duties and adding others. Moreover, they expected
to be heard and to retain their posts regardless of their attitude toward the
government, and irrespective of how frequently and forcefully they expressed
their opinions. Before the advent of mass schooling, education in both Islamic
and Western European contexts was characterized by a lack of specialization;
the ideal scholar/teacher was a renaissance man, mastering various languages

1. Al-Sakakini, "Such Am I, O World," 672.

and overlapping fields of study.[2] Schoolteachers in the first decades of the twentieth century were likewise renaissance men and women, approaching teaching as dilettantes rather than career professionals.

During the 1920s and 1930s, government schooling integrated this wide variety of individuals and their not-precisely professional behaviors into mandate governments. Locals demanded government education due in part to its automatic connection to government employment. Meanwhile the mandate administrations refused to fund schools or to train sufficient teachers. Colonial officials, recalling anti-imperial uprisings in India and Egypt, were reluctant to pay for education and afraid of educating a class of bookish, rebellious, anti-imperial, and unemployed nationalists. This situation of high demand and scant supply allowed educators to leverage their scarcity and qualifications against governments' desire to prevent rebellion.

Military and mandate governments had to hire heterogeneous individuals who held widely disparate views on how to teach, and who constantly tested the limits of permissible activities. Educators possessed a range of social, geographic, and educational backgrounds. They wore different clothes, from suits to *abayat*.[3] They professed different sects of Islam, Christianity, and other religions. Some had Kurdish, Turkish, Persian, or Arab origins. Several were wealthy, many were middle class, and others came from nearly destitute families. Moreover, they could choose from a variety of political ideologies and agendas, none of which ruled out employment by the mandate administrations.

The habitus of these male and female educators included particular types of agency, as teachers maneuvered through the haphazard and contradictory rules, ideals, and policies of the mandate governments' education systems. By using "*habitus* (or a system of disposition), practical sense, and strategy" to investigate educators,[4] we can see the productive nature of educational irregularities, but also the limits of educators' actions within these frameworks. Educators' practical concerns, knowledge, or even feigned ignorance of the overlapping rules of their profession defined their relationship to their governments. Jacques Bouveresse notes how, when rules include "a reasonably large

2. Hazri, "Religious Education and the Challenge of Modernity," 714–15.

3. *Abaya* (plural *abayat*) are long, black robes often worn by women outside in Iraq but can also refer to long robes worn by men in the Gulf and Greater Syria.

4. Bourdieu, in Pierre Lamaison, "From Rules to Strategies: An Interview with Pierre Bourdieu," 111.

margin of indeterminacy," actors must be inventive. They must understand the rules but also have the option of ignoring, adapting, or even breaking them "intelligently."[5] While the rules, according to Bouveresse, are present and known, adherence, partial adherence, and outright rejection are all options. Indeed, one of Bourdieu's questions, which he hoped habitus could resolve, was: "How can behaviour be regulated without being the product of obedience to rules?"[6] Habitus as a concept underscores "vagueness and indeterminacy" or "a generative spontaneity which asserts itself in an improvised confrontation with ever-renewed situations."[7]

The possibilities for teachers' actions were shaped by circumstances, as well as gendered policies, rules and frameworks. However, public schooling, and indeed governance, occurred in the contested space between rules and their execution, and between the definition of a teacher and who educators actually were. Diverse educators and civil servants used their elite status to redefine the parameters of teaching and to shape the authority of their governments overall.

Timothy Mitchell posits that in order for us to perceive the state as its own entity, imbued with authority and divided from society, state and nonstate actors need to engage in banal and repetitive actions. Mitchell focuses his analysis of these actions on regulation of space, time, bodies, and/or populations.[8] The Arab provinces and the mandates certainly experienced some degree of increasing oversight, regulatory measures, and government intrusion. But what of those carrying out these measures, marking the point at which the "state effect," or separation between state and society, was meant to be seen and experienced? Moreover, rules were, as in the Ottoman era, irregular. What is the significance of the unsystematic implementation of these processes, such as inspection, which were meant to regulate the mandate populations?

I argue that in the mandates, civil servants, specifically educators, capitalized on the processes forging the "state effect" that Mitchell describes. Educators enjoyed and promoted participation in government. They received state paychecks and carried out inspections. They recorded and reported attendance and misbehavior. They also used the wiggle room granted to them by

5. Bouveresse, "Rules, Dispositions and the *Habitus*," 55.

6. Bourdieu, *In Other Words: Essays towards a Reflexive Sociology*, 65.

7. Bourdieu, 77–78.

8. Mitchell, "Society, Economy, and the State Effect," 185.

discrepancies between rules and their application strategically in ways that ran counter to their employers' goals. Educators also encouraged their students and their societies to try out the ideologies that fluctuated across the Middle East. These concepts ranged from the ends of cosmopolitan Ottoman identities, to dreams of a unified Arab state, to overlapping sentiments of Palestinian, Iraqi, Transjordanian, tribal, religious, and local notions of affiliation. Educators' political engagement contributed to but did not exist solely in the service of a nationalist project, whether that project was clearly defined or (as in the mandate era) fairly fluid. Their connections to governments tied politics to professionalism in a peculiar way, a relationship forged within a culture of petitions, notions of self-improvement, social mobility through schooling, literature, and local conflicts.

Imperial Antecedents: A Palimpsest of Ottoman and British Policies

British forces conquered the majority of the areas that would become Britain's Middle Eastern mandates in 1917–1918, although Basra fell in November 1914. Upon their arrival, British military leaders perceived that prewar promises had whetted local appetites for both education and self-government. As one report on Iraq described, the lack of schools was causing "great dissatisfaction among the population in general."[9] By reopening schools, British forces were not merely placating a dissatisfied and war-weary enemy population; they were taking over the responsibilities of the defeated Ottoman government, as required by Hague conventions regarding military occupation.

Rather than devoting time and funding to creating new educational laws and disrupting the status quo, British officials left Ottoman regulations in place. Until the enactment of the Education Law in 1929 in Iraq,[10] the British

9. "Third Meeting of the Advisory Council," India Office Records 3, IOR/L/PS/11/180, P 7965/1920, 16, BL.

10. In describing the Public Education Law of 1929, the high commissioner of Iraq complained that Iraqi law included all the Ottoman laws that were not specifically repealed and were promulgated before November 1914. He noted dryly, "I doubt very much whether any legist could be found in 'Iraq competent to draw up with certainty a complete schedule of all previous laws, regulations, or orders relating to education law that contradict the provisions of the new 'Public Education Law.'" Acting High Commissioner for Iraq Hubert Young, "To the Right Hon'ble Lord Passfield, Pc, Secretary of State for the Colonies, 25 October 1929," CO 730/149/6, Colonial Office Records, NA, 2.

Education Ordinance in Palestine in 1933,[11] and the Education Regulations in Transjordan in 1939,[12] the only laws specifically governing education were based on the Ottoman Regulation for Public Education of 1869. Ottoman government schools became the direct responsibility of the British, while schools deemed private or foreign under the Ottomans continued as nongovernment schools. The League of Nations required mandate administrations to allow freedom of worship, including "the right of each community to maintain its own schools for the education of its own members in its own language." This Ottoman-era and later mandate structure preserved the relative autonomy granted to institutions run by foreign missions and religious minorities, including schools managed and funded by the Zionist executive in Palestine.[13]

The British did not exercise direct control over Palestine's Jewish curriculums, methods of teaching, or language of instruction; this was left to the Va'ad ha-Hinukh, the Jewish Agency's board of education. The mandate government would use the carrot of grants-in-aid, which were provided to nongovernment institutions, to exert influence, mainly to make sure schools were up to hygienic standards. While the Yishuv relied on taxing its own community and foreign donations to support its schools, its representatives constantly protested the disparity in government funding between the Jewish and Arab educational systems. Later, after much lobbying, new Yishuv Jewish schools would technically be counted as a government system, receiving more financial help from the mandate government but little, and contested, oversight. This autonomy created an almost totally separate school system, part of the burgeoning Jewish state within a state.

British education policies combined a reliance on religious, foreign, and missionary schools, as well as a continuation of Ottoman laws and infrastructure with tactics they believed would suit any colonial possession. Officials viewed the schools newly under their jurisdictions as part of a late stage in the development of colonial education. They appraised their record of colonial schooling in an almost lachrymose fashion, regularly complaining about its adverse results. Yet they continued to institute the same policies over and over, with only slight variations. Harkening back to experiences in India and Egypt,

11. Tibawi, *Arab Education in Mandatory Palestine*,134.

12. Matthews and Akrawi, *Education in Arab Countries of the Near East*, 302.

13. Government of Palestine, "Palestine: Report of the High Commissioner on the Administration of Palestine, 1920–1925," London, 1926, 13.

the British deployed strategies of divide and rule (based on religion, class, and at times intellect) to maintain social and economic hierarchies, and above all to prevent the development of a class of educated, naturally rebellious unemployed.

In India, the British had initially sought to apply methods gleaned from the metropole. They introduced an elite public school-style education intended to produce a select class of educated Indians of strong character and morals, who thought like Europeans and would mediate between the British and the rest of the Indian population.[14] The English language was particularly important. As Thomas Babington Macaulay, one of the chief architects of Britain's education policy in India, argued: "English is better worth knowing than Sanscrit or Arabic. . . . The natives are desirous to be taught English. . . . It is possible to make natives of this country thoroughly good English scholars, and that to this end our efforts ought to be directed."[15] In 1835 the British chose this "Anglicist" policy, opting to educate a minority of the Indian population using the medium of the English language and Western-style institutions of education. The conduct of these graduates would mirror that of British gentlemen, and their thoughts would follow as closely as possible those of the "rational" British mind. British policy makers focused their attention on those they viewed as natural leaders of local society, or rather those that best fit British stereotypes of gentlemanly natives. They hoped to find and through schooling confirm an upper class, which would be amenable to British rule and encourage stability.

Instead, with growing dismay, British officials decried the growth of a disaffected group of the educated unemployed, who couched their demands in a Western rhetoric of nationalism. For colonial officials, this cadre represented a "warning example" of the type of citizen produced when British domestic

14. In "Wood's Education Despatch," from the Court of the Directors of the East India Company to the governor general of India in 1854, British authorities plainly stated "the education which we desire to see extended in India is that which has for its object the diffusion of the improved arts, science, philosophy and literature of Europe; in short, European knowledge." Yet that same dispatch, which would later be known as the Magna Carta of English education in India, suggested English would be the language of instruction for higher education, while the vernacular would be employed in the "education of the masses." Quoted in Grover and Grover, *A New Look at Modern Indian History*, 259.

15. Macaulay, "Minute on Indian Education," in Macaulay, Clive, and Pinney, *Selected Writings*, 249.

educational tactics, particularly its elitist qualities, and the teaching of English, were applied wholesale to a colonial polity.[16]

Correcting what they viewed as a mistaken policy in India, British officials in Egypt created a doubly divisive system during the period of their direct control, from 1883 through 1922.[17] This time, British officials sought to train an even smaller faction of upper-class, English-speaking bureaucrats, as well as a large, lower class of rural farmers who would increase agricultural productivity. To matriculate at an urban preparatory or even a technical school, a student had to be able to pass an exam in a European language and pay a fee. The British colonial administration only funded village schools that taught in Arabic, precluding village children from gaining both secular higher education and a career in the civil service.[18] These rural schools taught a basic level of literacy and mathematics as well as religious instruction, with the eventual addition of programs in hygiene, technical, and agricultural education.[19] In elite urban schools, curricular emphasis was placed on English, helping to cement a class divide along linguistic lines.[20] Having taken on Egypt's enormous debt, the British directed a large portion of their budget toward debt payments as well as infrastructure and agriculture. This situation limited educational funds overall, keeping schools rare.[21] As of 1918 there were only 134 elite primary schools and a total of 4,265 "vernacular schools"[22] for a population that numbered 12.72 million in 1917.[23]

English-speaking elites tended to benefit from an education system that shuttled them almost exclusively into government posts. Nevertheless, due to the harshness of British rule in Egypt, this symbiotic relationship was imperfect and could not last.[24] The arrest of Sa'ad Zaghlul, the founder of the Wafd Party and the former head of the Ministry of Education, sparked protests that finally led to limited Egyptian independence in 1922. Students at government

16. Chirol, *The Egyptian Problem*, 221.
17. Cochran, *Education in Egypt*, 38.
18. Starrett, *Putting Islam to Work*, 31.
19. Russell, "Competing, Overlapping, and Contradictory Agendas," 52.
20. Johnson, *Reconstructing Rural Egypt*, 5.
21. Tignor, "The 'Indianization' of the Egyptian Administration under British Rule," 637.
22. Lloyd, *Egypt since Cromer*, 14.
23. Owen and Pamuk, *A History of Middle East Economies in the Twentieth Century*, 30.
24. Russell, "Competing, Overlapping, and Contradictory Agendas," 51.

schools formed the first wave of protesters.[25] Humphrey Bowman, who spent twenty years as an education official in Egypt and the Sudan, described Egypt's revolts as the "Frankenstein monster," which paralyzed the Egyptian government through student demonstrations. Britain, according to Bowman, had become Dr. Frankenstein, shocked by the outcome of its ungrateful creation: rebellious students and graduates of British-controlled schools.[26] As British historian and diplomat Sir Valentine Chirol argued, and Bowman would later agree, "By whatever standard we judge the educational system devised for the youth of Egypt under British control, it has tended not at all to the salvation of the State. It is unquestionably the worst of our failures."[27]

After finishing his stint in Egypt, Bowman would become the director of education in Iraq from 1918 to 1920 and director of education in Palestine from 1920 to 1936. He was one of several officers employed in the mandates who had formerly worked in the Egyptian Ministry of Education. They brought colonial goals of stability and fears of revolution by the educated unemployed. The mandate governments initially relied on these formerly Egypt-based officials, as well as on Egyptian textbooks. They adapted policies that strove to separate a bilingual, government-employed elite from a contented class of economically productive agriculturalists and mothers. For reasons of economy as well as politics, however, British administrations hired non-British individuals to staff bureaucracies and schools. This cut costs and likely contributed to stability by granting locals a stake in governance. They were also cheaper than British, Indian, and even Egyptian employees (outside of Egypt), who formed the bulk of foreigners initially employed in the mandates.

Bowman articulated British educational goals clearly in annual reports on education in the mandate for Palestine. These goals were rife with gender-specific and contradictory expectations. Bowman argued that government schooling under British rule aimed to prevent the "village boy" from becoming urbanized, educated, and subsequently "unemployed or unemployable" and prone to nationalism.[28] Instead, the British would focus their energies on

25. Whidden, *Monarchy and Modernity in Egypt*, 15–16; Carman, "England and the Egyptian Problem," 70.

26. Bowman, *Middle-East Window*, 311.

27. Chirol, *The Egyptian Problem*, 221.

28. "Report by His Majesty's Government in the United Kingdom of Great Britain and Northern Ireland to the Council of the League of Nations on the Administration of Palestine and Trans-Jordan for the Year 1930," *Palestine and Transjordan Administration Reports, 1918–1948*, vol. 3: *1929–1931*, 65.

"elementary and primary education" as, according to Bowman, "it was obvious that to open secondary and higher schools before preparing the material to fill them would have been to follow the Turkish method."[29] Invoking the "Turkish method" as something to be avoided at all costs was somewhat disingenuous, as essentially all educational legislation during the first years of the mandates and nearly all secondary schools were holdovers from the Ottoman era. Nevertheless, Bowman asserted that secondary and higher schools were not to be prioritized until an indefinite future date when there would be sufficient elementary schools, in his and his colleagues' estimation.

In terms of the mandates' female inhabitants, Bowman asserted in his memoir that "the Moslem woman of the future" would, through schooling, become

> a wife capable of bringing up her children in clean and healthy surroundings. Some book-learning was of course needed to bring about such a reformation. The principles of domestic hygiene, almost completely absent in many Arab homes, once appreciated and acted upon, would revolutionise the coming generation, which, in its turn, would set the standard for the future. It was with this end in view that we formulated the system of female education [in Palestine].[30]

British policies dictated that the overwhelming majority of locals would receive a minimum amount of schooling in their vernacular, coupled with some vocational education and, for female students, domestic science. This form of education, the British hoped, would prevent urbanization, rebellion, or indeed any great change at all. Men were to be docile village laborers or craftsmen; women were to take their place at the head of the home, leading the fight for "domestic reform" and "domestic hygiene," which would create a healthier, more modern, and cleaner generation, without women's emancipation or politicization. Single-sex education from first grade to college, if not beyond, would preserve distinct masculine and feminine spheres.

Bowman grudgingly noted, however, that the mandate governments' needs went against its gendered ideals of modern womanhood and subdued masculinity. To train mothers, the mandate governments needed female teachers who would postpone motherhood and domesticity. Instead, generally

29. Captain H. E. Bowman, Director of Education, "Department of Education, Annual Report 1918, 20 of January, 1919," in *Records of Iraq*, vol. 1: *1914–1918*, 104–5.

30. Bowman, *Middle-East Window*, 259.

unmarried and childless female teachers would travel to educate the mandates' girls in gender-segregated classrooms. Staffing the mandates' growing bureaucracies required "clerks with knowledge of English." Teachers and other petty civil servants were meant to function as intermediaries between British officials and the rest of the population. Educators would gain the power to engage with British imperialists in their own language and on their own terms. The instability and inherent conflict between the needs of each mandate state and its educational goals likewise opened up a space for educators to make claims on their governments. The need for educators of different genders, coupled with the British desire to avoid educating the populations under their control, was productive, granting educators influence over the mandate governments.

To find teachers, the British were reduced to "combing the prison ships and camps."[31] Even if sufficient teachers could be found, British officials were reluctant to extend access to education, particularly secondary education, beyond that of their Ottoman predecessors. This meant that all students who remained in formal, government schooling past the age of twelve would have attended one of a handful of secondary or postsecondary institutions left over from the Ottoman era, located in urban areas. Between 1922 and 1932, al-Markaziyya was one of only three government schools in Iraq that offered intermediate or secondary classes.[32] There were no complete secondary schools for girls through 1933.[33] Iraq did, however, possess upper-level institutions training teachers, lawyers, doctors, and military officers. Palestine's twenty full secondary schools for girls were nongovernment schools; the lone government secondary institution, the Women's Training College (WTC), was located in Jerusalem. The Men's Teacher Training College, by 1927 renamed the Arab College of Jerusalem, was the only government secondary school in Palestine that offered the full four-year (as opposed to only a year or two) course for boys until the 1938–1939 school year. Even by 1940, both full secondary government schools for males were located in Jerusalem.

31. Dorothy Van Ess, "'Pioneers in the Arab World' Revised Draft, 1966–1975," Dorothy Van Ess Papers, 78-M124, folder 32, 2, SL.

32. Çetinsaya, The Ottoman Administration of Iraq, 17.

33. By 1933 only four schools offered the preparatory level for secondary classes; of these, only two schools (both male-only) included the final and fourth year: al-Markaziyya and the secondary school of Mosul. Wizarat al-Ma'arif Iraq, Al-Taqrir al-Sanawi 'an Sayr al-Ma'arif li-Sanawat [Annual report on educational progress for the year] 1930–31, 1931–32, 1932–33, 37.

Transjordan's situation in terms of secondary schools was still more meager than Iraq's or even Palestine's. The only secondary school in Transjordan to offer a full secondary course during the entire mandate era was the boys' school of al-Salt, founded by the Ottomans rather than the mandate government. There were no government secondary girls' schools with a full secondary course until Jordanian independence.[34] This dearth of institutions meant Jerusalem enhanced its Ottoman-era status as Palestine's educational center, particularly because of its bounty of missionary institutions. Because both Palestine and Transjordan were British mandates, Jerusalem supplanted Damascus as a destination for Transjordanian students.[35]

Overall, the more British control any given territory experienced, the less government education it would receive. The English-language instruction frugally granted in the few government schools available was to be as rationed as possible: English was taught in primary rather than elementary schools, and only in urban areas.[36] Although the British believed this method of dividing and conquering through schooling could work nearly everywhere under their control, they also nearly always voiced the same objections regarding the results. Despite British officials' increasing efforts at preventing higher education, they continued to fear the emergence of a surfeit of rebellious graduates, bent on careers in governments independent of Britain.[37] Paradoxically, colonial fears of the growth of nationalism solidified the connections between government education and work in the civil service. Teachers' agency within these frameworks rendered the extension of British authority into a locally driven, locally mediated process.

From Policies to Their Implementation: Local Variations

In Basra, the British revenue officer asserted that it was better to delay opening schools than to saturate "the *wilayat* with partly trained and partly immoral so called *muallimin* (teachers) to show a fine educational system on paper

---

34. Matthews, *Confronting an Empire*, 315.

35. Department of Education Government of Palestine, *Department of Education Annual Report 1941–42* (1942), 4–5.

36. Bowman, "Department of Education, Annual Report 1918, 20 of January, 1919," in *Records of Iraq*, vol. 2: *1918–1921*, 104–5.

37. Suzanne Schneider has argued that colonial fears of rebellion included a "politics of denial," namely, the British claim that education was apolitical. Schneider, *Mandatory Separation*.

[*sic*].["](38) Instead, schools were opened only when British forces deemed it absolutely necessary due to local demand. The teachers had to be moral men, academically qualified at least on a basic level, and "physically fit." Only twenty-one teachers were actually hired in Basra. However, both Gertrude Bell, the famous British traveler, spy, and 1918 Oriental secretary, and the district education officer emphasized the better quality of these teachers compared to those under the Ottoman regime. Their observations dovetail with Orientalist stereotypes of Ottoman-era teachers as "men of very bad moral character" and Ottoman schools as "hot-beds of vice to which respectable Arabs hesitated to send their boys."[39]

Reports like that of Gertrude Bell would foreground the role of Britain's military administration in the reconstruction of government education in Iraq. Yet British efforts across the mandates were almost completely dependent on local initiative, albeit with British inspection and constant criticism. This meant British education policies allowed for considerable local participation and control of government schooling. In the interests of economy, British officials encouraged those they had recently conquered to provide the funding for building schools and hiring teachers. Simultaneously, the British military administration sought to curb any destabilizing local impact on education policy.

One such example was the Education Committee of Baghdad, an organization explicitly meant to bark but not bite, allowing the Department of Education "to keep in close touch with different phases of religious and educational opinion."[40] By incorporating religiously and ethnically diverse representatives into consultative but not legislative roles, British officials hoped both to learn what Iraq's population thought of government education, and to increase that population's investment in their own schooling. Its members ranged from Abdul Karim al-Chalabi, the token Shi'ite notable, to Pere Anastase, "a Syrian catholic of Corsican origin and an Arabic language savant," as well as Haj Ali al-Allusi, a Baghdad Qadi, or religious judge.

Backing local educational committees across Iraq, Palestine, and Transjordan (without allowing those committees policy-level decision-making power)

38. Sg. A. L. Gordon, "Education, 1918," in *Iraq Administration Reports, 1914–1932*, vol. 1: *1914–1918*, 25.

39. Gertrude Bell, "Educational Measures in the Occupied Territories of Lower Mesopotamia," in *Records of Iraq*, vol. 1: *1914–1918*, 8; Gordon, "Education, 1918," 25.

40. "Note on the Organization of the Civil Administration of Mesopotamia April 1, 1920," IOR/L/PS/11/173, BL. 22.

FIGURE 2.1. *The Education Committee, Baghdad*, 1919: Abdul Karim Chelabi, E. H. Base, Père Anastase, H. E. Bowman, Hajji Ali al Allusi, H. B. Staffard Northcote, Yussef Beg, N. A. MacGurk. Photo by Humphrey Bowman. (Reproduced by permission from the Humphrey Bowman Collection, GB165-0034, Alb2-272, Middle East Centre Archive, St Antony's College, Oxford.)

was only one of the tactics the British military administration employed to inspire (or indeed require) support of public school systems. Municipal funds, collected by local rather than British officials, were earmarked to pay for government schools in Iraq.[41] In Palestine, and what would become Transjordan,

41. "Mesopotamia Administration Report, Kirkuk Division," IOR L/PS10/621, April 19, 1920, BL.

the British military administration urged local committees, founded during the Ottoman era, to raise funds and help villages to provide appropriate buildings for schools.[42] The mandate administration in Palestine stipulated that new village schools would be opened only if villagers paid for the construction or rent of suitable school buildings, while the mandate government would inspect the school and pay teachers' salaries. In Transjordan, villagers and town-dwellers alike were expected to pay for not only the school buildings and their maintenance but also teachers' salaries and school furniture.[43] This situation saved each government money but left much of schooling in local hands.

The clearest departure from the Ottoman system of schooling was the substitution of Arabic for Turkish as the language of instruction in most areas.[44] While this change sparked no protests in Palestine or Transjordan, in certain areas of Iraq, with large Turkish and Kurdish populations, there was resistance.[45] One British intelligence report raised the problems associated with trying to reduce a multiethnic Ottoman polity to an Arab, Arabic-speaking one, run by an Arab dynast. The report described "a strong local prejudice, both among the Turkish and Kurdish population, to Arab government," to the extent that the Boy Scout organization had to be renamed "Isji" (Turkish) rather than the Arabic "Kashafah."[46]

British administrations pledged to eventually offer standardized elementary schooling to "the whole population," an echo of the compulsory and gratis schooling the overly optimistic Ottoman law of 1913 had stipulated.[47] These government elementary schools, however, differed wildly across locales due to teachers' qualifications and proclivities and the relative wealth of their communities. For example, in Iraq there was little similarity between schools in Baghdad and those in surrounding villages. The Zakho School (figure 2.2) was located in northern Iraq, with a relatively large number of teachers as well as a modern school building.

42. Tibawi, *Arab Education in Mandatory Palestine*, 25.

43. "Decision of the Diwan Khas no. 6," February 1, 1931, in C. R. W. Seton and Transjordan, *Legislation of Transjordan, 1918–1930*, 803.

44. Palestine and Great Britain, Palestine Royal Commission, *Memoranda Prepared by the Government of Palestine* (London: H. M. Stationery Office, 1937), 117.

45. Captain E. H. Base, "Administration Report of the Department of Education for the Year 1919," Government Press, Baghdad, 1920, ST 34/16, 2, BL.

46. "Intelligence Report no. 28," December 1, 1921, IOR 420/A 1237, BL.

47. "First Meeting of the Advisory Council," IOR/L/PS/11/180, P 7965/1920, 15, BL.

FIGURE 2.2. *Zakho School, Iraq, 1920s.* Photo by Arthur Lionel Forster Smith. (Reproduced by permission from the Lionel Smith Collection, GB165-0266, Alb6-012, Middle East Centre Archive, St Antony's College, Oxford.)

In contrast, figures 2.3 and 2.4 show schools in more rural areas. The school at Sharqat (al-Shirqat) shows children of varying ages, including girls, as well as two teachers, all in long robes. An older-looking, rustic building sits in the background. The school in Bir Idhren (figure 2.4) has an Ottoman-era stone building with open, arched doors and windows. Pupils are dressed in what looks to be scouting gear, while the older schoolmaster, in a turban and long coat, smiles at the camera.

Relying on previous institutions reinforced disparities between urban and rural locations.[48] While Mosul boasted a large number of schools, particularly for girls, the Sharqat School, approximately 115 kilometers south of Mosul, lacked basic facilities. Similarly, in Palestine, Bowman noted how schools varied due to the input of local individuals.[49]

Foreign observers like Bowman tended to invoke local prejudices to justify the region's lack of female education rather than the more salient causes: colonial priorities and stinginess. Coming from the United States and the United

48. Bowman, "Department of Education, Annual Report 1918, 20 of January, 1919."
49. Bowman, *Middle East Window,* 278.

FIGURE 2.3. *Village School at Sharqat, Iraq,* 1920s. Photo by Arthur Lionel Forster Smith. (Reproduced by permission from the Lionel Smith Collection, GB165-0266, Alb6-009, Middle East Centre Archive, St Antony's College, Oxford.)

FIGURE 2.4. *Bir Idhren School, Schoolmaster and Three Pupils,* Iraq, 1920s. Photo by Arthur Lionel Forster Smith. (Reproduced by permission from the Lionel Smith Collection, GB165-0266, Alb6-010. Middle East Centre Archive, St Antony's College, Oxford.)

Kingdom, using and believing in gendered and Orientalist stereotypes, they assumed it was traditional biases against female education and empowerment that caused a lamentable dearth of girls' schools. They also presumed that schooling should make women more Western, whereas Westernization (and demands for national rights) were more problematic for male colonial subjects. Even for officials with firsthand experience of colonial policy, it was difficult to consider their role vis-à-vis the young, female inhabitants of the mandates as anything but magnanimous. F. B. Riley, writing in 1925 after his stint as commissioner of education in Iraq complained of a lack of schools for girls, asserting that Iraq's girls "sadly need the influence and training that only Western women can give them."[50] Riley blamed the absence of schools for girls on a deficiency of Western women, believing that their civilized, feminine example was superior to that which non-Western, educated women would offer.

These paternalistic and Orientalist ideas of Arab (Muslim) resistance to women's schooling tended to be exaggerated or wholly inaccurate. The American Monroe Commission in early 1930s Iraq stated that nothing regarding schooling in the country "offered more surprise to the members of the Commission than the very genuine interest that everywhere appeared in the education of girls and women." Despite, as the commission noted, the fact that the mandate government had been willing to sponsor very few schools for girls, these schools were well attended, and well supported by the local community.[51] Even in the early 1920s, local newspapers referenced the need to increase women's education to educate mothers to improve their societies and their nations. In Palestine, one article claimed girls' education would improve "social and literary life" due to women's role as mothers.[52] In Iraq, another argued that "the regeneration of Iraq should be wrought not only by the rough hands of men but by the soft hands of women," and that there would be no benefit to the "social life of the nation" without women receiving education. The writer held up Japan as a model of progress in this regard.[53] Mandate-era inspector of education and historian, the Palestinian Abdul Latif Tibawi declared that any assumptions of Arab/Muslim resistance to girls' schooling were untrue, and he faulted Palestine's mandate government for using the

50. Riley, "Education in a Backward Country," 4.

51. Educational Inquiry Commission Iraq and Paul Monroe, *Report of the Educational Inquiry Commission*, 56.

52. "Ta'alim al-Banat" [Girls' education], *al-Nafais al-Asriyya*, April 1, 1921, 115, NLIJ.

53. Article in *al-Iraq*, quoted in *Baghdad Times*, August 14, 1922, BL.

excuse of greater local demand for boys schools to justify a lack of expenditure on girls' education. Tibawi went so far as to state that the "unfortunate neglect of female education" was "in a way the most colossal of the failures of the Government educational system."[54] Tibawi had numbers to support his claim: in Palestine, demand for education for both boys and girls always exceeded the supply of overcrowded government schools. For example, in Hebron through the 1930s, approximately 77 percent of girls who applied to the lone government girls' school were rejected for lack of space.[55]

The supply of educators, both male and female, was low, and demand was high. This meant that a few qualified teachers (and petty civil servants) could manipulate their governments, promoting individual agendas as well as national, regional, religious, and local affiliations. Khalil al-Sakakini's process of resignation from his post at the training college in Palestine points to the bargaining power teachers could command, its limitations, and the ability of educators to move in and out of government service throughout the region. Al-Sakakini acted as principal of the Men's Teacher Training College in Palestine for only a year. He resigned, not because he could not teach what he wanted, but because he refused to serve a government he felt was acting unfairly (and because he had other job prospects). As principal, al-Sakakini took advantage of his position and the disorganized mandate government to foster a student-run newspaper. If they got into trouble at school, students would be brought before a group of their peers rather than professors to be disciplined. They also managed the college's household budget.[56]

In 1920, al-Sakakini resigned to protest the appointment of Herbert Samuel, an English Jew and Zionist, as high commissioner of Palestine.[57] In his final interview with Sir Ronald Storrs, the military governor of Jerusalem, al-Sakakini silently smoked a cigarette as Storrs tried to convince him to stay. In this one-on-one meeting, recounted in al-Sakakini's personal diary, Storrs alternated between criticizing and complimenting al-Sakakini. Storrs complained that al-Sakakini had been wandering the country, deploring government schools' lack of development and telling the Arabs they must depend on themselves for education rather than the government.[58] According to

54. Tibawi, *Arab Education in Mandatory Palestine*, 229–30.
55. Greenberg, *Preparing the Mothers of Tomorrow*, 51.
56. Al-Sakakini, *Yawmiyyat Khalil al-Sakakini*, 3:207.
57. Al-Sakakini, 3:223–24.
58. Al-Sakakini, 3:224–25.

al-Sakakini, Storrs had noticed al-Sakakini's advocacy of Arab control of education, and for schools to "instill in students the spirit of freedom, pride, independence, courage, sincerity, and other such principles that can serve to raise nations from the depths of degeneration and enable them to shake off the semblance of servitude they have worn for generations."[59] Storrs added, somewhat misguidedly, that Herbert Samuel would act in the interests of the English rather than the Jews. Rather than acquiesce to Storrs's speeches, which offered him no true guarantee of British goodwill or impartiality, al-Sakakini left Storrs's office without a word. Shaking off any "semblance of servitude," he asserted his independence and refused to compromise his principles any further. The fact that he already had an offer to work at the Arabic-language primary school attached to the Syrian Orthodox University in Egypt, with a salary five pounds higher than his current wage, certainly helped him to leave.[60] He could therefore push back against British policies, secure in the knowledge that his qualifications would secure him employment elsewhere.

Individual initiative had its limits, however, even within the loosely controlled framework of the mandate system of education. Pedagogical control, and the "generative spontaneity" of al-Sakakini's actions, such as his innovations at the Men's Teacher Training College, did not correspond to direct authority over the military system of education, or to the erasure of the Zionist project in Palestine.[61] Al-Sakakini could not force the British military government to require music as part of its syllabus throughout government schools, or to forbid corporal punishment, although he could enforce these policies in the institution he led. Moreover, he could not convince Palestine's government to fire its head, the high commissioner, and to end its support of the Zionist project in Palestine. Al-Sakakini's resignation constituted a particular gesture on the part of one civil servant of the British administration; it did not result in the replacement of Herbert Samuel.

Al-Sakakini's rejection of government employment because the mandate explicitly facilitated Zionism points to broader questions of politics and bureaucracy under colonial regimes. His resignation paralleled the actions of many other Palestinian Arabs who refused to form representative bodies, which would imply acceptance of the Zionist project embedded in the charter of the mandate

---

59. Al-Sakakini, quoted in Segev, *One Palestine, Complete*, 145.

60. Al-Sakakini, *Yawmiyyat Khalil al-Sakakini*, 3:223.

61. Bourdieu, *In Other Words: Essays towards a Reflexive Sociology*, 77–78.

government itself.[62] Yet these individuals were willing to staff the mandate bureaucracies: al-Sakakini would work as a government inspector of education for
over a decade beginning in 1926, after Herbert Samuel was replaced as high commissioner.[63] As an inspector, al-Sakakini wrote not only the grammar textbooks
used throughout the mandates but also political articles in various journals.

Al-Sakakini provides one example of a habitus, and what Ilana Feldman
terms a carefully nurtured "civil service persona," which existed across multiple, explicitly temporary regimes.[64] The civil servant would be ethical, self-
less, and motivated by the good of the population rather than personal gain.
Separating state services, such as health and education, and those who provided
these services from the politically repugnant purpose of the state itself allowed
individuals such as al-Sakakini to continue as civil servants, even when they
disagreed with their government's colonial goals and policies. Nevertheless,
staffing government services bolstered the mandate government's ability to act
with authority, although this form of local participation granted a different type
of legitimacy from what a legislative body might offer. Despite educators' government paychecks, mandate populations' perceptions of educators were usually
positive: modernizers rather than government stooges. It is important to remember that al-Sakakini was an outlier, both politically and in terms of his pedagogy.
Nevertheless, his ability to shape the education system but not change the pro-
Zionist course of the mandate points to the limits of local participation, limits
the British cultivated across Iraq and Transjordan as well.

The First Generation of Teachers

Mandate-era educators, including the thousands less famous than al-Sakakini,
were intermediaries, rabble-rousing civil servants, and pedagogues. A lack of
standardization in education, combined with the bargaining power teachers
possessed, renders the background and proclivities of individual teachers even
more important for understanding their contradictory roles. The disparate
sizes of the mandates, as well as varying degrees of British control over education, shaped the number of teachers and type of schooling each government
offered. However, the quantity of teachers in the mandates' government

62. Khalidi, *The Iron Cage*, 33–35.
63. Government of Palestine, *Civil Service List 1938: (Revised to the 1st January, 1938)* (Jerusalem, 1938), BL.
64. Feldman, *Governing Gaza*, 96–97.

schools remained low during the first decade of British hegemony, granting them more power in relation to their governments and employers.

British control over schooling fluctuated over time and across its three Mandate territories. Due to the Iraqi revolt in 1920, British officials decided to hold up education as an example of Iraq's ability to function without British tutelage.[65] From 1923 on, "no administrative order [was] given by a British official in the Ministry of Education."[66] Instead, the British and the newly installed King Faysal hired Sati al-Husri to be director of the Department of Education. Al-Husri quickly became one of the most important figures in the mandate education system, though British officials remained in Iraq in an advisory capacity. Competing local factions under watchful and increasingly discomfited British supervision fought over how much and what type of schooling to implement, but Iraq's capacity to open schools and to train and import educators increased whenever British influence faded.

In Transjordan and Palestine, education and educators remained limited, albeit for different reasons. In Transjordan from 1922 to 1924, the British-supported monarch Abdullah sought to increase the government's role in schooling. His budget was constrained, however, both by British frugality and by his own extravagances. Legally separated from Palestine only in 1923,[67] the mandate for Transjordan devoted little funding to schooling after the British consolidated their administrative control over Abdullah's finances in 1924.[68] Almost completely staffed by individuals from the mandates, Transjordan's fledgling education system was more of an afterthought, falling under the general curricula and policies of the mandate for Palestine.

Palestine experienced the greatest degree of British control over education, as British colonial officials staffed the top echelons of the educational bureaucracy, allegedly to preclude complaints of bias by either the Jewish or the Arab communities. In one infamous incident, the wealthy and well-traveled George Antonius, born in Lebanon and raised in Egypt, with a degree from King's College Cambridge, was appointed assistant director of education in 1921.[69]

65. The series of uprisings between June and November 1920 required the British to deploy approximately sixty-five thousand soldiers, spending one hundred million pounds overall. Abbas K. Kadhim, *Reclaiming Iraq*, 1.
66. Great Britain, Colonial Office, *Special Report*, 224.
67. Anderson, *Nationalist Voices in Jordan*, 41.
68. Alon, *The Making of Jordan*, 136.
69. Tibawi, *Arab Education in Mandatory Palestine*, 28.

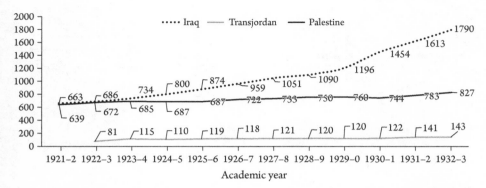

FIGURE 2.5. Number of government teachers in the mandates. See note 71 for sources.

Despite his credentials, high social position, and perfect English, he was passed over for promotion in 1927. Jerome Farrell, the British civil servant who took the position, argued that Antonius was "not an educationist" and, because Antonius was Arab, he could not be put "in charge of both Jewish and Arab education."[70] In reality, British officials occupied the upper ranks of the mandate government as a whole, due to the impossible goals articulated in the Balfour Declaration. To found one nation within another, British officials would maintain authority over education of the majority Arab population and would increasingly deploy force to keep this population in line.

The amount of British control over schooling is clearly reflected in the number of teachers hired in each mandate; where the British retained close control, educational expansion was slow, as shown by the chart depicting total government school teachers in the region from 1921 to 1932 (figure 2.5).[71]

The number of teachers in Iraq increased faster than in Palestine and Transjordan, particularly after 1923. The total number of teachers relative to

70. Jerome Farrell to Lionel Smith, October 8, 1927, Smith papers, GB165–0266, Box I, File 3, Letters from Jerome Farrell 1926–29, DS 113, 1, MECA.

71. The charts in figures 2.5 and 2.6 are composed from statistics from the following sources: Government of Palestine Department of Education, *Department of Education Annual Report 1929–30* (Jerusalem, 1930), table 11; al-Hilali and Khalil, *Tarikh al-Ta'lim fi al-'Iraq fi al-'Ahd al-Intidab al-Baritani, 1921–1932* [The history of education in Iraq during the era of the British Mandate, 1921–1932], 106; Ireland, *Iraq: A Study in Political Development*, 126; al-Tall, *Education in Jordan*, 40; Mahasina et al., *Madrasat Al-Salt* [The school of al-Salt], 1:115; Matthews and Akrawi, *Education in Arab Countries of the Near East*, 140, 236.

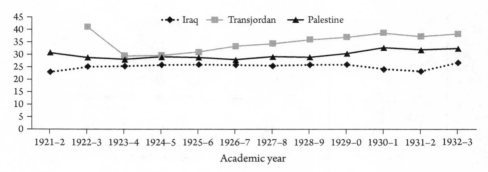

FIGURE 2.6. Student-to-teacher ratio. See note 71 for sources.

students remained relatively constant, however, indicating a continually high demand (figure 2.6).

The teachers employed in government schools during the early years of the mandates had gained their academic credentials (such as they were) during the Ottoman period. They represented a wide range of qualifications, skills, and interest in teaching; however, they shared certain characteristics: they tended to be urban and, at least in Palestine and Transjordan, in their twenties or early thirties.[72] These demographics reflect patterns of access to education in the late Ottoman period and the consistency with which mandate Departments of Education continued to rely on Ottoman structures of schooling. In Transjordan, for instance, teachers' training ranged from elementary school, to a few years at college, to a degree from the Sorbonne.[73] In Iraq and Palestine, educators, particularly at secondary or postsecondary institutions, would have studied abroad, at institutions like al-Azhar or AUB.[74]

72. "Abdul Majid Khurshid Kafr Kama V.S" 1019 4 M, ISA; "Hamed Saʿid el-din," 1020 4 M, ISA; "Khalaf Sabbagh," 1017 10 M, ISA; "Helwa Ismail Abdu," 1019 10 M, ISA. In Transjordan, of the 348 educators whose employment began before 1932, 152 birth dates are available. Of these, 3 were born before 1890. Eleven teachers were in their thirties when they began teaching, 80 were in their twenties, and 58 were teenagers. HRD. In 117 personnel files for teachers who taught before 1932 in Palestine, 104–105 of the teachers were born around the turn of the century, a few were born between 1890 and 1900, and 4 were deemed "old."

73. HRD. Saʾid Bahrah was a Sorbonne graduate and principal of the Boys Secondary School of al-Salt. Mahasina et al., *Madrasat Al-Salt*, 78.

74. See, for example, Muhieddin Yahia Naser, who studied at al-Azhar and then taught in Ein Hod, Palestine ("Mohd. Yahia Naser," ISA 1016 5 M), while there were increasing numbers of AUB graduates in Iraq. Wizarat al-Maʿarif Iraq, *al-Taqrir al-Sanawi ʿan Sayr al-Maʿarif* [Annual report on educational progress for the year] *1928–1929*, 38.

In both Palestine and Iraq, certain sects were overrepresented among educators. In the mandate for Palestine, a large proportion of teachers taught in
nongovernment schools. This indicates both the lack of government schools
and the religious significance of Palestine as part of the Holy Land, as missionary
and foreign institutions competed with one another for the souls of the area's
inhabitants. Over 25 percent of Palestine's government teachers were Christian
during the 1920s, although Christians constituted only a little over 10 percent of
the non-Jewish population in Palestine.[75] Palestine's Ottoman-era Christian
schoolchildren often attended missionary schools, but, like Omar al-Barghouti
and Ahmad Samih al-Khalidi, it was not uncommon for Muslim students to
attend Christian schools. This, among other factors, contributed to Christian-
Arab Palestinians having greater educational qualifications than Muslim-Arab
Palestinians. For example, in 1931, 14 percent of the Muslim population over age
seven was literate (25 percent of males, 3 percent of females), while 58 percent of
the Christian population (72 percent of males, 44 percent of females) could
read.[76] The proportion of Christian teachers remained constant during the 1920s,
as did the overall population of Christians in Palestine.[77] The administration of
the Department of Education was also disproportionately Christian: it included
seven Christian administrators, two Jewish (from the new Yishuv), only one
Muslim, and three British (Christian) officials.[78] In 1923 there were significantly
more teachers (1,701) in nongovernment schools than government ones (685).
The teachers in nongovernment schools, however, included the Yishuv as well
as foreign and Christian missionary institutions.[79]

Similarly, Iraqi teachers reflected (though not proportionally) the religious
diversity of their country, and different groups' access to education. Shi'ites,
who formed the largest proportion of Iraq's inhabitants, were underrepre-
sented. Ottoman government schools had tended to target and cater to Sunni
Muslims, while Shi'ite religious schools, including the madrasas of Najaf,
served the Shi'ite population. It is not possible to determine the exact proportion of Shi'ite to Sunni teachers, as reports on education after 1923 carefully

75. Krämer, *A History of Palestine*, 183
76. Ayalon, *Reading Palestine*, 16.
77. By the 1931 census there were 759,700 Muslims (including, according to the British, the
Muslim nomadic population), 88,907 Christians, 174,606 Jews, and 10,101 others. Anglo-American
Committee of Inquiry, *A Survey of Palestine*, 141.
78. In Palestine and Iraq, the British defined educators and education by religion, followed
by language.
79. Government of Palestine Department of Education, *Department of Education Annual
Report for the Year 1923*, 13, 20, 23.

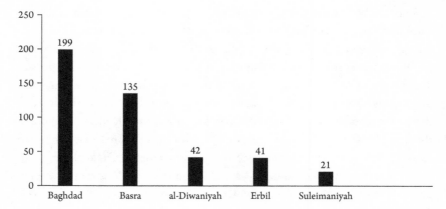

FIGURE 2.7. Iraqi government school teachers, 1928–1929. (Wizarat al-Ma'arif Iraq, *al-Taqrir al-Sanawi 'an Sayr al-Ma'arif 1928–1929*.)

avoided defining teachers by religion. There is no list of Christian/Jewish/ Shi'ite/Sunni teachers once the British stopped composing educational reports. Sati al-Husri and other education officials desired an Arab and Iraqi unity among teachers but perhaps also wanted to downplay a lack of Shi'ite educators overall. Evidence from 1918–1923 underscores how few Shi'ite teachers and students there were, relative to their numbers in Iraq; only approximately 20 percent of students were Shi'ite.[80] The 1918 report on education mentioned requiring that a Sunni and a Shi'ite teacher be employed in each government school but added that this suggestion "has not proved to be necessary or even desirable" as most schools were located in majority Sunni or majority Shi'ite areas. The British also touted their own skills at selecting teachers who would bridge sectarian divides, as they were "instructed to avoid as much as possible sectarian differences and to emphasize points of common ground."[81]

Moreover, Iraq's few educators were clustered in urban areas. In 1928–1929 the urban districts of Baghdad, Basra, and Mosul had between 261 and 135 teachers, whereas in more rural districts there were between 45 and 21 (figure 2.7).[82] The numbers for female teachers (figure 2.8) were even more stark: only two female teachers were willing to live and work in either Erbil or Kut.[83]

80. "Irak Report on Education, Report on the State of Education for the Year 1922–23," S T 34/15, 7, BL.

81. Bowman, "Department of Education, Annual Report 1918," 103.

82. Wizarat al-Ma'arif Iraq, *al-Taqrir al-Sanawi 'an Sayr al-Ma'arif 1928–1929*, 1.

83. Wizarat al-Ma'arif Iraq, 8.

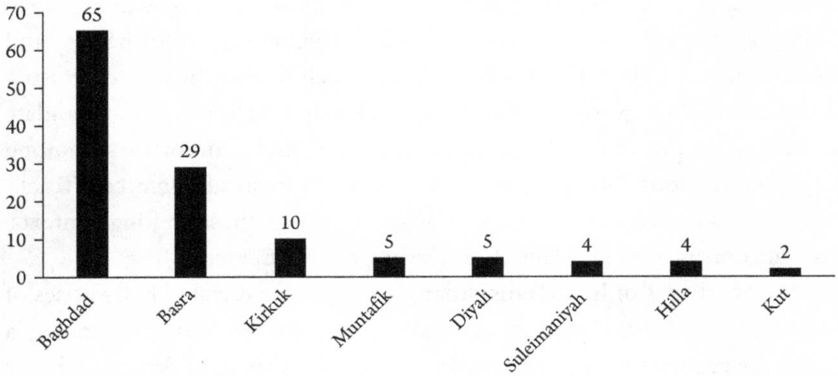

FIGURE 2.8. Female teachers in Iraq, 1928–1929. (Wizarat al-Ma'arif Iraq, *al-Taqrir al-Sanawi 'an Sayr al-Ma'arif 1928–1929*.)

The scant number of mandate-era teachers shared a privileged position relative to their employers and their societies. The haphazard implementation of educational regulations, excess demand for schooling, as well as a lack of oversight (and of replacement teachers) extended considerable leeway to the heterogeneous public school educators of the 1920s Middle East. Moreover, when these teachers entered government service, they marked one of the points at which the mandate states met society. The educators who appear as statistics in annual reports were state employees who had almost daily contact with each state's youngest subjects. Education policies, conflicting definitions of the teaching profession, and educators' individual agency combined in the habitus of mandate teachers and in the workings of the mandate governments themselves.

Prescriptions and Methods: The Model Teacher in the Mandates

What the profession of teaching lacked in standardization, it made up for in expectations. Economizing and modernizing colonial governments hoped teachers would fill a variety of functions: promoting hygiene, fitness, order, and development.[84] Village teachers in particular were to be "punctual" and

84. One teacher was severely reprimanded for refusing to attend a course on hygiene held in Nazareth in 1923. Letter from District Inspector of Education, Galilee, to Director of Education, November 19, 1934, "Sadi Muhammad Shihadeh," ISA 1019 15 M.

"industrious" disciplinarians, instructing students of various ages in a range of subjects, such as "Arabic, Arith., Geog., Hist., Hygine [*sic*], Nature Study and M. Religion."[85] Urban male teachers were to teach English, history, chemistry, and penmanship, in collared shirt and preferably a tie.[86] While the mandate governments prescribed syllabuses, dress codes, and comportment, among other multifarious duties, few regulations were systematically enforced. Teachers' habitus therefore included improvisation within these shifting contexts, as educators protested, adapted, and leveraged requirements.

The syllabuses of Iraq, Transjordan, and Palestine dictated hefty doses of Arabic, arithmetic religion, and, in later years, English.[87] Approximately a third of weekly classes were devoted to the study of the Arabic language, by far the most of any subject.[88] The Iraqi syllabus in 1919 argued that the purpose of so much Arabic-language instruction was not only to allow Iraqis to communicate but also to inspire a love of Arabic literature. The Palestine syllabus in 1925 was more explicit, asserting that the main purposes of Arabic-language instruction were to promote a linguistic style "in accord with the tradition of the classical writers and adapted to the needs of modern life" as well as "to interest the pupil in the classical and modern literature of the Arab nation."[89] Sati al-Husri went still further, arguing that "language is the soul and the life of the nation, but history is its memory and consciousness."[90]

Although history and geography syllabuses portrayed the mandates as defined territorial entities, they also told a regional/national story that was fundamentally Arab. In Iraq and Palestine, and in Transjordan at upper levels, geography and history were explicitly taught together, linking territory and a shared past that extended beyond the mandates. Iraqi students spent their second year learning specifically about the peoples and geographical features

85. A.S. Inspection Report ʿAbdul Ghani Sharaf, January 18, 1924, "Abd el-Ghani Sharaf Kafr ʿAin V.S.," ISA 1016/11 M.

86. Hussein Ruhi, "Confidential Report on Teaching Staff, Arafat Duwaik," September 7, 1931, and Mr. Hogben, "Inspection of Ramle Boys' School," October 17, 1939, "Arafat Duwaik Haifa Boys School," ISA 1041/6-M/.

87. Government of Palestine, Department of Education, *Elementary School Syllabus: Revised Edition* (Jerusalem, 1925), 7, Wizarat al-Maʿarif Iraq, *Manhaj al-Dirasa al-Ibtidaʾiyya* [Elementary school syllabus] (Baghdad, 1931), 2–10; al-Tall, *Education in Jordan*, 73–76.

88. Followed by religion, presumably for its moralizing and authentic character.

89. Department of Education Palestine, *Elementary School Syllabus*, 6.

90. Husri, quoted in Bernhardsson, *Reclaiming a Plundered Past*, 199.

of Iraq, followed by the rest of the world, focusing on Arabic-speaking areas.[91] Similarly, in the syllabuses for Palestine, students would begin by learning about their local geography, followed by the geography of their "region," encompassing the Arab world—Palestine and Syria in particular.

Beyond content, syllabuses explicitly called on educators to improvise, and to use their creativity and critical thinking to convey subject matter to their students. They exhorted teachers to do more than simply transmit information and instead to consider their role as that of an artist, rather than a cog in an educational machine. For instance, the Palestine syllabus in 1925 stated that despite its "somewhat detailed advice to teachers . . . it is not desired that the teacher's liberty to choose and develop his own methods should be restricted by too close an adherence to minute instructions."[92] By 1940 teachers in Iraq had to provide a positive atmosphere for students, fostering their "unique talents and passions" while also monitoring their hygiene, encouraging a "love of discipline," "good behavior," and sports, not to mention students' "capacity to prepare for lessons on their own." "[93] Precisely how one was to do this while teaching thirty-two periods a week was not explained.

The optimism of each syllabus notwithstanding, they were neither enforced nor standardized. As late as 1940, Transjordan's minister of education wrote to the principal of the secondary school of Kerak inquiring as to the resolution of a parent's complaint that their secondary school student was expected to learn geography from one textbook in Kerak, focusing on the "New World," whereas in Amman they studied the geography of Europe from ancient times.[94] Textbooks, curriculums, and subject matter were not equivalent even within Transjordan's narrow borders.[95]

Educators often could not or would not teach to the syllabus. Inspectors' reports in the mandate for Palestine criticized teachers for failing to, or indeed

91. Department of Education and the Education Committee of Iraq, "Syllabus of the Primary Course of Study, Government Schools of Iraq," 1919, in *India Office Records and Private Papers*, 20, BL.

92. Department of Education Palestine, *Elementary School Syllabus*, 5.

93. Wizarat al-Ma'arif Iraq, *Manhaj al-Dirasa al-Mutawasita* [Intermediate school syllabus], 1–2.

94. Letter from the Minister of Education to the Principal of the Secondary School of Kerak, *Al-Mudaris al-Thanawiyya: Manhaj al-Geographiyya* [Secondary schools: Geography syllabus], April 1, 1940, NLJ Personal Documents, Ministry of Education Collection, NLJ.

95. Mahasina et al., *Madrasat Al-Salt*, 1:154

being unable to, "adhere to the syllabus,"[96] or even for "sitting crossed legs on the chair smoking and giving lessons in geography" while refusing "to follow the syllabus."[97] Teachers were quite clear, particularly in the 1920s, that the Palestine government syllabus provided guidance at best. When one teacher, the ornery Muhieddin Haj 'Isa, was caught by a colleague teaching a lesson "which did not correspond to the lessons mentioned in the fixed time table,"[98] he yelled, "This is none of your business, this is my own work and you have no right to interfere in my school. Don't enter into my school!"[99] It seems rare that educators, even if they were willing to try, were able to get their students through the 1925 Palestine syllabus at all. One inspector's report lauded a teacher as "one of the very few . . . able to carry out the new syllabus."[100]

The model teacher combined not only these exhaustive educational obligations but also medical duties. Teachers were frequently the only government officials treating "the simpler and more common diseases" their students suffered, particularly in Iraq.[101] Humphrey Bowman, reflecting on teachers in mandate Palestine, stated that in "addition to his other responsibilities, village welfare was regarded as one of the main duties of the schoolmaster." Welfare for Bowman meant cleanliness, reduction of pests, improvements in agriculture, and administering eye drops to prevent trachoma.[102]

Teachers were to be farmers as well as doctors. Tending school gardens was a key responsibility in Transjordan and Palestine. By 1932 the Transjordanian government required every government school to have a garden and to carefully document how many and what kind of plants it contained. Educators also had to guard those gardens from vandalism or looting during school vacations.[103]

96. "Confidential Report on Teaching Staff, 'Abdallah al-Khatib," July 4, 1936, "Abdallah Al-Khatib Lubia V.S.," 1017–9/M, ISA.

97. "Confidential Report on Teaching Staff. Sh. Abdul Qadir Qaddumi," January 28, 1931, "Abdul Qadir Qadumi," 1020/8-M, ISA.

98. District Inspector of Education for the Galilee, "To the Director of Education, Jerusalem. Subject: Safad Town Schools. Reference: This Office Letter No. 89/En of 16th March 1926," March 23, 1926, "Muhieddin Haj 'Isa" 5112/2 M. ISA.

99. Rushdi Sha'th, "To the District Inspector of Education for the Galilee. Subject: The Headmaster of Sawawin School," March 11, 1926, "Muhieddin Haj 'Isa" 5112 2 M. ISA.

100. "Kamel 'Izzidin, 'Ain al Zaitun Village School" January 27, 1928, "Kamel 'Izzeddin Fir'im V.S.," 1020/1-M, ISA.

101. Akrawi, Curriculum Construction in the Public Primary Schools of Iraq, 177.

102. Bowman, Middle-East Window, 371–72.

103. Kalisman, "The Next Generation of Cultivators," 158.

FIGURE 2.9. *Tyreh: The School Master and His Boys at Work in the School Garden*,
Palestine, 1932. Photo by Humphrey Bowman. (Reproduced by permission from the
Humphrey Bowman Collection, GB165-0034, Alb3-020, Middle East Centre Archive,
St Antony's College, Oxford.)

In figure 2.9, a photograph taken by Bowman, the modern, Western-dressed
village teacher incongruously poses in the school garden and is depicted as an
enlightening force for his charges. The young boys, with hygienic short hair
and varied local and more European-style clothes, work in the garden (which
does not appear to be particularly fruitful at the time). Bowman chose to
photograph students outside of the classroom, without books or any sign of
literary or academic pursuits, presenting them as juvenile productive villagers
rather than future urban clerks. The young and enthusiastic teacher wears a
tie: a symbol of education and authority. Indeed, as one British education official asserted, in "hot weather there was no objection to a teacher removing
his jacket and even his tie but a collar was essential."[104]

Beyond this idealized image of the collar-wearing schoolmaster, teachers
might even provide extracurricular village services such as preaching or
performing marriage ceremonies. For example, the venerable Shaykh Abdallah

104. "Mr. Hogben Inspection of Ramle boys' school," October 17 1939, "Arafat Duwaik Haifa
Boys School," 1041 6 M, ISA.

Yehia and his local mukhtars (village leaders), elders, and notables successfully petitioned Palestine's government to allow Yehia to act as a marriage registrar as well as teacher.[105] Although, as the district inspector of education (DIE) for the Galilee asserted, a "sweeping majority of the Sh. (Shaykh) Category have already yielded to the Dept. request and consequently resigned their posts as marriage registrars."[106] Yehia was able to retain both positions simultaneously.

Marriage posed another sort of challenge for the mandates' female teachers, who faced different constraints from those of their male counterparts. They wrestled with the incongruities within their profession, on the one hand, and the gendered ideals of marriage, child-rearing, and domestic life, on the other. While the model male teacher would creatively impart syllabuses keeping the British mandates' boys contented and rural, the model female teacher had to put off or even forgo married life to modernize and nationalize children, often circumventing the colonial goals of their education systems in the process. Reconciling colonial ideals of womanhood with teaching was almost impossible. However, women used not only their scarcity but also paternalistic notions of modesty, tradition, and women's role in society to their own advantage.

Negotiating the Profession

Within a web of Ottoman and British policies, ideals, and gendered stereotypes, educators negotiated, cajoled, manipulated, and made claims on their governments. The regional shortage of educators granted them a surprising degree of freedom. One such teacher was the headmistress of the girls' school in Gaza, Bahiya Farah, who objected on principle to inspection itself. Farah claimed that district inspectors had no right to come into her school unannounced.[107] In response to demands from the director of education, then Bowman, Bahiya argued that it was "unseemly" for the male DIE to enter a

105. Two mukhtars of the Moslems at Nazareth, Two members, Thirty five notables, "To the District Officer, Nazareth. Mazbaata," September 1, 1925, "Abdalla Yehia," 1010/34 M, ISA.

106. Sgd. Khalil Abdel Nour, District Officer Nazareth, "To the District Commissioner, Northern District. Haifa. Reference: Attached Translated Copy of a Mazbata Together with a Copy of Letter from D.I.E. Galilee," September 15, 1925, "Abdalla Yehia," 1010/34 M, ISA; Sgd. Ibrahim, District Inspector of Education of the Galilee, "To the District Officer, Nazareth. Subject: Sheikh Abdallah Yahia. Reference: Your Nz/16/19 of 7th September 1925 and Enclosed Mazbata," September 12, 1925, "Abdalla Yehia," 1010/34 M, ISA.

107. Bowman, "To Miss Bahiyeh Farah, Headmistress Gaza Girls School, Thro' D.I.E Gaza," March 29 1922, "Bahiya Farah," 1010 6 M, ISA.

school wherein the majority of the female pupils were Muslim.[108] Bahiya's argument foregrounded tensions within the Department of Education and the mandate. While British officials often sought to uphold what they deemed to be traditional segregation of the sexes, or "harem conditions," for the sake of stability, the government was also required to modernize the mandates' inhabitants. Farah's refusal of inspection, a clear tool of modern governance on the premise of traditional gender norms, put the director of education in an awkward position. Farah was eventually required to allow inspections, but she received no punishment for her rebellion.

Bahiya Farah's views contradicted both British expectations and those of the villagers who placed their daughters under her authority, yet again raising questions of how British officials invoked tradition in the mandate education system. Farah dismissed the daughters of a Gazan notable because they came to class wearing henna. The DIE informed her that "this is an old custom of the country and it cannot be avoided at once by pressure."[109] Farah also became entangled in village affairs, fighting with her staff. She was sued by an angry parent after beating his daughter.[110] The Department of Education rationalized the conflict in a paternalistic fashion: "to put the case in a nutshell, an excitable woman dealt rather foolishly with a petty incident and thereby hurt a parent's pride."[111] Yet the DIE was displeased; he wrote to Bowman, "it seems that the headmistress desires to follow her own rules and she thinks she is free to do whatever she likes without the approval of the department."[112] Farah remained defiant. Still, she was not fired. Moreover, she requested a raise, alleging that one of her teachers received a higher salary. In her letter, Farah called out the director of education's sense of fair play and impartiality, one of the key justifications for the legitimacy of the mandate government. After noting the disparity in salary, Farah exclaimed "Do you think it fair? Or do you call this justice?"[113] A month later her salary was increased.[114]

108. Bowman, "To Miss Bahiyeh Farah."

109. District Inspector of Education Jamil Khaled, "Subject: Headmistress of Gaza Girls' School. Reference: Attached Petition," April 2 1924, "Bahiya Farah," 1010 6 M, ISA.

110. Jamil Khalid, "To the Director of Education, Jerusalem," March 23, 1924, "Bahiya Farah," 1010 6 M, ISA.

111. Khalid, "To the Director of Education, Jerusalem."

112. Khalid, "To the Director of Education, Jerusalem."

113. Headmistress of Gaza Girls' School Bahiya Farah, "To D.I.E," November 1, 1923, "Bahiya Farah," 1010 6 M, ISA.

114. Bowman, "Extract from Increment Warrant," December 26, 1923, 1010 6 M, ISA.

Bahiya Farah was eventually transferred from Gaza to the post of teacher in the Acre Girls School.[115] Teachers were often transferred if they were incompetent, involved in politics, or even "immoral."[116] Without sufficient numbers to replace teachers who failed to meet villagers' expectations of propriety, modesty, and dignity, the Department of Education's first choice was not to dismiss poor-performing teachers but to transfer them. Once in Acre, Farah resigned her post, citing her planned marriage.[117] Marriage, followed by raising healthy, hygienic children, constituted the Department of Education's primary goal for female education. As Bowman noted in his memoir, the Department of Education in Palestine "had the satisfaction of knowing that every teacher who married would be an asset in domestic reform."[118] Farah's surprise announcement, however, caused trouble for the department, faced with finding a replacement in the middle of the semester. The marriage bar exacerbated the already existing shortage of female educators.[119] Adherence to notions of a woman's domestic role hindered the spread of education on a very concrete level while granting female teachers leeway with the mandate governments.

On the other hand, the freedom enjoyed by female teachers in Palestine fluctuated in direct proportion to the number of graduates produced each year by the Women's Training College. As the mandate government often refused to open new girls' schools, in some years graduates of the WTC exceeded demand. Non-WTC graduates could find themselves dismissed simply because they were not legally contracted to teach for the government or because they had studied at an institution under Ottoman rather than mandate jurisdiction. For example, in 1928 the department decided to transfer or (if a transfer was not possible) to end the service of twelve female teachers, all but one of whom were likely Muslim. The lone Christian teacher, Melia al-Sakakini, sister of Khalil al-Sakakini, continued her employment as a teacher

115. Director of Education, "To the D.I.E. Southern. Subject: Sitt Bahiya Farah-Transfer," September 4, 1924, "Bahiya Farah," 1010 6 M, ISA.

116. Greenberg, "Between Hardships and Respect," 306.

117. District Inspector of Education for the Galilee, "To the Director of Education, Jerusalem. Subject: Bahiya Farah, Resignation. Reference: Telephone Conversation with Chief Clerk (H.Q.) and Attached," "Bahiya Farah," 1010 6 M, ISA.

118. Bowman, *Middle-East Window*, 259.

119. Forty-one percent of the 212 female teachers who resigned their posts from 1920 to 1948 stated that their resignation was due to impending or already completed marriages. Greenberg, "Between Hardships and Respect," 300.

for another decade in the nongovernment Islamic Girls' School in Jerusalem.[120] This occurred despite the fact that in 1927 the government had been unable to round up sufficient female staff for at least one new government girls' school.[121] Moreover, in 1937 the government again asserted that it could not open more schools for girls, particularly in villages, because "it was impossible to find women teachers."[122]

Antoinette Burton argues that gender possesses the "capacity, as contingent and highly unstable systems of power, to interrupt, if not to thwart modernizing regimes. This is in part because they are not simply dimensions of the sociopolitical domain, but represent its productive and uneven effects."[123] Teachers like Bahiya Farah redefined gendered notions of competency and tradition, while seeking to hold the mandate government to its modernizing promises of fairness and justice, or at least to use those promises to make claims on the government. They seized the chance to redefine societal norms within formidable constraints. Bahiya Farah's actions indicate how teachers used British notions of tradition and modernity, as well as educators' scarcity, to push the uneven limits of the teaching profession as a whole.

Educators often found the mandate governments' approach to teaching to be too burdensome; they lobbied their employers to relieve them of certain onerous duties. For example, Sati al-Husri refused the requests of Yusuf Zainal, a young Iraqi teacher who hoped first hoped to reduce his workload (which he complained was more demanding than that of professors at AUB) and second to teach extra classes on the side to supplement his income.[124] Zainal could not force al-Husri to change his hours or further bend the boundaries of the profession. Zainal, however, had already gotten away with far more: he had been arrested in 1928 for leading a political demonstration of schoolboys against Zionism and British imperialism. Despite his antigovernment politics

120. Teachers who ended their service were Adibeh 'Atallah, Naefa Haddad, Nabiha Fares, Kulthum Ghazal, Helwa Abduh, Wafiya Tubaileh, Sadiqa Sharaby, Nadiya 'Aql, Shuhrat Haikal, Raqikya Daudi, Sadiqa Saegh, and Melia al-Sakakini. Greenberg, *Preparing the Mothers of Tomorrow*, 118; Sakakini, *Jerusalem and I*, 27–28.

121. Miller, *Government and Society in Rural Palestine*, 105–6.

122. Khalil Totah, Palestine Royal Commission, Great Britain, "Palestine Royal Commission: Minutes of Evidence Heard at Public Sessions (with Index)," 338.

123. Burton, "Introduction," 1.

124. Al-Husri, *Mudhakkirati fi al-ʿIraq 1921–1941* [My memoirs in Iraq 1921–1941], 88–89.

and frequent complaints to his superiors, as an in-demand graduate of AUB he could maintain his job in the Ministry of Education.[125]

Zainal's peers in Palestine and Transjordan, particularly those who had gained at least a secondary education, also frequently manipulated their governments, redefining what it meant to be a teacher. The personnel files of Judeh Farah Docmac, a young English-speaking Arab Palestinian who would end up as the headmaster of the Lutheran School in Bethlehem,[126] and 'Abd al-Qadir al-Tannir, the composer of Jordan's national anthem, indicate each government's reluctance to allow educators to resign, as well as the ability of teachers to negotiate with the government for individual gain. Al-Tannir's file is brief for his long service, but when he tendered his resignation from his post as principal of the preparatory school in Irbid, the government's response was not merely acceptance but also rather exuberant thanks for his work.[127] This was shortly followed by a letter inquiring if al-Tannir would prefer to rescind his resignation and continue as a principal, or take up a teaching position at the top government boys' school in al-Salt.[128] Al-Tannir, born in Lebanon, was one of Transjordan's rare graduates of AUB. His services and loyalty commanded not only praise but also premium posts: he remained in government service throughout his life, ending his career with the Ministry of Education as one of its highest-ranking employees, before becoming the head of the Income Tax Department of the Ministry of Finance.[129]

In Palestine, the slightly less qualified Docmac sought to renegotiate compensation for his labor; failing that, he sought greener pastures. As teachers like Docmac contested their duties, the mandate bureaucracies became mired in local disputes. Hired in 1923, at the age of nineteen, Docmac was the type of young, English-speaking, Christian teacher the British preferred.[130]

125. For a discussion of Yusuf Zainal and this incident, see Kalisman, "Bursary Scholars at the American University of Beirut," 599–617.

126. Sirignano, "Mother and Child in Palestine," 168.

127. Letter, Director of Education to the Principal of the Preparatory School Irbid, October 23, 1929, "'Abd al-Qadir al-Tannir," 40, HRD.

128. Letter, Director of Education to 'Abd al-Qadir al-Tannir, Principal of the Preparatory School Irbid, November 20, 1929. "'Abd al-Qadir al-Tannir," 40, employee number 0000040, HRD.

129. Letter, Minister of Finance and Economics to 'Abd al-Qadir al-Tannir, May 5, 1945, "'Abd al-Qadir al-Tannir," 40, employee number 0000040, HRD.

130. Letter, Director of Education Jerome Farrell to the District Inspector of Education Galilee, December 27, 1923, "Judeh Farah Docmac," 1010 4 M, ISA.

Glowing inspectors' reports described him as "noticing all of his students when introducing the lesson" and "thirsty for knowledge."[131] Although Docmac, like Zainal, was not technically permitted to take time away from his teaching to either teach or take formal lessons, he was encouraged to study in his free time and to sit for the Teachers Higher Certificate exam, which, if completed, would lead to further increases in salary.[132] By 1927, citing ill health and the tiring effects of teaching, Docmac submitted his resignation.[133] The DIE initially refused his request, urging the teacher to reconsider.[134] Nevertheless, after multiple letters, the inspector reluctantly submitted the resignation to the director of education, stating that Docmac had given "unsound reasons for his relinquishing the service . . . but I understood from some of his close relatives that he has found a more attractive post with the Germans in Bethlehem."[135]

In Docmac's case, the government, through the education bureaucracy's highest officials, was in close contact with the teacher's family. Village society and kinship networks took priority in the day-to-day affairs of government schools, teachers, and inspectors. A framework of local concerns, professional ambitions, and the assumption that the state would function in an intrusive but personalized fashion shaped Docmac's sense of himself as well as that of his district inspector. The inspector considered knowledge of Docmac's personal wishes to be relevant to the Department of Education, and also that Docmac should be reasoned with and accommodated. Similarly, al-Husri in Iraq considered Zainal's background and his experiences at AUB as key factors in his desire to teach either more or less than required. Memoirs of those

131. Principal of Zawiya School, "Subject: Judeh Effendi Farah," undated, "Judeh Farah Docmac," 1010 4 M, ISA; "Confidential Report on Teaching Staff No. 402/En. Teacher: Judeh Effendi Farah Docmac," January 20, 1926, 1010 4 M, ISA.

132. District Inspector of Education for the Galilee, "To the Principal of Zawia School. Subject: Private Lessons of Salah Al Din Abbasi and Judeh Farah Docmac," February 10, 1926, "Judeh Farah Docmac," 1010 4 M. ISA.

133. Judeh Farah Docmac, "To the District Inspector of Education for the Galilee: Cc the Principal of Zawia Secondary School," November, 20 1927, "Judeh Farah Docmac," 1010 4 M. ISA.

134. District Inspector of Education for the Galilee, "To Mr. Judeh Farah Docmac Cc: The Principal of the Zawia Secondary School," November 26, 1927, "Judeh Farah Docmac," 1010 4 M, ISA.

135. District Inspector of Education for the Galilee, "To the Director of Education, Jerusalem. Subject: Judeh Farah Docmac, Zawia Boys' School, Safad. Reference: Attached Letter of Resignation," 1927, "Judeh Farah Docmac," 1010 4 M, ISA.

within Iraq's education system also note the importance of personal relationships (including nepotism) to the system's functioning. For example, Abdul Karim Uzri, one of the few educated Shi'ites granted access to the civil service in Iraq, received a government scholarship to study economics in the UK. Upon his return, he met with multiple ministers, officials, and relatives before finally being given a post as a teacher.[136]

Pedagogues or Ideologues? Teaching Local and National Politics

While some teachers, like Docmac and Farah, pressured the department for personal reasons, others promoted political ideologies through the writing of pamphlets, poetry, and newspaper editorials. Modes of affiliation and political ideology fluctuated widely between religious, local, national, and regional affiliations, along divisions that did not necessarily match the mandates' borders. As teachers articulated dissenting ideologies from within state service, they pushed those governments to accommodate both critical individuals and their criticisms. The political was also personal; individual teachers' arguments with peers and superiors, as well as educators' varied types of participation in the mandates' burgeoning public sphere, complicate the idea that public education automatically gives rise to territorial nationalisms. Instead, local entanglements and squabbles, as well as religious and regional affiliations, moved with educators through and across the mandate education systems.

Interpersonal dynamics extended to local politics. Teachers in Palestine, like the syllabus-refusing Muhieddin Haj 'Isa, elevated their own concerns over the dictates of their profession. The irregular frameworks combined with agency, strategy, and practicality are, as the framework of habitus shows, fruitful and dynamic. Educators' practices and goals rendered education, one of the key sites connecting governments with their populations, into an idiosyncratic and subjective job, defined by individual educators rather than mandate-wide rules. 'Isa, a headmaster in several schools in northern Palestine, caused numerous headaches for the district inspector of Galilee as well as the director of education himself. 'Isa's challenges to the administration that employed him ranged from interfering with local elections to writing anti-British poetry. His experiences with the government also point to the state's own haphazard

136. Uzri, *Tarikh fi Dhikrayat al-'Iraq* [A history of Iraq in memories], 17–19.

nature. 'Isa was accused by the mufti of Safad of meddling in the elections for the Supreme Muslim Election Council.[137] While the charges against the teacher were dropped, the elections themselves were annulled due to "irregularities" in voting procedure.[138] This act was itself irregular, as it was based on "different grounds in each district."[139] Later, 'Isa was transferred to Nablus before being permitted to return to the secondary school of Safad.[140] His personnel file attributes 'Isa's transfer to both his inability to control his teachers and his intervention yet again in local elections. In hindsight, 'Isa asserted that his involvement in the Muslim Youth Association, blamed for the Wailing Wall Riots of 1929, forced the department to transfer him.[141] Arab politics at local and national levels in the mandate for Palestine was fractured and contentious.[142] Even the Young Men's Muslim Association was at times divided between civil servants and intellectuals, workers, and others.[143] Although teachers like Muhieddin Haj 'Isa were members of the civil service, their involvement in localized forms of political engagement meant the mandate government as a whole reflected their affiliations.

Even the DIE in the Galilee, meant to impartially judge teachers' performance, seemed mired in a feud with 'Isa. This district inspector's annual reports constantly complained that 'Isa had a troublesome nature and undue interest in law classes. For example, the confidential report of 1927 noted that 'Isa was too knowledgeable, "suspicious, and cunning" for his job and therefore spent all of his time doing "mischief." The DIE recommended 'Isa's transfer "if Safad town is to keep its peace at all."[144] However, the mandate government's criticisms of 'Isa ended with that DIE. The new inspector, appointed

137. The Supreme Muslim Council (a British innovation) oversaw the "administration and supervision of Muslim religious endowments, proposing candidates for Qadis (judges) in the Sharia (Muslim religious) courts, appointment of Muftis, appointment-and dismissal, if needed of all Waqf property; and introducing changes in the management of the religious endowments." Hirsch, Housen-Couriel, and Lapidoth, Whither Jerusalem, 166.

138. Eisenman, Islamic Law in Palestine and Israel, 96.

139. Kupferschmidt, The Supreme Muslim Council, 30.

140. District Inspector of Education for the Galilee, "Confidential Report on Teaching Staff. Muhieddin Haj 'Isa," July 25, 1928, "Muhieddin Haj 'Isa," 5112 2 M, ISA.

141. Al-Haj 'Isa, Min Filastin wa-Ilayha [From and to Palestine], 6.

142. Khalidi, The Iron Cage, 65.

143. Matthews, Confronting an Empire, 60–62.

144. District Inspector of Education for the Galilee, "Confidential Report on Teaching Staff. No 247/En. Muhieddin Haj 'Isa," July 18 1827; "Muhieddin Haj 'Isa," 5112 2 M, ISA; District Inspector of Education for the Galilee, "To the Director of Education, Jerusalem. Subject: Safad

in 1928, had no such vendetta against ʿIsa, describing him as a "good discipli-
narian," possessing "good character," and supervising his school and teachers
"with great moderation."[145]

Despite his involvement in local politics, ʿIsa served the Department of
Education through the end of the mandate. Moreover, he never devoted his
time exclusively to teaching. He possessed experience, having taught for the
British administration since 1921, as well as credentials; he studied at Ottoman
Sultaniye, first in Damascus, then in Beirut, the short-lived Salahiyya School
in Jerusalem, and at the law school in Damascus. As the first DIE had feared,
ʿIsa completed his study of law on the Department of Education's time (and
dime). He never sat for any of the teaching examinations meant to streamline
and improve the teaching profession because he had a high rank already and
could become a lawyer if he chose. His combination of legal training and
teaching points to education's relatively high status and to the difficulty of
practicing law in the mandates. ʿIsa also wrote overtly political poetry.[146] One
1930s poem, addressed through the British high commissioner to the British
government asked, "Is this [the mandate] the rule of justice? Will this satisfy
the Jews? Is there anything more other than killing [us] unjustly that you intend to do? While the Arabs cherish the hopes given to them by the West, all
of a sudden, the promises turn into threats."[147] It is unclear if ʿIsa's poems
circulated. Although a short play he wrote that critically highlighted divisions
within Arab society was used in secondary schools during the mandate period,
collections of his poetry were published only posthumously.[148]

ʿIsa's participation in politics, while ignoring the criticisms of the exasper-
ated DIE and writing literature on the side, characterized the tactics of educators in relation to the mandate governments. Without adequate replacements,
mandate governments had no choice but to accept the educators available,
with all their extracurricular activities. ʿIsa's idiosyncrasies were incorporated
into his government's bureaucracy; local and even individual concerns, rather

Town Schools. Reference: This Office Letter No. 89/En of 16th March 1926." "Muhieddin Haj
ʿIsa" 5112 2 M, ISA.

145. District Inspector of Education for the Galilee, "Confidential Report on Teaching Staff.
Muhieddin Haj ʿIsa," July 25, 1928; "Muhieddin Haj ʿIsa," 5112 2 M, ISA.

146. Tamari, "The Great War," 118–19.

147. Muhi al-Din al-Haj ʿIsa, 1930, quoted in Sulaiman, *Palestine and Modern Arab Poetry*, 24.

148. Al-Haj ʿIsa, *Masraʿ kulayb* [The death of Kulayb]; al-Haj ʿIsa, *Min ahadath nakbat
Filastin: usrat shahid* [From the events of the Palestinian Nakba (catastrophe): The family of a
martyr]; al-Haj ʿIsa, *Min Filastin wa-ilayha.*

than clearly defined professional categories, shaped the mundane functions of mandate-era bureaucracies.

While 'Isa had been concerned with anti-imperialism and Palestinian politics, other educators explored liberal and even Marxist political currents. For example, in Iraq, two teachers who had worked together in the Haidari school in 1921, Mustafa Ali (who also authored a history textbook) and Ayuni Bakr Sidqi, created a "circle" or "club" with two law students, including Iraqi intellectual Husain al-Rahhal, a clerk in the office of posts and telegraphs.[149] This group was fundamentally concerned with social justice and had certain communist or proto-Marxist tendencies. The newspaper they published, however, did not promote overt political action. As Hanna Batatu, who was searching for the origins of Iraqi communism, argued, this group "had no definite program. All that they wrote, however, can be resolved into one dominant idea: the need to overthrow the power of tradition."[150] Nonetheless, what they meant was not a radical overthrow of the government or a Marxian revolution. Instead, they focused on the liberation of women. Despite their relatively radical ideas, both teachers remained in government service. Bakr Sidqi rose through the ranks, reaching the level of senior official by 1945.[151] Mustafa Ali served as minister of justice from 1958 to 1961.[152]

Palestinian teachers, even more than their Transjordanian and Iraqi peers, tended to reject the premise of the mandates overall, despite the fact that they technically represented the mandate governments as civil servants. Hamdi Husaini strove to further his anti-imperial and personal agendas as a teacher. Having worked for a mere seven months as an instructor in the government boys' school in Gaza, the continuously absent Husaini irritated the school's headmaster and was deemed by the inspector to be "disobedient, not

149. "Irak Report on Education, Report on the State of Education for the Year 1922–23," S T 34/15, 15, BL; al-Hilali and Khalil, Tarikh al-Ta'lim fi al-'Iraq fi al-'Ahd al-Intidab al-Baritani, 1921–1932 [The history of education in Iraq during the era of the British Mandate, 1921–1932], 418.

150. Batatu, The Old Social Classes, 390–95.

151. Iraq Government Gazette, no 13, April 1, 1945, CO 813 20, NA; no 3, January 19, 1947, CO 813 23, NA; and August 28, 1951, CO 813 33, BL.

152. Iraq Government Gazette, no 1, July 23, 1958, LLMC Digital Law Library Microform Consortium. Merkaz le-mehkar 'al shem Reuven Shiloah [Reuven Shiloah Research Center], Middle East Record, 2:260.

punctual," and, worse, "political."[153] Husaini resigned, precluding a formal reprimand and possible inquiry into his subversive actions. A few years later he was reappointed as a teacher, this time in Ramleh. Bowman justified his decision to rehire a difficult teacher by optimistically claiming Husaini's "misbehavior" was merely a personal dispute with the headmaster, and that he would "probably shape into a good teacher if he is properly and sympathetically supervised."[154] What Bowman's optimism concealed, however, was that Husaini was scrounged up to replace a vice principal who had recently resigned. There seemed to be few, if any, remotely qualified candidates for even the school in Ramleh, one of the larger towns in the mandate.

Husaini's political activities continued to escalate; he was reprimanded for refusing to stand when the high commissioner for Palestine passed by the café in which he had been sitting. The assistant director of education, George Antonius, threatened Husaini, noting that "a government agent who refuses to perform what he must for the head of the government out of respect . . . cannot remain a worker for the government."[155] Despite these threats and unanswered demands for an apology, Husaini was transferred to the boys' school in Acre (at the same rate of pay) rather than dismissed. This transfer was probably both punitive and preventive: to punish Husaini for his lack of respect for the state that employed him, force him to move to a less central location, and (hopefully) prevent him from continuing his rebellious activities in Ramleh. Husaini had other plans. He moved to his hometown of Gaza and stopped collecting his salary.[156] Abdul Latif Tibawi asserted that Husaini was "later dismissed."[157] Husaini's personnel file, however, contains no record of his discharge.

Husaini's later activities underscore the choices teachers had to work within and beyond the mandate government. Although Husaini's explicit rebellion

153. Headmaster of Gaza Boys School Nejib G., "To the Sub-Director of Education Forwarded from the Governor of Gaza: Report on Hamdy Eff. El Husainy," June 7, 1920, "Hamdi Husaini," 1010 25 M, ISA; District Inspector of Education Jamil Khaled, Southern District, "Annual Confidential Report on Junior Services Officials of the Government of Palestine: Hamdi Al-Husaini, Teacher at Gaza Boys' School, Gaza," July 26, 1921, "Hamdi Husaini," 1010 25 M, ISA.

154. Bowman, "To the District Inspector of Education, Jaffa. Subject: Hamdi Husaini."

155. Deputy Director of Education George Antonious, "To Hamdi Efendi Al-Husaini, Teacher of the Ramleh School C/O the Inspector of Education for Jaffa," July 3, 1925, "Hamdi Husaini," 1010 25 M, ISA.

156. District Inspector of Education for the Galilee, "Salaries of Officials: Hamdi Husaini, Acre School," November 7, 1925, "Hamdi Husaini," 1010 25 M, ISA.

157. Tibawi, *Arab Education in Mandatory Palestine*, 198.

against the legality of the mandate led to threats of dismissal, it appears he chose to reject his post. He would go on to represent British policy makers' worst fears. An outspoken journalist and a leader of the Pan-Arabist Istiqlal (Independence) Party as well as the International Anti-Imperialist League, Husaini was described in a *New York Times* article in 1930 as "the most prominent [Communist Arab] agitator" in the mandate for Palestine.[158] He also explicitly employed tactics of protest and noncooperation influenced by Gandhi's resistance in India.[159] One of Palestine's most notorious anti-imperialists, he relied on youth associations and communist organizations to work against the mandate government and to advocate pan-Arabism, as well as Palestinian nationalism.[160]

Tibawi acknowledged that "an Arab teacher could not, even with a severe stretch of imagination, have been expected to foster loyalty to a government that in his opinion was daily undermining the national existence of his people." Teachers were clearly not loyal to the British-run mandate governments. However, they generally continued to work for them, and enjoyed the benefit of steady employment as in-demand civil servants. Tibawi concluded, "Every teacher concerned acted according to his own lights. They all thus followed narrow and often discordant aims of national or other ideological character. If this was so, it can be said that teachers tended imperceptibly to impair the authority of the established Government."[161] The mandate governments, unable to rein in the limited cadre of government teachers, instead found their authority and image "impaired" by the actions of their civil servants. Bearing little to no resemblance to any clear, abstract, or modern incarnation of disciplinary authority, teachers acted as individuals. The sum of their decisions defined not only the teaching profession but also the mandates' bureaucracies as a whole.

———

Teachers who continued to work for the mandate governments, despite frequent rejections of their legitimacy, show how civil servants within a colonial bureaucracy cannot simply be classified as collaborators with the colonial state

158. Levy, "Red Propaganda Rife in Palestine," 11.
159. Matthews, "Pan-Islam or Arab Nationalism?," 5, 10.
160. Matthews, *Confronting an Empire*, 61, 140.
161. Tibawi, *Arab Education in Mandatory Palestine*, 151, 152.

or rebels against that state. Public education did not easily result in indoctrination, or indeed loyalty to the governments that sponsored that education. Educators' scarcity created a space in which to negotiate better wages and transfers, to teach subversively, and to participate in politics. The concept of a habitus encompassing educators learned but still improvisational strategies help bring to light the aggregate consequences of their individual decisions. Although the effects of the leeway educators enjoyed varied, it nevertheless led to a peculiar form of interaction among purportedly modernizing colonial states, their staff, and their subjects.

During the 1920s and 1930s, the newly created mandate governments engaged in regularizing processes, promulgating rules and regulations, inspecting educators and children, and quantifying and documenting their populations. These processes, according to scholars of state building, create the appearance of coherent state authority.[162] However, those taking part in regularizing practices, namely, educators, did so in fundamentally irregular ways.

Educators formed a particularly prominent segment of the mandate governments. While there were institutions that, in theory, represented the mandate populations, these institutions lacked the power to implement significant political or legal changes. Instead, local individuals who staffed administrative and educational posts acted as intermediaries; in many villages, the government school teacher represented the only "extra-village authority" as well as the person who would improve local children's future prospects.[163] On the other hand, the ability to rise through the civil service, which education offered, meant educators were more than just intermediaries: they were part of the mandate governments. The varied qualifications of teachers, their freedom to act as they saw fit, and the Department of Education's dependence on them precluded standardization, not only between town and village schools, as desired by British policy makers, but also on the level of individual institutions.

This chapter has focused on the importance of irregularity, spontaneity, and strategies inherent in the habitus of interwar-era teachers. Gendered frameworks and expectations frequently opposed education policies or the practicalities of teaching, circumscribing the rules of the educational game, particularly for female teachers. The following chapter traces the habitus and impact of

162. Migdal, *State in Society*; Mitchell, "Society, Economy and the State Effect."
163. Miller, *Government and Society in Rural Palestine*, 47–48, 63.

educators across national borders. Shared school days, youthful rebellions, and government service defined this regionwide group. Diverse individuals came together within the few higher institutions of the mandates. Their limited numbers belie their disproportionate influence on the literary and political trends that swelled across the Middle East, trends that would last until the arrival of mass education in the 1950s.

3

"Borders We Did Not Recognize"

TRAVEL, TRANSNATIONALISM, AND HABITUS IN THE INTERWAR ERA

YUSUF SAYIGH, briefly a teacher in Iraq, then a leading Palestinian economist, professor, activist, and consultant for the Palestinian Liberation Organization, attended the American University of Beirut during the 1930s. For Sayigh, as for Omar Saleh al-Barghouti during the final years of the Ottoman Empire, moving from the small towns and villages of his childhood to the city of Beirut as a young man was a revelation. There, Sayigh met and mingled with a few thousand other young, politically engaged, and excited men and women "from all over the Arab World, as well as from Ethiopia, America and other places." He stated that, "to students coming like me from traditional high schools, university was new and exciting. AUB had its own mystique—we used to sing *nahna awlad al kulliyeh*, we are the children of the university, when we went down to the cinema, filling the tram. We felt that we were a special breed."[1]

The "special breed" that Sayigh joined when he matriculated at AUB was a transnational, elite group. Study, growing political awareness, and engagement, as well as enjoyment of the sophisticated pursuits Beirut had to offer, separated students from their homes and families. Through common experiences, they came to perceive themselves as youthful leaders of culture, intellectual trends, and politics, despite their different backgrounds and birthplaces. The mobility required to attend school helped create elite, transnational social spaces. Coveted university degrees broadened these spaces, as credentials permitted further travel. Students, later schoolteachers, gained employment along alumni networks that cut across territorial borders.

1. Sayigh and Sayigh, *Yusif Sayigh*, 109, 114.

I argue that public education grew and supported *nationally* bounded in-frastructures while facilitating *regional* networks, methods of political engage-ment, and ideologies. A shortage of secondary schools meant students needed to travel for higher education, as they had during the Ottoman era. When graduates of the few secondary and postsecondary institutions available in the region made the transition from student to civil servant and educator, they tended to move as well, particularly if they advanced in government employ-ment. In the Ottoman era, educational and professional journeys took place within the empire. In the post-Ottoman world, these journeys often crossed national rather than provincial borders. Mandates and, in the case of Iraq, postmandate governments divided formerly Ottoman territories, separating cities from their hinterlands, schools from their potential pools of teachers, and states from a sufficient assortment of prospective employees.

These administrations had little choice but to accept anyone remotely qualified. Therefore, during the key period of state building in the Middle East, those constituting ever-increasing government bureaucracies were often not nationals of those governments. Transnational hiring went against global trends, as other state bureaucracies worked to consolidate the alignment of civil servants, citizenship, and governments.[2] In contrast, those tasked with teaching the early generations of Palestinian, Iraqi, and Transjordanian children had either been trained within a broader Ottoman national space or, in the wake of post-Ottoman divisions, traveled and/or worked abroad. Edu-cators tended to promulgate concepts of nation that ill fit states' borders. By serving multiple states and advocating for expansive, anti-imperial ideologies, educators challenged the mandate governments' territoriality and sovereignty while simultaneously extending each government's bureaucracy. Educators themselves embodied regionalism and transnationalism. These prodigal sons (and daughters) of their frustrating governments would decry imperialism but would frequently return to state service.

This chapter uses transnational alongside comparative frameworks as both method and analytic for understanding the interwar period. The suffusion of new government bureaucracies with noncitizen employees added a different layer to the correspondence among states, nations, and territories. The aspira-tional concept of self-determination, so prominent during the interwar era, aligned the category of nation with the territory it inhabited, and—the very

2. For example, in 1919 Britain barred foreign citizens from its civil service. Spencer, *Migrants, Refugees and the Boundaries of Citizenship*, 6.

thorny question of minority rights notwithstanding—with a state that represented and controlled that nation and territory. This was a fraught and often violent process, as governments aimed at homogenizing populations, forcing them to learn one language and pledge allegiance to one government.[3] The transnational cadre of teachers and civil servants discussed in this chapter formed a vanguard group who sought to implement various types of educational tactics as well as ideologies they learned abroad. However, the fact that they frequently worked for countries other than their own meant that public education functioned as more than a national institution, tied to the development of territorial nationalism aligned with the land each state controlled. Instead, new borders had the unforeseen result of prompting teachers to cross these boundaries for work, constituting a roving elite that carried wide-ranging, fluid ideas of nationalism and identity along with them.

The abrupt and arbitrary transition from the Ottoman Empire to the polities of the interwar era meant that the degree to which individuals considered themselves foreign, or transnational, is questionable. For example, Yusuf Sayigh was Palestinian, but his family spilled over the border zone between Palestine and Lebanon. Although modes of affiliation necessarily changed with the Ottoman Empire's end, they did not clearly match the new mandate structure. The nation students learned about from their worldly teachers was often a regional, pan-Arab one, with overlapping national, social, and religious sentiments.

The states through which educators moved differed in their use of citizen or noncitizen teachers. Iraq's mandate officially ended in 1932. Transjordan was subject to less British oversight than Palestine and had fewer schools, students, and teachers. Iraq's greater degree of sovereignty and Transjordan's need for personnel led both countries to import educators from or educated in Egypt and Greater Syria, including Lebanon and Palestine. These newly foreign individuals often achieved high-ranking positions. In Palestine, state consolidation differed due to the mandate's divided nature, between Jewish and Arab Palestinian inhabitants, and its more tightfisted British control. The highest echelons of Palestine's government were reserved for British officials, while the Yishuv busily worked on its own state-building project, including government education. Nevertheless, educated Palestinians, like their Iraqi and Transjordanian peers, staffed mandate governments at multiple levels.

---

3. Smith, *Nationalism and Modernism*, 39–40.

Historians have defined various segments of educated, modern, and Western-dressed individuals in the interwar Middle East as the new *effendiyya*. A sobriquet of religious learning and a bureaucratic designation during the Ottoman period, by the twentieth century *effendiyya* (singular *effendi*) denoted a young, educated, and politically active portion of the Middle Eastern population. Scholars' analyses of both the term and the group it describes have tended to use a national rather than regional lens, concentrating on Egypt and, to a lesser extent, Iraq.[4] They have sought to determine whether the effendiyya could provide an indigenous counterpart to a European or Western definition of an urban, professional middle class, and to highlight the role of the effendiyya in national politics.[5] This group, as Christoph Schumann argues, shared a unique social habitus or "patterns of world- and self-perception" shaped by similar experiences and practices, particularly of education. Despite the varied economic statuses of the effendiyya in interwar Syria and Lebanon, Schumann asserts they possessed relatively large amounts of at least one of three different "capitals: property, education, and social prestige."[6] Building from Schumann, I argue that mobility was inseparable from the achievement of educational capital, and a crucial aspect of educators' region-spanning habitus.

Their mobility, the regional nature of their political expression, and their entanglement with multiple governments are key, and somewhat overlooked, factors in the effendiyya's political impact. Iraq's suited teachers and poets were likely to have been born in and return to Latakia or Jerusalem, as well as Baghdad. Peter Sluglett claims that the effendiyya form a poor unit for class analysis, because these individuals were disenfranchised and disconnected from the tenuous mandate states, out of touch with the real "social forces" at work in the region.[7] Yet they joined their governments, becoming civil servants from the lowest to the highest ranks of various government bureaucracies. The promise of engagement with the state and their thoughts on what the state could and should do led educated individuals, as Sluglett rightly notes, to play

4. Gershoni and Jankowski, *Rethinking Nationalism*, 16, 18–19, 23; Jacob, *Working Out Egypt*, 46–47, 103–4; Eppel, "Note about the Term Effendiyya"; Eppel, "The Elite"; Bashkin, *The Other Iraq*, 2; Bashkin, *New Babylonians*, 8, and chap. 3; Efrati, "The Effendiyya," 375–77; Ryzova, *The Age of the Efendiyya*.

5. Watenpaugh, *Being Modern in the Middle East*, 17–20.

6. Schumann, "The Generation of Broad Expectations," 190, 191.

7. Sluglett, "The Urban Bourgeoisie," 85–87.

a more complicated role than simply harbingers of modernization and democracy. They spread alternative ideologies, along regional as well as national lines, through the institutions of multiple states. Teachers both trained and formed a key segment of this modern, educated, interwar society, possessing a particular mentality of civil servant cum antigovernment rebel.

Schooling and Habitus: The Making of an Educated Elite

It would have been easy to pick students of the Arab College of Jerusalem out of a crowd. Wearing their "green jacket(s), with the motto of the college on its left side pocket (the black hawk against a circular white background), and gray wool pants, a white shirt, and a green tie,"[8] these young men would have spoken English and formal Arabic, recited poetry, studied Latin, played sports, and had their privileged intellectual status reinforced by peers and professors alike. The school admitted the top boy or two (if of appropriate age) from each government school across the mandate, generally offering a scholarship for that boy to become a teacher. The competition to attend the school was fierce.

Flush with their intellectual success, students left their parents and often their villages behind to begin a strict and strictly supervised round-the-clock regimen of sport and study at the Arab College, punctuated by a bell. From when they were awakened at 6 a.m. until lights-out at 9 p.m., students would march in precise order from one class to another, to collective meals, to "mandatory athletic activities, such as soccer and basketball," and to study hall, watched over by proctors from the senior class.[9] The formal, regimented, and supervisory character of the Arab College fostered a sense of elitism, pride, and responsibility in its students as it emphasized the distinctness of its pupils from their less-educated peers.

The college was unique due to its meritocratic admissions policies and innovative curriculum. Yet, during the interwar period, its students shared the experience of being set apart by travel, dress, language, and learning with peers in other mandate institutions, such as the Women's Teacher Training College in Jerusalem, the boys secondary school of al-Salt in Transjordan, al-Markaziyya high school, the teachers colleges in Baghdad, and, the pinnacle of mandate-era education, the American University of Beirut. Graduates of these institutions, with their expectation of a guaranteed government career

8. ʿOdeh, "The Arab College in Jerusalem," 53.
9. ʿOdeh, 53.

with one state or another, resulted in a new, socially, and physically mobile elite. Attaining the habitus of secondary school graduates involved a series of ruptures, of which the few students and fewer educators of the mandates' secondary and postsecondary institutions were extremely cognizant. Through the journey to school, socialization among peers, new styles of pedagogy, the examples of transnational teachers, and the possibilities education promised, students honed the habitus that they sought to reproduce when they too became educators.

The explicit desire to use secondary schooling to produce a limited number of elites was by no means restricted to British colonial officials. Local, transnational, and colonial educators endeavored to transmit the "cultural capital" they had achieved, but also to preserve it as an elite accomplishment.[10] For example, the Arab College of Jerusalem combined a liberal education, draconian discipline, and selectivity thanks to the public school–trained assistant director of education Jerome Farrell and a succession of principals: Khalil al-Sakakini, the Quaker pacifist and pedagogue Khalil Totah, and Ahmad Samih al-Khalidi, who led the college for most of its history. Khalidi, an AUB graduate, put his educational theories—gleaned from a wide range of European and American sources—into practice with the college's limited student body. He argued that expanding secondary school too quickly, as had been the case in Europe, would result in a class of half-educated graduates of middling intelligence who would decrease their country's status and productivity.[11] Farrell likewise claimed that "the maximum percentage of those capable of a high standard of achievement . . . is very small . . . fixed by nature . . . and cannot be increased by education."[12] For Farrell, a graduate and Fellow of Jesus College, Cambridge, as well as a former assistant-master at Rugby and Haileybury, education systems, be they colonial or domestic, should find and select a particular elite.

Al-Khalidi, from a leading Palestinian family, was a staunch believer in merit, measured by academic achievement rather than aristocratic birth. In 1927 Prince Nayyif, son of Transjordan's King Abdullah, was sent to the Arab College to prepare him, as his father hoped, for further education in England.

10. Harker, "On Reproduction, Habitus and Education," 118.

11. Ahmad Samih al-Khalidi, from a speech of 1929, quoted in *Khams wa Saba 'un Sana 'ala Ta 'sis al-Kulliya al- 'Arabiyya fi al-Quds* [Seventy-five years after the founding of the Arab College in Jerusalem], 15.

12. Jerome Farrell, Circular no. 38, "Secondary Education," February 12, 1941. ISA 127/1 M.

al-Khalidi viewed Nayyif as "ineducable," not up to the college's standards. Instead, the boy attended Victoria College in Alexandria.[13] In Yusuf Sayigh's family, the strictness of the institution was legendary. His brothers Tawfiq and Munir also attended (on academic scholarships). Tawfiq, later a poet and academic, had been "terrorized" by Ahmad Samih al-Khalidi due to his lack of skill in more technical subjects. Tawfiq thought their youngest brother, Anis, was too sensitive for the Arab College's rigorous discipline, stating "don't send him to that school or he will never smile again."[14]

Ahmad al-Khalidi's younger son, Tarif Khalidi, noted that while the mandate government hoped to create an educated cadre, "at the same time the nationalists were keen on producing a kind of educated elite because there were Zionists coming at them from all over the place and they wanted some sort of answer to this quickly. So, this is one area where I think the mandate policy and nationalist policy were coincided."[15] Arab Palestinians hoped that creating this elite as quickly as possible, through the mechanism of the college, would further their cause. Belief in this elitist model of education was not universal: there were criticisms, particularly in hindsight, that the college was too limited, and too academically oriented to benefit Arab Palestinian society.[16] For its graduates though, the college's selectivity, academics, discipline, and career prospects meant training for leadership, albeit one limited by the constraints of the mandate for Palestine.

Patrick Joyce argues that in the late eighteenth and early twentieth centuries in Britain, elite liberal education was marked by "the cultivation of distance and detachment going hand-in-hand with formalism and authoritarianism in liberal pedagogy."[17] Leaving homes and parents at tender ages, boarding in urban institutions, and learning from international professors cultivated a sense of superiority and status in the young men and women of Britain's Middle Eastern mandates. The socialization into higher institutions forms a key component of their memoirs and senses of self. Even if they were born in rural areas, in economic straits, and were from minority religions, schooling

13. Wilson, *King Abdullah*, 93. As Wilson notes, British officials tended to agree with al-Khalidi's assessment.

14. Sayigh and Sayigh, *Yusuf Sayigh*, 97–98, 100.

15. Author interview with Tarif Khalidi, Beirut, Lebanon, January 20, 2012.

16. Yusuf, "The British Educational Policy in the Arab Public Schools of Palestine during the Mandate," 185.

17. Joyce, *State of Freedom*, 1.

FIGURE 3.1. *The Arab College Jerusalem*. Dining hall, Palestine, between 1919 and 1962. Photo by Frank Hurley. (Reproduced by permission from the National Library of Australia.)

and the allure of a secondary school degree ushered them, with varying degrees of difficulty, into state service and, minimally, into the lower middle class.

The teachers' colleges of Iraq, like that of Palestine, nurtured a feeling of estrangement in their graduates from those who did not receive this same level of education. Bodily aspects of socialization were perhaps just as important as the intellectual. How graduates dressed, cut their hair, ate, and drank became part of a promised future: a career in education and government service, if not necessarily governance.

Figure 3.1 shows young boys, with cropped hair and collared shirts, in the dining hall of the Arab College of Jerusalem. Seated at long tables, they enjoy a communal meal from matching plates, talking and laughing with one another. Abdul Latif Tibawi, an Arab College graduate, wrote that through "education he [the educated villager] had dropped the dialect, the dress, the habits of feeding and drinking of his parents and adopted new habits. More important, he had modified his moral outlook."[18] The college drew its students from

18. Tibawi, *Arab Education in Mandatory Palestine*, 246.

mainly rural areas, producing dozens of "educated villagers" who would have found themselves yet more separated from their origins, by language, dress, and career.[19] The school's graduates are a who's who of Palestinian and Transjordanian intellectuals, politicians, scientists, Palestine Liberation Organization (PLO) officials, engineers, university presidents, optometrists, businessmen, and ministers.[20]

Likewise, in Iraq, Shakr ʿAli Takriti resorted to hyperbole to describe his years at the teachers college in Baghdad and the "new life" he found there.[21] Matriculating in 1927, Takriti noted that what he learned, not in classes but from the proctors who managed boarding students, became "the reason for our success in practical and educational life later." In his home of rural Tikrit, Takriti had experienced a different lifestyle, which he contemptuously shed as he became a modern, cultured young man. He detailed the training of students' conduct, including discipline, how to speak at an appropriate volume at meals and in class, and how to behave at table, using knife, fork, and spoon.[22] For Takriti, the teachers college was a gateway to a new, all-encompassing mode of being, changing body, mind, and future.

Takriti and others who attended the college used school-day connections to spark careers in journalism, education, and government service. Rafaʾil Butti, born in Mosul, was the sole breadwinner for his household after his father died, and part of Iraq's Christian minority. He viewed the teachers college as a stepping stone to better-paid work, and to joining Iraq's cadre of politicians and civil servants. After graduating, he had hoped to continue his education abroad, and was even offered a government scholarship to study at AUB, but, with tears, had to decline to support his family. Instead, he chose to matriculate at the law college in Baghdad, writing to his mother that this step was necessary because "there is no rich teacher found anywhere in the world." The law school would permit him to learn "about higher culture" and its "deep connections to journalism, literature and politics." On a more practical level, Butti could work and financially support his family while attending.[23]

Butti and Takriti became frequent civil servants. Butti's political actions were absorbed, as he was, by Iraq's government. After graduating, he used

19. Nashabeh, "Al-Kulliyya al-ʿArabiyya fi al-Quds" [The Arab College in Jerusalem], 144.
20. Odeh, "The Arab College in Jerusalem, 1918–1948," 54–56.
21. Takriti, Mudhakkirati wa-Dhikrayati [My diary and my memories], 15.
22. Takriti, 20–21.
23. Butti, Rafaʾil Butti, Dhakira ʾIraqiyya [Rafaʾil Butti, Iraqi memory], 54, 61.

various connections to find work in Iraq's government bureaucracy: as a clerk in the Department of Agriculture, then assistant secretary in the Ministry of the Interior. He was fired for two months for giving a speech deemed too political at a party of luminaries in honor of Sa'ad Zaghlul's visit to Baghdad. However, after much maneuvering among the highest levels of Iraq's bureaucracy, Butti was appointed a translator in the Department of Defense, and his two months of missed salary were repaid to him by none other than the minister of defense himself.[24] Takriti taught, received promotions in the Ministry of Education, worked in the Department of Propaganda, and then in the Ministry of the Interior and back again. Takriti and Butti's instructors also moved from teaching to other posts in the civil service, such as director of waqfs, or secretary to the Iraqi Senate, solidifying overlapping networks between state schooling and government employment.[25]

In Transjordan, the bottleneck in education and therefore networking was even more extreme. The only full secondary government school in the entire country for the duration of the mandate was the secondary school for boys in al-Salt. Students traveled from throughout Transjordan, while teachers came from the wider region. Opened in 1919, the school occupied a series of dilapidated rented houses and lacked both an access road and water. By the end of the 1920s, the institution boasted a laboratory and a library. It was one of the few places schoolbooks (in multiple languages) and educational journals were accessible to Transjordan's limited student population.[26]

In hindsight, graduates tended to recall, and likely to exaggerate, the school's role in their own politicization and nationalism. For these students, al-Salt was clearly a site of political awakening. They described their teachers and peers as models of patriotism.[27] Teachers often moved into other government posts. Therefore not only the habitus but also the networking of school days directly linked graduates and teachers to government officials.

24. Butti, 78–84.

25. Rusafi and Rashudi, *Al-Rasa 'il al-Mutabadala bayna al-Rusafi wa-Mu 'asirihi* [Letters exchanged between Al-Rusafi and his contemporaries], 187; Mehmoud Zeki, "The First Graduates," *Iraq Times*, no. 10470, January 9, 1953, 3.

26. Mahasina et al., *Madrasat al-Salt*, 1:78–79, 103, 90–92.

27. Betty Anderson cites schooling as the key arena of politicization, noting that Jordanian nationalist memoirs frequently describe an inspiring teacher whose classroom lectures broadened their students' political horizons, most often in a pan-Arabist, although at times Marxist, direction. Anderson, *Nationalist Voices in Jordan*, 71.

Boys' secondary education unequivocally conferred an elite status that combined political awareness, networking, and travel. Female secondary education however, and the mobility required for both study and teaching meant different and more difficult contradictions. The mandate governments viewed teachers' transnationalism as a necessary evil. Like male teachers, female educators achieved a distinctive status through schooling and travel. Yet both government officials and nationalists tended to connect the female gender to ideals of domesticity and development, constructs much at odds with the processes through which female teachers achieved their distinctive status.

Professional Domesticity: Women's Teacher-Training Institutions

While promoting overlapping regional and national identities, geographic mobility also pitted local, colonial, and nationalist ideals of femininity against the need for female teachers who would impart—but could not represent— notions of domesticity, modern housewifery, and motherhood.[28] Women attended institutions that embodied these paradoxes, as conflicting perceptions of the ideal woman and the realities of the teaching profession contributed to a divide between curricular goals and their results. At teacher-training schools in Iraq and Palestine, curriculums included different amounts of subjects specifically targeting female students, most frequently domestic science and associated classes. However, traveling to, living at, and graduating from training colleges pushed female teachers, like their male counterparts, into a new transnational sphere, increasing their participation and investment in their governments. As most professionals were men, women who became teachers occupied an ambiguous space, necessary for colonial and national visions of women's progress, but also rebelling against these ideals.

Teacher-training institutions for women in Iraq and Palestine projected a complex view of the type of woman graduates were meant to be. Some of these schools aimed at enrolling rural, generally Muslim, young women, with the

---

28. As Ela Greenberg and Ellen Fleischmann argue in the case of Palestine, women's education, hygiene, domestic science, and modern motherhood were inextricably connected. Ela Greenberg, *Preparing the Mothers of Tomorrow*; Fleischmann, *The Nation and Its "New" Women.* Sara Pursley demonstrates that attenuating gender difference was a key policy of modernization through schooling, tied to issues of national sovereignty in Iraq. Pursley, *Familiar Futures,* 83, 103; Bowman, *Middle-East Window.*

goal of training them to teach in overcrowded village schools, where they might educate (and ideally become) hygienic, modern housewives. This type of school included the Rural Teachers' Training Centre (RTC) in Palestine, the Elementary Teachers College for Women in al-Diwaniyah, later the Primary Teachers College for Women in Baghdad, and Baghdad's Home Arts School. In contrast, the Women's Training College in Palestine and Queen Aliya College in Iraq combined high academic standards with gendered curriculums that were meant to be specifically feminine.

The universal prestige of a matriculation certificate and the promise of peripatetic government employment belied notions of propriety, and training in gendered subjects, at the elite academic WTC in Palestine and Queen Aliya College in Iraq. Global educational trends equated manual or practical work of various kinds with development. This meant both schools wavered between offering female-focused classes such as domestic science, needlework, or even secretarial training and more academic subjects that would grant female teachers higher qualifications (and salaries). Policy makers sought to balance their students' ambitions with gendered notions of modernization and colonialism as well. At Queen Aliya, as Sara Pursley argues, gender differentiation was tied to modernity and ideals of practical education, tailored to specific subsets of Iraq's population.[29] Although boasting experts in physics, economics, zoology, and mathematics, the college attempted to specialize, particularly in later years, in home economics, dress designing, applied art, social welfare, and English.[30] At the WTC, colonial emphasis on the subversive nature of too much "book learning" pushed British officials in Palestine to be, as Ellen Fleischmann notes, wary of making education too academic.[31] Graduates of these institutions, however, were guaranteed a job in the civil service. Their training and socialization at these colleges, whether the subjects they studied were construed as feminine or masculine, beckoned steady employment rather than domesticity.

The WTC targeted upper-class girls in both Palestine and Transjordan, opening the profession to women who were not motivated by economic necessity to teach. The government hoped that these girls would set an aristocratic example, modeling education and teaching as a well-regarded but temporary stage in Palestinian or Transjordanian women's progress from girls to

29. Pursley, *Familiar Futures*.

30. Queen Aliya College Prospectus, 1953–1954, Iraq, Box 29, Folder 9. SS. 15.

31. Fleischmann, *The Nation and Its "New" Women*, 38–40.

wives. In the 1930s Ruth Woodsmall wrote that "hitherto teaching has been considered as a respectable profession, but in the general public mind no girl would enter teaching except as an economic necessity, and certainly no girl of social position would teach. The Training College is successfully changing this idea."[32] The college would therefore train already-privileged examples of femininity while making teaching itself elite, and to some degree feminine. The WTC was also, despite its focus on the upper class, an institution that offered a few intelligent girls free tuition if they agreed to teach after graduation. This made it even more desirable. As Najwa Kawar Farah, later an author and staunch Palestinian nationalist, noted, "To win a place (at the WTC) was an honour, an acknowledgement of intelligence." She emphasized how selective the school was, and how talented its students were. Her mother was particularly proud of Farah's admission to the school, after "strict written and oral exams." The government's interest in training thrifty domesticity was offset by the competitive nature of the school, and the career opportunities it granted ambitious girls, prepared to take Palestine's difficult Matriculation examination alongside their male counterparts. Moreover, the school was not immune from politics. Students came from "all over Palestine," and during the 1936 revolt they passionately discussed the effects of the rebellion on their families and their country. For Farah, the school was both a hallmark of her intelligence and a political site where she would become socialized into the ranks of educated elites.[33]

Students like Farah shared the paradoxical experience of travel, intellectual challenges, and academic rigor at the hands of internationally born and educated teachers, on the one hand, and the limitation, on the other hand, particularly in the early years, that they be trained only to teach in elementary schools and to participate in manual work. As Hilda Ridler, the British inspector of girls' schools who graduated from the University of London in 1909,[34] asserted, "We lay great stress on developing what is latent in every girl—a taste for design. Neatness and dexterity is a tradition with the Arabs, so it is not surprising that they excel in handwork. Every girl is given a complete domestic course and the students do the housework of the college under trained supervision."

32. Woodsmall, *Moslem Women Enter a New World*, 191.

33. Farah, *A Continent Called Palestine*, 22–24.

34. "University of London, the Historical Record: (1836–1912) Being a Supplement to the Calendar, Completed to September 1912," first issue.

Students, irrespective of religion, were also to be protected in accordance with "Moslem ideas of seclusion," and there was to be no discussion of religion in history classes.[35] Ridler perceived Arab girls to be naturally predisposed to particular kinds of modesty, domesticity and gendered labor. By pushing students, future teachers, toward needlework rather than controversial or even rigorous historical discussions, Ridler formed part of a colonial apparatus that hoped to keep colonized women, as well as men, occupied with manual professions rather than nationalism. Moreover, this curriculum sought to tie teaching to modern domesticity. Farah noted that she disliked, but also paid little attention to, the sewing and other domestic subjects required of her as a student.[36] Instead, she preferred academic subjects, intending to become a teacher. A frequent participant in anti-British and anti-Zionist protests, she particularly hated Ridler.

Institutions that enshrined ideals of more "practical" training, casting rural women as emissaries of modern housewifery, hampered those women's careers by excluding them from more elite levels of the teaching profession. The Rural Teachers Training Centre in Ramallah, Palestine, targeted Muslim girls who would ideally come from and return to their villages, increasing literacy and improving their village's health and economy.[37] The school charged no tuition. Students were expected to clean the school buildings, do laundry, and cook. The Department of Education's annual reports emphasized the school's practicality. One touted the girls' training: two years of "child-welfare, house management and general village hygiene . . . women's agricultural occupations . . . [and] practice in the sole management of a school containing 30–40 children of varying grades and ages."[38] The teacher produced in this school was therefore to be a model of efficiency, possessing practical scientific knowledge and yet able to singlehandedly control dozens of children while improving the hygiene of the village to which she was assigned. This school, like its counterparts in Iraq, aimed at training women to modernize the home

35. "Dominion Teachers Visit London for Imperial Exhibit," *Christian Science Monitor*, July 10, 1923, 2.

36. Farah, *A Continent Called Palestine*, 23.

37. Greenberg, "Between Hardships and Respect," 290.

38. Government of Palestine Department of Education, *Department of Education Annual Report for the Scholastic Year 1935–1937*, Jerusalem, 1937, 34; Government of Palestine Department of Education, *Department of Education Annual Report for the Scholastic Year 1945–1946*, Jerusalem, 1946, 9.

but graduated teachers who, as young single women, were poorly equipped to
garner the respect of experienced housewives in fields such as child rearing
and household management.[39]

The RTC's mission to rapidly supply female teachers suited to modernizing
village life had adverse consequences for its graduates' careers, throwing into
sharp relief the gap between what the teaching profession was meant to be and
what roles women were meant to play. The course in Ramallah was brief (two
to three years), while that at the WTC included four years of a "modified secondary syllabus," including preparation for the matriculation exam.[40] Therefore RTC graduates would lack a secondary school certificate and the chance
to sit for the matriculation exam. Their certificates did not automatically en-
title them to a classified post, and their training did not prepare them to teach
the full range of subjects offered, even in village schools. Government inspectors therefore frequently derided these graduates, deeming the standard of the
schools they ran to be too low.[41] A lack of academic expertise barred these
young women even from the middle ranks of civil service. The gendered image
of a thrifty housewife without impractical academic training had the rather
impractical result of rendering RTC graduates unable to be or train teachers,
even at a village school level. A similar situation occurred at Iraq's Primary
Teachers College for Women and the Home Arts School in Baghdad. Graduates sought to use their degrees to rise through the ranks of the civil service
rather than simply improving the health and hygiene of Iraq's rural population.
Graduates' degrees, however, allowed them less social mobility than those of
the more academic colleges.[42]

These teacher-training institutions were caught by idealized gender norms
that fit neither the teachers they produced nor the facts on the ground, particularly the need to travel. Women faced unique and mundane challenges that
differed from their male counterparts: how to balance individual ambition
with the demands that family, society, and governments placed on women.
This paradox was especially pronounced for the pioneering women who

39. Pursley, "Building the Nation through the Production of Difference," 136.

40. Government of Palestine Department of Education, *Annual Report for the School Year
1939–1940*, Jerusalem, 1941, 3.

41. See, for example, "Ali Abu Humeida Tarshiha Girls School," ISA 1033 14 M; "Balqis el-
Sheikh Tarshiha Girls School," 1035 9 M, ISA; "Saniya Zu'bi I'bilin Girls School," 1038–18 M,
ISA.

42. Matthews and Akrawi, *Education in Arab Countries*, 187–88.

attended universities; their movement across national borders disrupted the feminine domesticity prescribed in the syllabuses they taught. Their journeys, made necessary by the lack of higher-level schooling in the mandates, shook connections between the local and the home as a predominantly feminine space, and the transnational and the school as masculine ones.

The Transnational American University of Beirut

When Palestinian, Transjordanian, or Iraqi students graduated from secondary school and sought higher education, they moved from national hubs of schooling and politics to international ones, most frequently the American University of Beirut. Originally named the Syrian Protestant College, the institution was founded in 1866 under the auspices of the American Board of Foreign Missions. By the interwar era, AUB became a more hybrid institution, reconciling American interests, in the form of philanthropic and/or missionary organizations aimed at extending American soft power, with the university's placement in the Middle East. AUB combined the American liberal arts education of its founders with the goals of its students and local employees: an emphasis on Arabic, Arab history, and—at various times and in different configurations—Arab nationalism.[43] The prestige of the institution and its increasing numbers of Arab faculty meant that students and parents tended to separate AUB from American politics, albeit with difficulty as the United States became more directly and militarily involved in the region after World War II.[44]

Despite its contradictions, this institution played a crucial role, socializing students into the habitus of transnational educated elites and transnational ideologies, and, on a more practical level, facilitating students' work for various governments. Once one AUB alumnus was in place, they often hired fellow alumni. Graduates would possess bachelor's degrees, as well as desirable skills in English, regardless of their majors (and, at times. whether or not they completed their degrees). They obtained employment throughout the region, leveraging their credentials as a means of securing job stability. As a laudatory article in the *Christian Science Monitor* noted, "There is always a demand for

43. For a discussion of bursary scholars, see Kalisman, "Bursary Scholars at the American University of Beirut."

44. Bertelsen, "Private Foreign-Affiliated Universities," 298–99.

A.U.B. graduates; indeed there is no unemployed graduate known of by the Alumni Office, who wants a job; in fact there are more jobs waiting than there are men for them."[45]

The demand for credentialed employees, rendered more severe by restrictions on secondary and postsecondary schooling, allowed AUB graduates to dominate key positions in each mandate's education system. The absolute numbers of Iraqis, Palestinians, and Transjordanians attending AUB fluctuated during the 1920s and 1930s from dozens to hundreds, as the institution enjoyed a near monopoly on BAs and BScs.[46] This alumni network constituted a disproportionately large segment of Iraq's, Transjordan's, and Palestine's education bureaucracies. In 1934 AUB publicized the increasing numbers of graduates across the "Near East," particularly Iraqi, Syrian, and Lebanese graduates working for Iraq's government or the Iraq Petroleum Company, and alumni in Transjordan and Palestine.[47] As Khalil Totah remarked in 1932, referring to Palestine, "Practically all [teachers with postsecondary degrees] are secured from the American University of Beirut."[48] In the early 1930s AUB graduates constituted over half of the Arabs employed in the upper ranks of Palestine's education bureaucracy.[49] In 1939 two out of the three district inspectors in Palestine were graduates, as were seventeen of the thirty-five Arabs employed by the Department of Education.[50] By 1940 all three inspectors of education

45. "Sons of Iraq, Palestine, Syria and All Creeds Friends: American University of Beirut Merging Diverse Peoples Offers Western Teaching Suited to Near Orient," *Christian Science Monitor*, May 17, 1938, 1.

46. *Al-Kulliyah* 15, no. 7 (May, 1929); *Palestine and Transjordan Administration Reports, 1918–1948: Vol. 1, 1918–1924; Vol. 2, 1925–1928; Vol. 3, 1929–1931; Vol. 5, 1934–1935; Vol. 6, 1936–1937; Vol. 7, 1937–1938.*

47. The numbers of alumni were particularly striking in the case of Iraq, Palestine, and Transjordan, jumping from 28 to 110 in Iraq, and 182 to 402 in Palestine and Transjordan combined. *Al-Kulliyah* 20, no. 3 (February 1, 1934): 68–69.

48. Totah, "Education in Palestine," 157.

49. Only the upper ranks of Palestine's civil service were included in the civil service lists. For the Department of Education in 1932, out of twenty-five positions, thirteen were held by Arabs, seven of whom were AUB graduates. Government of Palestine, "Government of Palestine Civil Service List Revised to the 1st April, 1932," Jerusalem, Government of Palestine, 1932, CBS 127, BL.

50. Government of Palestine, "Government of Palestine Civil Service List 1939 Revised to 1st January 1939," Jerusalem, Government of Palestine, 1939, CBS 127, BL.

in Transjordan were AUB graduates.[51] In Iraq, graduates also achieved key positions in the Ministry of Education.[52]

As AUB alumni advanced throughout the Middle East, they formed extensive transnational networks. In contrast to secondary schooling in the mandates, where teachers might be international but students were not, at AUB the student body included a wide range of nationalities, from the Arab world but also from Romania, Mexico, Persia, Sudan, Zanzibar, Brazil, Greece, and France.[53] Students who would go on to work in Palestine, Transjordan, and Iraq mingled with peers of different backgrounds, languages, and goals and enjoyed Beirut's restaurants and cafes. As a nexus of schooling and a supplier for various governments' civil services, the specific experience of AUB also united students and graduates into a socially and culturally—but not economically—distinct class.

Exposed to the cosmopolitan environment of both AUB and the city of Beirut during their transition from adolescence to adulthood, students questioned their place in the world. They sought to locate themselves relative to their counterparts in other polities in the Middle East and to "the West," which they encountered in the books they read, in the lectures they listened to, and in the large percentage of American (and some European) instructors they learned from at AUB.[54] They viewed themselves as a vanguard generation, with the responsibility to advance their homelands to the level of developed countries.[55] As Betty Anderson has argued, the university hoped to train young men for character, not for subversive politics.[56] But the combination of imperial control of the Middle East and association with other young political engaged individuals meant that university graduates would become catalysts of protests throughout the region.

Students and pundits debated American and Western influence, focusing on language, nation, and nationalism. They sought to fit themselves and their understanding of Arab nations and nationalism into a new global perspective,

51. *Al-Kulliyah Review* 7, no. 3 (January 1, 1940): 18.

52. *Al-Kulliyah* 19, no. 5 (May 15, 1933): 152.

53. "Registration Report," *Al-Kulliyah,* 20, no. 2 (December 15, 1933): 39.

54. It was not until the 1960s that there were more Arab than American faculty. Anderson, *American University of Beirut,* 49–50.

55. Ahmed Sousa, speech at the Iraqi Students Club, November 19, 1924. Quoted in Sousa, *Hayati fi Nisf Qarn* [My life in half a century], 133–34.

56. Anderson, *American University of Beirut.*

against and entwined with the West. In 1924 Isa'af al-Nashashibi, the Palestinian textbook author, poet, sometime teacher of Arabic at the Jerusalem Arab College, and inspector of education, gave a speech to the "Committee for Encouraging the Study of Arabic" at AUB entitled "Arab Heart and European Mind." He asked, "What is a nation other than its language, literature, character?" After describing the glories of the Arabic language, he argued that Arabic would be accepted only "if Western Civilization became aware that Arabic is like the West, the owner of a civilization and its situation is accompanied by famous civilizations." He concluded by urging his audience to leave his lecture "bearing the task of achieving a European mind and also an Arab heart."[57]

Al-Nashashibi offered AUB's students a way to synthesize what they and their instructors believed to be the rational, scientific, and material innovations of the "West," while retaining pride in their heritage and language. During the 1920s, classes at AUB were taught in English, but students, particularly from the pan-Arab student club al-'Urwat ul-Wuthqa petitioned for Arabic to be the language of instruction in more classes, indicating that they agreed with al-Nashashibi's platform and ideas of the Arab nation.[58] For these young, self-conscious, and increasingly politically informed students, traveling to AUB meant becoming part of a regional class of uniquely educated individuals. There they gained prestige and ready access to government posts, but they also became more acutely aware of the weakness of their region relative to the colonial powers that dominated it during the interwar period.

Students at AUB accessed Europe and America in a hybrid space, located firmly in the Middle East. This further pushed a transnational identity among graduates: they were at home with others who shared their unique experiences of travel and acculturation. They spoke English and colloquialisms picked up from their school days. Moreover, AUB was neither funded nor run by the imperial powers that then controlled the Middle East, allowing students to explore aspects of Western culture from more neutral ground. Nevertheless, they frequently used what they had learned at school to criticize imperialism. For example, Akram Zu'aytir, who attended AUB, published a pamphlet

57. Isa'af al-Nashashibi, "Qalb 'Arabi wa-'aql Urubbi" [Arab heart and European mind), al-Kulliyah 10, no. 7 (May 1924): 310, 314, 316.

58. "A Memorandum to the Trustees and Faculty from the Arabic-Speaking Students Committee on the Revival of Instruction in the American University of Beirut," July 1923, Student Life 1882–1980s Collection, AA 4.3, Box 1, File 6, American University of Beirut University Archives, Lebanon, 5–6.

during the 1936–1939 revolt against British rule and Zionism in Palestine arguing for "no taxation without representation," a clear jibe at British imperialism, showing an understanding of American history likely gleaned from his days as a student.[59]

This blend of Western, European, and American learning with Arab nationalism and love of the Arabic language proved a potent but difficult combination for AUB's graduates.[60] As Hisham Sharabi, an AUB graduate and later one of the most prominent Arab intellectuals of the twentieth century, described, his teachers, "the leaders and intellectuals" of a middle to upper class, "hated the West and loved it at the same time. The West for them was the source of all that their souls desired and, at the same time, the source of their humiliation and misery. They ingrained in us an inferiority complex toward the West, as well as a complex to sanctify it."[61] Sharabi expanded on his discussion of this group in the 1950s in a similarly critical vein. He argued that Arab intellectuals did not form a cohesive political class but could be analyzed as a whole, because they were "cultural hybrid[s]." While he lambasted them for their lack of political engagement and ambition, the solution he proposed, like that of Isa'af al-Nashashibi, sought to make Western learning compatible with a variety of Arab nationalisms and anti-imperial politics. He wrote:

> Muslim Arab culture is not Eastern, nor is it alien to the West, for the basic edifice of Islam is based on the same cultural origins which support the present civilization of Christian Europe and America. A deep and true understanding of Western tradition, therefore, can only lead to a new revival of the mind and spirit which declined in the Arab World four or five centuries ago. The great challenge of the Arab intellectual at the moment is to rise above himself and above the present confused situation of his half-awakened, bewildered society. The historic challenge now is to seek that true knowledge of the West at the very moment when the West itself seems no longer capable of transmitting to others its great tradition of humanism.[62]

59. Zu'aytir and Hut, *Watha'iq al-Haraka al-Wataniyya al-Filastiniyya* [Documents of the Palestinian national movement], 802.

60. Although Isa'af al-Nashashibi did not graduate, he was a frequent contributor, both financially and culturally, to AUB. *Al-Kulliyah* 11, no. 1 (November 1924–1925): 29.

61. Sharabi, *Embers and Ashes*, 9.

62. Sharabi, "Crisis of the Intelligentsia in the Middle East," 193.

Sharabi advocated for the sense of estrangement he and other Arab intellectuals felt from their society, as he thought it necessary to advance that society. He also argued that his culture was not, in fact, Eastern. This pronouncement integrated his heritage and status with the subjects he learned (and loved) at AUB and at the University of Chicago. It allowed him to criticize both West and East, calling on other Arab intellectuals to pull their societies into modernity and pointing out the hypocrisy of Western imperialism in the face of its humanistic tradition. Sharabi, like so many other graduates of AUB, exemplified the contradictions of an American liberal arts education, in the English language, with a political orientation toward anti-imperialism and pan-Arabism.

Networks of AUB graduates expanded this type of intellectual and political engagement. The number of alumni branches and their activities increased during the interwar period, from Cairo, Jerusalem, Beirut, and Brazil in the early 1920s to Baghdad, Mosul, Nablus, Khartoum, New York, Damascus, Aleppo, Homs, Hama, Sidon, Zahleh, Tripoli, Jaffa, and Nazareth in the 1930s.[63] These branches consciously worked to keep AUB's transnational graduates connected—to one another, to global, social, and intellectual trends, as well as to the communities in which they found themselves. For example, in the 1930s the Nazareth branch of the alumni association defined its goals as raising funds for scholarships, "holding periodical receptions and entertainments," and to "be advised by council as to how alumni can meet the needs of the country."[64] Events tended to attract alumni but also foreign dignitaries and local politicians, solidifying AUB graduates' connections to politics. By inviting AUB alumni, organizations helped codify transnational networks. The Baghdad branch of the alumni association brought together graduates from Iraq, Syria, Palestine, and Lebanon, such as Salma Khuri Makdisi, BA 1929, the Lebanese-born daughter of an AUB professor and a teacher of social science and math in the Women's Teacher Training College in Baghdad.[65] At the reception in 1930, guests included the high-ranking Iraqi Matta Akrawi, then director of the Teachers Training College in Baghdad, as well as the Palestinian educators Darwish al-Miqdadi and Mohammed Khorshid, who composed a poem for the occasion.[66]

63. Al-Kulliyah 20 (1933): 32, 205, 211.
64. Al-Kulliyah 16, no. 1 (November 1929), 19.
65. Al-Kulliyah 16, no. 4 (February 1930): 100; al-Kulliyah 16, no. 2 (December 1929): 52.
66. Spreading AUB's alumni network further, Khorshid would return to Palestine in the 1930s, changing his name to al-Adnani and publishing poetry. "Report of Progress Baghdad

For female graduates of AUB, becoming the first women in the region to hold higher degrees set them apart to an ever-greater extent than their male counterparts from gendered norms of work and travel. These highly educated women crafted transnational identities, defined, at times unwillingly, by their divergence from the roles of home-bound wife and mother. Salwa Nassar, the first Arab woman to gain a PhD degree in physics, articulated this paradox, noting that her education outweighed gender biases, but that it pushed her away from the home and family she believed women should have. Nassar, a Lebanese graduate of AUB, taught in Iraq and Palestine. She then received scholarships to attend Smith College and to work on atomic physics at Berkeley.[67] At MIT's centennial celebration in 1961, Nassar, one of only two women attending the 151-person event, asserted that the lack of scientists in the Middle East, regardless of their gender, offered women opportunities. As she put it, "There is no set tradition against women in science and not much competition, either from men or women."[68] For Nassar, the rarity of her expertise allowed her to break boundaries, rendering her gender less important. She joined regional and global intellectual circles, choosing education and research over marriage, but regretted that she had to decide at all. One former student remembered, "Probably because of social conditioning, she always told us that her success was nothing compared to a baby in her arms, advising us, her female students, not to miss our chances to marry at an early age!"[69] In contrast, Milia Malik Kheir, who received her BA degree in 1937 and then taught in Iraq and Cairo for several years before marrying an AUB graduate (and classmate of her brother), argued that her education prepared her for motherhood, although she complained her years teaching "dragged on" as she waited for her fiancé.[70] Teaching for Kheir, like many of her male counterparts, was not to be a profession but rather a temporary stop on the road toward a real vocation: the civil service, or, in her case, motherhood.

For these women, the divide between domesticity, home, and family, on the one hand, and teaching and travel, on the other, was both pronounced and

Branch," *al Kulliyah* 16, no. 4 (February 1930): 101; "Annual Confidential Reports," 1037 12 M, ISA.

67. Mohl, *History of the Israel (Palestine) Association of University Women*, 7; *al-Kulliyah* 25, no. 5 (May 1950): 34.

68. Gloria Negri, "Miss Drew Amazed: Only 2 Women at Centennial," *Boston Globe*, April 4, 1961, 6.

69. Hamadeh, "Wives or Daughters," 283.

70. Dounia Mrowa, "How They Met Their Husbands: Four Women Alumnae Tell Their Story," *al-Kulliyah* 14, no. 1 (January 1951): 10–11.

difficult. Nevertheless, AUB graduates, male or female, who became teachers often worked away from their birthplaces, representing to their students a type of nationalist engagement that spanned the mandates. Having traveled to Beirut from throughout the region, these graduates had experienced Beirut's city life, honed their English-language skills, been exposed to various strands of nationalism, and made lifelong connections with their classmates. When they became secondary school teachers, AUB influenced where and how they taught. They modeled and promoted a particular elite academic culture across the Middle East. As they participated in varied political ideologies, teachers claimed for themselves a modern and, ambivalently, a hybrid Western and local status.

Secondary School Teachers: Transnational Elites

Secondary school students learned from teachers who had by necessity traveled to receive a post–high school diploma and who were often born in or citizens of other mandates or nations. Educators' transnational origins and credentials helped disrupt the consolidation of government authority, creating a disjuncture between national institutions and transnational employees. As they sharpened in students a sense of nationality that spilled over mandate borders, educators also exemplified a cultured, transnational persona that students became eager to emulate.

These well-traveled teachers stressed transnational modes of affiliation, in part because so many came from or studied elsewhere. At the Arab College of Jerusalem, several educators came from Egypt, Lebanon, or Iraq but were more frequently trained abroad than born there.[71] Teachers in postelementary institutions in Iraq included English-, Egyptian-, Syrian-, and Palestinian-born instructors who studied either at the American University of Beirut or in Europe. For example, when Rafa'il Butti attended the Teachers College, five out of nine teachers and administrators were from abroad.[72] Combining the inconsistent statistics of the 1929 and 1930–1934 annual reports from Iraq's Ministry of Education, it seems that over half of Iraq's intermediate and secondary school teachers were imported from Syria, Egypt, Palestine, the United States,

71. These included the first principal of the college, who was Egyptian, Selim and Jibrail Katul from Lebanon, as well as the Egyptian-trained Itzhak Musa al-Husseini and Hussein Ruhi. Ma'arouf al-Rusafi also taught very briefly at the college.

72. Butti, *Rafa'il Butti, Dhakira 'Iraqiyya*, 50.

or the United Kingdom, with the bulk coming from Syria. About 50 percent of Iraq's female teachers were foreign, as were essentially all the female secondary school teachers.[73] Both educators and most civic officials in Transjordan through the end of the 1920s came from what became Syria, Palestine, Iraq, and the Hijaz. All the teachers in al-Salt had studied or been born abroad. Students therefore interacted on a day-to-day basis with peers from throughout each mandate and teachers from the region.

Public school teachers, the civil servants who had the most, and most mundane, interactions with mandate society, frequently were not from the state they represented. Yet essentially all such "foreigners" had very lately been fellow Ottomans or, after World War I, fellow Arabs. A logical consequence of nonlocal Arab teachers was the growth of an idealistic, inclusive, and anti-imperial pan-Arabism. 'Abd al-Karim al-Gharaibeh, a graduate of the secondary school of al-Salt and later a member of Jordan's Senate, explicitly connected al-Salt's secondary school with Arab unity. He wrote that the school "played an important role in building national (pan-Arab) unity" as students came from throughout Jordan, "learning in one class and being taught by teachers coming from across the political borders whose existence we did not recognize."[74]

Interwar nationalisms, however, must be taken on their own terms. A former student in Kerak, later a professor in Jordan, recalled how, as there were no political parties when he attended school in Kerak, each teacher's nationalism "would manifest in his attention to the reforms of the conduct of the students in both his knowledge and his style."[75] Here, nationalism does not appear to refer to a territory or even political representation. The Transjordanian government's repression of dissent and of political parties altogether contributed to a clear disconnect between the significance of nationalism as a stance and a coherent political platform. Nationalism meant cultivating a particular culture among the students, including style, character, and moral conduct, rather than introducing these students to a codified ideology.

A complicated, fluctuating pan-Arabism is a frequent subject of reflection in the recollections of intellectuals and politicians who were students during the mandate era, as well as in the hagiographic texts devoted to the

73. Wizarat al-Ma'arif Iraq, *Al-Taqrir al-Sanawi 'an Sayr al-Ma'arif* [The annual report on] *1930–1931, 1931–1932, 1932–1933*, 33.

74. 'Abd al-Karim al-Gharaibeh in Mahasina et al., *Madrasat al-Salt*, 64.

75. Mutah and al-Turath, *Madrasat al-Karak* [The school of al-Karak], 69.

Arab College of Jerusalem and the secondary school of al-Salt. Here, national consciousness appears more coherent and unified than it likely was. In examining materials from this period, it is clear that identity, especially among educated individuals with the philosophical background and inclination to self-actualize in print, fluctuated with changing borders and professional opportunities. For example, Ahmad Lowzi, a Jordanian politician who attended and later taught at al-Salt, stated hyperbolically, "There is no doubt that the school of al-Salt was the pillar of my intellectual being, and the lighthouse that lit up all the stages of my life, sparking my long path of service, for myself, my family, my country (*watan*) and my people."[76] For Lowzi, writing in the biography of the school as one of its more famous alumni, al-Salt represented the point at which he became educated and inspired to serve his country. His use of the term *watan* indicates the consolidation of an attachment to Jordan as a separate territory. However, by defining his people as something separate from his *patrie*, Lowzi points to lingering differences among territory, citizenship, and national belonging, perhaps referencing divisions between Jordan's Palestinian and non-Palestinian populations.

Educational networks bred intellectual connections and government employment, even if they could promise their participants neither solace nor homeland. Arabism could overlap with more local affiliations, but these overlaps were not easy to sustain for those inhabiting post-Ottoman polities. The new divisions of the formerly Ottoman world forced individuals not only into a transnational Arabism and Arabic-language intellectual milieu but also national spaces that clashed with their identities and citizenship. At the Arab College of Jerusalem during World War I, the Iraqi-born poet Ma'arouf al-Rusafi became friends with local leading literary figures, including Isa'af al-Nashashibi and Khalil al-Sakakini.[77] Having criticized the Arab revolt in 1916, al-Rusafi was not particularly welcome in Iraq, so made his way to teach at the Arab College in Palestine. There, he garnered criticism for writing a poem his Arab Palestinian and Lebanese peers took to be too rosy toward the British and the Zionist high commissioner Herbert Samuel (whose appointment led to al-Sakakini's resignation). It also seemed overly positive toward Palestine's

76. Mahasina et al., *Madrasat al-Salt*, 49.

77. Khulusi, "Ma'ruf al-Rusafi in Jerusalem," 67. They also kept up correspondence. "Risala min Muhammad 'Isaaf Nashashibi li-al-Rusafi" [Letter from Muhammad 'Isaaf Nashashibi to al-Rusafi], August 12, 1921, in al-Rusafi and Rashudi, *al-Rasa'il al-Mutabadala bayna al-Rusafi wa-Mu'asirihi* [Letters exchanged between Al-Rusafi and his contemporaries], 31.

FIGURE 3.2. Maruf al-Rusafi foundation ceremony of
Al-Tifayidh School, Iraq, 1928. (Photograph reprinted from
Wikimedia commons.)

Jews, albeit with fears of Zionism, "expulsion, exile, and the policies of a state that seized our nation by force." A Palestinian poet-educator-bureaucrat retorted, in verse, that although al-Rusafi's poetry was "truly unique among the pearls of speech . . . this sea you [al-Rusafi] have entered is the sea of politics." The poet complained of British colonialism and denigrated al-Rusafi's political statements.[78] In his defensive, open-letter response, al-Rusafi described himself as "a man who, wherever he went today, he did not find a political homeland (*watan*)."[79]

Al-Rusafi (figure 3.2) was embedded in regional literary and intellectual currents. His lack of a "political homeland" may have indicated his frustration not just with his critics but also with post-Ottoman partitions, and his lack of support for the Hashemite dynasty. Al-Rusafi worked less than a year in Palestine before traveling to Iraq to edit a new opposition newspaper, although he claimed this was by request of the Iraqi government.[80] Despite his short tenure at the college, his poems continued to be taught there, and he maintained friendships he made in Jerusalem. Moreover, once in Iraq (after a brief deportation to Ceylon for being too critical of the British-controlled government), he continued to work as a teacher and later as a member of Iraq's

78. Wadiʾ Bustani, quoted in Jones, *The Dangers of Poetry*, 78–79.

79. Khulusi, "Maʾruf al-Rusafi in Jerusalem," 67–68; "Risala min Maʾruf al-Rusafi li-Suleiman al-Taji al-Faruqi" [Letter from Maʾruf al-Rusafi to Suleiman al-Taji al-Faruqi], February 6, 1921, in al-Rusafi and Rashudi, *al-Rasaʾil al-Mutabadala bayna al-Rusafi wa-Muʾasirihi*, 21.

80. Khulusi, "Maʾruf al-Rusafi in Jerusalem," 68.

Senate, while keeping up his poetry and correspondence. Leslie Tramontini argues that al-Rusafi's position as a nationalist and anti-imperial poet and an employee of an imperial government led him and others "to make contradictory statements in their poems," which she blames on these poets' personal "ambitions."[81] Educators and intellectuals across the region, however, held a similarly ambivalent stance toward the British and mandate governments. This nationalism encompassed their work in state service and their complicated relationships to the mandate governments, even if at times it failed to accommodate their nationality and citizenship.

One of the most high-profile examples of an educator's disjuncture between nationalism and nationality was Sati al-Husri. Born in Yemen to a Syrian father, educated at the civil service academy, the Mülkiye Mektebi in Istanbul, and other schools throughout the region, al-Husri served as an educator and government official during the final years of the Ottoman Empire. By the end of the First World War, he was working as the minister of education in the short-lived independent government of Syria and came to Iraq with King Faysal to shape its schooling system along Arab-nationalist lines.[82] Although he advocated pan-Arabism, Arabic was not his mother tongue. As his biographer William Cleveland noted, al-Husri was, in post-Ottoman Iraq, nearly always a fish out of water: "a Syrian among Iraqis, a graduate of the *mülkiye* among individuals with military and traditional training, a cosmopolitan, French speaking intellectual and administrator among tribal shaykhs, local religious leaders and officers turned politicians, he never completely belonged. Even Arabic, to which he attached such importance in his nationalist ideology, was a third language to him."[83] During the era in which nationality was becoming ever more bureaucratically and narrowly defined, the identities of individuals like Sati al-Husri poorly matched the categories of citizenship applied to them. Even today Sati al-Husri's nationality is contested: in interviews with several Iraqis, he is described variously as Yemeni, Syrian, or Turkish.[84] For al-Husri, *qawmi* (pan-Arab) nationalism offered a means of accommodating his regional background, which a more exclusively Iraqi *watani* nationalism could not.

81. Tramontini, "Poetry in the Service of Nation Building?," 473–74.

82. Cleveland, *The Making of an Arab Nationalist*.

83. Cleveland, 65.

84. Interview by the author with Basel S., January 22, 2013; Abdullah M., February 15, 2013; Yeheskel Kojaman, February 28, 2013; and Kamal Majid, March 3, 2013.

Beyond the famous Sati al-Husri, other education officials, inspectors as well as teachers, born in one location and teaching in another, ran into disparities between their backgrounds and those of their students and colleagues. These contributed to the flexibility of the teaching profession but also undermined public education as a national project, because teachers' identities, and often their nationalities, failed to correspond to the governments for which they worked.[85] As these individuals crossed slowly consolidating borders, their hybrid nationalities were difficult to fit into *watani* or even the more expansive *qawmi* nationalist narratives. Moreover, they often inspired antipathy among their colleagues. There were instances of protest against so many foreign teachers, indicating some rather practical divisions between *qawmi* and *watani* nationalisms; Iraqis and Transjordanians desired government jobs and were loath to see others, Arab or no, in these positions.[86] While teaching pan-Arabism caught on with students, those seeking employment became frustrated when it denied them a coveted place in government service.

Students tended to react more positively toward teachers who, regardless of their origins, embodied transnationalism, modernity, and expertise. Both Takriti and Fadhil Hussein, another former student at Iraq's Teachers College, later history professor, recalled interactions with teachers, including the Palestinian history instructor Darwish al-Miqdadi, that emphasized their beneficial traits. Takriti remembered being shocked when a fellow student was expelled for sectarianism, something Takriti asserted he and his fellows did not understand. The teachers Takriti approached about the expulsion were poets, holding anti-imperial and generally Arab nationalist views.[87] One told him that sectarianism was against Islam, another that it was encouraged by imperialism, and the third, Darwish al-Miqdadi, argued passionately that sectarianism would destroy Arab unity, which was necessary to combat

85. See, for example, Husayn Ruhi. Kalisman, "The Little Persian Agent in Palestine," 65, and the story of Jibrail Katul and his son's discomfort with his national identity. Lauren Gelfond Feldinger, "The House on Rehov Graetz." *Jerusalem Post*, March 12, 2010. http://www.jpost.com/Magazine/Features/The-house-on-Rehov-Graetz.

86. Al-Husri, *Mudhakkirati fi al-'Iraq 1921–1941* [My memoirs in Iraq 1921–1941], 2:249. Betty Anderson also describes rebellions in Transjordan against the placement of so many Syrians and Hijazis in positions of power in the army and bureaucracy, though not specifically education. Anderson, *Nationalist Voices in Jordan*, 43.

87. One teacher was the father of the famous poet Nazik al-Malaika, and another was the poet Naji al-Qishtaini, who held pan-Arab views through at least the 1950s. Naji al-Qishtaini, "Thikra Shu'ban," *al-Ai'man*, no. 4 (April 1, 1953): 261–62.

imperialism.[88] If these conversations took place as Takriti recorded, educators clearly promoted anti-imperialism as well as Arab unity, while decrying differences within regional, and Arab communities. Hussein, who attended the college a few years later, similarly remembered al-Miqdadi assigning the exam question, "What of the study of Arab-Islamic history has benefitted you?" The young Hussein answered, hyperbolically, that "the Arabs were a great nation, which had contributed to the utmost extent to human civilization." He then brought the concerns of history to the present, arguing that it was "now possible to turn back and restore their [the Arabs'] great historical role and to contribute to contemporary human civilization." Al-Miqdadi was pleased with this pan-Arab answer and commended Hussein to the rest of the class.[89] Both memoirs were written in hindsight, likely overstating their authors' political engagement, acceptance of the idea of Arab unity, and rejection of sectarian divides. Yet Hussein and Takriti viewed school as the site in which they joined a world of politics and poetry and where regional issues became entwined with adolescent and academic concerns.

Traveling Texts: Curriculums between Nation and State

The individual experiences of induction into a pan-Arab cultural and political sphere at the hands of literary, well-traveled teachers characterized secondary and postsecondary education in the mandates. However, curriculums also reinforced transnational ideas, and transnationalism. The songs students sang as well as the textbooks they read underwrote notions of territorial affiliation that did not precisely align with the states of Transjordan, Iraq, and Palestine. Will Hanley notes that "governments and bureaucracies, borders, flags, anthems, textbooks, passports, visas, and critically, nationals" are the main constituents of nationality.[90] In Britain's Middle Eastern mandates, however, especially in their secondary government schools, these components did not agree. For example, every morning students at the secondary school of al-Salt would sing nationalist songs for states beyond Transjordan. As late as the 1940s, students would sing a popular anthem of Arab unity, "The Arab Lands Are My Country," with

88. Takriti, *Mudhakkirati wa-Dhikrayati* [My diary and my memories], 21
89. Al-Hussein, "Jam'iyat al-Jawwal" [The rover society], 245.
90. Hanley, *Identifying with Nationality*, 3.

lyrics by a Syrian politician and music by a Lebanese composer.[91] This song was sung by students in Iraq as well; the first line of the chorus is "from Greater Syria (al-Sham) to Baghdad."[92]

Likewise, the mandates' textbooks, and often their authors, crossed from one classroom and country to another. History, civics, and geography textbooks generally tell the story of a nation, tied to the state where they are produced: a state that has the capacity and will to define its own national narrative. In the interwar years, Palestine, Transjordan, and Iraq imported textbooks on a variety of subjects, unable or unwilling to craft national narratives from within. Historians have underscored the mandate textbooks' contributions to a militant pan-Arabism in Iraq,[93] whereas in Palestine and Transjordan they have concentrated on Palestinian complaints that censorship prevented them from writing their own national history. Famously, Omar Saleh al-Barghouti and Khalil Totah's textbook was banned in Palestine due, according to Totah, to a "very inoffensive reference to Zionism."[94] While Palestinians faced more stringent restrictions over their curriculums in comparison to Iraqis and Transjordanians, the structural factors that rendered educators transnational precluded the mandate states' dominion over textbooks as well. Instead, textbooks, like their authors, were part of a regional sphere of productive dissonances among states, nations, and politics.

During the Ottoman era, few if any textbooks were published in the areas that became Britain's mandates. Once severed from the Ottoman Empire, the region's textbooks traveled from an eclectic range of countries. In Basra in 1918, books came from Egypt, the reserves of the American Mission School, and even India, while in Kirkuk, according to the British, "Turkish-school books" would remain, despite "some political unsoundness."[95] Transjordan's students could expect to learn about mathematics, grammar, literature, and even civics

---

91. Mahasina et al., *Madrasat al-Salt*, 2:51.

92. Zaki and Jawdat, *Memoir of an Iraqi Woman Doctor*, 30.

93. Dawn, "An Arab Nationalist View," 355; Simon, "The Teaching of History in Iraq," 42.

94. Khalil Totah, Palestine Royal Commission, Great Britain, "Palestine Royal Commission: Minutes of Evidence Heard at Public Sessions (with Index)," 352. This would change during the 1950s. See Mezna Qato, "A Primer for a New Terrain," 26; Anderson, "Writing the Nation," 5–14.

95. "Kirkuk Division Report," in "1919 Division Reports," cited in Diskin, "The 'Genesis' of the Government Educational System in Iraq," 352, 250.

from Egyptian, Palestinian, and Syrian textbooks.[96] Through the 1920s, Egyptian textbooks suffused Palestine's schools.[97]

Over time, the mandate governments sought to regularize, if not nationalize, the production and certification of textbooks. Despite these efforts, all three governments assigned many of the same textbooks. In Palestine, an education committee, in consultation with "expert teachers," would determine whether a textbook could be used in schools. Although Palestine's Department of Education considered producing its own textbooks, only three were "adapted and translated."[98] Instead, inspectors, teachers, and other educated individuals composed textbooks on their own, undermining standardization while solidifying the role of educators in shaping education systems. The bulk of Transjordan's hodgepodge of textbooks used through the 1950s were written and produced abroad.[99] In contrast, Iraq's Ministry of Education in the 1920s touted its success at inducing Iraqi authors to write primary school textbooks while admitting that Iraqi authors were loath to write for the limited intermediate and secondary schools, as there were simply not enough students to make the labor profitable.[100] Instead, the Iraqi government would import textbooks, and teachers, from surrounding areas.

The region's shared sphere of textbooks was acutely prominent among certain subjects and countries; textbooks on Arabic literature, grammar, history, and to a lesser extent civics, as well as math sciences and object lessons, tended to travel from Egypt, Palestine, and Syria to Iraq and Transjordan, more so than to Palestine. Iraq and Transjordan relied on Egyptian grammar books,

96. In 1926–1927 for example, all thirty textbooks assigned to the students of Transjordan were published in Iraq, Lebanon, Syria, Palestine, or Egypt, although two of their authors (born in Lebanon or Syria) were working as educators in Transjordan at the time. Mahasina et al., *Madrasat al-Salt*, 1:155–56.

97. Furas, *Educating Palestine*, 207.

98. Tibawi, *Arab Education in Mandatory Palestine*, 95–96.

99. The biggest problems cited during the mandate era seem to have been those of textbook distribution, as the government would loan poor students books gratis and then fail to get those books back for various reasons. "Letter from a teacher of the school of Jadita to the director of the district of al-Koura," "al-Kutub al-Madrisiyya" [Textbooks], August 9, 1931, Government Documents Collection, 7/1/9/22, NLJ: "Letter from the principal of the school of al-Koura to the director of the District of al-Koura," "al-Kutub al-Ma'ara" [Loaned books], October 6, 1935, Government Documents Collection, 59/1/9/22, NLJ; "Letter from the mutasarrif of Ajlun district to the Qaimaqam of Jabl Ajlun," July 31, 1940, Government Documents Collection, 101/1/9/22, NLJ.

100. Wizarat al-Ma'arif Iraq, *al-Taqrir al-Sanawi 'an Sayr al-Ma'arif 1929–1930*, 31–32.

occasionally using Khalil al-Sakakini's works.[101] Both countries also used history books written by Palestinian authors, mainly ʿIzzat Darwazeh.[102] The Iraqi government went so far as to publish Darwish al-Miqdadi's and Akram Zuʾaytir's works, thereby assuming some of the costs and lowering the prices for students.[103] These were assigned through the Anglo-Iraqi War in 1941, after which only texts coauthored by Zuʾaytir and other Iraqis were permitted.[104] Transjordan used geography and history books written explicitly for the schools of Palestine, such as those of the AUB graduate Wasfi ʿAnabtawi.[105]

101. In 1933–1934, Khalil al-Sakakini's new book for teaching the alphabet was used in Iraq and Transjordan, and likely in Palestine as well. Al-Sakakini, *Dalil al-Awal lil-Jadid al-Awal fi al-Afaba* [The first guide to the new, the first in the alphabet]. This book was found in the textbook museum of al-Salt and referenced in Wizarat al-Maʿarif Iraq, *al-Taqrir al-Sanawi ʿan Sayr al-Maʿarif 1933–1934*, 18. The books most often used for Arabic grammar, however, were those written by the Egyptian novelist, poet, and educator ʿAli al-Garem and Mustafa al-Amin, then an inspector of education in Egypt. These were used in Iraq through the 1950s. Wizarat al-Maʿarif Iraq, *al-Taqrir al-Sanawi ʿan Sayr al-Maʿarif 1953–1954*, 176; *al-Taqrir al-Sanawi ʿan Sayr al-Maʿarif 1929–1930*, 31–32.

102. Darwazeh's *Mukhtasar Tarikh al-ʿArab wa-al-Islam* [A brief history of the Arabs and Islam] was used (and indeed lost) by students in early 1930s Transjordan. "Letter from the teacher of the school of Judayta to the director of the district of Kura," August 9, 1931, 7/1/9/22, Government Documents Collection, NLJ.

103. Wizarat al-Maʿarif Iraq, *al-Taqrir al-Sanawi ʿan Sayr al-Maʿarif 1938–1939*, 37.

104. The Iraqi government explicitly forbade the teaching of Darwish al-Miqdadi's *Tarikh al-Umma al-ʿArabiyya* [The history of the Arab nation]. Wizarat al-Maʿarif Iraq, *al-Taqrir al-Sanawi ʿan Sayr al-Maʿarif 1943–1944*, 91. However, through 1954, *al-Mutalaʿa al-Arabiyya*, by Izzeddin al-Yasin, ʿAbd al-Razzaq Muhieddin, Muhammad Nasser, and Akram Zuʾaytir was assigned. Aside from Zuʾaytir, the authors were all Iraqis, although the poet ʿAbd al-Razzaq Muhieddin had studied in Egypt. Wizarat al-Maʿarif Iraq, *al-Taqrir al-Sanawi ʿan Sayr al-Maʿarif 1953–1954*, 176; Yousef ʿIz al-Din, *al-Shuʿaraʾ al-ʿIraqiyyun fi al-Qarn al-ʿAshrin* [Iraqi poets in the twentieth century], 229.

105. Wasfi ʿAnabtawi and Saʿid Sabbagh, *Jughrafiyya Filastin wa-al-Bilad al-ʿArabiyya* [Geography of Palestine and the Arab countries]. Even in 1949, Jordan's government assigned students ʿAnabtawi's geography textbooks. The Ministry of Education noted that there was no textbook for geography at the fourth secondary level, so they decided to use ʿAnabtawi's *Geography of Palestine and the Arab Countries* for the 1949–1950 school year. "Letter from the Minister of Education to the principal of the secondary school of Kerak and the principal of Maʾan Secondary," December 19, 1949, 148/7/9/22, History of Jordan Collection, Government Documents Collection, NLJ. The ministry had already recommended that students read ʿAnabtawi's geographies in their spare time. Wazir alʾMaʿarif [minister of education], "Official Communication no. 37 of 1949," December 1, 1949, 316/12/5/22, 317/12/5/22, History of Jordan, Government Documents Collection, NLJ.

Transjordan's civics and history textbooks included works from Syria and Egypt, which goaded teachers to tailor their history lessons to "ancient Egypt" and to "the area in which the school was located," followed by stories of Cairo and Giza.[106]

Iraqi Ministry of Education reports and the shelves of the textbook museum in al-Salt, Jordan, demonstrate that, over time, governments did reduce the number of imported textbooks. In Iraq, the percentage of imports decreased from well over half in the 1930s to only about 1 percent by 1947.[107] In Jordan, the process is more difficult to quantify, but all the textbooks used before independence were, with few exceptions, produced in Egypt, Palestine, Syria, or Lebanon. Moreover, the books themselves stated the curriculum to which they belonged. For example, one physics textbook was translated from French by Damascus-born educator 'Izz al-Din al-Tanoukhi, who had studied in Palestine, Egypt, and France before teaching at the Higher Teachers' College in Iraq. The book's cover proclaimed it was "assigned by the Iraqi Ministry of Education to be taught in the Teachers College and Secondary Schools."[108] It nevertheless found its way to Transjordan. Even books written by Palestinian authors, to be used in Palestinian schools, synthesized diverse sources. Surveying the bibliographies of Palestinian history textbooks, Yoni Furas argues that "no Palestinian history textbooks during the Mandate were, in themselves, quite Ottoman, Egyptian, Lebanese, English, French, or American: rather, they were an amalgamation, a mixture of all these sources."[109]

The authors of domestically published textbooks also shared similar transnational experiences with one another: the majority had studied at the American University of Beirut. The government of Transjordan imported works written by AUB graduates; with the exception of the famous poet Husni Fariz, these were all written by non-Transjordanian authors and published beyond Transjordan's borders.[110] In interwar Iraq, AUB graduates' textbooks were also

106. Wizarat al-Ma'arif al-Umumiyya [Ministry of education, Egypt], *Manhaj al-Dirasa al-Ibtida'iyya li-Madaris al-Banat* [Elementary school syllabus for girls' schools], 78.

107. See the annual reports from the Iraqi Ministry of Education from 1929–1947.

108. Fernan Meyer, *al-Mabadi'al-Fiziyya, al-Ustadh 'Izz al-Din al-Tanoukhi* [Principles of physics, Professor 'Izz al-Din al-Tanoukhi], Arab Academy of Damascus, http://www.arabacademy.gov.sy/ar/page16240, accessed June 17, 2001.

109. Furas, *Educating Palestine*, 109.

110. Fariz wrote several textbooks used in Jordan from the 1950s through the 1980s such as *Tarikh al-'Abbasiyun wa-al-Fatimiyun lil Soff Al-Khamis al-Ibtidai* [The history of the Abbasids and the Fatimids for the fifth elementary class] and *Stories from the Arab World*.

used, regardless of whether the authors were Iraqi or not.[111] Even when Iraqi-written textbooks replaced those written and produced overseas, AUB graduates were often their authors. These include Matta Akrawi, Rashid Salbi, and 'Abd al-Majid Kazem, who wrote primers on Arabic reading, replacing those written in Egypt by the late 1930s and early 1940s, thus gaining an important voice in the curriculums of the mandates. Moreover, as AUB alumni as well as individuals with higher degrees gained importance, the overlapping roles of textbook authors, educators, and ministers were blurred. In Iraq, authors such as Amin Zaki, a former defense minister, or Taha al-Hashimi, minister of defense and later prime minister, both wrote textbooks used during the late 1930s.

What, then, of the ideologies these textbooks promoted? Beyond connecting students to locations they might never see, such as the girls of Transjordan reading about field trips to Giza, textbooks reinforced slippage between the mandates' borders and an Arab culture, language, and nation. However, even the most politically charged narratives of Arab unity kept borders, potential policies, and political futures, perhaps unsurprisingly, vague.[112] The most explicitly pan-Arab textbooks in the mandates, by Zu'aytir and al-Miqdadi, extended the concept of Arab unity back into the past while incorporating various civilizations into a pan-Arab canon.[113] In *Tarikhuna bi-Uslub Qisasi* (Our history in stories), first published in 1935, Darwish al-Miqdadi and Akram Zu'aytir combined a heady mixture of religion, nationalism, and pedagogy. In the dedication to the book, they asserted, "Each teacher of history who is not eager to preserve his nationalist opinion in the souls of his students, will multiply his own hurt above his benefit; its evil is greater than its good."[114]

111. Works known to be used in Iraq included Darwish al-Miqdadi's *Tarikh al-Umma al-'Arabiyya* [The history of the Arab nation] as well as Anis Nusuli's *Al-Dawla al-Umawiyya fi al-Sham* [The Umayyad state in greater Syria]. Simon, "The Teaching of History in Iraq," 42. *Al-Kulliyah* 19, no. 6 (July 1, 1933): 190, describes with pleasure the publishing of *The Principles of Natural History* by Jamil M. Jammu'ah, BA 1930, and Jalil M. Jawad, BA 1930, with the approval of the Iraqi Ministry of Education. This book was to be used in secondary schools.

112. Al-Miqdadi generally uses a bodily image, as do many influenced by the Semitic wave theory, to define the Arab region. There are questions of language, but there is no essential political program, no idea of federation, just simply Arab unity.

113. Simon, "The Teaching of History in Iraq," 92–93; Lewis, *The Arabs in History*, 19; Hurvitz, "Muhibb Ad-Din Al-Khatib's Semitic Wave Theory and Pan-Arabism," 118–34; Harte, "Contesting the Past in Mandate Palestine," 157.

114. Zu'aytir and al-Miqdadi, *Tarikhuna bi-Uslub Qisasi* [Our history in stories], 3.

In essence, their argument was that nationalism in a teacher did no good unless that teacher sought to instill it into their students' very "souls," thereby strengthening the Arab nation.

The stories in their textbook are framed by Islamic history but emphasize the integrity of the Arab world, the physical connection between land and Arab history, and ideals of independence, militancy, and nationalism over and above historical accuracy. For example, they include the story of Zenobia, a third-century queen regent of Palmyra, now in modern-day Syria, then a vassal state of Rome. Zenobia expanded her kingdom at Rome's expense before being defeated. Her ethnic origins are not known with certainty, but for Zu'aytir and al-Miqdadi she was a prime example of a successful female Arab ruler. In introducing her story, the authors situate Palmyra in a modern context, noting how far it is from Damascus, and that the ruins still exist today. The story further argues that Zenobia's husband sought "independence" and territorial expansion. For al-Miqdadi and Zu'aytir, this strong, Arab queen perhaps idealizes a modern Arab woman. They emphasize her anti-imperialism, courage, beauty, and intelligence, and that she chose to die when she lost her independence (now a disputed part of the story).[115]

Other history and geography textbooks were more sedate in their analyses of Arabism and the Arab World. For example, Wasfi 'Anabtawi and Sa'id Sabbagh's geography, adopted by the mandate for Palestine and also used in Transjordan, did not call for teacher-nationalists to inspire their students' souls. Nevertheless, as it took its young readers around the Mediterranean and "Al-Sharq al-Adna" (the Near East), it emphasized the importance of Arab history and the Arab language, for example, describing the city of Damascus as having specific institutions in which subjects such as medicine and law could be studied in Arabic.[116] Another work, published in Syria but used in Jordan's girls' schools (written by a Syrian educator who had taught in Iraq), began with a section on "The Patriots" (*Al-Wataniyyat*), including a poem, "The Spiritual Homeland," by Shafiq Jabri, a Syrian author.[117] The textbook on modern history written by Rafiq al-Tamimi, a member of Palestine's Arab Higher Committee and Ottoman-era graduate, like Sati al-Husri of the Mülkiye Mektebi in Istanbul, and later of the Sorbonne, included a more pointedly political section on Palestine entitled "The Cause of Arab Palestine," describing

115. Zu'aytir and al-Miqdadi, 12–14.

116. 'Anabtawi and al-Sabbagh, *Jughrafiyya al-Sharq al-Adna* [Geography of the Near East], 32.

117. Al-Seqal and Hindawi, *al-Mukhatar fi al-Qira'a wa al-Insha' wa al-Muta la'a wa al-Istithahar* [Selections in reading, composition, perusal, and recitation].

"Palestine and the efforts of her people to defend her against evil." He wrote that after the "tragedy" that ended the Arab Kingdom, which Arabs everywhere sought as the pinnacle of their national aspirations, "in Palestine the people rose up after the announcement of the British mandate and its intention to found a Jewish national home, and to defend against the Zionist evil and the aggression of colonial greed from their holy places."[118]

The Arabism of the mandates' textbooks was one of anti-imperialism and anti-Zionism rather than specific political programs. Even Darwish al-Miqdadi's textbook, *Tarikh al-Umma al-'Arabiyya* (The history of the Arab nation), offered no prescription for drawing the Arab nation's borders.[119] Nor did it describe the type of political formation best suited to that nation, except to gesture toward strongman politics. Al-Miqdadi's writing signifies an understanding of current literature and a desire to achieve modernity. Yet it was not in any sense a program for governance. His textbook evinced a sense of solidarity encompassing Islam, Arabic, and a general notion of civilization.

This pan-Arabism was transnational and fluid. In his analysis of al-Miqdadi's textbook, historian of Arab nationalism C. Ernest Dawn asserts he can find "all the elements of the self-view set forth by later Ba'athist and Nasserist writers." Although Nasserism and Ba'athism are both pan-Arab ideologies, they were not the same and would eventually oppose each other. Ba'athism, particularly during its early years, emphasized socialism as the means to unify and strengthen the Arab world, whereas Nasserism involved not only socialism, but also anti-imperialism, nonalignment, and pan-Arabism under Egyptian leadership. The differences between these ideologies, both of which Dawn traces back to al-Miqdadi, indicate that al-Miqdadi's politics constituted an anti-imperial liberation movement rather than a codified state ideology. Pan-Arabism would shift as it changed hands from educator-elite state functionaries like al-Miqdadi to the military leaders of Ba'athist Iraq, Syria, and Nasser's Egypt.

During the interwar era, as educators came to write the textbooks circulated through the mandates, they joined a transnational group of educated elites. They participated in regional literary as well as political networks. The large proportion of foreign educators employed by Iraq's and, to a lesser extent, Transjordan's governments, as well as the almost universally foreign-trained teachers, inspectors, and administrators in all three of Britain's mandates, meant that each system of public education fit uneasily within the government

118. Al-Tamimi, *Tarikh al-'Asr al-Hadir* [History of the current era], 301.
119. Harte, "Contesting the Past in Mandate Palestine," 159.

that oversaw its administration. Foreign-trained and foreign-born educators, as well as internationally written and published textbooks, stymied state building projects, which would otherwise link nationalism to nationality on a daily basis. The oldest generation of these educators, not only born but educated during the final years of the Ottoman Empire, found themselves poorly suited to the mandates' new categories of nationality and citizenship. Instead, they and their peers advocated and embodied more flexible forms of national affiliation. They were able to do so from a privileged position, as secondary education represented a foothold in the civil service for students as well as educators and civil servants.

Politicization: Pushing the Limits of the State

In his memoirs, Shakr ʿAli Takriti described his participation, along with his fellow students, in a series of nationalist demonstrations. Storming out of classrooms and taking to the streets, students in the interwar era began to form a politically active bloc, which could be called on by other organizations. Students' involvement in anti-imperialist strikes and demonstrations overlapped with more prosaic concerns, such as the desire to miss school or to prove their manhood through politics.

Takriti claims that the students at al-Markaziyya and the teachers college formed the backbone of support for nationalist resistance, making connections and honing forms of political engagement that shaped Iraq's limited political sphere. For Takriti, this type of nationalism was anti-imperial. It signaled resistance and the desire for independence rather than clear links to a territory. For example, several founders of the Iraqi political organization al-Jamaʿat al-Ahali not only studied together at al-Markaziyya but also became aware of and involved in politics because of their experiences as students. In one incident, the British teacher of English at al-Markaziyya found himself transferred (apparently put on forced, albeit paid, leave) due to student complaints regarding his views on the Anglo-Iraqi Treaty in 1924. The English teacher, a Mr. H. Goodall, told his students that Iraqis were "stupid" for not supporting the treaty, which granted Britain control over much of Iraq's affairs, and for not "appreciating what Britain was trying to achieve." After Goodall described those opposing the treaty as "fools and donkeys," students became incensed. Inspired by their pride and resentment of the British, and led by the future founders of the al-Ahali group, students refused to attend the teacher's classes, wrote letters to their principal as well as the Ministry of Education, and, with the support of the rest of their teachers, succeeded in having Goodall trans-ferred.[120] They brought their politics to bear on the classroom. Al-Ahali would become particularly influential in the 1930s, one of the few Iraqi organizations that advocated an explicitly democratic platform.

The experiences Takriti described, learning from foreign and pan-Arabist teachers and then participating in demonstrations with an anti-imperial bent, are characteristic of his peers across the region. British imperialism and Zion-ism were the main targets of student ire. Scholars tend to focus on these pro-tests within the confines of each mandate, seeking to connect each public school system's politics to the growth of nationalism within those states. How-ever, as the education systems in Iraq, Transjordan, and Palestine expanded, they tended to employ individuals from beyond their purview. Students' and teachers' concerns were, to differing degrees, regional. Therefore, rather than considering protests as exemplary of nationalism tied to the borders of each mandate, we should consider their forms and effects on a wider scale. The similar ideas and idioms of antigovernment protests in schools are less surpris-ing when we note that several of these teachers were in fact leading demonstra-tions against multiple governments, while also employed by them.

The strike at the Arab College in 1925 and protests at the Central Secondary School of Baghdad in 1927 against government policies are linked by individu-als and styles of protests. Through these demonstrations, educators under-mined public education's role as a national institution meant to shore up the borders of its state, and that state's (or those states') authority. At AUB, par-ticularly in the meetings of the pan-Arab al-ʿUrwat ul-Wuthqa club, students forged lasting relationships with their peers from throughout the mandates. Here we will follow a small nexus of influential individuals who, having been in classes with one another, brought their anti-imperial, pan-Arab politics with them when they dispersed to teach.

In 1925 the Arab College of Jerusalem and several other government schools went on strike, led by teachers as well as students, to protest the visit of Lord Balfour to Palestine on the occasion of the founding of Hebrew University and the Balfour Declaration. George Muʾammar of the Arab College of Jerusalem, along with Darwish al-Miqdadi and Jalal Zurayk, played leading roles in organ-izing the strike. All were graduates of the American University of Beirut.

---

120. Amin, *Jamaʾ at al-Ahali* [The al-Ahali association], 72; *Iraq Government Gazette*, Colonial Office Records, NA, CO 813 1, July 24, 1924.

Mu'ammar and al-Miqdadi were born in what would become Palestine; Zurayk, in Syria.[121]

When they went on strike against Balfour's visit and the Balfour Declaration, educators and schoolboys publicly rejected imperialism, Zionism, and the premise of the government that ruled over them, chanting: "Allah-u akbar la nurid al-Tura fa-inkas 'ala 'aqbayka ya Balfoura" (God is great and we don't want al-Tur [the location of the high commissioner's residence], so turn on your heels and go, [Lord] Balfour).[122] Yet the mandate government was lenient with its scarce teachers: they would be fired only if they acknowledged their role in provoking rebellion. The teachers involved were disciplined but not dismissed.[123] The director of education in Palestine noted in his diary that despite his misgivings, the teachers would remain. He wrote that although Mu'ammar was "the worst of the three recalcitrants . . . I do not really think either of the other two are really suitable for teaching posts as long as they hold the views they do but we can wait and see."[124] Mu'ammar was transferred to another school, at the same salary; Zurayk and al-Miqdadi were not fired. Al-Miqdadi shortly thereafter resigned, in part to lead a nongovernment, nationalist scout group. All three could have remained employed by the government they had denounced as illegitimate. They preferred to leave the Education Department of the mandate for Palestine; Mu'ammar became an attorney,[125] while Zurayk moved to Iraq. However, schoolchildren's strikes against the Balfour Declaration became a yearly occurrence.

This type of nationalist fervor appeared to be carried, like the virus to which the British likened nationalism itself, to Iraq. Both Zurayk and Miqdadi found work in Baghdad, alongside fellow AUB graduates Matta 'Akrawi, Anis Nusuli, Abdullah Mashnuk (who had already taught in Hama),[126] and others. Most were former members of al-'Urwat ul-Wuthqa.[127] In the late 1920s, students

121. Hisham Nashabeh, "Al-Kulliya al-'Arabiyya fi al-Quds" [The Arab college in Jerusalem], 139; American University of Beirut Directory of Alumni, 154.

122. Al-Khalidi, "Al-Kulliya al-'Arabiyya fi al-Quds I" [The Arab college in Jerusalem I], 48, quoted in Davis, "Commemorating Education," 190–204.

123. Executive Council, *Minutes of the Executive Council, Sixty-Second Meeting Held at the Government Offices on the 1st May, 1925*, Government of Palestine, CO 814/21 (Jerusalem, 1925), 15, NA.

124. Humphrey Bowman, April 13, 1925, Humphrey Bowman Collection, BOWMAN GB165–0034, Box 3b, MECA.

125. *Al-Kulliyah* 19, no. 2 (December 15, 1932): 62.

126. *Al-Kulliyah* 12, no. 1 (November 1925): 27.

127. *Al-Kulliyah* 7, no. 8 (June 1923): 139–40.

and teachers from both al-Markaziyya and the teachers college demonstrated to reinstate the Lebanese secondary school teacher, Nusuli, who had been fired for publishing and distributing a history textbook whose content was offensive to Shi'ites.[128] Iraqi and non-Iraqi teachers, naturally the above-mentioned AUB graduates, staged a protest, urging students at the secondary school and the teachers college to come out in force to protest Nusuli's dismissal.

In their list of demands, students (including founders of al-Ahali) empha-sized not just that their teacher was unfairly fired but that they needed freedom of speech and "liberty of thought."[129] While several students and teachers were expelled, they were allowed to return within a few months, after student peti-tions to the Iraqi government, although Nusuli returned to Lebanon.[130] On the one hand, these anecdotes, related in hindsight, project an anti-imperial nationalist spirit back into the past and perhaps overemphasize the role of the future al-Ahali members who recounted the events. On the other hand, when we combine discussions of the Balfour and Nusuli strikes as representative of a trend, we see the transnational reach of AUB and its educators, that the edu-cation system was a site of protest, and also that it offered teachers leeway to lead and participate in specific types of rebellion. Moreover, historians usually frame these protests as nationalist: Palestinian and Iraqi rather than pan-Arab or anti-imperial.[131] The protests do show the development of Iraqi and Pales-tinian nationalisms, tied to the mandate territories. However, at least two in-dividuals were involved in both protests. The protests functioned in compa-rable ways, using schoolboys as political blocs to cause disruption and create publicity. AUB graduates had shared similar experiences as part of the

128. Muhammad Mahdi al-Jawahiri, then a poet, wrote in praise of the decision by the min-ister of education (his fellow Shi'ite) to dismiss Nusili, which led to his being appointed as a teacher in Baghdad. Jones, *The Dangers of Poetry*, 98–100.

129. Davis, *Memories of State*, 73; Batatu, *The Old Social Classes*, 399.

130. Kahati, "The Role of Some Leading Arab Educators," 436, 473. For a fuller discussion of this incident, see Kalisman, "Bursary Scholars at the American University of Beirut."

131. Historians have argued that the protests illustrate the growth of Palestinian nationalism against Zionism, although Betty Anderson connects the protest to a broader, Arab nationalist consciousness. Marco Demichelis argues that the Arab College produced intellectual elites, but he ties that argument to the idea that the college specifically produced Palestinian nationalists, rather than emphasizing its place in the Arab world. Demichelis, "From Nahda to Nakba"; Anderson, *The Street and the State*, 99–101; Davis, "Commemorating Education." With the Nu-suli incident in Iraq, historians underscore Iraqi nationalism or alternatively emphasize sectarian divides; Baram, Rohde, and Zeidel, *Iraq between Occupations*, 45; Bashkin *The Other Iraq*, 48–49.

pan-Arab al-ʿUrwat ul-Wuthqa club and in teaching together across the region. These educators transmitted their experiences and the tactics of protest to a second generation, who would continue their school day rebellions into the 1940s, spreading a regional view of politics and schooling.

———

For Hisham Sharabi, the American University of Beirut in the early 1940s was a halcyon period,

> full of enthusiasm and patriotism. . . . Arab students (Palestinians, Syrians, Iraqis, and Saudis) took part in the demonstrations with their Lebanese schoolmates, as though the country were theirs and the French enemy their enemy. No states, no sovereignties yet divided the Arabs. We used to feel really that Lebanon was our homeland and that we were all one nation. How happy those days were. Who could dream then that fifteen years later, in 1958, Lebanon would turn into an arena for civil war, or that in 1975 it would become a stage for massacres unparalleled in the twentieth century.[132]

Sharabi voices an almost painful nostalgia for the interwar era, regardless of British and French control of the region. Despite the decades-old borders of the Mandates, he asserts that these divisions meant nothing in the face of his schoolmates' love for their Arab homeland. For Sharabi and his fellows, pan-Arabism and anti-imperial nationalisms were lived experiences rather than studied ideologies, forged through travel as they came of age. When students and educators moved along networks created by schooling, their writings and employment within multiple states enforced regional as well as national ties. They fought against imperialism rather than against one another.

Nationally bounded education systems nevertheless brought about transnational and regional ideologies. The networks formed by students, texts, and educators across the interwar Middle East were intrinsic to the establishment of state bureaucracies. Without traveling civil servants, the mandate governments could not have expanded. Students, teachers, and administrators inhabited life worlds that spanned new and contested political borders. The processes educators were involved in, working for governments, writing textbooks, and presenting curriculums are key hallmarks of state and nation building. Educators' travels, however, disrupted the links between the idea of the nation

---

132. Sharabi, *Embers and Ashes*, 10–11.

they offered their students and the national boundaries that circumscribed them. Although these borders were new, their validity was questioned by those who taught those borders' history and geography. A more regional identity persisted due to the formative experiences of teachers and civil servants who traveled and studied transnationally. The next chapter details the ideas of nation that educators advanced, from the violent rebellions of the 1930s and early 1940s through the revolutions of the 1950s. Despite protests, rebellions, and coups, educators could stay employed by their governments due to the fluidity of the ideologies they learned and taught, as well as their rare status. However, stronger states, released from British colonial rule, rendered those ideologies, and their practitioners, obsolete.

4

Educators and Governance

REBELLIONS FROM NATION TO STATE

Akram Zueitar (Zu'aytir), schoolteacher, frequently addresses hot-headed
youths, mostly recruited from boy scouts and his own students. . . . He spoke
of sacrifice and the boycott of foreigners, he mentioned de Valera and Gandhi,
he commended training as soldiers and fighting for independence, he hoped
to see the young men as soldiers fighting for their country.

—PALESTINE: POLICE SUMMARIES, MARCH 10, 1933

AKRAM ZU'AYTIR, the Palestinian schoolteacher immersed in Iraq's interwar
political scene, was the quintessential educator-nationalist.[1] He dramatically
fulfilled British colonial officials' fears that allowing colonized individuals access to education would lead to anti-British protests. On multiple occasions,
he rallied "hot-headed youths" to take to the streets, from Nablus to Baghdad.
Zu'aytir inducted students and boy scouts into the global quest for independence from colonial rule, while emphasizing the particular case of Arabs and
the threat of Zionism. Less concerned with classroom subjects than with elec-
trifying national identity, he used schools as a nationalist platform, and his
students as an audience. He interspersed stints as a primary or secondary
teacher in government and nongovernment schools with interludes as a

---

1. A website devoted to Zu'aytir includes a section of quotes from Palestinian intellectuals.
Nasher, http://www.akramzuayter.org, accessed April 5, 2014.

140

journalist, political activist, textbook author,
and historian.[2] His activities did not go unno-
ticed by the governments he protested: he was
subject to imprisonment, fines, internal and
external exile by multiple regimes. Historians
and political theorists have mined Zu'aytir's
memoirs and polemics for their contributions
to pan-Arab and Palestinian nationalism as
well as insight into events in the Middle East
during the twentieth century.[3] Yet his later
job titles included ambassador, government
minister, and senator in the Hashemite Kingdom of Jordan.

FIGURE 4.1. Ustadh fi Baghdad
(a professor in Baghdad), 1934.
(Reproduced by permission
from Sari Akram Zu'aytir,
Akramzuayter.org.)

Figures like Akram Zu'aytir represent many
of the tensions and contradictions inherent in
educators' politics, between the upheavals of
the interwar era and the early decades of statehood or exile. Zu'aytir, like Darwish al-Miqdadi,
Suleiman al-Nabulsi, and others, constitute an
elite and well-studied group, self-proclaimed nationalists first and educators
second.[4] Yet, at least during the interwar era, they could always find employment with governments, even when they fomented protests against them.
Their nationalism, both within and outside of schools, made them infamous
in the eyes of British and mandate officials. Anti-imperialists, rule-breakers,
and self-styled revolutionaries, they nevertheless continued their work in the
civil service until independent nation-states divided the region. After independence, teachers, as well as interwar-era elite politicians, would scramble to
maintain their positions and their beliefs.

Histories, newspaper articles, memoirs, and popular accounts have lionized
teachers, from the lowliest unclassified village schoolteacher to professors in

2. Mattar, *Encyclopedia of the Palestinians*, 566–67; Palestinian Academic Society for the
Study of International Affairs, "Personalities" (PASSIA 2006), http://www.passia.org/palestine
_facts/personalities/alpha_z.htm, accessed April 17, 2014.

3. Matthews, *Confronting an Empire*; Anderson, *Nationalist Voices in Jordan*.

4. This group generally also includes Talib Mushtaq, Anis Nusuli, at times Muhammad 'Izzat
Darwazeh.

Iraq's colleges, as nationalist heroes. Educators appear as the mouthpieces of violent, peasant, or popular revolutionary uprisings, in contrast to vilified elites and notables.[5] Schools themselves are repeatedly described as "hotbeds of nationalism."[6] In these narratives, educators preach to legions of angry young men and women, inspiring them with "the spirit of nationalism" and "resistance to imperialism," thereby inciting and participating in anticolonial rebellions.[7] Yet contrasts between elite notables and peasants elide the complex experience of the growing number of individuals who fell between these categories. Moreover, in searching for a unified Palestinian cause, a Jordanian sense of nationalism, and Iraqi unity (or sectarianism), historical actors as well as historians have downplayed educators' ambiguous role as government-subsidized antigovernment nationalists and the nature of interwar politics overall.

Assuming that expanding public schooling automatically spreads nationalism subsumes divergent ideological platforms into a linear story of national awakening. By looking across Iraqi, Palestinian, and Transjordanian borders, we see a transnational structure of schooling in which individuals acted in similar ways with multiple governments. In his seminal work on education and state building, Andy Green argues that government education "can only be understood in relation to the process of state formation," including "not only the construction of the political and administrative apparatus of government and all government-controlled agencies which constitute the 'public' realm but also the formation of ideologies and collective beliefs which legitimate state power and underpin concepts of nationhood and national 'character.'"[8] The growth of state institutions, bureaucracy as well as the ideologies that

5. Matthews, *Confronting an Empire*, 50, 57, 73; Mattar, *Encyclopedia of the Palestinians*, 25; Simon, *Iraq between the Two World Wars*; Wien, *Iraqi Arab Nationalism*; Eppel, "The Elite," 233; Reich, *Political Leaders*, 35; Bowman, *Middle-East Window*; Swedenburg, *Memories of Revolt*; Anderson, *Nationalist Voices in Jordan*; Davis, *Memories of State*; Dodge, *Inventing Iraq*; Antonius, *The Arab Awakening*, 405–7.

6. Anderson, *Nationalist Voices in Jordan*, 98; Palestinian Academic Society for the Study of International Affairs, "Personalities: Dr. Khalil Totah (1886–1955)" (PASSIA 2006), http://www .passia.org/images/personalities/totah-khalil/khalil-text.htm, accessed April 17, 2014; Rush and Priestland, *Records of Iraq*, 9:397; Mari, *Arab Education in Israel*, 17–18.

7. Abu Gharbiyah, *Fi Khidam al-Nidal al-ʾArabi al-Filastini*, 19; Great Britain Palestine Royal Commission, *Palestine Royal Commission Report*, 133–34, 340.

8. Green, *Education and State Formation*, 77.

Green presumes swell along with the state itself, are fundamentally tied to public education.

This narrative, however, fails to explain not only the pan-Arabism of the interwar years but also its more restrictive variety of the 1950s and early 1960s, to say nothing of the myriad transnational platforms attempted and dissolved during these years. Instead, I argue that nationalisms, and more clearly transnational political platforms such as communism, fascism, or anti-imperialism, did not easily align with growing state institutions, either in opposition to the mandate states or in support of them, until the end of British colonial rule. The ideals teachers promoted differed from the codified territorial nationalisms or political parties of later years. Moreover, even during key moments of nationalist fervor, revolutions were undermined by the imbrication of civil servants in the mandate states as well as their transnational nature. Limited education under colonial rule fostered a particularly open type of anti-imperial politics that did not require armed rebellion, even among its most active proponents. Despite their rebellious reputations, then, educators seldom participated in the armed uprisings that swept the region.

The formation and cooperation of nationalist educators within the government schools of interwar Iraq, Palestine, and Transjordan bolstered the status quo, undermining radical changes in governance. Educators' interests were often more closely aligned with those of politicians rather than peasants. Political and economic elites as well as government-employed educators depended on the state for their livelihoods and prestige. They benefited tangibly from the mandate governments, in contrast to workers and *fellahin* who did not. Nevertheless, due to the scarcity and value of education, educators in particular did not draw local ire for their part in the generally reviled government systems. In contrast, those denied the benefits of education in Palestine or excluded from a clear career path through the civil service in Iraq led violent rebellions.

"Nationalism" itself is a complex term, especially in the context of the many different nationalist and anti-imperial uprisings in the twentieth-century Middle East. The shifting meanings of the word (or in Arabic, words), can make studying its history difficult: hunting out the seeds of modern-day ideas can blind us to what those terms meant to people at earlier times. Uncovering the shifting meanings of nationalism during the 1930s requires abandoning anachronistic searches for the origins of well-defined pan-Arab (*qawmi*), communist, socialist, Islamist, or territorial (*watani*) affiliations. For teachers, nationalism and rebellion did not rule out employment by the very regimes they resisted. Invocations of nationalism and patriotism signified political engage-ment, erudition, and anti-imperialism on a regional scale, not in a specific territory or political system. However, the division of the Arab world into rival countries and the codification of pan-Arabism into federations or alliances after World War II would accompany the codification of ideologies, educator-politicians' ouster from power, and teachers' loss of their elite status.

By closely examining interwar educators as proponents and practitioners of anti-imperial nationalism, and as a crucial part of the civil service, a more nuanced picture forms of how educated individuals engaged in politics while paving the way for revolutions on the part of other social groups across the region. By comparing Iraq, Transjordan, and Palestine across the transition from mandate to independence or occupation and diaspora, this chapter shows how government education can affect regime stability. During the in-terwar era, the incorporation of educated individuals into government service tempered their nationalisms and curbed their protests. Their place as government-subsidized nationalists, supported by consistent demand for schooling, excluded educators and the educated alike from revolutions, as groups barred from the civil service took up arms. Following the mandates' end, educator-politicians sought to fit themselves into midcentury nation-states, despite these states' differences. They faced a changed world of stronger, more codified, and more exclusive ideologies, squeezed into the new map of the Middle East.

Nationalism across Borders: Akram Zu'aytir between Iraq and Palestine

From a very early age, future politician Akram Zu'aytir was exposed to the values of government service and agitation against that government, and also the assumption that the purpose of schooling was, above all, a nationalist one. Zu'aytir was born in 1909 in Nablus. His father worked as a teacher and was the sometime mayor of Nablus during the Ottoman period. On the other hand, the Ottoman government also sentenced his brother to death during World War I for participating in the Arab Revolt. For at least a generation, then, Zu'aytir's family had been enmeshed in the connected domains of edu-cation, government service, and antigovernment activities.[9] One of the first

---

9. Palestinian Academic Society for the Study of International Affairs, "Personalities." Zu'aytir took part in the 1916 Arab revolt, fighting on the side of the Hashemites. Kabaha, *The Palestinian Press*, 13.

graduates of al-Najah, a private school in Nablus, Akram Zu'aytir internalized the school's anti-imperial, anti-Zionist, and pan-Arab atmosphere. There, he sang national songs, read Arab history, and, during the early 1920s, listened to the nationalist lectures of then principal and future Arab Higher Committee member Muhammad Izzat Darwazeh, who hoped to heighten students' "national consciousness."[10]

Zu'aytir later studied at the American University of Beirut. Even though illness prevented him from graduating, his short stint in higher education granted him sufficient credentials to teach, as well as access to alumni networks that would facilitate his, and many of his contemporaries', transnational careers. In al-'Urwat al-Wuthqa, he met individuals who would combine nationalist teaching with government service, first as educators and later as ministers.[11] Zu'aytir also joined an Arab nationalist secret society, composed of cells and various executive committees, which utilized a vanguard model, requiring its members to influence other nationalists and even other secret societies.[12] More concretely, Fadhil al-Jamali and Matta 'Akrawi, once they became high-ranking officials, explicitly hired Zu'aytir to teach in Iraq because of their shared connections to AUB.[13] For Zu'aytir, like many of his generation of educator nationalists, access to higher levels of schooling meant integration into "the big leagues," allowing him to participate in the highest ranks of political movements, which were also connected to the civil service.

Before teaching in Iraq, Zu'aytir taught in the government schools of mandate Palestine, using his credentials and knowledge of English as leverage to negotiate with the government that employed him while also pushing his luck protesting against it. He combined bargaining with the Department of Education regarding banal matters with, as he put it, seizing the chance "to inflame nationalist sentiments!"[14] His requests included whether he could attend (and receive a scholarship) to any law school in the United Kingdom without passing an examination (he could not); whether the Higher Teachers Examination he took would be a sufficient credential to enable him to matriculate at the Sorbonne (it would not); and whether the department would transfer him

---

10. Darwazehh, *Mudhakkirat Muhammad 'Izzat Darwazeh,* 533. Zu'aytir's peers included Farid al-Sa'ad and Hikmat al-Masri.

11. These included Wasfi 'Anabtawi, Thabit al-Khalidi, Arafat al-Duweik, and Fadhil al-Jamali, among others.

12. Choueiri, *Arab Nationalism, a History,* 94.

13. Zu'aytir, *Bawakir al-Nidal: 1909–1935,* 662, 644, 667, 673.

14. Zu'aytir, 65.

to Jerusalem to allow him to take law classes while teaching (it could not in time to suit his ambitions).[15] While he received few if any positive answers, his constant questioning shows an intimate relationship with the state he both served and criticized. He was also ambitious, seeking to gain an education (and legal credentials) by any means possible. Meanwhile, he wrote political tracts in Egyptian and Palestinian newspapers, wrestled with his supervisors, and contacted other self-described nationalists both within and beyond government service.[16]

As an avowed public nationalist, he was nevertheless able to combine work in education with agitation against the governments that employed him, to a degree. He resigned as a teacher in Palestine in 1929, then studied law in Jerusalem while editing a newspaper, writing articles, and giving well-documented speeches advocating independence.[17] These speeches underscored ideals of freedom and anti-imperialism, repeatedly using concepts of nation and patriotism. For example, in celebrating political prisoners in February 1930, Zu'aytir described prison as "the house of dignity, the base of loyalty, the national (*wataniyya*) beacon and the source of strength. The nation (*umma*) which does not recognize slavery, and does not accept it, and struggles against injustice and colonialism is a free nation (*umma*)."[18] After calling for "Jihad for the sake of Palestine in every sensible and peaceful way," he was arrested.[19] Forbidden from leaving Nablus for a year (except to complete his law studies), Zu'aytir found work in education; he taught at al-Najah and organized a youth

15. Akram Zu'aytir, "Director of Education Jerusalem, through the Official Channel," December 15, 1928; Jerome Farrell, "D.I.E. Galilee, Subject:- Akram Zu'aiter," December 22, 1928; Zu'aytir, "To the Director of Education Thro the Principal of the Salahiyya School," February 17, 1928; Farrell, "D.I.E. Galilee Subject:- Akram Zu'aitar," March 21, 1928; Zu'aytir, "Letter to the Director of Education, through the Inspector of Education and the Principal of the Secondary School Esq.," April 6, 1929; Farrell, "D.I.E. Galilee Subject:- Akram Zu'aitar," May 11, 1929; "Akram Zuaiter," 1012 15 M, ISA.

16. Zu'aytir, *Bawakir al-Nidal: 1909–1935*, 28.

17. Palestinian Academic Society for the Study of International Affairs, Jerusalem, "Zu'aiter, Akram (1909–1996), Palestine Personalities," http://www.passia.org/palestine_facts/personalities/alpha_z.htm, accessed April 17, 2014; Kabaha, *The Palestinan Press*, 22.

18. Akram Zu'aytir, "Al-Sijn Bayt al-Karama: Khitab al-Ustadh Akram Effendi Zu'aytir fi haflat nukarim mua'taqli Jaffa fi kulliyat rawdat al ma'arif" [Prison is a house of dignity. A lecture by Professor Akram Effendi Zu'aytir at the party in honor of the detainees in Jaffa at the Rawdat al-Ma'arif College], *Al-Jami'a al-Arabiyya*, February 23, 1930, 1, NLIJ.

19. "Al-Ustadh Zu'aytir fi al-Sijn" [Professor Zu'aytir in prison], *Az-Zouhour*, April 19, 1930, 6, NLIJ.

bloc also seeking independence.[20] From 1933–1935 Zu'aytir used his connections from AUB to become a professor in Iraq, spending his school vacations as a rabble rouser in Nablus and a founding member of Palestine's Istiqlal (Independence) party.[21] In Iraq, Zu'aytir's negotiations only increased along with his rank in the civil service. He lobbied the Iraqi government to protest journals and political organizations that he felt did not support his type of nationalism and the cause of Palestine or that denigrated "Syrians."[22] He threatened to resign on multiple occasions and solicited help from politicians to discredit his "rivals": those who preferred Iraqis to hold posts in the Iraqi government.[23] He also brought together other young, educated men to advocate anti-imperialism and Arab unity in the face of Palestine's political divisions.

Zu'aytir's influence was sidelined as the rise of Nazism in Germany and restrictive immigration policies in other countries led to increasing Jewish immigration to Palestine. Palestine's Arab population rebelled, stoked by fears of an exclusively Jewish state in all the mandate.[24] Although the vast majority of Jewish immigrants moved to cities, the policy of *avoda ivrit* or "Hebrew labor "contributed to a situation wherein Jewish immigrants supplanted Arab agricultural workers.[25] Unemployed villagers flocked to urban areas such as

20. Zu'aytir, *Bawakir al-Nidal: 1909–1935*, 139–43; Matthews, *Confronting an Empire*, 70–71. Matthews claims that Zu'aytir was expelled from the law classes, but Kabaha claims he became an attorney. Kabaha, *The Palestinian Press*, 14. Zu'aytir asserts that he was able to take the law exam, albeit under police guard. Zu'aytir, *Bawakir al-Nidal: 1909–1935*, 185–86.

21. For example, in January 1933 he held a meeting at a mosque in his hometown of Nablus, sending telegrams to the high commissioner in Palestine and King Abdullah of Transjordan protesting the leasing of land in Transjordan to Jews. "Sale of Transjordan Lands," *Palestine Post*, January 1, 1933.

22. Zu'aytir, *Bawakir al-Nidal: 1909–1935*, 617–19.

23. Anderson, *Nationalist Voices in Jordan*. For example, in his memoirs, Zu'aytir offers his resignation because certain newspapers were publishing anti-Syrian articles. He recalled meeting with Sami Shawkat, then director of education, who begged him to rescind his resignation. Zu'aytir did, and the newspapers who had denigrated him and Adel Arslan published apologies, which satisfied him. Zu'aytir, *Bawakir al-Nidal: 1909–1935*, 617, 662.

24. In the first eight months of 1933, 16,000 Jewish immigrants entered with permission, compared with 4,070 in 1931 and 10,000 in 1932. There was also illegal Jewish immigration. Great Britain Colonial Office, *Report by His Majesty's Government in the United Kingdom of Great Britain and Northern Ireland to the Council of the League of Nations on the Administration of Palestine and Trans-Jordan for the Year 1933*; "Riots in Palestine," *Sunday Times (Perth)*, October 29, 1933. Although some pro-Palestinian demonstrations took place in Transjordan, they were also put down by the Transjordan frontier force, which was called into Palestine.

25. Beinin, *Workers and Peasants*, 94; Nadan, *The Palestinian Peasant Economy*, 5, 8.

the port city of Haifa, seeking unskilled jobs.[26] Their frustrations and lack of opportunities escalated into petitions, strikes, protests, and riots.[27]

While educators and educated individuals like Zuʾaytir sought to encourage schoolboy protests, others, the most famous being religious leader and activist Sheikh ʾIzz al-Din al-Qassam, formed small cells of armed "revolutionaries," particularly among Haifa's pious and illiterate workers. Al-Qassam was killed in a skirmish with the British. One of his followers, leading a group of guerilla fighters, killed two Jewish travelers in 1936, sparking retaliations. The mandate government declared a state of emergency. Local groups set up national strike committees, while elite leaders struggled to catch up to the tide of revolution, showing solidarity by joining together in the Arab Higher Committee.[28] A general strike continued for six months, ending by order of the committee in 1937.[29] Although the strike was relatively peaceful, there was no resolution to Arab Palestinian demands, and fighting resumed.[30]

When Zuʾaytir heard of the growing ferment, he returned to Palestine from Iraq to participate.[31] His involvement took the form of fiery speeches and demonstrations urging others to take up arms. The Zionist English-language daily, the *Palestine Post*, having first criticized Zuʾaytir for preaching rebellion while remaining comfortably employed in Baghdad,[32] lambasted him from late 1935 through early 1936 as an "extremist leader," goading schoolchildren and fellahin to arm themselves and strike.[33] The authorities quickly lost patience with him. As he was no longer an employee of the government of Palestine, Zuʾaytir lacked the bargaining power he had held as a civil servant.

26. Lockman, *Comrades and Enemies*, 406.

27. For example, there were twenty-one Arab worker strikes in 1935. Taqqu, "Arab Labor in Mandatory Palestine, 1920–1948," 149.

28. Matthews, *Confronting an Empire*, 253.

29. Bowman, "Diary June 1935–Oct 1936," October 11, 1936, Humphrey Bowman Collection, Box 4 B, GB165–0034, MECA.

30. Kimmerling and Migdal, *The Palestinian People*, 130.

31. Zuʾaytir, *Bawakir al-Nidal: 1909–1935*, 747, 748.

32. "A Palestinian's Patriotism Queried: Istiklalist Who Remained in Baghdad," *Palestine Post*, February 6, 1934.

33. "Arabs Denounce Britain and Jews on Balfour Day," *Palestine Post*, November 3, 1935; Staff Correspondent, "Arab Parties Divided over Protest Strike," *Palestine Post*, November 13, 1935; Our Own Correspondent, "Large Crowds at Burial of Three Arab Terrorists," *Palestine Post*, November 22, 1935. Zuʾaytir was busily publishing materials calling for strikes and martyrdom. His preferred audience involved students. Our Own Correspondent, "Tulkarm Kadoorie School," *Palestine Post*, February 24, 1936; "More Arabs Exiled," *Palestine Post*, May 26, 1936.

The mandate government first exiled, then arrested him.[34] Within the year he returned to Iraq and to the Ministry of Education, where he worked as an inspector and teacher.[35]

In retrospect, Zu'aytir defined his teaching in Palestine as a nationalist platform. What he meant by those nationalist sentiments is harder to tease out. He was clearly against Zionism and imperialism and unmistakably for an Arabism, which included Palestine. But his nationalism was one of broad strokes rather than specific details. His former student Mahmoud al-Musa al-'Ubaydat, later a Jordanian army officer, recalled that Zu'aytir was "beloved by all the students because of his nationalist tendencies, his enthusiasm for the Palestinian cause and because of his correct reasoning."[36] Writing in Jordan, and in hindsight, al-'Ubaydat separates "nationalist tendencies" from the Palestinian cause. This classification underscores different meanings of political engagement; nationalism, especially in the eyes of students, signified particular activities, paramount among them, discussing the idea of the nation and its oppression by imperial powers (which al-'Ubaydat repeatedly describes). The Palestinian cause, tied to both a territory and a more specific enemy, existed alongside a more all-encompassing anti-imperialism. Al-'Ubaydat's phrasing must be attributed in part to contemporary concerns, due to conflicts between Palestinian citizens of Jordan and Jordanians. Nevertheless, in memoirs and scholarly works, authors frequently invoke nationalism, particularly in schools and in reference to Zu'aytir, as a public articulation of anti-imperial and often pro-Arab ideas rather than as a defined political program.

As the mandate for Iraq officially ended, nationalist educators like Zu'aytir flocked to Iraq's schools and cities, eager to make the intertwined educational and political systems a platform for nationalist indoctrination, a platform that increasingly combined militarism with anti-imperial Arabism. The ability to both express antigovernment sentiments (more virulently in Iraq than Palestine or Transjordan) and stay a civil servant framed intellectuals' political stances, facilitating political engagement but circumscribing the form of that engagement to discussion and vanguardism rather than action.

34. "Receptions Given for Syrian Exiles," *Palestine Post*, April 20, 1937.

35. *Iraq Government Gazette* 24, June 11, 1939, CO 813/14 NA.

36. Kahati, "The Role of Education," 38; 'Ubaydat, *al-Mujahid al-'Aqid Mahmud al-Musa al-'Ubaydat*, 33.

Education, Militarism, and Gender

In 1932 Iraq was admitted to the League of Nations, granting its government some independence, although Great Britain continued to dictate Iraq's foreign policy. Less British involvement meant more funding for schooling, permitting a large increase in the number of educators employed by Iraq's government, in comparison to Transjordan and Palestine. Despite the upturn in hiring, teachers remained relatively limited, particularly at a secondary school level. The lack of British oversight, coupled with Iraq's heightened status as an importer of teachers, meant Iraq's bureaucracy and education system functioned as a stage for nationalist educators from throughout the region. These educators, including Akram Zu'aytir, found Iraq to be the best location from which to combine state service with political agitation.[37]

More independence with regard to Iraq's budget also led to increases in the number of soldiers recruited into Iraq's army and subsequently a greater political role for upper-ranking military figures. Beginning in 1936, a series of military coups reshuffled the government, adding military leaders to the limited seats available in parliament but leaving the Hashemite monarchy intact. The fluid nature of Iraq's government extended to its education system. Across both, an elite cadre of individuals moved frequently in and out of official posts. As this group circulated ministerial or educational positions among themselves, they also stepped in and out of power, and in and out of government employment.[38] Legislation facilitated these frequent transitions, absolving government employees from any "political crimes" they may have committed during one or another of the elites' turns as prime minister. Individuals could be ousted and even punished for disagreeing with whichever political configuration was in place and yet return to ministerial and education jobs without permanent penalties.[39]

The political movements available to educators during the 1930s were almost always anti-imperial, due to consistent British involvement in both

---

37. Talhami, *Syria and the Palestinians*, 19. This also meant a deterioration in the status of Iraq's Jews, despite their overwhelming lack of support for Zionism (and pan-Arabism). Abd al-Latif, *Mudhakkirati*, 20–23.

38. Ayad Al-Qazzaz, "Power Elite in Iraq." From 1936 through 1941, military figures at the head of armed forces became part of this limited group. They became not only politicized but also a tool for adjusting politics. Tarbush, *The Role of the Military in Politics*.

39. See "The State Officials Discipline Law, no 68 of 1936," *Iraq Government Gazette* 27, July 5, 1936, CO 813/10, Colonial Office Records, NA.

foreign and domestic policy. Britain's enemies modeled different ideologies and methods of resistance, which some educated individuals across the Arab world found appealing, aligning nationalist concepts with the trappings of militarism. In Iraq, the rise of the military in politics paralleled some officials' growing interest in German fascism, notably that of the minister of education during the 1930s, Dr. Sami Shawkat.[40] Other educators and civil servants, however, would amend, critique, or satirize this militarism, participating in regional and global political trends, from within or only briefly outside of the Iraqi state.

Shawkat's interest in militarism, as well as global understandings of the military potential of organized youth groups, led to a reinvention of the government's scouting program. Scouting connected military strength and masculinity with a fascist-esque Arab nationalism that some of Iraq's government elites and educators believed was well-suited to their political goals, including promoting feelings of country-wide unity. During the first years of British control of the region, boy scouts and girl guides had been pet projects of colonial officials in both Iraq and Palestine. These were fairly sedate organizations, which aimed at improving students' minds, bodies, and above all their characters. By 1932, with Iraq's official, albeit compromised, independence from British rule, Baghdad's boy scouts were participating in nationalist rituals tied to the Iraqi state, as in the parade pictured in figure 4.2.

However, narratives connecting scouting, state education, and territorial nationalism poorly describe the interwar Middle East. Exposure to and performance of nationalist ideologies did take place in the schools of Iraq, but those participating in Iraq's wide range of nationalist movements and scout groups included educators from beyond Iraq. Scouting was explicitly transnational. Scouts traveled from one district or town to another, and even to other countries; Iraqi scouts acted as emissaries to Beirut and to the Hijaz during the 1930s.[41] These trips were construed not only as a part of Iraqi youth's physical education but also as international diplomacy, geared toward strengthening "the bonds of friendship and national (*qamiyya*) ties between the youth of Iraq on one side, and that of the Hijaz on the other."[42] In Palestine, nongovernment scouting groups in 1934 chose King Ghazi of Iraq to be their honorary leader,

40. Simon, *Iraq between the Two World Wars*, 103.

41. "Irakian Scouts at the A.U.B.," *Al-Kulliyah* 18, no. 5 (May 15, 1932): 107–8.

42. Wizarat al-Maʿarif Iraq, *Al-Taqrir al-Sanawi ʿan Sayr al-Maʿarif li-Sanawat* [Annual report on educational progress for the years] *1934–35, 1935–1936,* 62.

FIGURE 4.2. Iraq (Mesopotamia), *Celebration of Iraq Becoming a Member of the League of Nations, October 6, 1932, Baghdad*. Schoolboys pay their respects at the palace. Photo by American Colony, Photo Department. (Reprinted from the Library of Congress, G. Eric and Edith Matson Photograph Collection.)

connecting the ideals of scouting with a pan-Arab educational sphere.[43] Darwish al-Miqdadi, who had resigned in protest over his desire to set up a nongovernment scouting group in Palestine, was instrumental in establishing a governmental one in Baghdad in 1931. After just four years of independence, al-Miqdadi's scouts would transform Iraq's state-sponsored boy scouts as a whole.[44] Figure 4.3 depicts the new version of its boy scouts, the *futuwwa*, in 1936.

The futuwwa was a government scouting and youth organization composed of students from secondary and intermediate schools, both public and

43. Degani "They Were Prepared," 204.
44. Cohen "The Anti-Jewish *Farhud*," 6.

FIGURE 4.3. *Janib min futuwwa mutawasita al-Karkh yu 'adun al-tahiyya al-'askariyya* (A portion of the intermediate futuwwa of Karkh making a military salute), Iraq, 1936. (Reprinted from Sati al-Husri, "Al-Khidma al-'Askariyya wa-al-Tarbiyya al-'Amma" [Military service and public education], *al-Mu 'allim al-Jadid* 1, nos. 3 and 4 [June and September 1936]: 276.)

private. The word *futuwwa* emphasized a specific category of Iraqi student and citizen; it means masculine youth or "youthful masculinity."[45] Implemented shortly after the law of compulsory military service in 1934, the futuwwa became mandatory for students five years later. The overtly militaristic purpose of the futuwwa by 1939 was "to give the youth of the country such various forms of military training as to accustom them to rough life, hardships and devotion to duty, and to foster in them the military spirit and manly, chivalrous and other kindred qualities of love of discipline." The minister of education was granted the title of prince or *Amir* of the futuwwa. Futuwwa officers were to wear a badge including sword and pen. Older students used arms and live ammunition in their training.[46] They were required to pass a test on "military information" each year and to attend "military training, military lectures, and camps" in order to advance to the next class.[47] As Peter Wien argues, the futuwwa represented a physical, concrete, modern, and masculine ideal in which

45. Pursley, "The Stage of Adolescence," 178.

46. Zu'aytir, *Bawakir al-Nidal: 1909–1935*, 673. He also mentions Matta Akrawi, Darwish al-Miqdadi, and others as participating in this military training as teachers.

47. *Iraq Government Gazette*, no. 47, November 19, 1939, CO 813/13. NA, 628–31.

youth, nationalism, and education would be embodied, displayed, and indeed advertised to a new generation of Iraqis.[48]

The "living through" of this particularly militarized masculine ideal, including its attendant militant pan-Arabism was, unsurprisingly more complicated than its official articulation.[49] Drills, camps, and parades were memorable, although the patriotism they imparted in students tended to be more show than substance: a militaristic anti-imperialism that incorporated global political elements, without importing fascism wholesale.[50] Contrasting memories from the Jewish Heskel Haddad and the Muslim Khalid Kishtainy point to the sectarian tensions this militarism encouraged. Kishtainy, an Iraqi author, journalist, and artist, remembered school-day parades in the late 1930s. He stated that "once or two times a year, we formed lines and would march, all of us in uniforms . . . with a band with at least one drum."[51] Similarly, Haddad, the precocious son of a well-off plumber, viewed the futuwwa as a means of "integration," which made him proud to wear his scouting uniform and to participate in the same activities as other Iraqis, regardless of religion.[52] Kishtainy thought that these practices were "very nationalistic" and that a lot of "Nazi influence" manifested in "khaki uniforms" and "nationalistic songs." He took care, however, to argue that the 1930s were in fact a period of tolerance "with regards to religion and beliefs," despite parades and nationalistic history lessons focused on Islamic civilization and Arabic heritage. For the young Kishtainy, nationalism was self-evident: an idea of Arab and Islamic civilization in which Iraq could play a leading role, tied to practices rather than any particular political platform. For Haddad, these policies led to disillusionment with the Iraqi government, and the idea of Arabism as an ideology that could overcome religious differences.

Despite the best efforts of Haddad's Jewish school scout troop, they never won the public scouting competitions that took place in "Baghdad's biggest stadium." His father told him that no "dhimmi" would ever be permitted to win against a Muslim, underscoring the strength and durability of religious prejudices over and above notions of Arabism or Iraqi nationalism. Haddad,

48. Wien, Iraqi Arab Nationalism, 99–101.

49. McNay, Gender and Agency, 36–37.

50. Israel Gershoni and James P. Jankowski, in Confronting Fascism in Egypt, have shown that the bulk of Egyptian intellectuals did not embrace fascism.

51. Author interview with Khalid Kishtainy, December 12, 2011.

52. Haddad and Rosenteur, Flight from Babylon, 30–31.

a Jewish Iraqi, also experienced antisemitism attached to fascist tactics and encouraged by anti-Zionism. While walking in his scout uniform, he and his baby sister were attacked when a group of Arab youths realized he was Jewish. Haddad shouted at them, to no avail, that he "was a fellow Scout . . . an Arab brother." His attackers retorted that he was "just a Jew. . . . No Jew is brother to an Arab."[53] Haddad, in the increasingly politically volatile atmosphere of the 1930s, could not find purchase in Arabism regardless of the unity it promised. For both Haddad and Kishtainy, the lasting influence of parades and scouting activities was not Shawkat's message but their own experiences.

The message Shawkat sought to convey through both the futuwwa and Iraq's education system was one of militarist resistance against imperialism, as well as anti-intellectualism in favor of a strong, masculine ideal. Government teachers, in Shawkat's view, were a type of soldier, imparting a militant anti-imperial "strength" rather than any academic subjects. In a famous speech in 1933, he told the teachers at the Teacher Training College that education and a robust economy were not enough to win independence. He highlighted the examples of strongmen, such as Harun al-Rashid, Ataturk, Reza Shah Pahlavi, and Mussolini, bombastically arguing that these leaders possessed the necessary "strength," through "iron and fire," to successfully resist imperialism and even to reclaim their past empires.[54] He also asserted that government teachers must teach the "'history of the fatherland, and the past of the nation'—without giving too much attention to historical facts. They should promote patriotism while being careful not to "oppress the memory."[55] Other educationalists, particularly Sati al-Husri, the sometime director general of public instruction in Iraq, could not support Shawkat's anti-intellectualism. Nevertheless, Husri believed militarization could still inculcate nationalism across different groups, making "the army a tool to defend the nation, deriving its strength from all the classes of the nation."[56]

The military posturing of the solely male futuwwa points to a particularly masculine notion of state-sponsored nationalism, which followed global trends strengthening links between governments and the sharpening category

53. Haddad and Rosenteur, 34

54. Shawkat, "The Profession of Death," 97–99.

55. Simon, *Iraq between the Two World Wars*, 41.

56. Sati al- Husri, "Al-Khidma al-ʿAskariyya wa-al-Tarbiyya al-ʿAmma" [Military service and public education], *al-Muʿallim al-Jadid* 1, nos. 3 and 4 (June and September 1936): 273–74.

of youth.[57] As Sara Pursley describes, policy makers in Iraq, particularly in education, linked gender differentiation to modernity. According to these policy makers, the more different students' education was, in terms of subject matter or even level of study, along gender lines, the better suited the products of that education would be for modern life, and Iraq's advancement.[58] While schoolboys were to be soldiers, schoolgirls were to be trained, as Beth Baron argues in the case of Egypt, as "Mothers of the Nation" who would in turn instill "their sons with love for the nation."[59] As we have seen, female teachers' travel as well as their postponement of marriage and motherhood often contradicted gender-specific curriculums. In imparting nationalism, and in participating in nationalist movements, female teachers likewise had to decide when it was useful to use gendered stereotypes or to downplay or to break them.

Women's prominence in the various nationalist movements of the twentieth century included a strategic ambivalence around gender: when it was acceptable or useful to underscore their femininity, women did so. More frequently, however, when women took on the role of politically active teacher, they spoke in the language of national resistance, often eliding specific references to women in favor of more masculine erudition and expertise. Separating their gender from their intellectual and nationalist works, women wrote in a universal, nationalist parlance that made no mention of women specifically, with few exceptions. Nationalism had the potential, as Sati al-Husri noted, to overcome gender differences and thereby to offer women a different role in interwar politics.

In the article "Arab Education" (1939), Bahiya Farajallah, an Egyptian instructor of education in the Women's Teachers College in Iraq, described a long Arab history of education, triumphs of Arab civilization, and the importance of literacy. She addressed her essay to the "sons of Arabism," and to a new generation beginning to remember the "glories" of their past and to recover this legacy for the present.[60] There is no separate mention of women. Instead, she displays a global expertise in both Arab and European authors, juxtaposing

57. Although, as Peter Wien notes, women could claim specific roles even in relation to the futuwwa. Peter Wien, "Watan and Rujula," 18.

58. Pursley, "Building the Nation."

59. Baron, *Egypt As a Woman*, 36.

60. Bahiya Farajallah, "al-Tarbiyya wa al-Taʿalim ʿaind al-ʿArab" [The education the Arabs possess], *al-Muaʿllim al-Jadid*, no. 1 (April 1939): 78.

Pestalozzi with Ibn Khaldun to make her case. Farajallah situates herself within a masculine intellectual world, claiming her right to be there based on her education, while underscoring an inclusive Arab rather than exclusive Iraqi or Egyptian affiliation. Farajallah thereby showed educators like herself to be intellectuals and experts. Publishing in an official government magazine in the late 1930s, she likely had little freedom to advance a feminist agenda, whether or not she desired to do so. Instead, her presence on the page pushed at the boundaries of authority on issues of Arab history and nationalism, but not at the gendered nature of those fields.

The lack of reference to women in nationalist discourse by no means meant that they were excluded from political activity. Female teachers also joined women's organizations, separating their profession from their gender while using both to advance their politics. During the interwar era, teachers' unions were either forbidden or subject to intense surveillance (as in 1940s Iraq), but women's associations did not receive the same level of government interest or repression. It was at times easier for women to participate in Iraq's, Palestine's, and Transjordan's restricted political spheres as women rather than as teachers. Young, educated female teachers formed the foot-soldiers of women's organizations, using their free time and their ability to travel to organize, speak, and write.[61] As Ellen Fleischmann argues, Arab women's associations in the mandate for Palestine dealt with a variety of issues that cannot easily be limited "to simplistic categorizations such as 'nationalist,' 'feminist' or 'reformist.'"[62] Instead, these organizations asserted that they possessed the capacity and the right to engage with Palestinian and pan-Arab politics, which overlapped with issues of women's social and economic status.

Throughout the interwar era, nationalisms and politics intertwined with notions of gender, erudition, and education. For female teachers, education and the ability to travel allowed them to shape the region's nationalist discourse and join organizations both public and secret. For example, the transnational Najla Abu Izzeddin, the first woman PhD holder from the Arab World, was a member of the secretive pan-Arab Red Book Group in early 1940s Iraq.[63] In later years she would advance nationalist arguments that defined women's liberation as part of a broader national struggle. For educators,

61. Fleischmann, *The Nation and Its "New" Women*, 146.

62. Fleischmann, 119.

63. *Iraq Government Gazette*, January 21, 1940, 37; Al-Rashoud, "Modern Education and Arab Nationalism," 96–97, 217, 257.

this struggle encompassed a variety of ideological stances that could absorb the growing numbers of women who shaped these movements, as well as the entanglement of teachers with their governments.

While the pan-Arabists Shawkat and al-Husri agreed on the value of a masculine militarism and its connection to anti-imperial Arab nationalism, Iraq's educators did not as a whole form a monolithic bloc of militant demagogues. Many did not appreciate either the militarization of schoolboys or the emphasis on racial pan-Arabism. To appreciate the consequences of teachers' privileged role as ideologues and civil servants, we need to move beyond simply viewing educators as transmitters of nationalist ideologies. Teachers adhered to different political sentiments, which were themselves fluid and overlapping. Educators also did not necessarily support the automatic links between schooling and government employment, even as they benefited from these connections. Government employees explored a range of ideologies, including leftist and Marxist. Dhu al-Nun Ayyub, an educator, author, and sometime politician, held beliefs different from those of his pan-Arabist peers. Nevertheless, the form his political engagement took was similar: writing subversively from within the ranks of the civil service rather than outright revolt.

A native of Mosul, born in 1908 and an embittered product of Iraq's government school system, Dhu Ayyub wrote fictional works that satirized Iraqi government officials and their lack of commitment to the militant nationalisms they espoused.[64] In his short story "A Pillar of the Tower of Babel" and the longer, and even more subversive novella "Doctor Ibrahim," Ayyub made no secret of his disapproval of the education system and its promotion of racial ideas of Arabism in a country filled with non-Arabs and a variety of sects, all of which participated in and cared about education. Ayyub's opportunistic protagonist, Dr. Ibrahim, uses Iraq's education system to move into the civil service. Having received a doctorate abroad from "the most progressive university in Britain," Dr. Ibrahim relies on his education, connections, and almost constant political machinations to become a high-ranking government official.[65] At one point, he and indeed all Iraq's politicians suddenly find themselves trying to prove their "Arabness."[66] Dr. Ibrahim is initially concerned but

64. Musawi, "Dhu Al-Nun Ayyub," 359.

65. Ayyub, "A Pillar of the Tower of Babel," 1.

66. Musawi, *Reading Iraq*, 99; Bashkin, *The Other Iraq*, 360; Matthews, *Confronting an Empire*, 161–62.

concludes he is safe in paying lip service to racialized Arabism without having to prove his own dubious ethnic purity, which was, in fact, impossible for almost anyone to do.

Ayyub criticizes equating pan-Arabism with race, as well as the connections between pan-Arabism and Iraq's government. As an educator and educated individual, he could disapprove of both his government and its leaders' conceptions of nationalism without losing his job, although he was censured because his character, Dr. Ibrahim, bore too strong a resemblance to Dr. Fadhil al-Jamali, the former teacher and then high-ranking official in Iraq's education system in the 1930s. Both character and minister achieved doctorates abroad, married foreign wives, and possessed Shi'ite ties.[67] The Ministry of Education banned the short story collection in which "The Tower of Babel" appeared, and Ayyub was transferred. Undaunted, he satirized his own punishment in his novella, inserting himself into his own story, blurring fact and fiction, to skewer Fadhil al-Jamali and the Iraqi government as a whole.

In the novella, Ayyub meets his fictional character Dr. Ibrahim at a café, blaming the character for Ayyub's difficulties with the Department of Education in real life. Dr. Ibrahim, angered by Ayyub's description of him in "A Pillar of the Tower of Babel," threatens vengeance, saying he will go to al-Jamali and will argue that Ayyub was upset at "not being given an important position in the Ministry of Education" and in retaliation created the character of Dr. Ibrahim to insult al-Jamali.[68] Here, Ayyub underscores accusations against him that actually took place, while showing how educated individuals expected high-ranking government jobs in Iraq's education system and bureaucracy. The disbelieving Ayyub objects that al-Jamali can't possibly be so simple as to believe Dr. Ibrahim, and that Dr. Ibrahim will only prove conclusively that Dr. al-Jamali is no "subtle schemer" like Dr. Ibrahim but rather a naïve, artless man caught easily in a trap. Ayyub was of course being disingenuous; by claiming that al-Jamali would clearly bear no resemblance to the conniving Dr. Ibrahim, Ayyub drew attention to al-Jamali's manipulative opportunism. Britain's ambassador to Iraq described al-Jamali in similar terms as "an intelligent, plausible and utterly unscrupulous self-seeker" who employed "subtle methods" of

67. Bashkin, "When Muawiya Entered the Curriculum," 359.
68. Ayyub, *Al-Athar al-Kamila li-Adab Dhi al-Nun Ayyub* [The complete works of the author Dhi(Dhu) al-Nun Ayyub], 3:23.

agreeing with a British official in person, while "intriguing against him behind his back."[69]

Ayyub, like so many other teachers in Iraq, Palestine, and Transjordan, was transferred, in his case to a town some 450 kilometers north, at the same rate of pay as his position in Baghdad. In the novella, Iraq's bureaucracy appears unnecessarily bloated: two officials from the Ministry of Education were apparently required to communicate Ayyub's punishment to him, each reading half of the two-sentence announcement. After Ayyub tells one official that his government was Machiavellian, the official states he has no idea who this Machiavelli is, as he hasn't read anything since he finished his studies and doesn't intend to read anything in the future.[70] These officials had used the education system to gain official positions but were poorly qualified and concerned only with narrow procedures rather than intellectual engagement.

Despite his transfer, Ayyub was able to disapprove both in writing and in conversation with his superiors without being fired from his post.[71] Moreover, although he censured his government as well as the pan-Arabism several key government officials promoted, the broad strokes nationalisms of the 1930s embraced Ayyub's work. Particularly during the 1930s, the intersection of political parties, anti-imperialism, government service, and fluid ideologies meant that multiple political parties used political tracts by Ayyub and his contemporaries, even if the authors themselves disagreed with those parties.[72]

Educators from the lowest to the highest ranks of the mandates' education systems passionately articulated nationalisms that were expansive and, to some degree, impractical. To understand educators' contributions to political ideologies, how Ayyub's tracts could be deployed by competing political factions, as well as how this combination of intellectual and political engagement actually shored up governments in the interwar Middle East, one must take the nationalisms of the period on their own terms. The political stances educators adopted were both wide ranging and overlapping. Nationalisms based on European-drawn borders did not necessarily conflict with pan-Arab or

69. Kinahan Cornwallis to Mr. Eden, "Reorganisation by Professor Hamley," Baghdad, April 30, 1943, E 2963 496 93, in Rush and Priestland, *Records of Iraq, 1914–1966*, vol. 9: *1941–1945*, 389.

70. Ayyub, *Al-Athar al-Kamila li-Adab Dhi al-Nun Ayyub*, 3:24.

71. Bashkin, "When Muawiya Entered the Curriculum," 364.

72. Al-Musawi, "Dhu Al-Nun Ayyub," 48.

left-wing political ideologies. Moreover, the states enforcing those borders were relatively weak in comparison to their successors. Educators' incorporation into government service fundamentally shaped their politics. Their nationalisms signified erudition and political engagement. They did not involve cohesive party platforms nor the intention to violently overthrow the government itself. For female educators, joining these nationalist movements also marked entry into a predominantly masculine sphere of elite, cultured political engagement. For women, however, nationalisms' gendered norms had posed a particular conundrum: the figure of the teacher-intellectual-nationalist was not a feminine one.

Pan-Arabism and Beyond: The Fluidity of Interwar Politics

Palestinian, Iraqi, and Transjordanian teachers, officials, and students were divided in their prescriptions for nationalism and for education policy. Officials, especially within the Iraqi education department, often worked at cross purposes. Amid the upheavals of the 1930s, educators in the government schools of Iraq, Palestine, and Transjordan as well as officials at the highest levels of the Iraqi bureaucracy used education as a means of promoting a variety of notions of political affiliation. Educated individuals frequently wrote communistic, pan-Arabist, fascistic, or territorial nationalist tracts extolling the benefits of the nation. Yet they generally could not, or chose not, to put the ideologies they expounded into practice, even when they reached top leadership positions in government service. Educators' continued reference to nationalism in publications, speeches, and debates at literary and political clubs indicated their status as intellectuals; engagement with various flavors of nationalism was a means of cultivating a modern intellectual sensibility. Although prone to militant rhetoric, educators' ability to promote ideologies without losing their posts meant that—to a certain degree—they supported the status quo over the revolutionary movements that sought to overthrow their governments.

Nationalist educators raised international ire for inciting protests. Scholars have somewhat uncritically taken these protests among schoolboys and villagers as indicators of the spread of nationalist consciousness from elites to the masses through the medium of public education. As we have seen, educators' transnationalism and transnational experiences meant the nationalism promoted through public schooling seldom corresponded to the borders of the state sponsoring that education. In addition, the nature of the protests they inspired did not necessarily indicate unified politics or even comprehension of the pan-Arabist and anti-imperial ideologies educators hoped to communicate.

At times, attempts to inspire nationalist sentiments beyond schoolboys failed even when they succeeded. For example, Suleiman al-Nabulsi, another AUB graduate and later a prime minister of Jordan, led a protest in Kerak against the Balfour Declaration, which symbolized British imperialism and Zionist incursions into Palestine. Al-Nabulsi sought to offer his students and the townspeople a vision of pan-Arab solidarity, united against imperialism anywhere in the Arab world. Al-Nabulsi's student, another prime minister, Haza' al-Majali recalled how al-Nabulsi did convince both students and indeed the town as a whole to demonstrate. However, he mentions that few who joined the protest actually understood the implications of the Balfour Declaration. According to Majali, while al-Nabulsi was yelling in English "Down with the Balfour Declaration," the surrounding crowd was shouting "Down with the Balcony! . . . Down with the one who is upstairs!" as well as "Down with Krikor." Krikor, a local shoemaker who was participating in the demonstration, in turn yelled, "Balfour! O group of Balfour," presumably in an effort to make sure he was not attacked.[73] Majali's recollections indicate the difficulties for historians in assuming protests led by educators were based in well-defined ideologies, Pan-Arab or not.

In another example of interwar nationalist resistance, educators mixed with government ministers in secret political societies. Modeled on the World War I Arab nationalist al-Fatat society, these groups generally balanced a public face, including a journal and possibly a club, with a cadre of leaders who worked secretly to manipulate politics.[74] The Arab Liberation Society (Jam'iyat al-Tahrir al-'Arabiyya), Arab Nationalists' Movement (Harakat/Kutlat al-Qawmiyyin al-'Arab), and the Red Book Society (Jam'iyat al-Kitab al-Ahmar), to which Najla Abu Izzeddin had belonged, formed the hidden vanguard of several other organizations, including the al-Muthanna club and the Rover Society (Jam'iyat al-Jawwal al-'Arabi).[75] Members were tied to one another through shared educational experiences and work in the civil service. For example, several members of the Rover Society studied with one another at the primary teachers college in Baghdad in the late 1920s and early 1930s, learning

73. Kedourie, *Arabic Political Memoirs*, 185.

74. Choueiri, *Arab Nationalism, a History*, 94.

75. Kahati, "The Role of Education," 37.

their Arab history and Arab nationalist stances from Darwish al-Miqdadi.[76] These pan-Arab associations would often dissolve into one another, particularly as more and more high-ranking educators and civil servants began to attract smaller groups to one or another association.[77] Joining the secret cells of Arab nationalist societies was quite exciting, involving oaths of loyalty sworn on a sword and the Qur'an.

Despite their accoutrements of revolution, the mission of secret Pan-Arabist societies was seldom violent, in part due to their members' symbiotic ties with their governments. They sought to influence other elites rather than leading mass political movements. Rover Society members pledged "to work for Arab nationalism and Arab unity through culture and education," as many of them were educators or soon to be educators employed by Iraq or Palestine's mandate governments.[78] Using schooling as a platform to instruct others in the value of Arab unity did not imply government overthrow. As the scholar of Arab nationalism Youssef Choueiri described, "Ideologues and cadres drifted in and out of established state institutions." The state institution through which the bulk of them made their entry into politics was public education. Choueiri castigates these individuals, arguing that their willingness to work with governments forced them to "compromise their initial political purity by accommodating themselves to the programs of local personalities and provincial policies."[79] The political purity Choueiri seeks is a chimera, however, particularly during the interwar era. Both secret and public political organizations were nebulous and in flux. The boundaries between state and nonstate institutions and individuals were porous. Ideologies themselves were flexible. These factors ruled out clearly defined, "pure," and static political programs, be they pan-Arab or not.

Pan-Arab ideologies that infused educators' and students' secret societies were neither the only option for politically engaged individuals nor the most codified creeds available. Communism, which by the 1940s would form the most established of Iraq's political organizations, advanced an ideology during the 1930s that was nearly as nebulous as its pan-Arab counterparts. Johan Franzen argues that through the late 1930s "the ICP [Iraqi Communist Party] was indistinguishable from other 'parties' made up largely of urban effendis." The

76. Al-Hussein, "Jam'iyat al-Jawwal," 244–45.

77. Al-Hussein, 247.

78. Al-Hussein, 248.

79. Choueiri, *Arab Nationalism, a History*, 94.

Soviet-trained Iraqi who reorganized the Communist Party in the early 1940s "deridingly dismissed them as 'Coffeehouse Communists' as they spent most of their time chatting in cafés rather than organizing the masses."[80] Similarly, Professor Kamal Majid, a Kurdish Iraqi Communist now living in London, noted that in the 1930s "there wasn't a Communist Party." Instead, he described one communist teacher as "just a person who has read about communism and liked it and wanted people to become communists, but he wasn't at all frightening the government. . . . This fellow, the first communist, he never managed to convince anybody."[81] For this teacher and his coffeehouse crowd, engaging with ideologies, whether nationalist or communist, signified erudition, membership in a politically active, middling class, and entry into the civil service. Educators could write communistic, pan-Arabist, prodemocracy, and Iraqist tracts extolling the benefits of the nation but generally could not, or chose not to, carry out these policies, even when they did reach the top leadership positions in government service during the interwar era. Many teachers, particularly in Iraq, participated in the more formal, if not necessarily official, politics of the region. Still more teachers, particularly in Palestine, led or joined popular protests. Yet very few broke their ties with their governments.

Educators and Palestine's Great Revolt

During the 1930s, educators' work in the civil service nearly always withstood their rebellions, whether they criticized their governments from the right or the left. This incorporation of intellectuals into the state and its concurrent moderation of their tactics of rebellion perhaps makes more sense in the cases of Iraq and even Transjordan than in Palestine. Less restrictive British control, and therefore greater opportunities for local participation in education and government, would seem more likely to reduce stigma against those who would continue to work for the states they disparaged.

In Iraq, schoolteachers and educated individuals joined, and at times combatted, their corrupt governments, striking blows with pen rather than sword, choosing one or another political faction without seeking an end to the government as a whole. In Transjordan, documents hint that students, not

80. Johan Franzén, "A History of the Iraqi Communist Party Interview with Univ. of East Anglia's Johan Franzén Musings on Iraq: Iraq News, Politics, Economics, Society," July 15, 2014, http://musingsoniraq.blogspot.com/2014/07/a-history-of-iraqi-communist-party.html.

81. Kamal Majid, interview with the author, London, March 3, 2013.

teachers, sought to demonstrate in support of Palestinians' revolt, rather than against their own government. In 1938 a circular went out to all government school principals and teachers with instructions for dealing with "students of the government schools who participate in the strike movements and the demonstrations, and who meddle in political affairs." The government cast student protests as a problem, but the instructions to inspectors and principals frame these individuals as part of the regime, empowered to suppress rather than instigate student activism.[82] Few if any teachers were disciplined from 1936 to 1939.[83]

In Palestine, the mandate government's heavy-handed tactics, lack of Arab representation, support for Zionism, and indeed popular rebellions against the government might have rendered government-employed Arabs into collaborators. Yet the prestige of government educators, the fact that they were overwhelmingly Arab, and the desirability and scarcity of education overall made teachers relatively immune to accusations of treachery. This allowed educators in Palestine to support the Great Revolt without picking up arms and while working for the government the revolt sought to undermine. While those denied education and its concurrent government benefits revolted, educators, with very few exceptions, were able to balance teaching in government schools with nationalism without losing favor in the eyes of the rebels.

During the six months of the general strike in Palestine in 1936, which preceded the more violent outbreak of the revolt, government-run schools were closed one by one, either due to "action of the government" or because of student strikes.[84] "Action of the government" included the closing of schools in anticipation of student strikes or their occupation by the army, as they were often the most suitable buildings for lodging soldiers.[85] In total, over half of

82. "Balagh 55: Ta'almat al-Mudaris [Communication 55: Teachers' instructions]" 11/20/8/22, December 25, 1938, History of Jordan Collection, NLJ.

83. Only three teachers ended their service by action of the government during Palestine's Revolt, out of 20 teachers who ended their service during these years. It is not clear if their termination was due to subversive activity or other, more mundane causes.

84. Government of Palestine, Department of Education, *Education in Palestine General Survey 1936–1946* (Jerusalem, 1946), 1.

85. Twenty-nine schools were occupied during the general strike. Even after the strike ended in January 1937, the army was still using four school buildings. Bowman, "Diary June 1935–Oct 1936," April 26, 1936, Humphrey Bowman Collection, Box 4 B, GB165–0034, MECA; Government of Palestine, Department of Education, *Annual Report for the School Year 1935–1936*, 20.

FIGURE 4.4. *Al-Shahid Ustadh Sami al-Ansari* (The martyr professor Sami al-Ansari). (Reprinted from *Filastin*, June 20, 1936.)

the schools, including all town schools, were closed during this period.[86] Within a year of the strike's beginning, however, schools were reopened, with teachers to staff them. Teachers, like the more elite nationalists who constituted the Arab Higher Committee and the Palestinian political parties, usually chose to remain at their posts and to negotiate rather than to take up arms. Government employment nearly always moderated educators' rebellion. Those denied government employment had a greater tendency to seek their government's overthrow.

Sami al-Ansari and Bahjat Abu Gharbiyah were both young and angry men during the revolt.[87] Their frustrations, their youth, and chance played key parts in their decisions to take up arms against the British and the Zionists. "Handsome . . . a tall boy, wiry, slender, sharp and adept . . . mad about sports, well-dressed,"[88] the upper-class al-Ansari, depicted in figure 4.4, and his less well-to-do friend Abu Gharbiyah, attended government schools together. Their activities and sentiments seemed to be a deadly combination of playing at becoming revolutionaries and actually participating in nationalist rebellions.

Both young men were anti-British, passionate about Arab unity, and frustrated with Palestinian politicians' lack of militant action.[89] As al-Ansari and Abu Gharbiyah pursued careers as teachers and civil servants, they entered the mandates' world of subversive, antigovernment politics. Al-Ansari was an excellent student, passing the Palestine matriculation certificate in 1934 and graduating from the Arab College of Jerusalem in 1935.[90] In contrast, Bahjat Abu Gharbiyah saw his hopes of higher education dashed when his father refused to pay his secondary school fees. Bahjat's older brother Nidam had

86. Government of Palestine, Department of Education, *Annual Report for the School Year 1936–1937*, 71–72, 78; *Annual Report for the School Year 1935–1936*, 20.

87. Abu Gharbiyah was twenty and al-Ansari was eighteen. Hughes, "A History of Violence," 725.

88. Khalil al-Sakakini, quoted in Segev, *One Palestine, Complete*, 366.

89. Abu Gharbiyah, *Fi Khidam al-Nidal al-ʿArabi al-Filastini*, 63.

90. *Palestine Gazette*, no. 468, September 27, 1934, CO 742/11, NA; Abu Gharbiyah, *Fi Khidam al-Nidal al-ʿArabi al-Filastini*, 66.

failed the medical exam necessary to serve as a teacher; despite connections and academic success, he could not gain the government post he had worked so hard to achieve. For Bahjat's father, the sudden realization that government education might not automatically result in a government job and a secure future meant he could not support his younger son's continued study. Instead, Bahjat Abu Gharbiyah worked in a nongovernment school and became increasingly militant, bringing his friend al-Ansari along in the process.

Abu Gharbiyah and al-Ansari became part of a small, "revolutionary group" in 1934. Named "freedom" by 1936–1937, this group was anti-imperial and secret (following the vanguard model), even from the more established Palestinian leadership. Struggling to arm itself, the group addressed itself to students (rather than teachers or parents), distributing pamphlets and meeting with student leaders in government and nongovernment schools alike.[91] The composition of the group was socially broad, including al-Ansari, a shoemaker-cum-Sufi sheikh, a religious school teacher, workers, students, petty traders, and, by 1936, the leader of Palestinian resistance in Jerusalem.[92] Al-Ansari at this point was teaching at al-Rashidiyya School, from which he and Abu Gharbiyah had graduated, participating in sports and "military drills" with his students while moonlighting as a rebel and setting fire to Jewish stores in Jerusalem.[93]

Abu Gharbiyah and al-Ansari attempted to assassinate Superintendent Alan Sigrist, a hated British police commissioner in Jerusalem. They chose Sigrist based on a combination of personal anger and local resentment because of his brutality and abuse of Arab Palestinians.[94] In the course of the attempted assassination, Sami was killed and memorialized as a hero by his friends and neighbors. A front-page article in the Palestinian paper *Filastin* described him as "The Martyr Professor Sami al-Ansari." It carefully documented his

91. It would reemerge in 1948 as the "Jaysh al-Jihad al-Muqaddas," the "Army of the Holy Jihad," Abu Gharbiyah, *Fi Khidam al-Nidal al-`Arabi al-Filastini*, 47–48, 63.

92. Abu Gharbiyah, *Fi Khidam al-Nidal al-`Arabi al-Filastini*, 47. Sheikh Yasin al-Bakri would go on to fight in the 1948 conflict at the head of a "Holy Jihad" group. Hillel Cohen describes this meeting with Jewish officials in 1947 in *Army of Shadows*, 210. He also worked as a teacher at al-Aqsa Mosque, and at the Ibrahamiyya school. Al-Hadi, *Documents on Jerusalem*, 2:132; Palestinian Academic Society for the Study of International Affairs, "Al-Husseini, Abdul Qader (1907–1948)," http://www.passia.org/palestine_facts/personalities/alpha_h.htm, accessed April 17, 2014

93. Abu Gharbiyah, *Fi Khidam al-Nidal al-`Arabi al-Filastini*, 66.

94. Hughes, "A History of Violence," 733–35.

educational achievements, but not how he died.[95] Sami al-Ansari's death, while noble, was a tragedy, as a young, educated, and employed man (with aristocratic connections and a violent streak) lost his life at only eighteen years old.[96] His compatriot Bahjat Abu Gharbiyah (who lived until age ninety-six) illustrates the futures Sami might have enjoyed, had he survived. Abu Gharbiyah participated in radical politics throughout his career, fighting in 1948, helping to found and lead a branch of the pan-Arab Ba'ath Party in Ramallah in the 1950s, becoming a member of the Palestinian Liberation Organization and an esteemed Palestinian nationalist. While Abu Gharbiyah's decision to take up arms against the government made more sense because he worked outside of it, Sami al-Ansari's rash decision to join him was an almost unique occurrence among government-employed educators, indicating government education's role in both politicizing educated individuals and incorporating them into the state. Al-Ansari is the exception that proves the rule of educators' tendency to avoid armed conflict during the revolt.

Government educators chose to avoid Sami al-Ansari's path of resistance in part because of education's role as a revered government institution. Many parents, and even rebels, were loath to stop their children's education, despite their participation in the strikes and revolt against the government that sponsored it. For example, a circular written by "The Central Committee of the Arab Revolt in Palestine" in February 1939 echoed later popular accounts that alleged the British government denied schooling in order to retard Palestinian national development. This circular addressed striking students directly while blaming the mandate government for closing schools, stating:

> Ye dear students, the throbbing heart of the nation, ye young men of the present and men of the future . . . we invite you to return to your classes and studies where you can get light for the proper path to follow. . . . Please note that the Government is anxious to suspend your studies. They send you weak hearted men to arouse you to strike. Beware such men and continue your studies whatever the case may be. . . . We declare that the Schools authorities have the full right to punish instigators for strike. Please note that schools should never be closed.[97]

95. "Al-Shahid Ustadh Sami al-Ansari" [The martyr Professor Sami al-Ansari], *Filastin*, June 20, 1936, 1, NLIJ.

96. Government of Palestine, *Annual Report for the School Year 1936–1937*, 29; Hughes, "Assassination in Jerusalem," 5.

97. Deputy Inspector General of the CID, "Appendix B, Criminal Investigation Department," 50/2/G/S., File 47/65, February 21, 1939, Haganah Archive, Tel Aviv. This document is

This circular, although partisan in nature and distributed toward the end of the revolt, indicates a desire for schools to remain open for the good of the nation and of its future. It asserts that gaining an education was in fact an act of rebellion and enlightenment. This circular shows the population's awareness that Palestine's government did indeed seek to restrict education for fear of nationalist upheaval. Such a positive view of education, even government schooling, meant that educators could maintain their nationalism, loosely defined, while working for the government that they believed repressed that nationalism. Similarly, the Department of Education asserted, perhaps overoptimistically, that even the Arab insurgents themselves did not see the village schools as extensions of the state because "in general the Arab insurgents left the schools unharmed and sometimes made money contributions (to their upkeep)."[98] It was not only government schools that remained open. Al-Najah, the national school that Akram Zu'aytir had attended after the general strike, remained open "with some slowdowns," despite the fact that several of its teachers were simultaneously acting as advisors to the rebels.[99]

Although teachers could continue to work for the mandate government without censure, they still struggled with safety and salary. The restriction on the number of teachers relative to the number of students was so extreme that villages petitioned the mandate government in Palestine to allow them to appoint teachers paid directly by the villagers. During the revolt, the extra money to support village teachers evaporated, forcing the discharge of seven teachers.[100] Many teachers did not feel safe, with good reason. At least two requested (and were granted) permission to carry arms for protection.[101] Several teachers died in bombings of public places. Gertrude Nassar was accidentally

---

a translation from a group called the "Central Committee of the Arab Revolt in Jerusalem," which supports the viability of the then banned Arab Higher Committee while denigrating the Nashashibi-led National Defense Party, the only political party that wasn't banned during the course of the revolt. The factional nature of this document may indicate the view of pro-Husayni factions toward schooling.

98. Government of Palestine, Department of Education, *Education in Palestine General Survey 1936–1946*, 1.

99. Darwazeh, *Mudhakkirat Muhammad 'Izzat Darwazeh*, 543, Porath, *The Emergence of the Palestinian Arab National Movement*, 2:93.

100. "Farah Khadr Rama Boys School," 1030 22 M, ISA; "Niazi Qadri Hafiz Zib," 1027 1 M, ISA; "Hanna Nasser Nazareth," 1029 4 M, ISA; "Abd El Hamid Zu'bi Hittin Vs," 1038 17 M, ISA; "Ahmad Muhammad Qasem Isa Sali," 1037 17 M, ISA; "Atwa Hanna Rama Boys School," 1032 4 M, ISA; "Amanda Sabbagh," 1029 22 M, ISA.

101. "Ahmad Tawfiq Najami," 1014 16 M, ISA. Khalil al-Sakakini requested permission to bear arms as well. Segev, *One Palestine, Complete*, 366.

shot by British soldiers while waiting outside her neighbor's door.[102] Many
government bureaucrats, including teachers, acted as intermediaries. They
hedged their bets by staying at their posts while donating a portion of their
salaries to the rebels.[103]

The military, as well as Jewish police forces, did not discriminate between
government officers and rebels.[104] However, teachers who were arrested frequently appealed to the Department of Education to secure their release.[105]
The same government that arrested these teachers actually paid them while in
prison, underscoring the extent of the rebellion but also the leeway teachers
enjoyed within the Department of Education. For example, Khaled Shukri
al-Qadi, a hardworking teacher, was arrested in 1939 by the military and imprisoned in a concentration camp. The principal of the school at which he
taught wrote the local British official, who forwarded the letter to the district
inspector of education. The teacher was freed "without any conviction." He
thanked the director of education for securing his release and returned to
work, being paid for his absence and in fact securing a raise.[106]

During the revolt, "civil administration of the country was, to all practical
purposes, nonexistent." Yet schools continued to function. Approximately
5,679 Arabs were "detained."[107] Out of these thousands, 90 out of approximately 1,300 teachers were arrested.[108] Only 10 of these teachers were dismissed.[109] Only one of the 140 teachers teaching during the revolt whose personnel files are available was fired due to political involvement, in his case by
the high commissioner, over the authority of the Department of Education.[110]

102. Gertrude Nassar, "Letter to Director Ispector of Education Galilee District. Subject:
Shooting Incident" October 17, 1938, "Gertrude Nassar," 1012 18 M, ISA.

103. Hughes, Britain's Pacification of Palestine, 93.

104. "I'tqal Arba'a, Ahaduhum Mu'allim Madrasa" [Four arrested including a teacher], al-
Difa 4, March 25, 1938, 5, NLIJ.

105. "Aziz Khuri," 1020 6 M, ISA; "Mahmud Arrabi," 101911 M, ISA; "Amin al Abdallah," 1018
1 M, ISA.

106. D.I.E. Galilee, "To the Asst. District Commissioner Acre," May 24 1939; Khaled Shukri
el-Qadi, "Letter to the DIE Galilee," June 13, 1939; "Yearly Increment," July 10, 1941; Khaled
Shukri El Qadi," 1029 10 M, ISA.

107. Khalidi, The Iron Cage, 107.

108. Matthews, Confronting an Empire, 236.

109. Miller, "From Village to Nation," 336; Tibawi, "Educational Policy and Arab Nationalism," 20.

110. "Letter from the Inspector of Education to Ibrahim Jadallah," February 1, 1937, "Ibrahim
Jadallah," 1018 6 M, ISA.

Yet, even the British director of education in Palestine stated that every Arab student and teacher "was a supporter of the Arab cause; everyone an ardent anti-Zionist."[111] These supporters, strikers, and protesters were still counted, and counted themselves, as employees of the Department of Education. Their ability to remain nationalists while protesting the policies of the government they served would lessen during the 1940s in Palestine, essentially ceasing in 1948 with the end of the mandate and the founding of Israel. The new Jewish state explicitly sought to restrict Arabs' political activities, erasing the elite position as government-subsidized nationalists that Arab Palestinians had enjoyed under the mandate government while drastically expanding both schooling and state capacity.

The case of Palestinians is unique. Nevertheless, even the educator-politicians of Iraq and Jordan found themselves, at least initially, on the wrong side of newly powerful states. In 1941, amid World War II, the British lost patience with Iraq's anti-British coups and activities. British armies cracked down on teachers' freedoms, buttressing Iraq's Hashemite monarchy, winning a month long Anglo-Iraqi War, and expelling non-Iraqi or even recently Iraqi nationalists, including Sati al-Husri and Akram Zu'aytir. While al-Husri went to Syria, Lebanon, and Egypt, working for the Syrian government and later the Arab League,[112] Zu'aytir moved to Turkey, Syria, and finally Jordan, whose government welcomed him with open arms as a trophy nationalist, and a Palestinian one to boot.[113] In 1962 Zu'aytir, shown speaking to the United Nations General Assembly in figure 4.5, acted as Jordan's ambassador to Syria and then Iran. He was appointed foreign minister in 1966 and minister of the royal court in 1967. He was a member of the Senate in 1984.[114]

Hugh Foot, a former British official in mandate Palestine, recalled in the late 1970s Zu'aytir's radical transformation from a "particular leader of the Nablus schoolboys who was especially violent" to an individual who was not only willing but happy to interact with his former enemy. Foot mused, "I exiled

111. Bowman, *Middle-East Window*, 311.

112. Cleveland, *The Making of an Arab Nationalist*, 326.

113. Palestinian Academic Society for the Study of International Affairs, Jerusalem, "Zu'aiter, Akram (1909–1996), Palestine Personalities," http://www.passia.org/palestine_facts/personalities/alpha_z.htm, accessed April 17, 2014.

114. Majlis al-Aʿyan l-Urduni, "Al-Majalis al-Sabiqa" [Previous parliaments]," http://www.senate.jo/ar/page/%D9%85%D8%B9%D9%84%D9%88%D9%85%D8%A7%D8%AA-%D8%A7%D9%84%D9%85%D8%AC%D8%A7%D9%84%D8%B3-%D8%A7%D9%84%D8%B3%D8%A7%D8%A8%D9%82%D8%A9, accessed April 24, 2014.

FIGURE 4.5. *Akram Zu'aytir, wazir al-kharijiyya al-Urduniyyi
yukhtabu fi al-Jam'iyat al-'Amma lil-Umam al-Muttahida
17-10-1966* (Akram Zu'aytir, Jordanian foreign minister, gives a
speech at the United Nations General Assembly, October 17,
1966). (Reproduced by permission from Sari Akram Zu'aytir,
Akramzuayter.org.)

him to the desert but I didn't meet again until he later. He was the Jordanian
ambassador and he came to the UN where I met him and we are now on the
most friendly terms."[115] Zu'aytir's participation in the Jordanian government, and his fraternization with the former imperialists he had rebelled
against, lent that government both pan-Arabist and pro-Palestinian credentials, helping to make palatable the perpetuation of a monarchy financed by
foreign donations.

The final incorporation of teachers like Zu'aytir into ministerial bodies
formed part of a moment of opening in Jordan's and Iraq's political systems.
Jordan's liberal experiment and the political upheaval of Iraq's transition from
monarchy to republic in the late 1950s allowed for some former educators to
work in greater numbers in parliaments. These educators successfully (at times
briefly) obtained, or retained, their elite relationship to their governments.
This was a pyrrhic victory. The expansion of education wrought by independence reduced teachers' status, disconnecting them from the upper ranks of

115. Thames Television, Gb165–0282 Thames Television Palestine Series Collection, Box 1,
File 18, Lord Caradon, 1978, MECA.

politics and from the anti-imperial nationalisms of the interwar era. The curtains that came crashing down on educators' political ambitions were Ba'athist dictatorships in Iraq, a foreign-backed monarchy in Jordan, Israel's Zionist project, and martial law. Increasing government control of education and expansion of schooling contributed to the growth of a more populist, state-centered form of politics whose proponents had little patience with the negotiations of teacher-politicians.

The Politics of Independence: Teacher-Politicians and the End of an Era

In December 1956 Suleiman al-Nabulsi's face loomed from the pages of the *New York Times* (figure 4.6). The specter of a communist Middle East drove U.S. interest in Jordan's political tumult. Al-Nabulsi, Jordan's newly elected prime minister, denied any Communist or authoritarian leanings. Instead, he described recent forced retirements and dismissals in Jordan's government as due to inefficiency, corruption, or lack of "sincere" nationalism. Al-Nabulsi defined this nationalism as pan-Arab, proclaiming that his country "cannot live forever as Jordan" but "must be connected militarily, economically and politically" in a federation of Arab states.[116] As a teacher, al-Nabulsi had sought to cultivate Arab unity. He had led the protests in Jordan against the Balfour declaration which had so alarmed Krikor, seeking to unite Transjordan with Palestine. These pan-Arab interwar ideals were now his to implement.

By the 1950s, former educators like al-Nabulsi reached the highest levels of governance, and in startling proportions. Six of the seventeen prime ministers who served in Jordan from 1946 to 1972 had worked as teachers.[117] Similarly in Iraq, six of the thirteen prime ministers who served from the 1950s through the 1960s were former teachers.[118] In contrast, only two of the nineteen Arab

116. Hanson W. Baldwin, "Arab Federation Urged by Jordan: Premier Says Country Must Be Connected with One or More of Its Neighbors Aid from Arabs Indicated," *New York Times*, December 17, 1956.

117. Suleiman al-Nabulsi, Fawzi al-Mulqi, Wasfi al-Tall, 'Abd al-Munim al-Rifai, Ahmad Touqan, and Ahmad Lowzi.

118. In Iraq, Mustafa Mahmud al-'Umari, Fadhil al-Jamali, Ahmad Mukhtar Baban, Tahir Yahya, Abdul-Karim Qasim, and Ahmed Hassan al-Bakr all worked at government school teachers before their stints as prime minister. Qasim worked for only a year before moving on to the military college. Khadduri, *Republican 'Iraq*, 74.

ARAB FEDERATION URGED BY JORDAN

Premier Says Country Must Be Connected With One or More of Its Neighbors

Associated Press

FIGURE 4.6. Premier Suleiman al-Nabulsi. (Reprinted from the *New York Times*, December 17, 1956.)

Knesset members (out of about 260 odd members) who served between 1949 and the mid-1960s were former educators.[119] These politicians fall generally into two categories: the old guard or a very limited wave of technocrats. The bulk were elites like al-Nabulsi, who had spent a few years teaching in the best schools of their country either before entering official politics, or when on the outs with whichever government was in power. Others found themselves in the political system through their educations. For example, the Palestinian Ibrahim Snobar, son of an illiterate father who worked in the shoe industry, would serve many years as an education official in Jordan and as a member of the Senate.[120]

As these former educators moved into increasingly powerful positions, their Arabism, honed in Beirut, Baghdad, Jerusalem, al-Salt, Mosul, and beyond, hardened into an idealistic but conservative variety. Its enemies were foreign domination and imperialism, yet its denizens shored up the British- or

119. Arabs made up approximately 18 percent of the Israeli population but only 7 percent of Knesset members. Mendales, "A House of Cards," 444.

120. Snobar, *Tadhakkurat Ibrahim Snobar* [The recollections of Ibrahim Snobar], 1, 9.

French-influenced governments that employed them. When European hegemony receded, the nature of politics, of Arabism, and of education's connection to both changed accordingly.

Across the Arab world and Israel, educators-turned-politicians, the pan-
Arab dreamers of the interwar era, saw their ideals and often their jobs usurped
by more rigid ideologies and new political players. Egypt's free officers in 1952
and Iraq's in 1958 advocated revolutionary Arabisms predicated on change and
realpolitik. As Gamal Abdel Nasser, the Pan-Arabist Egyptian military leader
whose removal of Egypt's monarchy would inspire the July 1958 coup in Iraq,
put it in May 1958, "Arab nationalism is something practical, not sentimental."
For Nasser, Arab nationalism was not a dream but a "strategy" through which
the Arab world could, through economic, social, and military improvements,
overcome its historic weaknesses.[121] However, this strategy also meant reckon-
ing with hierarchies of unified Arab countries and their affiliations to the West,
the Soviet East, or neither. Within Iraq, the idea of Arab unity espoused by the
free officers quickly degenerated into a conflict between Ba'athist ideas of
links with Egypt and Abdul-Karim Qasim's censure of pan-Arabism when it
conflicted with his regime's goals. Pan-Arab proponents began sniping at
Communists in the streets.[122]

Qasim's revolution and the end of Iraq's Hashemite monarchy overturned
its interwar pan-Arabism, along with the educator politicians who had so zeal-
ously promoted it in schools, clubs, and parliaments. Perhaps the quintessential
example is AUB graduate Fadhil al-Jamali. On the eve of Iraq's revolution, he
had finished his stint as prime minister and was juggling a portfolio as foreign
minister and a brief interlude as Iraq's representative to the United Nations. In
a detailed account of al-Jamali's 1953–1954 government, Michael Eppel argues
al-Jamali's worldview "was, on the one hand, extremely pan-Arab nationalist;
yet on the other, he held definite pro-western and anti-communist views" advocating "a combination of a rigid regime with social reform and economic
development and modernization." However, this "reformism was very limited
by his basically conservative outlook on society."[123] As a civil servant for the
bulk of his life, al-Jamali had held "radical" views and "conservative" tactics of
governance that had existed comfortably. While one might question how his

121. Desmond Steward, "Encounter with Gamal Abdul Nasser," *Middle East Forum, Al-
Kulliyah* 33, no 5. (May 1958): 18, 20.

122. Khadduri, *Republican Iraq*, 127.

123. Eppel, "The Fadhil Al-Jamali Government," 424–25.

"pro-Western" orientation and the anti-imperialism of pan-Arab nationalism in the era of European hegemony over the Arab world fit together, al-Jamali reconciled the two with a push for American assistance rather than British imperial involvement. His ability to preach pan-Arabism and to maintain interwar methods of governance would be erased as more defined, reformist versions of pan-Arabism gained control.

When Gamal Abdul Nasser began to advocate a new vision of Arab unity, tied to social reform, nonalignment, and the strengthening government he now controlled, the Iraqi state and al-Jamali struggled to adapt their politics as usual with growing, class-based movements that sought their governments' violent overthrow. A few months before Iraq's July revolution of 1958, al-Jamali was asked to explain how his previous advocacy for Arab unity fit with his animosity toward the United Arab Republic (UAR). The interviewer, for a magazine published by al-Jamali's alma mater, the American University of Beirut, told al-Jamali,

> You have always been a champion of Arab unity, including bilateral unity. In 1954 you submitted a memorandum to the Arab League in which you argued that the way to achieve Arab Union was for those states which felt they had present possibilities of union to go ahead and unite, while leaving the door open for others to join them later. Yet when Egypt and Syria united you called their union unnatural. What caused this change of view?

Al-Jamali replied that he remained a committed unionist, but that the links between Egypt and Syria were ones of "annexation" and not of "federation," and that Syria should unite with Iraq instead. He dismissed the possibility of Iraq's economic cooperation with the UAR, which he described as "collaborators with Communism." He concluded the interview by hearkening back to the interwar principles of Arab unity he knew, and to which he had tied his fortunes, arguing that the duty of his fellows Arabs was "to save the Arab world from what remains of Western domination, from Zionism and from Communism."[124]

Al-Jamali invoked the threat of communism to drum up Western, particularly American, support for his regime. When Iraq's free officer's movement overthrew the monarchy in July 1958, al-Jamali found himself imprisoned, with his property seized, along with others from the government to which he had

---

124. Mohammed Fadhil al-Jamali, quoted in Leila Shaheen, "Interview with Dr. Mohammed Fadhil Jamali, Foreign Minister of Iraq," *Middle East Forum, Al-Kulliyah* 33, no. 5 (May 1958): 13–14.

belonged for so many years.[125] The charges against him were themselves pan-Arabist: he was accused of trying to enact a coup in Syria "with imperialist backing," having "insulted President Gamal Abdel Nasser, rigged elections and squandered public funds."[126] Al-Jamali was found guilty of seeking a coup in Syria and asking for American and British help to do so, thereby "endangering Iraq's security and world peace."[127] However, his sentence was reduced to ten years, and he was permitted to leave the country.

In his political memoir, written from exile in Tunis in 1962, al-Jamali lambasted Gamal Abdul Nasser for egoism, "military logic," and being the biggest impediment to Arab Unity.[128] Al-Jamali did not explicitly criticize the various military regimes that succeeded Iraq's monarchy, including the one that had sentenced him to death. Instead, he railed against Nasser and the new generation of pan-Arab and territorial nationalists who had supplanted Jamali's own.

Al-Jamali had been a staunch promoter of pan-Arabism. His memoir is rife with references to his sense of kinship with individuals he met throughout the Arab world. Nasser's pan-Arabism, as opposed to al-Jamali's, meant a different relationship to the West, nationalization and land reform, the removal of Egypt's monarchy, and the brief unification of Arab governments, albeit with Egypt (and Nasser) at their head. In Iraq, Ba'athist pan-Arabism and the overthrow of Iraq's Hashemite monarchy led to a more restrictive, codified, and exclusive notion of nationalism as well as a social and economic revolution.

In contrast, the interwar era's nebulous and overlapping Transjordanian and pan-Arab ideologies faltered in the 1950s, only to return, changed but recognizable, a decade later. Jordan's Hashemite monarchy endured, incorporating former pan-Arab nationalists, such as Zu'aytir and al-Nabulsi, if not their nationalism. From an elite family, al-Nabulsi had moved in and out of government favor and government service throughout his life. His career vacillated from teaching to officialdom, exile to parliament, arrest to the Senate.[129] After having resigned from his post as a teacher, he worked as a bank official, then

---

125. "3. Notification No. (1) of 1958," *Weekly Gazette of the Republic of Iraq*, January 14, 1959, 21; "Internal Political Situation in Iraq. Fornightly Report from Baghdad, 24th October to 5th November, 1958," November 6, 1958, FO 371/133072, Foreign Office Records, BL.

126. Reuters, "Ex-Premier of Iraq Sentenced to Death," *New York Times*, November 11, 1958.

127. "Court of Iraq Decrees Death to Ex-Premier," *Chicago Daily Tribune*, November 11, 1958.

128. Ghareeb and Dougherty, *Historical Dictionary of Iraq*, 357; al-Jamali, *Arab Struggle*, 344, 446, 564.

129. Anderson, *Nationalist Voices in Jordan*, 164; Bidwell, *Dictionary of Modern Arab History*, 292; Majlis al-A'yan al-Urduni, "Dawlat Suleiman al-Nabulsi" [The state of Suleiman

was forced to the Transjordanian town of Shobeck in 1945 for protesting a Jewish company's mining concession, or as the government put it, for ignoring continued warnings against "broadcasting false advertisements in order to promote an unfair and harmful view of Arab interests and Transjordan's reputation."[130] Almost immediately after this exile, he served as minister of finance and economics, before again being arrested for opposing Jordan's treaty with Great Britain in 1948. He would go on to serve as foreign minister, ambassador, and prime minister from 1956 to 1957, was foreign minister again, put under house arrest, then appointed to the Senate in 1963 and again in 1967.[131] Al-Nabulsi's meandering through state service was both turbulent and persistent. He could serve both as nationalist, when politics was more open, and as nationalist symbol, when political activity was more restricted.

Al-Nabulsi was a key figure in Jordan's "liberal experiment." The year 1956 was a watershed in Jordanian political history: the brief culmination of five years of political freedoms under the rule of then-young King Hussein. This period and the liberties educators briefly enjoyed were cut short by the swift defeat of democratic initiatives due to internal conflicts over Jordan's participation in the Baghdad Pact, the role of the monarchy, and its dependence on foreign funding paid by the United States according to the Eisenhower doctrine.

Yet al-Nabulsi's political career survived the brief rebellion of the 1950s, if not with the same luster, due to both the flexibility of his interwar-honed political beliefs and the nature of Jordan's monarchy. In Jordan's 1954 election, the Communist Party, known as the "popular front," the Ba'athists, and al-Nabulsi's National Socialist Party all advocated varieties of transnational linkages, sought an end to feudalism, to create more employment, and adopted an anti-imperial stance. The Communist Party also called specifically for the distribution of feudal estates to peasants, and for creating more jobs through new industries. Pan-Arabism was de rigueur: even the Muslim Brotherhood supported "Arab unity" as a precursor to Muslim unity.[132]

al-Nabulsi], Jordanian Senate: Hashemite Kingdom of Jordan, http://www.senate.jo/en/node/404, accessed March 20, 2015.

130. "Transjordan," September 9–19, 1945, 15/67, 1–384. HMA.

131. Bidwell, *Dictionary of Modern Arab History*, 292, Majlis al-A'yan al-Urduni, "Dawlat Suleiman al-Nabulsi."

132. The Communist Party in 1951 was able to win three out of the eight electoral positions it applied for, in Nablus and Hebron.

Al-Nabulsi's National Socialist Party was anti-imperial but possessed a "relatively conservative platform, in support of the monarchy but against the abuses of government."[133] It was then typical for interwar pan-Arabism: against imperial intervention, but for the perpetuation of state institutions. However, the interwar era had ended. Al-Nabulsi's party, and al-Nabulsi, had to adapt to the possibility of actual Arab unity between nations. The party therefore advocated pan-Arab unity but on a limited basis: a failed alliance with Hashemite Iraq rather than an expansive Arab nation that might subsume Jordan and its government's political interests under Egyptian hegemony. Al-Nabulsi's party platform sought to reduce gaps between classes, to nationalize "productive forces," and to promote anti-imperialism as well as a loose notion of an Arab homeland based on "the citizen's feeling of belonging to one nation . . . not based on racial, material or ideological basis." It also made frequent reference to "our Arab nation."[134] This party, known to historians for its leftism and radical nature relative to Jordanian politics, was in fact a transition between interwar era Arab unity and postwar Arab state politics.

Jordan's monarchy used Palestinians' ability to enter the state as a means of both co-opting nationalists and expanding a more rigid state apparatus. Many educators-turned-politicians were well-known nationalists during the 1930s and 1940s. They were called on repeatedly to mitigate the continuing difficulties in assimilating Palestinians while preserving Palestinian identity and the stability of the Jordanian government. For example, Akram Zuʾaytir composed the introduction to a compilation of the writings of Jordanian prime minister and former educator Wasfi al-Tall. Al-Tall, a son of Mustafa al-Tall, is known for his role in "Black September": the purge of Palestinian Fedayeen fighters from Jordan and his subsequent assassination by the "Black September" group in revenge. Wasfi al-Tall's attempt to curb a then new, militant Palestinian nationalism had gotten him killed, underscoring the divisive nature of Palestinian, Jordanian, and Arab politics. Over time, however, the rhetoric of interwar pan-Arabism and of interwar pan-Arabists returned in the 1980s to rehabilitate al-Tall and to downplay the divisive nature of Jordan's midcentury nationalisms. Zuʾaytir's introduction describes frequent meetings between himself and al-Tall, honing a broad message of Arab unity and supposed plan, although carefully leaving military action to the military. The Palestinian activist politician and the Jordanian monarchist together agreed that "the cause of

133. Anderson, "The History of the Jordanian National Movement," 158.
134. Aruri, *Jordan*, 109.

Palestine is the cause of Arab unity, and Arab destiny."[135] In hindsight, Wasfi al-Tall had to be recast in narratives of Arab unity rather than emphasizing his assassination at the hands of a young Palestinian, thereby balancing the borders of Jordan with the national aspirations of Palestinians. Zu'aytir's broad strokes style of nationalism, his Palestinian origins, and past dislike of Nasser allowed him to bring these concepts together after the turbulence of the 1950s and 1960s. As he had in the past, Zu'aytir chose to work with rather than against states, in his case across the Arab world.

In contrast, for Palestinian politicians living in Israel during the first years of Israeli statehood, their understanding of pan-Arabism was necessarily tempered by their place within a non-Arab, and indeed anti-pan-Arab, state. In Israeli public forums, Palestinian citizens of Israel appealed to ideas of civic and state-based nationalism, rendering the boundaries of their territory more important and deemphasizing transnationalism in the process. The exclusive nature of nation-states, particularly those based on ethno-religious and/or ethno-nationalist bases meant those who found themselves within those states but outside of the prevailing category had to turn to other notions of national belonging. Palestinians had to call on the Israeli state and its nationalism to be either distinct from or inclusive of nationalisms based on race and language.[136] For example, Rostam Bastouni, one of two former Palestinian educators-turned-Israeli-MKs sought to integrate Arabs into the new Israeli state using the state-development model of Habib Bourguiba in postcolonial Tunisia.

Rather than argue for the Arab unity of the interwar era or the pan-Arabism of Nasser, Bastouni lobbied for an Arab identity that could encompass Palestinians within Israel, allowing Jewish Israelis to accept Palestinians' existence within a Jewish state.[137] Having come of age during the final years of the mandate and choosing to attend the Technion, Bastouni experienced an education and a career that were bounded by state borders. Asserting that "Bourgibists" were just as good Arabs as "Nasserists," he endeavored to fit pan-Arabism into the new reality of Israel, namely, how to find a model of nation-state that would allow for connections between Arabs across borders but also to facilitate his acceptance into Jewish Israeli society. He also sought to reject ethno-nationalist exclusivity, protesting exclusionary policies such as absentee property legislation that targeted Palestinian citizens of Israel. He worked to end

135. Al-Tall, *Kitabat fi al-Qadaya al-'Arabiyya* [Writings on the Arab cause], 7.
136. Lustick, *Arabs in the Jewish State*, 116.
137. Oscar Jarzmik, "'Adjusting to Powerlessness' in Occupied Jerusalem," 91.

military rule over "certain Arab districts," arguing that Arabs suffered much more than other citizens of Israel. However, Ben Gurion responded, in hyperbolic fashion, that the suggestion was "libelous and totally unfounded" and that instead "both economically and culturally the Arabs in Israel were better off than in any of the neighbouring countries, and it was a matter for the greatest regret that the neighbouring countries did not follow Israel's lead both in the matter of education and as regards the freedom enjoyed in Israel even by persons who slandered and libeled the State, and who did their utmost to fan hatred and enmity between the two peoples." According to Ben Gurion, in contradistinction to Bastouni's hopes, pan-Arabism was omnipresent, and in such a way that Arabs were always the enemy, always a fifth column, and never full citizens. Rather than comparing their status to that of their Jewish Israeli peers, he divided them into an Arab category that transcended national borders, and a group who should be happy they could criticize their government at all.

Bastouni's vision found little support among either Jews or Arabs within Israel. He sought to negate the Zionist project and to define Israel, to use more recent terminology, as a state of all its citizens, and for Israel's Palestinian population to renounce their ties to the rest of the Arab world. Bastouni would move to the United States in 1969, "bitterly disappointed by the attitude to his movement on the part of the authorities. He charged that the officials charged with carrying out Government policy not only disregarded his efforts [at Arab/Jewish coexistence] but actively hindered them."[138]

Bastouni relegated ideas of nationality based on language and race to the nineteenth century, at the same moment that Arab world politicians and intellectuals worked to place an Arab nation unified by language and culture into the twentieth-century world of relatively independent nation-states. The shift from the ideologies carried by the educators of the interwar era to the pan-Arab alliances from the Second World War to the 1950s was not immediate. Sati al-Husri continued to ply his trade, advising on education and culture from within the borders of multiple nation-states and the Arab League. Darwish al-Miqdadi worked as the director of education in Kuwait, importing Palestinian educators and a pan-Arabism supportive of their cause.[139] A new

138. Jerusalem Post Reporter, "Rustum Bastuni Leaves Israel to Live in U.S.," *Jerusalem Post*, December 10, 1964.

139. Kuwait's education system employed Palestinians almost exclusively in its upper levels during the early 1950s, and nearly 50 percent of the total number of teachers in 1966–1967. Al-Rashoud, "Modern Education and Arab Nationalism," 216.

generation of Palestinians would join diaspora liberation movements, including sometime educators such as Ghassan Kanafani, Yasser Arafat, and Mahmoud Abbas (Abu Mazen).[140] Although these men were participating in secret cells, propaganda, and armed resistance rather than vague pronouncements of Arab unity, teaching functioned in certain ways as it had during the mandate era: a readily available profession for educated individuals when others were closed to them, without the elite social and economic status educators had enjoyed during those years.

The rhetoric of Arab unity and of communism remained important frameworks for political understanding. A fundamental shift had occurred, however, from imagined nations to divided and strengthened states. The educator politicians of the interwar era met with ambivalence rather than enthusiasm the prospect of Arab unity in the divided climate of 1950s nation-states: an environment that resulted in a new politics of educators, from the highest to the lowest ranks of the civil service.

———

British, Iraqi, and Palestinian officials, as well as scholars today, connected the advent of mass education with political instability. However, they often downplayed both the strength of state required and its effects.[141] In 1956 a governor of a southern province of Iraq (where the poor condition of the peasantry was particularly pronounced) noted that as long as Iraq's peasants

> remain ignorant and illiterate, they will continue to show their respect to the authority of the government, to obey the law of the land, to accept the social system as it is and to be happy. But once they are educated, come troubles. They will demand land reform, land distribution. They will begin to speak of their rights. Of course I am not against the enlightenment of the people. I only believe that it is dangerous to awaken the people to new needs when we are not prepared to satisfy those needs.[142]

140. Washington Institute for Near East Policy, "Fatah Central Committee Profiles," 2015, https://www.washingtoninstitute.org/uploads/Documents/pubs/FCCProfiles2.pdf.

141. Great Britain Palestine Royal Commission, *Palestine Royal Commission Report*, 120; "Administration Reports for the Year 1918 of Certain Departments of the Civil Administration of the Occupied Territories of Iraq," in Rush and Priestland, *Records of Iraq*, 1:99.

142. Quoted in Clark, *Compulsory Education in Iraq*, 4–5.

This governor asserted that ignorance allowed for stability, while education meant political awareness and not only rebellion but the economic changes post-Hashemite regimes would advocate. In both Iraq and Palestine, however, those whom the official would deem "ignorant and illiterate" led rebellions calling for social justice, while those who "began to speak of their rights" more frequently manipulated their governments from within their ranks.

Analyses, including that of this mid-twentieth-century Iraqi official, that focus on the causal links between mass education and regime stability generally fail to adequately consider how the absence of mass education, or rather the denial of schooling, affected politics as well. In Iraq, Palestine, and Transjordan, limited education did incorporate educated individuals into government service, which made them less likely to rebel against that government as a whole. During the interwar era, educators preached anti-imperial and anti-government nationalisms while remaining civil servants, thereby contributing to the stability of their governments. Those who lacked access to government schooling and a clear path of upward mobility through the civil service, like the unemployed or underemployed workers and former *fellahin* of Palestine, or even the would-be government employee Bahjat Abu Gharbiyah, were more inclined to seek to overthrow mandate governments. In contrast, for the vast majority of educators, government employment was symbiotic; it sustained stability by offering a steady job that served the nonrepresentative regimes teachers criticized.

Nevertheless, the reverse was also true. The strengthened states of the mid-twentieth century would extend mass education to citizens within their borders. As nation, state, and territory came to align with one another, teachers would be forced into more nationally bounded forms of political engagement. These states would likewise erase the role of elite teacher–civil servant– nationalist and politician of the interwar era, revolutionizing their ideologies in the process. The following chapter moves from the end of teacher-politicians' extraordinary careers, and of their interwar nationalisms, to the swelling ranks of ordinary Palestinian, Jordanian, and Iraqi teachers. Their growing numbers eroded their socioeconomic status, as well as their political power as individuals, transforming the profession of teaching, and its politics, forever.

5

The Professional Teacher and the Hazards of Mass Education

IN 1944 a group of male and female teachers from all levels of schooling founded the Iraqi Teachers Association, Iraq's first teachers' union.[1] Its charter advocated solidarity, as well as improved living and professional standards. Its members vowed to raise the concerns of their colleagues to their government, defending their moral and material rights. They resolved to set up a fund to care for needy teachers and their families. In addition, they created a teachers' club in Baghdad and voiced the intention to found others across Iraq, in order to facilitate communication between educators and the Ministry of Education.[2]

It was no coincidence that this organization, aiming to support teachers as a collective and to take their concerns to the government with which teachers had been so entwined, was founded in Iraq during the mid-1940s. As the mandates ended, whether because their inhabitants gained independence or faced occupation, governments devoted more attention and funding to education. Politicians, policy makers, and an ever-increasing number of students, teachers, and professors sought to move away from imperial notions of education's civilizing mission toward modernization, development, and nationalization of schooling. Education bureaucracies, exams, and school inspections became

1. Hassan al-Dajili, "Jam'iyat al-Mu'allimin" [The Teachers Association], al-Mu'allim al-Jadid 8, no. 3 (May 1944): 271–72.

2. Al-Dajili, 272. Anyone who worked in education could join. Dues were half a dinar for membership outside of Baghdad, or one dinar for teachers in the secondary schools in Baghdad and its environs. Teachers in the primary schools of Baghdad and its environs had to pay 750 fils, with the knowledge that these dues might go up.

more comprehensive, centralized, and uniform, extending countrywide. Teaching became a standardized profession within national borders.

As national governments consolidated their control over state education, teachers' relationship to state- and nation-building projects changed. During the 1950s former teachers reached the peak of their power, gaining ministerial posts in Iraq and Jordan's newly independent governments. They were the final generation to do so. Teachers who began their careers during the 1940s in Iraq, after 1948 in Israel, and the 1950s in Jordan generally remained teachers. Even as they expanded state bureaucracies, they were cut off from their governments' upper levels.

In the process, educators forfeited their elite social and economic status. Scholars have linked the relatively low status of teaching globally to its feminization.[3] In Britain's former mandates, however, the depreciation of teaching as a profession occurred despite its remaining an overwhelmingly masculine profession. While male teachers almost worldwide have wrestled with "historical and cultural frameworks that define most teaching as women's work," in Iraq and Jordan, and for Palestinians, teaching did not conjure up images of women in the front of the classroom.[4] Teachers became less elite as they became more plentiful, not because disproportionate numbers of women became teachers.

The separation of teachers from high politics and their declining social and economic position changed their tactics of resistance. No longer elites or latent politicians, educators confronted their states en masse. They raised their voices as a collective, as an important political bloc, but in the process, they lost their "privileged access" to administrative posts, which had been so exceptional during the interwar era.[5] Instead, educators banded together to the extent each government permitted, seeking better wages and economic protections as well as the ability to engage in formal politics.

I argue that three related factors limited educators' individual claims on their governments and teachers' politics: teachers' increasing numbers, their professionalization, and the nature of each postmandate state. A surfeit of teachers meant these formerly rare, educated individuals could neither capitalize on their scarcity nor bargain with the governments that employed them. When governments increased in size, power, and independence, they cared

3. Etzioni, *The Semi-professions*.
4. Skelton, Francis, and Smulyan, *The SAGE Handbook of Gender and Education*, 476.
5. Gellner and Breuilly, *Nations and Nationalism*, 37.

more about education as a means of developing their economies, inculcating loyalty, and surveilling their populations. Teachers no longer marked the point at which society became incorporated into modern states. Rather than future government functionaries and ministers and therefore part of governance, teachers found themselves positioned as subjects. They faced strengthened states that enforced previously flexible policies, which teachers had been able to bend or break. When they could no longer negotiate with their governments on an individual basis, educators turned to collective action.

Teachers' professionalization went hand in hand with their political neutralization as individuals; both were facets of strengthened postcolonial states. Independence for Iraq and Jordan, or occupation and diaspora in the case of the Palestinians, led not to representative governments for these populations but to narrow autocracies, nonrepresentative parliaments, and martial law. These governments had little interest in permitting teachers the educational and political leeway they had enjoyed during the interwar era. Instead, they standardized teaching, more strictly monitored educators' performance in the classroom, and more stringently curtailed their participation in antigovernment protests, including written critiques. Punishments for political activity, particularly public criticisms of government, changed from reprimands and transfers to imprisonment, exile, or even, in 1960s Iraq, execution. These repressive measures severely limited the intermediary position teachers had enjoyed in previous decades.

Mass education and the inhibition of teachers' politics did not occur simultaneously across the region, nor did they have the same immediate causes and consequences. Therefore this chapter relies more on a comparative rather than transnational analytic. Education expanded in each country at different rates, causing teachers to lose their elite status at different moments. The story of Palestine and of Palestinians is fundamentally different from that of the other mandates. Palestine did not become a nation-state as Iraq and Transjordan did. Israel, the nation-state that extended into the former territory of Palestine, not only changed the region's political landscape but also had a distinct national project, which failed to accommodate the Palestinians who became its citizens. The situation of Palestinians under Israeli rule, or stateless in the diaspora, also differed from that of Iraqis and Jordanians, even when they worked alongside one another in government schools and government service.

Despite these differences, the eventual outcome of educational expansion and standardization was the same: teachers became more professionalized, but they lost the intermediary role they had enjoyed during earlier decades. The strengthening of ties between each nation-state and its education system, brought about by independence, weakened the links between that system and government employment. Guarantees of a job in the civil service, which government school graduates had enjoyed during the mandate era, began to dissolve as degree-holders increased beyond the capacity of each government to employ them. Independence also led to an opening-up of the private sector, tourism, and, in Iraq, control over oil revenue, providing other, even more appealing opportunities for educated individuals. Those who did become public school teachers found themselves in a career rather than a brief stop on their way to the top of the civil service. With independence, public education served to connect nation- and state-building projects. The end of teachers' elite status and intimate relationship with their governments were unintended casualties of these processes.

Colonial to National: Educational Expansion and State Capacity

The colonial-run governments of mandate Iraq, Palestine, and Transjordan generally had different goals regarding education's role in state building than their successor states. British policy makers sought not to develop each polity for its own sake but rather to benefit Britain, and to avoid costing the British taxpayer for these foreign adventures. Budgets reflected colonial parsimony. As Palestine was under British colonial control throughout the duration of the mandate, the percentage of Palestine's overall budget devoted to education remained relatively constant (see figure 5.1).[6] Officials claimed that the paucity of funds, in terms of percentage of the total budget spent on education, was due to the requirements of security and administration. Yet the mandate government actually had a significant revenue surplus from 1932 to 1936, and again from 1939 to 1942.[7] As late as 1946, one Arabic newspaper demanded the government justify and ameliorate the "teachers' crisis," arguing that the number of teachers produced only filled vacancies without expanding the

6. Matthews and Akrawi, *Education in the Arab Countries of the Near East*, 222; Government of Palestine, Department of Education, *Department of Education Annual Report for the School Year 1936–1937*, 5; *Department of Education Annual Report 1939–1940*, 2.

7. Wolf, "Selected Aspects in the Development of Public Education in Palestine 1920–1946," 138.

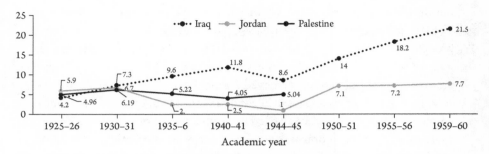

FIGURE 5.1. Percentage of total budget devoted to education. See note 6 for sources.

education system.[8] In Transjordan, the percentage of the budget devoted to schooling decreased during the 1930s and 1940s, indicating British prioritization of regional stability. Budgetary growth during this period directly served British rather than local interests; additional funds went to support the Arab Legion (and King Abdullah) as Britain's ally in the region, but not Transjordan's education system.[9]

In contrast, the independent governments of Iraq, Jordan and Israel had a much greater stake in their education systems. Education represented a panacea for a variety of ailments, particularly the political instability of the 1950s and 1960s. Officials and official reports describe schooling as crucial in improving economies, augmenting state power, and inculcating national values. Policy makers were conscious of the need to create new generations, physically and mentally fit to develop their countries but also loyal to their governments. For example, the army officers who overthrew Iraq's British-influenced Hashemite monarchy sought to use schooling to preclude discontent and protests while improving the country's global standing. A few months after the revolution, Major General ʿAbd al-Karim Qasim, prime minister of the new republic of Iraq, proclaimed, "Our aim will be to raise the prestige of the nation, to raise the prestige of the people, to raise the standard of education which is the basis (of everything)."[10] The education budget reflected Qasim's assertions: almost a quarter of government funds were devoted to public education in

8. Mustafa al-Taher "The Honourable, The Chief Secretary" February 18, 1946, *Al-Wihda Newspaper,* "Shortage of Government Teachers," 129/9-M, ISA.

9. Al-Tall, *Education in Jordan,* 65.

10. ʿAbd al-Karim Qasim, "Speech by Major General ʿAbd Al-Karim Qasim, Iraqi Prime Minister and Commander in Chief of the Armed Forces. Delivered at the Congress of Arab Lawyers," in *The Arab States and the Arab League,* 36.

1959–1960.[11] On the other hand, as each state became stronger, its capacity to target those criticizing its actions increased: teachers as well as students experienced more stringent disciplinary measures. Qasim's rise to power coincided with government purges and waves of arrests, including arrests of teachers.[12] Increasing education was part of independence, a stronger state, and authoritarian governance.

The education laws proclaimed by Iraq, Jordan, and Israel in the 1950s articulated clear and ambitious expectations for education. They demanded a harsher, more intimate relationship between each state and its citizens. Iraq's republican regime viewed education as a way of pleasing and uniting large swathes of its population, instilling patriotism in young and often recalcitrant students and their parents. The education law of 1958, promulgated a few months after the revolution, defines schooling's goal as creating a new, moral, loyal, and literate generation, while bringing it firmly under the state's purview. The duty of the Ministry of Education was to "build a conscious and enlightened generation that believes in God and the homeland (watan) . . . armed with scientific knowledge and sound character" and thereby able to "strengthen the position of the Iraqi people (sha'ab) and the Arab nation, and to secure its right to freedom, security and a decent life." To achieve these goals, the government advocated expanding public education and eradicating illiteracy as rapidly as possible, carefully monitoring schools, be they government or nongovernment, and incorporating the youth of the nation into government-sponsored organizations. The law also explicitly prohibited "partisan political propaganda" or anything that could corrupt morality, national unity, or Arab nationalism in schools.[13] Casting education as a tool of surveillance, development, and nationalism, the law required that as much of the Iraqi population as possible attend school. Arab nationalism remained prominent, but the Iraqi people formed a clearly defined subset of the "Arab nation." More concretely, teachers' and students' nationalisms had to match the nationalism of their government; anything else was forbidden.

---

11. UNESCO International Bureau of Education, International Yearbook of Education 20, 184; International Yearbook of Education 23, 186; International Yearbook of Education 21, 219.

12. Farouk-Sluglett and Sluglett, Iraq since 1958, 70–71. His replacement by the Ba'ath regime coincided with arrests, particularly of teachers deemed to have Communist leanings or affiliations. Wagner, Iraq, 58.

13. Ministry of Education, Law no. 39 of 1958, October 11, 1958, Iraq law book, 2015, https://iraqld.hjc.iq/LoadLawBook.aspx?page=1&SC=141220058855844.

In Jordan, the Hashemite monarchy called on education to pacify its population and to render it into moral, loyal citizens, protected explicitly from teachers' corrosive nationalisms. Jordan annexed the West Bank after the war of 1948, granting citizenship to Palestinians, thereby more than doubling its existing population. A Palestinian-Jordanian assassinated King Abdullah in 1951. Subsequently, there was a brief liberalization of Jordanian politics followed by a crackdown on political freedoms. Due to these upheavals, the state curtailed teachers' roles as government-subsidized nationalists moving in and out of education. Jordan's law of public education in 1955 forbade teachers from "undertaking or allowing directions that lead to corruption of morals or of religious doctrine or of nationalism or discrimination and discord, or affect respect for the Arab nation, or to use education a means of political propaganda."[14] This rather Orwellian law banned teachers from engaging in or even permitting criticisms of nationalism as well as religion. The punishments for those who disobeyed this law extended the reach of the state beyond its official purview. Even nongovernment schools were forbidden from hiring teachers who had been fired for the reasons stated.[15] Fearing educators while emphasizing morality, supervision, and a muted pan-Arabism, Jordan's government clearly sought to control its population. It aimed at neutralizing teachers' politics while promulgating a pan-Arabism that could, the government hoped, compete with that of Nasser and the free officers in Egypt. This pan-Arabism was also meant to absorb the nationalism of Jordan's new Palestinian citizens, who generally had more educational qualifications than their Jordanian counterparts.

Globally, mass education aimed at developing each country's economy and international standing, and to inculcate a national culture. Palestinians under Israel or other countries' control, or ministered to by the United Nations Relief and Works Agency for Palestinian Refugees in the Near East (UNRWA), ill-fit schemes of national incorporation and were often excluded from them. In Israel proper, Palestinians represented a problem for the Zionist aims of education. The education law of 1953 defined the goals of state education as based on "the values of Jewish culture and the achievements of science, on love of the homeland and loyalty to the state and the Jewish people, on practice in agricultural work and handicraft, on *chalutzic* (pioneer) training, and on

14. Law no. 20 of 1955: the law of public education. *Al-Jarida al-Rasmiyya*, April 4, 1955, no. 1224, NLJ.

15. Law no. 20 of 1955, article 5.

striving for a society built on freedom, equality, tolerance, mutual assistance, and love of mankind," with the caveat that in non-Jewish educational institutions, the curriculum could be modified in some way.[16] All school subjects were meant to fulfill this Zionist vision. As the minister of education in 1956 argued, the goal of teaching literature was to convey to students (including Arab ones) "the entire story of our (Jewish) courageous effort to build our nation and correct our way of life; it [literature] will revive the entire story of daring and courage of our struggle for independence."[17] For Arab Palestinians, loyalty to the Jewish people was not a valid option. Palestinians did not function as part of the Zionist national project. While Jewish immigrants from Middle Eastern countries were grudgingly integrated through schooling, non-Jews could not easily squeeze or be squeezed into Zionist national categories.

After the end of the mandate in 1948, the Israeli state made education at the elementary level compulsory for all citizens.[18] Following some debate as to whether schooling should take place only in Hebrew with one unified curriculum, the Israeli government resolved to permit the separate system of Arabic-language government schools that had existed under the mandate to continue, but with several changes. In this "separate but equal" system (and indeed as equal as segregated schooling in the United States), Arab students studied in Arab schools that were underfunded and understaffed compared to their Jewish counterparts.[19] Their strictly controlled textbooks were produced by the new Israeli government.[20] Education at the secondary level and above lagged for Arab Israelis and continues to lag behind that of their Jewish counterparts, due to the lower standard of Arab education, the Israeli government's priorities, and fears of the "demographic danger" well-educated Arabs represented.[21]

16. Israel State Education Law, 5713–1953, 113, https://www.adalah.org/uploads/oldfiles/Public/files/Discriminatory-Laws-Database/English/24-State-Education-Law-1953.pdf.

17. Ben Zvi Dinur "About the New Curriculum," in Hofman, "The Politics of National Education," 446.

18. In 1948 there was only one government Arab secondary school, increasing to seven by 1959 and thirty-five in 1969. Al-Haj, *Education, Empowerment, and Control,* 80.

19. This comparison has been made repeatedly through to the present. See, for example, Golan-Agnon, "Separate but Not Equal," 1075; Jabareen, "Law and Education."

20. Hofman et al., "Education and Social Change," 313.

21. The Arab population of Israel has remained approximately 20 percent since the beginning of the state, but the high school age population is often higher—today about 26 percent. In the 1950s, however, less than 2 percent of secondary schools and less than 4 percent of secondary school students were Arab: only 50 percent of Arabs who applied to secondary schools were

Similar to British colonial goals for Palestinians' schooling, Israel's government asserted Arab graduates should work in agriculture.[22] Government officials advocated closing off white-collar jobs to Arabs altogether, fearing their integration into government employment had the potential to undermine the state, or at least its Jewish majority. As the Israel Yearbook put it in 1958, "The problem of how to absorb [Arab] secondary and high school graduates who cannot or do not want to go into agriculture continues to exist."[23] The assumption was that all Arabs should be gainfully employed on the land rather than in positions of economic, social, or political leadership. The Ministry of Education also noted that Arabs were unable to go into the civil service due to the martial law they were subject to, as well as "a lack of peace" between Israel and its neighboring countries. Moreover, the ministry explicitly asserted that Arab secondary education was too expensive, and that limited funds should be devoted only to the elementary level.[24] When an Arab minister raised the issue of a lack of high schools for Arabs, the minister of education blamed a lack of funds, while another, more radical minister stated that educating Arabs at all constituted a "danger to the existence of the state of Israel." He further argued that the government should endeavor to "make their lives miserable, to cut off funds. Let them go to an Arab country."[25] Although Arab Israelis with advanced degrees have remained relatively limited, this limitation has not resulted in the same bargaining power with the government, due in part to the nature of the Israeli state and the educational attainments of the Israeli population as a whole.

In the diaspora, Palestinian educators used their diplomas, certificates, and experience as teachers to survive and, at times, to thrive. However, the growing importance of nation-states, and Palestinians' exclusion from them, rendered their positions fundamentally precarious. The UNRWA struggled with the impossibility of reconciling humanitarian relief, including long-term educational and economic programs, with Palestinians' political commitment to

accepted. Al-Haj, *Education, Empowerment, and Control,* 43; letter from Aviezer Yellin to Dr. B. Ben Yehuda, director of the Department of Education and Culture in Jerusalem, February 13, 1951, "Irgun ha-morim ha-melamdim be be'it sefer aravim" [Organization of teachers that teach in Arab schools], GAL 1631/7, ISA. Through the 1980s, less than 13 percent of the total number of high schools in Israel were devoted to its Palestinian population. Israel, Central Bureau of Statistics, "Schools, Classes and Students in Secondary Education," April 9, 2018, table 8–12.

22. These suggestions also took place amid land transfers that made agricultural work increasingly difficult for Palestinian Israelis. Lustick, *Arabs in the Jewish State,* 14–15.

23. Israel Yearbook 1958, 111.

24. Israel Yearbook 1958, 82–83.

25. Quoted in Kalekin-Fishman, *Ideology, Policy, and Practice,* 116.

returning to their homes.[26] Moreover, governments and NGOS alike questioned what refugees were supposed to do, and how to keep the population
economically stable (and quiescent). In surveying UNRWA during the early
1950s, Matta Akrawi, then working for UNESCO, both complained of the lack
of teachers capable of teaching at a higher level and argued that "no more than
a very limited number of refugees should, for the time being, be encouraged
to seek secondary education for their children." Instead, Palestinians were to
be given more vocational training or "manual training" in order to provide
"skilled labor" and perhaps, in echoes of British colonial policy, to keep them
quiescent.[27] The shortage of UNRWA teachers was in part due to higher-paid
positions open to Palestinian educators in the Gulf. For example, Kuwait's
education system employed Palestinians almost exclusively in its upper levels
of education during the early 1950s. Palestinians formed nearly 50 percent of
the total number of teachers in 1966–1967.[28] In this fledgling education system,
Palestinian teachers, particularly under the leadership of Darwish al-Miqdadi,
maintained a privileged academic as well as political role.[29] Kuwait and the
Gulf countries represented something of an anomaly for Palestinians, as they
enjoyed relative success due to the scarcity of schooling among the local population, its government's desire for modernization, and Palestinians' placement
at upper levels of Kuwait's education bureaucracy in particular. However, laws
increasingly favored Kuwaitis over non-Kuwaitis in work and education. As
growing numbers of Kuwaitis became educated, and as political currents
shifted during the 1970s, the status of Palestinian teachers deteriorated in the
Gulf as elsewhere.

Mass Education without Feminization: The Decline in Teachers' Socioeconomic Status

The stark difference between colonial governments that feared expanding
schooling would cause the rise of a clerical class and national governments that
seized on schooling as a means of controlling and improving their populations
resulted in a clear pattern: with greater independence came greater investment

26. Al Husseini, "UNRWA and the Refugees," 8.

27. Middle East Educational Relief Programme, "Historical Background of the Program,"
Working Party, Paris, 1952, REH/ME/CONF.1, WS/061.61. UNESDOC, 3–4, UNESCO Digital
Library.

28. Al-Rashoud, "Modern Education and Arab Nationalism," 216.

29. Al-Rashoud, " 240; Lesch, "Palestinians in Kuwait," 43.

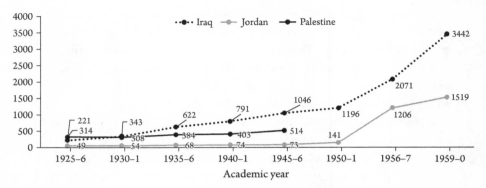

FIGURE 5.2. Number of schools, 1925–1960. See note 30 for sources.

in government schooling, increasing the quantity and—to a lesser extent—improving the quality of education. These increases had the effect of devaluing teachers' credentials and salaries, erasing their formerly elite standing, but without feminizing the profession as a whole.

The expansion of educational facilities, students, and personnel in the 1950s and 1960s in Iraq and Jordan are particularly striking, as teachers went from an elite cadre to part of the society they served.[30] Causes beyond each government's budgetary priorities contributed to these skyrocketing numbers. Jordan's annexation of the West Bank was one such factor.[31] Iraq's oil revenue in the 1950s was another.[32] More pupils in each school led to overcrowded classrooms that were difficult to manage, particularly as the number of schools

30. The information for the charts in figures 5.2–5.4 was taken from the following sources: Al-Tall, *Education in Jordan*; Government of Palestine, Department of Education, *Department of Education Annual Report for the Scholastic Year 1923, 1924, 1925–1926, 1927–1928, 1928–1929, 1929–1930, 1930–1931, 1931–1932, 1932–1933, 1933–1934, 1945–1946*; Matthews and Akrawi, *Education in Arab Countries of the Near East*; Ministry of Education Iraq, *Ministry of Education: Educational Statistics, Annual Report 1960–61*; Ministry of Education Iraq, *Annual Report [on] Educational Statistics 1946–1947 Taqrir Al-Sanawi, Al-Ihsa Al-Tarbawi*; Unesco International Bureau of Education, *International Yearbook of Education 20, 21, 23*; al-Mamlaka al-Urduniyya al-Hashimiyya, Wizarat al-Tarbiyya wa-al-Taʻlim, *Al-Taqrir al-Sanawi—Wizarat al-Tarbiyya wa-al-Taʻlim* [The Hashemite Kingdom of Jordan, Annual report—Ministry of Education], *1953/1954, 1955/1956, 1956/57, 1957/58, 1958/59, 1960/1961*.

31. Issawi and Dabezies, "Population Movements," 385; Al-Tall, *Education in Jordan*, 128.

32. Although oil profits were generally channeled toward irrigation, benefiting large landowners, 30 percent went directly to the Iraqi government's budget, which meant more funding for schooling. Tripp, *A History of Iraq*, 138–39; Haj, *The Making of Iraq*, 74–75; Reich, *Political Leaders*, 470–72.

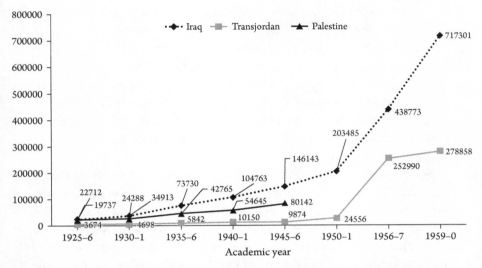

FIGURE 5.3. Number of students, 1925–1960. See note 30 for sources.

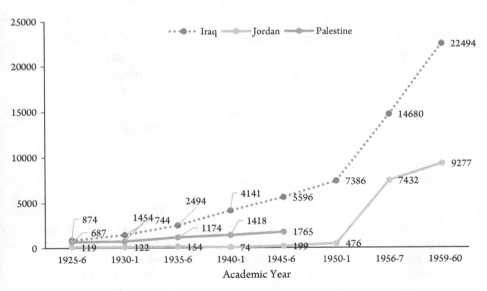

FIGURE 5.4. Number of teachers, 1925–1960. See note 30 for sources.

lagged behind the increasing number of students.[33] Despite the huge budgetary surges, the level of funding did not keep up with demand.

Increasing the number of teachers trained and requiring more years of training cheapened their educational qualifications; a high school education gradually became the norm. Detailed statistical information from Jordan shows that almost a third of teachers hired during the 1920s (whose degrees were documented) had less than a secondary education. Only about 14 percent of teachers hired in the 1950s whose degrees were documented had less than a secondary education.[34]

Simultaneously, teaching became a career in and of itself rather than a means of climbing to the highest ranks of the civil service or an interim measure between other, more prestigious government positions. Between the 1920s and the 1960s, the number of teachers in Jordan who moved in and out of teaching dropped, from over 40 percent of teachers having left the profession at least once through the end of the mandate to only about 9 percent having done so from the mandate's end in 1946 until 1960. The length of the terms they served increased. In the 1920s more than a third of teachers served two years or less: only 20 percent served more than twenty years. In contrast, approximately 37 percent of the teachers who served from 1946 through 1960 worked twenty years or more and achieved middle- to high-ranking positions within the Ministry of Education rather than in the government as a whole.[35] When men or women became teachers in the 1950s, they expected teaching to be their career rather than a temporary position.

Historically, the expansion of schooling and teaching's supposed lack of professionalization contributed to its feminization in countries ranging from France and England to China and the Soviet Union.[36] For example, as the English and American governments extended education from the late

33. Between the 1930s and 1940s in Palestine and Transjordan, the number of students admitted rose and the number of schools built stagnated. Only in Iraq did the 1940s mark an increase in schools without a comparable increase in students, in part because the government began renting houses in both urban and rural areas. Matthews and Akrawi, *Education in Arab Countries of the Near East*, 152–53.

34. HRD. Approximately 4,467 teachers, with documented degrees, were hired in the 1950s. Of these, 609 had less than a high school education.

35. HRD. Approximately 42 percent of teachers hired between 1946 and 1960 had a rank of 6 or higher.

36. Drudy, "Gender Balance/Gender Bias," 316–17; Basten, "A Feminised Profession"; Trouvé-Finding, "Teaching as a Woman's Job"; Fischman, "Persistence and Ruptures"; Fu,

nineteenth century, they employed women as teachers because they could pay them less than men and thereby support a greater number of schools. When women entered teaching with relatively low salaries, the profession became less prestigious.[37] In rural nineteenth-century America, as teaching became a long-term career at a lower salary, men left the field for more lucrative work, and women took their places.[38] Similarly, among Jewish teachers in the new state of Israel, the desire to expand education rapidly and cheaply meant lowering the desired qualifications alongside teachers' remuneration. With the failure to attract male teachers, particularly to lower levels of teaching, the number of female teachers increased from approximately 50 percent of the total in 1952 to about 67 percent ten years later.[39] Despite increasing external criteria and improving qualifications over time, "occupational sociologists and historians" and particularly female teachers have complained that teaching is not classified as a profession, due to its low status.[40]

In Iraq, Palestine, and Transjordan/Jordan, the professionalization of teaching, namely, its becoming both standardized and a career, also meant its degradation, but without the substitution of female teachers for male ones. In Jordan, only 19 percent of teachers who began their service from 1920 to 1940 were female. From 1946 through the 1960, although the number of teachers swelled drastically, the percentage of female teachers did not.[41] In mid-1950s Iraq, the number of female elementary school teachers approached 50 percent, yet even with the unlikely assumption that all pre-elementary school teachers were female, only 40 percent of teachers overall were women.[42] During the mandate for Palestine, the numbers of female teachers were generally not reported in official publications. However, 17 percent of government schools were girls' schools and 21 percent of students were female in 1944, the last year statistics were available.[43] The percentage of female teachers, then, is likely to have been

"Initial Exploration of the Phenomenon of the Feminization of Teachers"; Griffiths, "The Feminization of Teaching."

37. Apple, *Teachers and Texts*, 56–57.

38. Strober and Tyack, "Why Do Women Teach and Men Manage?," 498.

39. Braham and United States Office of Education, *Israel, a Modern Education System*, 135–36.

40. Biklen, *School Work*, 30, 41.

41. HRD. Female teachers formed 18 percent of the total.

42. Iraq Wizarat al-Ma'arif, *Al-Taqrir al-Sanawi 'an Sayr al-Ma'arif* [Annual report on educational progress] 1955–56, 7, 16.

43. Tibawi, *Arab Education in Mandatory Palestine*, 49.

between 17 and 21 percent, although possibly lower. After the end of the mandate, only about a third of Arab Palestinian teachers in Israel were female as late as the 1970s.[44] Gender segregation in schooling, persistent misalignment between familial and professional expectations for female teachers, and a lack of options for educated men preserved teaching as a male-dominated profession, even as it degenerated from an elite to an economically struggling vocation.

The women and men who worked as teachers from the 1940s had reason to fight against their governments: their salaries decreased in real value over time, downgrading teachers' social and economic status. In the mandate for Palestine, teachers had frequently received modest salaries. Although, as we have seen, salaries were disrupted during the 1936–1939 revolt,[45] at least in villages they were sufficient for "a good life."[46] Even without a university degree, teachers could receive up to 280 pounds per year. If they held a university degree and passed the higher teaching exam, they could be paid up to 500 pounds per year.[47] Comparisons to unskilled laborers, on one hand, and urban Jewish Palestinians, on the other, indicate the salary of a teacher approached middle-class status.[48]

The United Nations Relief and Works Agency noted that in the immediate aftermath of the *Nakba*, teachers either worked as volunteers or were paid less than cleaners. Teachers had to choose between rations and unemployment, or working for pay that would barely provide even a subsistence level for their families. By 1950 Palestinian teachers in UNRWA schools and in Jordan were being paid significantly less than during the mandate period.[49] Palestinian

44. Mar'i, *Arab Education in Israel*.

45. In 1937 the exiled former mayor of Jerusalem Hussein Fakhri al-Khalidi (brother of Ahmed Samih al-Khalidi) noted that "with the exception of Britishers, two or three heads of department, all officers are very underpaid—a girl teacher is lucky to get a post at Rs. 5 per month." Husseini, *Exiled from Jerusalem*, 62.

46. Ibrahim Othman, interview with author, April 16, 2012, Amman, Jordan.

47. To reach 600 pounds per year, teachers had to advance to being inspector or assistant inspector, in addition to fulfilling all previous qualifications. District inspectors and the principal of the Arab College could receive up to 800 pounds. Matthews and Akrawi, *Education in the Arab Countries of the Near East*, 224–25.

48. Unskilled laborers such as railroad workers received between 24 and 30 pounds per year during the 1940s. Urban Jewish Palestinians were counted as middle class if they earned 360 pounds a year. Jewish Palestinians also earned 1.264 times what their Arab counterparts made. Bernstein, *Constructing Boundaries*, 180; L.F.A, "The Family Budget: Results of a Survey," *Palestine Post*, December 5, 1947, NLI; Metzer, *The Divided Economy of Mandatory Palestine*, 124.

49. *Assistance to Palestine Refugees, Report of the Director of the United Nations Relief and Works Agency for Palestine Refugees in the Near East*, September 28, 1951, United Nations Digital Library; MeasuringWorth, "Qustandi Quanaze," 1016 12 M. ISA; Al-Tall, *Education in Jordan*, 68.

teachers in Israel were paid half the amount of their Jewish counterparts until 1952, when teachers' protests led to raises, making their salaries equivalent to those of Jewish teachers.[50]

In Jordan, standardizing educators' salaries meant their official depreciation. Through 1966, the relationship between academic qualifications, rank, and salary was not clear-cut. Anecdotally, village teachers in government schools could enjoy a social status equivalent to that of storekeepers and craftsmen: better than most farmers but below landowners and those who had held higher government posts.[51] However, teachers were often paid irregularly or not at all, particularly if villagers were responsible for educators' salaries. For example, in 1954 the principal of a village school near Irbid wrote to a local official noting that the villagers had not paid the salary of a supernumerary teacher. He urged the official, "for the sake of educational progress," to send the district's tax collector to collect the required amount from the villagers. He also complained that the villagers "had been warned on several occasions, and that they had, until now, done nothing they were ordered to do."[52] In 1959 a village in Hebron requested government funds as various issues that year, including a drought, made residents unable to pay their taxes or the salaries of their teachers.[53] In 1966 a new civil service regulation was implemented, stipulating that teachers were to have the same qualifications and salary scale as civil servants.[54] While teachers' salaries officially increased, the cost of living increased still more. The procedure for recruiting teachers resulted in an increase in nepotism, while the new abundance of teachers precluded promotion because of a lack of room in upper ranks.[55]

The Iraqi government had more resources at its disposal than Jordan did and therefore paid its teachers more. As in Jordan, however, wages did not keep up with the cost of living. From 1931 through 1951, teachers' salaries

50. Al-Haj, Education, Empowerment, and Control, 162.

51. A village teacher in 1960 could expect a salary between 180 to 300 dinars per year. Lutfiyya, Baytin, a Jordanian Village, 32–33.

52. Letter from the principal of the Samu'a school to the Qa'im Maqam of the area of al-Koura: Teachers' salary October 13, 1954, 79/7/10/22, NLJ.

53. Petition from the mukhtars of the people and dignitaries of the village of Sa'ir. July 2, 1959, 165/1/5/37, NLJ.

54. In Ahmad al-Tall's work on education in Jordan, a discussion of rules for teachers' salaries between 1950 and 1966 is conspicuously absent. Al-Tall, Education in Jordan, 68, 207–9.

55. Al-Tall, 207–12.

equaled those of other civil servants with the same level of education.[56] However, by 1953, after the Teaching Service Law of 1951, teachers' salaries were no longer commensurate with those of similar qualifications in other branches of the civil service, although teachers' salaries were still technically on the same scale.[57] Moreover, civil servants' salaries had increased 125 percent at lower levels since 1939; at higher levels the increase was 25 percent between 1939 and 1956. In contrast, the cost of living in Iraq increased by 400 percent during the same period.[58]

The depreciation in the real value of teachers' salaries had political as well as economic ramifications. To deal with their reduced economic circumstances, teachers began to take on extra lessons outside of class time, often to help well-off students pass their exams.[59] Teachers and other civil servants participated more and more in mass protests, particularly as part of the Iraqi Communist Party. Its calls for social justice resonated with the former middling-class educators. Hanna Batatu, in tracing the origins of Iraq's Communist Party, underscores, perhaps too simplistically, the attraction of communism as an ideology to teachers due to these economic shifts. When teachers' salaries declined relative to inflation after World War II, their numbers increased, and they experienced a drop in both purchasing power and status. Batatu asserts that in this situation of relative decline it "was natural enough under the circumstances that the teachers, the most socially conscious of the adversely affected classes and the poorest and neediest of the Iraqi intelligentsia, should come to be estranged from the prevailing order, and to seek in other protest movements a way of escape from the hardships that afflicted them."[60] Whether social decline naturally leans toward communism is debatable. However, the point that teachers were rapidly becoming alienated from their government and seeking collective movements (and collective

56. In Iraq, the salaries for government posts were revised in 1942. Teachers had been paid approximately 298 pounds per year before this revision. Kadhim, "A Plan for the Reconstruction of Teacher Education in Iraq," 62.

57. Majid, "Guides for the Improvement of Teacher Education in Iraq," 184; "The New Teaching Service Law of 1951," *Iraq Government Gazette*, no 2, January 11, 1953 19. LLMC Digital Law Library Microform Consortium; Samiuddin, *Administrative Development in the Arab World*, 42.

58. F. R. C. Bagley, "Iraq to-Day," *International Journal* (Summer 1957): 202.

59. Khalid Kishtainy, interview with author, December 12, 2011, London.

60. Batatu, *The Old Social Classes*, 646–47.

bargaining) indicates the erosion of their previous status vis-à-vis their societies and governments.

Across Iraq and Jordan and for Palestinians, declining salaries, coupled with educators' increasing numbers, removed government teachers and administrators from the elite class to which they had formerly belonged and brought them into new forms of conflict with their governments. For teachers, then, state investment in education coupled improved qualifications with deteriorating working conditions and the erasure of the elite status a high school or bachelor's degree had guaranteed. Increased state capacity included greater ability and interest in promoting loyalty to government and territory while eradicating dissent.

Standardization: Redefining the Teacher

Over time and with growing independence from British rule, teaching became increasingly defined and restrictive. During the 1940s and 1950s, when education became more widespread and more standardized, teachers found themselves less able to adapt their posts to their needs. Instead, their governments increasingly circumscribed educators' activities, prospects, and politics within national rather than transnational borders. Teachers were required to adhere to the rules, no longer able to negotiate and circumvent regulations. Governments also sought to replace foreign teachers with national ones. While this meant improved standards of schooling and solidified connections between each state and the idea of the nation promoted within its borders, it defined teachers as a specialized, professional, lower-status group.

With the advent of independence, Iraq, Jordan, and Israel attempted to render government schooling a nationally bounded institution. In May 1957 Iraq's still British-supported monarchy sought to purge the country of Egyptian educators. The *Baltimore Sun* enthusiastically reported this as a means of combating communism. It may have been Nasser's bid for a non-Western-aligned pan-Arabism and—more pointedly—the overthrow of Egypt's British-supported monarchy, however, that caused the Hashemite regime in Iraq to move away from Egyptian influence, including in education. Twenty-five Egyptian teachers were dismissed, "charged with having helped incite student riots" in response to the Suez crisis. As a high-ranking Iraqi official noted, the numbers of imported Egyptian teachers were being cut as the government sought to become more self-sufficient. Further, the official pointed out, although it was necessary to retain Egyptians in Iraq's Colleges, the fact that these institutions were only in Baghdad would allow the Egyptians to be "watched carefully." As the article adds, "It would have been more difficult to maintain surveillance of high schools which are scattered over the country."[61] Egyptian educators were to be grudgingly permitted to stay, while being surveilled for signs of Nasserist pan-Arab activity.

During the final years of Iraq's Hashemite dynasty, there was a pointed effort on the part of the government to make its education system more Iraqi and (it was hoped) less disruptive. By 1960, although expanding primary education was straining the number of teachers relative to schools, the government considered having high school graduates teach, rather than importing foreign instructors.[62] Officially, all teachers needed Iraqi citizenship.[63] By the early 1980s, the refusal to import state personnel was reversed as Iraqis were forbidden to travel outside the country except on government-sanctioned endeavors.[64]

Israel and Jordan likewise, albeit for different reasons, took steps to avoid the movement of teachers from one country to another. In Israel, a lack of peace with Arab countries, the desire to save money on Arab schooling, and the goal of restricting the number of Arabs in the country overall precluded the possibility of importing foreign educators. In Jordan, the government fought to keep its qualified teachers as they sought better pay in the Gulf.[65] With the influx of educated Palestinians and the creation of the University of Jordan, hiring foreigners became less financially sound and less appealing due to the divides between Arabic speakers of one stripe or another.

61. Philip Potter, "Iraq Expelling Egyptian Teachers, Recalls Students," *Baltimore Sun*, May 15, 1957.

62. "American Embassy Baghdad to the Department of State Washington. Subject: Developments in the field of Iraqi education," March 1, 1960, Folder 003120-011-0067, United States Intelligence and the Middle East, http://primarysources.brillonline.com.ezp-prod1.hul.harvard.edu/browse/us-intelligence-on-the-middle-east, accessed February 16, 2020.

63. Doori, "The Administration of Education in Iraq," 45.

64. Yousif, *Human Development in Iraq*, 162.

65. Abdul-Hadi, "The Place of the Urban Teacher in Modern Jordanian Society," 156–57. Displaced Palestinians in particular traveled to staff the rapidly expanding education systems of Algeria and the Gulf countries. In Algeria, there were about fourteen Palestinian teachers during the first years of the Fatah organization. Within two years, the number of Palestinian teachers increased to four hundred, and later up to a thousand, due to the efforts of Khalil al-Wazir to increase Fatah's strength in Algeria. Shemesh, *The Palestinian National Revival*, 138–39.

Beyond rendering teaching a national profession, the governments of Iraq, Jordan, and Israel sought to homogenize educators' credentials and classroom activities. A key mechanism for judging teachers' performance, determining their level of professionalization, and, for our purposes, illustrating the changes in teachers' status was inspection. Inspectors' reports on teachers' activities and their professional and, at times, their personal lives clearly connected government regimes with educators. These reports formed the basis of teachers' promotions within each education system, showing both ideal standards and how much teachers could get away with relative to those ideals. When the format of these reports, their content, and inspectors' qualifications became standardized, they redefined the teaching profession, reducing its flexibility and prestige. Strengthening states used inspection to enforce national as well as pedagogical ideals, in the process changing teachers from relatively independent and variable actors to the more interchangeable bureaucrats of modern governments.

Inspections featured prominently in education policy from the first years of British control. During these visits, government inspectors would arrive, generally unannounced, unless the teacher or principal subject to inspection was lucky enough to know the inspector personally. Inspectors would watch the teacher in action, rate their performance, and observe the dress, comportment, cleanliness, and health of the students. Their reports would later appear in the personnel files of teachers in Palestine and Jordan, and likely Iraq.[66] Adverse reports could result in teachers being transferred or occasionally dismissed, based on interactions the inspectors observed between teachers and principals or students. In Palestine and Transjordan/Jordan, a poor inspector's report could also lead to withholding a teacher's annual raise.

Through the 1940s, inspectors' reports could be arbitrary but were generally diverse, unsystematic, and personal.[67] Inspectors' qualifications varied. Their ties to teachers, families, villages, and politics were strongly in evidence in their reports.[68] For example, an inspector's report in 1924 on one teacher, Khalaf Sabbagh, in a village near Nazareth complained of his lack of use of the blackboard and described the teacher as "a man of age. Looks delicate. Constantly coughing and suffers from chronic asthma. He has a good knowledge of Arabic but it is extremely difficult for him to teach. I consider that he is not worth

66. Teachers' personnel files for Iraqi teachers are unavailable.
67. "Press Supplement, Intelligence Report, December 1, 1921," IOR/420/A/1237, BL.
68. Tibawi, *Arab Education in Mandatory Palestine*, 31.

keeping at all owing to his state of health and advanced age. A good candidate who should know sufficient English may be appointed to replace him."[69] The inspector cited village politics, described Sabbagh in intimate detail, and made recommendations based on Sabbagh as an individual rather than according to professional standards. As we have also seen with Bahiya Farah and Judah Docmac, inspectors—and through them the mandate governments—became minutely and personally involved in teachers' personal lives and families.

During the 1940s and the 1950s, the procedure of inspections became standardized, streamlined, and tightly controlled. Inspectors possessed advanced qualifications, and nearly all had worked as teachers.[70] In Transjordan and especially Iraq, inspectors changed from elite generalists with broad, ill-defined powers, to trained specialists, inspecting particular subjects, schools, and students.[71] For these individuals, and for the teachers they evaluated, inspection functioned not only as a key regulatory mechanism of the education system, but also as a way of defining and restricting the profession of teaching as a whole. Inspectors enforced adherence to the syllabus and modern pedagogical methods and sought to weed out those teachers they deemed "not of the type to be retained in the service."[72] Consolidated bureaucracies demanded a new role for educators: one of compliance with national ideals that subordinated their idiosyncrasies and personal desires to the dictates of their profession, and of their governments.

As Iraq's inspectorate became more specialized and bureaucratic, criticisms of its "rigidity," particularly on the part of American or of American-educated Iraqi observers, became increasingly strident. Formerly wide political

69. "Khalaf Sabbagh," June 26, 1924; "Petition from the Muslim and Christian Villagers of Maslul," September 8, 1924; "Khalaf Sabbagh," 1017 10 M, ISA.

70. Many inspectors shared similar qualifications, usually a degree from either a teachers college in Iraq or the American University of Beirut. See, for example, Ibrahim Ismail, *Iraq Government Gazette*, no. 49, December 3, 1939, CO 813/12. NA. Similarly, Hasan Jawad had graduated from AUB. Khalil Salem, another inspector, also had a B.A. degree. *Al-Kulliyah* 28, no. 5 (May 1953): 3. By 1958 in Iraq, all inspectors had to have a post–high school diploma and experience in education. Iraq Legal Database, "Nizam Wizarat Al-Maʿarif" [The regulation of the Ministry of Education]," no. 29, July 7, 1958; United Nations Development Programme, https://iraqld.hjc.iq/LoadLawBook.aspx?SC=120120016618718.

71. Matthews and Akrawi, "Education in the Arab Countries of the Near East," 126–27; Yasin, "Education for All Iraqi Youth," 50; Government of Jordan, *Al-Taqrir al-Sanawi 1953–1954— Wizarat Al-Tarbiyya wa-al-Taʿlim.*

72. For example, "Sadi Muhammad Shihadeh," 1019 15 M, ISA; "Abdullah Faraj Hunin," 1016 10 M, ISA; "Ahmad Shaʿban ʿAidi," 1014 2 M, ISA; "Abd el Ghani Sharaf," 1016 11 M, ISA.

divisions between nationalist and academic schooling, as opposed to practical and psychologically oriented pedagogy, would narrow along with teachers' depleting freedoms within the classroom. Sati al-Husri, the sometime head of Iraq's education system in the 1920s and early 1930s, had viewed inspection as a tool for streamlining and expanding schooling. He promoted an academic curriculum while unifying Iraq under the banner of Arab nationalism and maintaining adherence to a pan-Arab ideology.[73] His antagonists included American and American-educated educationalists (most prominently Fadhil al-Jamali) who censured the inspectorate for holding teachers to standards that supposedly stifled their creativity.[74]

These educationalists argued that the growing rigidity of the curricula and strictness of inspection over time reduced teachers' ability to teach beyond the prescribed syllabus and to shirk their duties for political and/or personal gain. It also meant, however, a more direct correspondence between the state's prescriptions and its teachers' actions. Matta Akrawi wrote in his Teachers College dissertation in 1942 that "blame must be put for the rigid application of the course at the doors of the inspectors. These seem to have misunderstood the course of study just as much as the teachers, and have usually insisted on a strict application." Akrawi contended that fear of inspectors caused teachers to adhere blindly to the syllabus.[75] A few years later, another Teachers College graduate lambasted inspectors' unending focus on the syllabus and "whether the class is controlled by the teacher and is perfectly quiet," as well as their ability to report any teacher whose students failed to answer questions correctly as "inefficient." She asserted that this situation not only suppressed innovation but also prevented teachers from improving the state of their schools and their own professional lives.[76]

Teachers College Columbia, as Sara Pursley argues, promoted a child-centered curriculum, which would help children develop according to principles of psychology. However, when educators applied this curriculum to

73. Al-Husri, *Mudhakkirati fi al-'Iraq 1921–1941*, 2:206, 210.

74. By the early 1950s, Teachers College graduates tended to reiterate the critiques of their predecessors. For example, in 1953 Hammoudi Abdul Majid cited Paul Monroe's, Matta Akrawi's, and Fadil al-Jamali's earlier complaints about the system of inspection, namely, that inspection was "too rigid," leading to "mechanical and highly formal teaching." Abdul Majid, "Guides for the Improvement of Teacher Education in Iraq," 14.

75. Akrawi, "Curriculum Construction in the Public Primary Schools of Iraq," 206.

76. Khaddouri, "Suggestions for the Improvement of Instruction in the Urban Primary Schools of Iraq," 10–11.

America's lower classes, African American populations, or indeed Iraq's population as a whole, they promoted an ideal of stability, hoping practicality and vocational training would prevent social mobility or political rebellion.[77] Criticisms of inspection as rigid, then, tied into ideals that children should have time to play and to be spontaneous but also should not gain the academic knowledge and training necessary for social mobility or to disrupt the political and economic status quo. Teachers College graduates argued that in Iraq, inspections and exams led teachers and students to prize rote memorization of abstract academic knowledge, precluding the critical thinking that characterized Western democracies. Regardless of the power relations embedded in ideals of American education as liberal and flexible, or Iraqi graduates' idealized (or at least advisor-pleasing) view of American schooling, their consistent criticisms of inspectors point to an increasingly inflexible system that reduced teachers' idiosyncratic interpretations of the syllabus, as well as their ability to criticize their governments.

In 1945 Daoud al-Qasir, one such demonized inspector, wrote back advocating increased standardization and inflexibility. A specialist inspector at the Iraqi Ministry of Education, AUB graduate, and textbook author, al-Qasir published a model of what an Iraqi inspector's report should be.[78] Al-Qasir's take on inspection focused on efficiency and impersonality rather than the more collaborative or creative approach advocated by Teachers College alumni. In contrast to the reports of Palestine and Transjordan, the hypothetical Iraqi report would be a standardized, fill-in-the-blanks form, leaving little space for personal observations or comments on character. Instead, the inspector would answer a series of questions with a letter grade. These questions focused on the state of the school, the teacher, and the lessons, with an eye toward hygiene and modern efficiency. The questions included, "Does the school have enough light, heat and ventilation?" and "Is the necessary school equipment in a suitable state of organization?" The ideal school was to be modern, well-equipped, and hygienic. The inspector would grade the teacher on the degree to which he or she possessed qualities such as tact, self-discipline, determination, enthusiasm, kindness, and a sense of justice. The teacher was

77. Pursley, "Education for Real Life," 96–99.

78. He received his Ph.D. degree from Columbia in mathematics, on a scholarship from the Iraqi government. He graduated with a B.A. degree from AUB in 1916. *Al Kulliyah* 15, no 1 (November 1928): 226. He was appointed inspector in 1944. *Iraq Government Gazette* 45, November 5, 1944, CO 813/9, NA.

also to take into account any students with disabilities, such as those hard of hearing or visually impaired, who might be in the classroom. The lessons were to take place at the appointed times, and students were to ask questions clearly, to be answered, and to complete the necessary work during class.[79] Only at the end did the report give the inspector an opportunity to phrase his observations in his own words, namely, what the best aspects of the school were, and which aspects required the most improvement.

Although there is no indication that this type of report was ever used wholesale in Iraq, it highlights inspectors' concerns: their, and indeed their state's, views of the ideal way to evaluate teachers. The Ministry of Education clearly supported the document's goals to some degree, as it published al-Qasir's report in the official teachers' journal. Moreover, the inspectoral law of 1958, implemented shortly before the revolution, like al-Qasir's idealized report, required inspectors to focus on the physical condition of the school, its hygiene, and that of its students rather than on individual teachers.[80] The fictional report demonstrates an intense desire for efficiency as well as objectivity: rather than completing a detailed, personalized report for each teacher, the inspector just had to check off a few grades. The teacher became less of an individual and more of a professional. The physical aspect of the school was just as important as the conduct of the teacher, even though it was almost assuredly beyond the teacher's control.[81] Connecting the teacher with the state of the school (rather than focusing on individual performance) helped redefine teaching as a profession. Instead of creating a better teacher, these reports sought to fashion a better school. The teacher became a cog in the Iraqi educational machine rather than the standard-bearer of Iraqi advancement. He or she would improve education standards but should not inspire students or go beyond the curriculum.

Likewise, in Palestine, inspectors' reports during the 1940s changed character, considering teachers less as individuals and more as functional parts of a school. The gradual expansion of inspection, a bureaucratic form of

---

79. Daoud al-Qasir, "Dalil al-Mufattish fi Taqrir Kifayat al-Tadris" [The inspector's guide for teaching efficiency], al-Mu'allim al-Jadid 9, no 2 (March 1945): 79–82.

80. Iraq Legal Database, "Nizam Wizarat Al-Ma'arif," 7, 1958.

81. The desire for efficiency may also have been tied to the lack of inspectoral personnel compared to teachers. Oddly, the Ministry of Education reports do not list the number of inspectors. In 1945 there were only two inspectors of English for all levels of education. Hakim, A Critical Assessment of Teaching Materials, 147.

governance, began to delimit teachers' idiosyncrasies and intermediary role. New forms attached teachers' performance to the academic situation of the school, emphasizing their professional connection to education rather than their individual concerns and achievements. Inspectors had always evaluated teachers in Palestine on their character and how they did their jobs. For example, inspectors would comment on teachers' morals, family life, how well they presented class material, how organized their notes were, and how much use they made of the blackboard.[82] In the 1940s, reports expanded to encompass how the school functioned as a whole. These evaluations focused on the "academic state" of the school, assessing all teachers and all subjects in the same document, urging teachers to work for the greater good of the school rather than to improve themselves or their own qualifications. Out of 402 available files of teachers who taught in the 1940s, 104 or approximately 26 percent had adverse reports on the state of the school, urging teachers and principals to "raise the academic standard," and often the health and cleanliness of its students as well. Considering the teacher as part of the school rather than a frequently transferred free agent indicates a gradual professionalization and collectivization of teaching.

In Transjordan/Jordan, even more so than in Palestine and Iraq, inspectors' reports from the 1920s through the 1950s became more regular, but also more cursory. At least on paper, the scant number of inspectors bore a tremendous amount of responsibility for the functioning of the education system as a whole. They would act not only as inspectors but demographers, informing Jordan's government about their growing population. The crushing volume of tasks inspectors were meant to perform gradually contributed to a standardized method of evaluating teachers and schools. In 1925 Transjordan's government gazette published an overview of the education system. The position of inspector required writing reports on numerous topics relating to education, educators, and the system as a whole. Biannually, the inspector had to analyze the entire school system, with an eye to its laws, regulations, and syllabus, and supervise all the schools, focusing on health, discipline, and the competence of each principal and teacher. In addition to inspecting government schools, inspectors had to inspect every private school and give a report regarding new schools. In each report, the inspector had to include the number of inhabitants of each town or village and the number of students attending a school near

82. "Khalaf Sabbagh," 1017 10 M, ISA; "Khalil Suleiman," 1016 15 M, ISA; "Ahmad Subhi Khalifa," 1016 14 M, ISA; "Gertrude Nassar," 1012 18 M, ISA; "Hilda Nassar," 1010 67 M, ISA.

them.[83] While this may indicate the government's interest in using schooling as a means of surveilling and therefore knowing its population, it also points to the limited nature of both schooling and bureaucracy in Transjordan; lacking sufficient personnel to count its inhabitants, the government resorted to its three educational inspectors to perform this duty.

The limited body of inspectors notwithstanding, inspection reports were a key means of observing and even altering teachers' actions while extending the reach of the state to monitoring ever larger proportions of its population. In 1940 the minister of education and later six-time prime minister of Jordan, Samer al-Rifai, wrote to the principals and teachers of Jordan regarding adverse inspectors' reports. Al-Rifai complained of how students were "mechanically" moving their bodies, putting pencils in their mouths while whispering answers to each other, and waggling their index fingers and shouting "I know!" when the inspector asked them a question.[84] Al-Rifai then turned his attention to teachers, noting that many of them taught their students a secret code, including clothes-fiddling, nodding, or thinly veiled hints, in order to help students give the correct answer during an inspection. As these irregularities reached al-Rifai, there may have been adverse consequences for educators; there was a slight surge in teachers being removed from their positions between 1940 and 1942.[85] In addition, after al-Rifai's public admonishment of educators, there were no similar critiques. Inspectors' reports continued in the formulaic way of simply noting the percentage of students who answered questions correctly.

Al-Rifai's criticisms illustrate the shifting nature not only of who teachers were but also who the government expected them to be during the 1940s and 1950s. As the education systems gradually became more standardized, educators found the profession to be a more clearly delineated and limited one. Although the extension of mass education did bring about teachers' professionalization, coupled with the loss of their elite status, this process was by no means linear. Teachers' changing demographics and experiences created a new professional cadre. Enjoying much more limited social and

83. "Nizam al-Mudarris" [The school system], *Al-Jarida al-Rasmiyya*, June 1, 1925, no. 106, 10–11, NLJ.

84. Letter from Minister of Education Samie al-Rifai to school principals, May 8, 1940, Miscellaneous Hamad School, Smakieh, 7/37/8/22, NLJ.

85. Twenty-seven teachers were removed, in contrast to the fifteen fired between 1938 and 1940 and the fourteen removed between 1942 and 1944, HRD.

political opportunities than its predecessor, this cadre was also less well-traveled, changing the nature of teachers' engagement with their nations and states.

Unionization and Repression

As teachers became more and more dissatisfied with their relationships to their governments, they sought means of increasing their leverage as a collective. They joined teachers' unions, as well as better-organized and increasingly rebellious political parties. Government policies that marginalized teachers and eroded their privileges contributed to the growth of political unrest. However, the expanded capacity of Iraq's, Jordan's, and Israel's governments, as well as those across the Arab world in which Palestinians lived and worked, checked educators' ability to advance their agendas, as individuals or as union and party members.

Iraq's teachers' union was founded in the mid-1940s. A "semigovernment association," it worked to promote teachers' interests in a variety of ways. In addition to bringing teachers together and advancing their concerns to their government, it also offered financial incentives to members (such as helping them purchase new houses) and, in keeping with its close relationship to the Iraqi government, helped draft a law meant to improve the status of the teaching profession.[86] As early as 1944, female teachers were inducted into the Iraqi teachers' society, open to male and female teachers from any school, government or private.[87] For example, in 1946 'Izzat al-Istarbadi, an activist who had earned her MA degree at Teachers College, Columbia University, intellectual, and lecturer at Queen Aliya College during the 1950s, was appointed to be the assistant secretary.[88] By the end of the 1950s, the association had become Iraq's largest vocational organization, pointing to both its importance and the swelling numbers of teachers in Iraq.[89]

In the absence of democratic elections, or indeed the ability of Iraq's population to participate in legally sanctioned formal political activity, the teachers' union and its leadership became an alternative political site. The Communist

---

86. UNESCO International Yearbook of Education, 1948, 196; Iraq, Education in Iraq, 17.

87. Al-Mu'allim al-Jadid 10 (May 1946): 187.

88. "Queen Aliya, Prospectus, 1953–4," 10; "Barid al-Majalat: al-Hayat al-Idariyya al-Jadida li-Jami'yat al-Mua'llimin" [Post of the new teacher: The new administrative life of the teachers association]," al-Mu'allim al-Jadid 10 (1946): 178.

89. Batatu, The Old Social Classes, 950.

Party, Iraq's best-organized political party, held the loyalty of a majority of the association's voting members and control over its leadership. Students, and teachers to a lesser degree, formed a key segment of the Communist Party and its public front, the National Liberation Party.[90]

Peter and Marion Farouk Sluglett have argued that the Communist Party was forced to "operate and organize a political party along lines that could only work properly in a functioning democratic system. In the absence of such a system, in which a party could test its own popularity in elections, it either had to go underground, or work within the existing system and try to obtain power by force, or accommodate itself to the political realities."[91] The political parties working around and within the constraints of Iraq's political system did use the methods the Slugletts describe, namely, union elections, street demonstrations, and secret political cells, in order to change Iraqi politics overall. The teachers' union, which allowed elections, was one means for the Communist Party to "test"—or rather demonstrate—its popularity, to try to convince the government to adopt its platforms.

In January 1948 students, civil servants, workers, and Communists poured into the streets of Baghdad. Driving the uprising were the country's increasingly dire economic conditions, as well as leaked news that the Iraqi government planned to preserve the British hegemony written into the 1930 Anglo-Iraqi Treaty in the slightly edited Portsmouth Treaty of 1948. Deaths of demonstrators at the hands of the government escalated the protests, causing top government officials not only to resign but to flee Baghdad. Protesters demanded bread, land reform, social justice, and free elections, calling their rebellion the *Wathba* or leap.[92] However, after brutal suppression, martial law, censorship, and hanging of Communist leaders, the near-revolution was ended by the close of the year.

Orit Bashkin has argued that, building from the *Wathba*, the state's capacity to regulate educators, particularly Communist ones, and their strengthening ties to students began to lessen.[93] As she stresses, the expansion of schooling to nonelites meant more politically radical educators, connecting the teaching profession to more antigovernment politics. Even as the state's policies

90. Thompson, "The 1948 Wathba Revisited," 133–34.
91. Farouk-Sluglett and Sluglett, *Iraq since 1958*, 75.
92. Batatu, *The Old Social Classes*, 552–53.
93. Bashkin, "To Educate an Iraqi-Jew," 175–76.

frustrated and radicalized teachers, however, the state itself strengthened, as did its ability to control educators and its population as a whole.

By the revolution of 1958, which intensified the push toward mass education in Iraq, the government restricted teachers' political activities, including the ability of the teachers' union either to act independently of the government or to promote alternative political agendas. In the wake of Qasim's military coup and the destruction of the monarchy, there was a brief, chaotic window in which political parties were permitted to function, albeit without official sanction. Anti-imperialism had united Iraq's clandestine opposition parties, including the Communist Party, against the Hashemite regime. The teachers' association elections of 1959 were overwhelmingly supportive of Communist candidates. Over 80 percent of the 11,488 voting delegates supported the "pro-Communist list." By 1961 the elections indicated a more restricted political climate and, by 1962 less than 30 percent of teachers' association delegates supported Communists. Although this likely points in part to Iraq's narrowing political sphere, the state's crackdown on teachers represented a general trend toward repression of the formerly powerful Communist Party. Moreover, teachers' ability to advocate multiple political positions publicly and comfortably within state employ had ended.[94]

In 1963, during the final months of Qasim's rule, a new law was promulgated in order to regulate the teachers' union. The law removed the union's revolutionary capacity, rendering it a government-controlled rather than antigovernment organization. The reimagined teachers' association was designed to increase the connections between state and citizens while forbidding those citizens power over the state. Teachers were not permitted to form any other organizations, restricting their political activities further. The second article of the law, after the establishment of the Iraqi (and Kurdish) teachers' unions, asserted that its primary objectives were "to support the Iraqi Republic as part of the Arab nation and to defend it by all means and in all possible fields, especially in the field of education." It added that this association must fight "trends and ideas that contradict the republican system in Iraq." Rather than supporting teachers and making their wishes known to the government as the teachers' association of the 1940s had sought to do, the teachers' union of the 1960s was designed to back the government and its ideology. A further goal of the union was to "work to raise the social and financial status of the teacher, and to help them to achieve a better life and social prestige." The need for an

94. Batatu, *The Old Social Classes*, 950–53.

organization to improve teachers' lives and explicitly their "social prestige" affirms that they no longer possessed it.[95]

Over time, teachers also experienced drastic changes in their professional lives due to Iraq's changing politics. For example, an Iraqi teacher, Dalal, a Communist in the teachers' union during the 1970s, recalled, "When I said I was in the teachers' union, I was approached by a colleague who said all teachers are required to attend a speech directly coming from the Ba'ath party every Thursday. All teachers should deliver the content of the speech to all their students even if they are not members of the Ba'ath Party. I refused and went to the head of the teachers' union. He said: 'I might be able to accept your refusal now, but within one year all teachers should be Ba'athi.'" The government clearly took an increasing interest in the activities and views of its teachers, requiring a strict party affiliation and constant practicing of a particular notion of nationalism. Dalal had to flee Iraq within the year.[96]

In contrast, Jordan's teachers' union began precisely as the separation between government education and governance occurred. When education became part of Jordan's state- and nation-building project, it lost its automatic connection to the civil service. Bereft of the potential to become officials, teachers were no longer able to negotiate with their government as part of that government. Instead, they joined ranks, lobbying as a collective. During the early 1950s the government of Jordan generated new positions in the civil service and government bureaucracy while attempting to open vocational schools and to restrict the number of secondary school graduates overall.[97] The goal of these measures was to combat the potential unemployment of secondary school graduates, particularly as college and university opportunities were limited. Until the late 1950s the government was able to provide jobs for all secondary school graduates in the country.[98] The increase in the number of graduates beyond the capacity of the government to employ them broke apart the connections between government schooling and government

95. "Qanun Niqabat al-Mu'allimin" [Teachers' Syndicate Regulation], no. 59 (1963), http://wiki.dorar-aliraq.net/iraqilaws/law/1502.html, accessed August 19, 2018.

96. Ali, *Iraqi Women*, 119.

97. Jordan had five vocational schools by 1959. Wizarat al-Tarbiyya wa-al-Ta'lim Jordan, *Al-Taqrir al-Sanawi—Wizarat Al-Tarbiyya Wa-al-Ta'lim* [The annual report of the Department of Education] 1958–9, 225.

98. Al-Tall, *Education in Jordan*, 139, 106.

employment, as these individuals had to find work either in the private sector or outside of Jordan.

Jordan's teachers found their union to be an easy target for government surveillance and repression, singled out even more than their counterparts in trade unions. The first incarnation of the teachers' union was part of Jordan's liberal experiment. In 1956, after the union was formed, nearly five thousand teachers went on strike, seeking higher pay.[99] This brief opening up of the political arena, including the freedom for Jordanian teachers to band together and demand change from the regime, ended in 1957, along with trade unions and political parties.[100] While other unions were permitted to reconstitute shortly after the ban, the teachers' union was not, despite repeated calls to do so. The rationale for preventing the union was explicitly political: it had been accused of seeking the destruction of the state. A number of teachers were later imprisoned when they attempted to create a preparatory committee to found a union in 1975. As in Iraq, the union of teachers was viewed as inherently volatile by the government, which employed these teachers as civil servants. The Jordanian teachers' union would not be allowed to form again until 2012.[101]

Israel's teachers' union functioned differently for its Jewish and Arab members; the union Palestinians experienced was more a tool of the Israeli state than a means of bargaining with it. For Jewish Israelis, the teachers' union had a relatively long, storied, and generally Zionist history. Founded in the early twentieth century, the teachers' association had translated textbooks into Hebrew, helped standardize curriculums, held conferences, and offered certification as well as exams.[102] During the mandate for Palestine, the teachers' union represented a means of organizing for ideological reasons (advocating and promoting the Hebrew language) as well as practical ones (organizing strikes for better pay and better working conditions). The first strike undertaken by the teachers' union occurred in 1925. For their part, Arab Palestinians had sought to form a teachers' union in 1937. Despite teachers' assertions that "they were only interested in professional problems, not in politics," founding an

99. Rugh, "Issues and Trends in Arab Teacher Education," 322; "Jordanian Teachers Strike," *New York Times*, April 10, 1956.

100. "Jordan Unions Banned; More Reds Rounded Up," *Washington Post*, May 2, 1957, 1.

101. Jordanian Teachers Syndicate, "al-Sira al-Tarikhiyya lil-Niqaba" [The biography of the syndicate], 2021, https://www.jts.org.jo/.

102. Halpern and Reinharz, *Zionism and the Creation of a New Society*, 114–15.

association in the midst of the Great Revolt was a nonstarter for the British director of education, who refused to permit the union's establishment.[103]

When Israel became a state, the General Teachers Union, and by the early 1960s a somewhat separate and antagonistic Secondary Teachers Association, carried on traditions of collective bargaining, as well as strikes, for teachers' wages and working conditions, and to adjust education policies.[104] Palestinian teachers within Israel, however, were given a distinct division within the teachers' union and were not permitted to elect the head of this division, who was, in all cases, Jewish.[105] While the union of teachers itself functioned as an advocate for educators, Arab teachers were not permitted to use the organization as a political platform. The Arab branch of the union couched its demands in practical and humane terms. These demands also indicate the reduced status teachers faced in the early 1950s. They requested a family supplement, a supplement for principals, and permission for their children to study at high schools, noting that only 50 percent of applicants were accepted.[106]

Within Israel, the secret service (Shabak or Shin Bet) was, since the beginning of the state, involved in the appointments and dismissals of Arab teachers and principals. Officially, various administrative bodies, namely, the military government, the Education Ministry's Arab section, as well as the Council on Arab Education, were responsible for Arab education within Israel. The leaders of all these organizations were Jewish. While in internal correspondence Palestinian Arab citizens of Israel were disqualified from leadership positions because they had not "taught in Hebrew schools," this seems fairly insincere.[107] Unofficially, the Shabak also had a heavy hand in Arab schooling. There was always a representative of the Shabak in the Ministry of Education. A series of documents released in 2018 revealed the Shabak's interference in Arab education in Israel during the 1970s. These documents explicitly show that teachers were being dismissed for voicing political opinions against the Israeli state, or even having relatives who did so. As one Arab professor in Haifa described,

103. Tibawi, *Arab Education in Mandatory Palestine*, 70.

104. Medding, *Mapai in Israel*, 211.

105. Mar'i, *Arab Education in Israel*, 55.

106. Eviezer Yellin, Letter from Dr. Ben Yehuda, manager of the Department of Education and Culture, February 13, 1951, "Irgun ha-Morim ha-Melamdim be Beti Sefer Aravim" [The organization of teachers in the Arab schools], GAL 1631/7 ISA.

107. Dr. B. Ben Yehuda, manager of the Department of Education, letter regarding a vacant position for an inspector of Arab schools, May 25, 1950, "Ha-hinukh ha-Aravi" [Arab education], 789/6-G, ISA.

there was an atmosphere of fear and snitching at the time. Everyone was afraid someone would snitch on them, and if someone snitched on you, you didn't get an appointment, you didn't get a job. People suspected each other and were afraid to open their mouths in public. I kept hearing the saying "walls have ears." . . . A lot of slots in the education system, Arabs' niches, were filled with pathetic rather than dignified figures. They chose their own people.[108]

In Jordan, the crackdown on popular protests targeted teachers and schools specifically: Amman's schools were closed, as a punitive measure, to discourage teachers and students from gathering or demonstrating in the wake of the government reshuffle of 1957.[109] Defense Minister and Military Governor Suleiman Toukan stated that Amman's secondary schools would not be reopened "until their staffs give satisfactory proof that they have purged themselves of disloyal elements: "Juvenile communists guilty of nothing but schoolboy effervescence can escape punishment by public renunciation of subversive doctrines but no quarter will be given to adult Communists who carried out indoctrination in the schools."[110] In June 1957 a further seven teachers were arrested, accused of trying to topple the government.[111] From the 1950s, then, Jordanian, Palestinian, and Iraqi teachers bore the brunt of mass education and mass politics. Participating in and often leading the region's political parties, they also were subject to increasingly repressive measures on the part of their governments.

———

In 1957 Muhammad Yasin Abdullah, a teacher in the Iraqi city of Tal Afar, 75 kilometers west of Mosul, wrote in to a special section of *al-Mu'allim al-Jadid* (The new teacher), composed solely of teachers' letters. Since its first issue, teachers, scholars, and administrators from across the region had contributed articles to the journal, underscoring their expertise and erudition. Here, however, Abdullah humbly asked his government whether teachers had the "right"

108. Ramzi Suleiman, quoted in Guy Lieberman and Lior Eilati, "The Shin Bet's Secret Activity in Israel's Arab Achools," *Yedioth Ahronoth*, January 1, 2018, https://www.ynetnews.com/articles/0,7340,L-5071236,00.html.

109. "Jordan Cutting Meat Intake to Tighten Belt," *Chicago Daily Tribune*, May 5, 1957.

110. Robert C. Doty, "More Extremists Seized in Jordan," *New York Times*, May 10, 1957.

111. "Jordan Seizes 8 in Plot." *New York Times*, June 27, 1957.

to contribute to the annual reports that determined teachers' yearly bonus, and if principals' opinions, on which the reports were based, could be proved by "official evidence." In a language of competence, fairness, rules, and bureaucracy, Abdullah requested greater power for teachers over their promotions. Rather than negotiate privately with either his principal or his government, Abdullah resorted to making his concern general and public. The response of *al-Mu'allim al-Jadid* reinforced teachers' low status within the Ministry of Education's hierarchy. Teachers would receive their yearly bonus according to the opinion of their principal, which would be reviewed by the principal's immediate superior, and so on. This opinion was to be based on a variety of the teacher's qualities, from the "strength of his character" to "the extent of his ability to benefit the students and his keenness to observe the rules," his ability to work with his colleagues and "his conduct inside the school and out." Teachers had, in this situation, no right to request a reconsideration of their principal's judgment.[112]Abdullah as an individual had little recourse; his conduct was to be severely scrutinized. He was locked into a self-checking and self-perpetuating bureaucracy. Even his demands were couched in bureaucratic and professional language. Abdullah was subject to a powerful, hierarchical, and well-defined state.

For teachers like Abdullah, the transition from limited and colonial to mass and national education meant more than increased government attention and funds granted to schooling. It also reduced educators' social and economic status, as well as their power to negotiate with and participate in the governments that employed them. The dissolution of Britain's Middle Eastern mandates marked a transition toward more extensive, and more regulated, education. Independence from colonialism meant drastic expansions in educational facilities, students, and personnel. The weaker colonial states of the mandate era, and their lack of interest in schooling, had left teachers with a relatively free hand and a relatively close relationship to their governments. With independence, teachers became less powerful as individuals, forcing them to leverage their rising numbers rather than their elite standing. For Iraqis, Jordanians, and Palestinians, the profession lost its stature without becoming feminized.

As the profession of teacher became more clearly and exclusively defined, so did the postmandate governments themselves. The flexible nature of educators' employment paralleled the more nebulous nature of nationalism: both

---

112. "Barid al-Mu'allim al-Jadid" [Post of the new teacher], *Al-Mu'allim al-Jadid*, no. 4 (September 1957): 173.

were a result of colonial government policies. By the time strengthened states locked teachers into a more limited, degraded profession, these states also more stringently policed their ideological, political, and territorial boundaries. The standardized bureaucracies that educators had helped to grow during the interwar era swelled to fit the borders teachers had formerly crossed. The more powerful governments of Iraq, Israel, and Jordan reduced teachers' role in shaping nationalism, even as they incorporated them more tightly into nation-states. Moreover, the downgrading of educators' political and economic status that took place with the expansion of schooling became permanent.

Epilogue

IN SEPTEMBER and October of 2019, tens of thousands of public school teachers went on strike. In Jordan, eighty thousand teachers, led by the Jordanian teachers' union, demanded pay raises, arguing that their salaries could not keep up with basic living costs. They told reporters that even though it was illegal to take on other work while teaching in government schools, many of them drove taxis or waited tables to survive. Teachers criticized the government for its harsh measures in suppressing earlier protests, as photographs of riot police attacking teachers amid clouds of tear gas went viral.[1] A little over a year later, the teachers' union was dissolved and its board imprisoned, supposedly for inciting "hatred and causing riots."[2] To Jordan's northeast, Iraqi teachers likewise went on strike, following the orders of their union and in solidarity with demonstrations against government corruption. In Baghdad and the South, all schools were closed between October 28 and November 7, 2019. After the Iraqi Army threatened to detain school administrators, schools reopened, but teachers continued to join their students in protests after class. Hundreds of protesters have been killed.[3] In the West Bank, the

1. Andrew Chappelle, "Jordan Teachers Strike: One Million Pupils Stay Home," *al-Jazeera*, September 16, 2019, https://www.aljazeera.com/news/2019/09/jordan-teachers-strike-million-pupils-stay-home-190916175221540.html.

2. Dana Gabriel, "Istimrar Azmat Niqabat al-Muʿallimin: Hal al-Niqaba wa-Manʿ al-Iʿtisamat amam al-Nuwwab" [The continuing crisis of the teachers' union: Dissolving the union and preventing sit-ins in front of (the house of) representatives], January 14, 2021, 7iber.com, https://www.7iber.com/politics-economics/%d8%ad%d9%84-%d9%86%d9%82%d8%a7%d8%a8%d8%a9-%d8%a7%d9%84%d9%85%d8%b9%d9%84%d9%85%d9%8a%d9%86-%d9%88%d9%85%d9%86%d8%b9-%d8%a7%d9%84%d8%a7%d8%b9%d8%aa%d8%b5%d8%a7%d9%85%d8%a7%d8%aa/.

3. Dima Abumaria, "Iraqi Teachers Union Stands with Protestors," *Media Line*, November 3, 2019, https://themedialine.org/by-region/iraqi-teachers-union-stands-with-protesters/.

FIGURE E.1. "Min I'tisam al-Mu'allimin fi 'Amman" (From the teachers' sit-in in Amman).
Photo by Khalil Mazrawi, APF, September 5, 2019. (Reproduced by permission from
Mohammed Gobari, "li-Madha yu'tasam Mu'allimu wa-Mu'allimat al-Urdun" [Why do the
male and female teachers of Jordan strike], *7iber*, September 5, 2019.)

Palestinian Teachers' Union called for strikes throughout 2020, demanding
that their salaries be paid.[4]

The sight of amassing Jordanian, Iraqi, and Palestinian public school teachers storming from their classrooms and streaming into the streets to protest a
variety of issues has become a regular occurrence in the twenty-first century.

4. Basil Mughrabi, "Ittihad al-Mu'allimin al-Filastiniyyin yu'linu al-Idrab Ihtijajan 'ala
siyasat sarf al-rawatib" [The Palestinian Teachers' Union declares a strike to protest the salary
payment policy], *Arab 48*, December 2, 2020, https://www.arab48.com/%D9%81%D9%84%D8
%B3%D8%B7%D9%8A%D9%86%D9%8A%D8%A7%D8%AA/%D8%A3%D8%AE%
D8%A8%D8%A7%D8%B1/2020/12/02/%D8%A7%D8%AA%D8%AD%D8%A7%D8%AF-%
D8%A7%D9%84%D9%85%D8%B9%D9%84%D9%85%D9%8A%D9%86-%D8%A7%D9%84
%D9%81%D9%84%D8%B3%D8%B7%D9%8A%D9%86%D9%8A%D9%8A%D9%86
-%D9%8A%D8%B9%D9%84%D9%86-%D8%A7%D9%84%D8%A5%D8%B6%D8%B1%D8%
A7%D8%A8-%D8%A7%D8%AD%D8%AA%D8%AC%D8%A7%D8%AC%D8%A7
-%D8%B9%D9%84%D9%89-%D8%B3%D9%8A%D8%A7%D8%B3%D8%A9-%D8
%B5%D8%B1%D9%81-%D8%A7%D9%84%D8%B1%D9%88%D8%A7%D8%AA%D8%A8.

FIGURE E.2. Banner reading "Haybat al-Muʾallim min Haybat al-Watan. Uʾidu lil-Muaʾllim Karamatahu" (The prestige of the teacher is part of the prestige of the nation. Give the teacher back his dignity), Jordan, 2011. (Reprinted from "Idrab al-Muʾallimin yashal Muʾazm Mudarris al-Mamlika, wa yudakhil bi-Quwwa ila Amman wa-Irbid wa-al-Zarqa" [Teachers strike includes most of the schools of the kingdom and enters with force into Amman, Irbid, and Zarqa], Kol al-Urdun, March 20, 2011.)

Teachers have demanded better evaluations of their performance, higher salaries and back wages, reshuffled cabinets, and even a new political landscape.[5] They have framed their protests using the term "dignity,"[6] thereby underscoring their degenerating economic status, their frustration, and what they

5. Lailah Azzeh, "Teachers Take to the Streets to Voice Demands," *Jordan Times*, May 29, 2014, http://www.jordantimes.com/news/local/teachers-take-street-voice-demands; Rana Hussein, "75,000 Public School Teachers Stage Partial Strike," *Jordan Times*, April 27, 2018, http://jordantimes.com/news/local/75-000-public-school-teachers-stage-partial-strike %E2%80%99; Diaa Hadid and Rami Nazzal, "Strike by West Bank Teachers Gains Momentum, Challenging Government," *New York Times*, March 7, 2016.

6. "Idrab al-Muʾallimin yashal Muʾazm Mudarris al-Mamlika, wa yudakhil bi-Quwwa ila Amman wa-Irbid wa-al-Zarqa" [Teachers strike includes most of the schools of the Kingdom and enters with force into Amman, Irbid and Zarqa], *Kol al-Urdun*, March 20, 2011, http://www .allofjo.net/index.php?page=article&id=9830. This article garnered over forty comments, generally in solidarity with the strike.

perceive as the injustice of their place in society.[7] Linking their dignity to their country or nation's future, they seek respect from and power against their governments.

Teachers' loss of prestige, though it took unique forms across Britain's former mandates, was part of global trends in the relationship between state and school: education became a right rather than a privilege. In 1920 the League of Nations covenant included no provision for schooling. The mandate charter for Palestine and Transjordan as well as the Anglo-Iraqi Treaty of 1922 merely noted that each community should not be prevented from educating its own. While "child welfare" was the responsibility of the international community, education was specifically defined as a national concern.[8] British colonial officials assumed that education not only was a national responsibility but also inevitably led to national awakening (and anti-imperialism). This meant that increasing the number of schools, teachers, and students constituted a dream for the colonized and a nightmare for colonizers. Government schooling during the interwar era was a national institution, the feared or desired harbinger of the nation-state.

In contrast, article 26 of the United Nations Declaration of Human Rights, promulgated in 1948, asserted that "everyone has the right to education. Education shall be free, at least in the elementary and fundamental stages. Elementary education shall be compulsory. Technical and professional education shall be made generally available and higher education shall be equally accessible to all on the basis of merit."[9] This document was a "program of principles" rather than a binding legal contract. But, at least in theory, a broad international consensus supported making education available to all. The acquisition of education would no longer be the purview of a limited elite. Schooling was to be prevalent, specialized, and meritocratic. As new countries disaggregated from imperial formations, government education became a given: a tool to advance rather than bring about the nation-state.

Restricting schooling during the mandate era engendered a particular type of political agency, status, and habitus among the privileged few who both studied and taught in government schools. This group used their rarity, as both

7. Mai Abu Moghli, Mezna Qato, "A Brief History of a Teacher's Strike," *Middle East Report Online*, June 5, 2018.

8. United Nations, "The United Nations and the Human Person: Universal Declaration of Human Rights," http://www.un.org/en/documents/udhr/, accessed June 18, 2021.

9. Kunz, "The United Nations Declaration of Human Rights," 318.

teachers and civil servants, to gain social mobility and to freely express their political views. They inhabited a transnational social space, only loosely bounded by mandate borders. Their travels, the texts they read and wrote, their language, and their school-day memories extended their habitus regionally. Their fortunes fell with the rise of independent governments.

Without colonial restrictions, mass schooling fundamentally altered teaching as a profession, eroding educators' capacity for bargaining with their governments and increasing educators' repression. During the 1970s Iraq's education system became one of the most renowned in the Arab World. The Ba'athist government prioritized mass education as a means of "political indoctrination" and "political, economic, and social progress."[10] A government campaign to eradicate illiteracy took on military overtones. Iraqis who were illiterate and refused to attend classes could technically be fined or even imprisoned.[11] This expensive and comprehensive campaign, subsidized by Iraq's oil, was quite successful in achieving its goals: literacy rates, particularly among Iraqi women, improved dramatically.[12] By the 1980s, however, the expansion of mass education and the results of sanctions against Iraq further depleted teachers' status. Educators began selling cigarettes before class to make ends meet.[13]

In Jordan and Israel as well as for Palestinians, the story of depleting status is similar, even without the crippling sanctions of Saddam Hussein's Iraq. When education became more prevalent in Jordan, jumping from approximately 20 percent of school-age children enrolled in 1960–1961 to 74 percent by 1976–1977, teachers in rural schools in particular complained of low salaries and poor working conditions.[14] In 2014 Jordan's teachers noted that their salaries were well below the poverty line.[15] In Israel proper as late as 2013, over 15 percent of public school teachers, including both Jewish and Palestinian

10. Ba'athist sixth and eighth national congresses, quoted in Lucas, "Arab Illiteracy," 78.

11. Lucas, 82.

12. By 1979, 80 percent of Iraq's women were literate. Ismael and Ismael, *Iraq in the Twenty-First Century*, 183.

13. Arnove and Abunimah, *Iraq under Siege*, 179.

14. Al-Tall, *Education in Jordan*, 97, 132.

15. Khetam Malkawi, "Teachers to Continue Strike Despite Gov't Promises," *Jordan Times*, March 25, 2010; Ali al-Rawashdah and Laila Azzeh, "Teachers Extend Strike to Monday," *Jordan Times*, November 18, 2012; Omar Obeidat and Raed Omari, "Teachers' Strike Splits Educators as Students Seen Main Victims," *Jordan Times*, August 18, 2014.

Israelis, made less than minimum wage.[16] West Bank Palestinian teachers' succession of strikes in the twenty-first century were due to low salaries and disproportionately low benefits in comparison to other civil servants.

These strikes and laments for teachers' lost dignity have their origins in the mandate period; educators' nostalgia for a higher social and economic status is based in historical fact. The professional grievances they articulate in slogans and banners as well as on social media are collective demands for a birthright enjoyed by the scarce, elite educators of the interwar era. For those limited few, public schooling was a means of social mobility, intellectual advancement, and imbrication in government service across multiple governments. Today, educators' protests not only are directed against their states, they are contained within them. Their mandate-era forbearers had rebelled from within government bureaucracies, extending states' reach into society while expanding ideologies that broke connections between those governments, the territories they controlled, and the political beliefs of their subjects. Understanding this history, we see the plight of educators today as a casualty of mass education, collateral damage of the modern nation-state.

16. Lior Dattel, "15% of Israeli Teachers Still Earn Less Than Minimum Wage: Teaching Remains One of the Lowest Paid Professions in the Public Sector," *Haaretz*, January 6, 2013. Although wages were raised in 2018, newly hired teachers make below the national average, and teachers have complained about irregularity in pay. Sivan Klingbail and Lior Dattel, "Whiteboard Jungle: One of Five Israeli Teachers Quits within Three Years," *Haaretz*, August 16, 2019, https://www.haaretz.com/israel-news/.premium-for-many-israeli-teachers-schools-are-a-whiteboard-jungle-1.7688587.

BIBLIOGRAPHY

Archives Consulted

Archives and Special Collections Department, Jafet Memorial Library, American University of
    Beirut, Beirut, Lebanon
The British Library, London, UK. Abbreviated as BL.
Central Zionist Archive, Jerusalem, Israel
Haganah Archive, Tel Aviv, Israel
Haifa Municipal Archive, Haifa, Israel. Abbreviated as HMA.
Hoover Institution Library & Archives, Stanford, CA
Human Resources Department, Archive Section, Ministry of Education of the Hashemite King-
    dom of Jordan, Amman, Jordan. Abbreviated as HRD.
Israel State Archive, Jerusalem, Israel. Abbreviated as ISA.
Jerusalem Municipal Archive, Jerusalem, Israel
Library of the Institute for Palestine Studies, Beirut, Lebanon
Middle East Centre Archive. St. Antony's College, Oxford, UK. Abbreviated as MECA.
National Archives, Kew, UK. Abbreviated as NA.
National Library and Center for Documents and Documentation, Amman, Jordan
Schlesinger Library, Radcliffe Institute, Harvard University, Cambridge, MA. Abbreviated
    as SL.
Sophia Smith Collection of Women's History, Smith College, Northhampton, MA
Textbook Museum, al-Salt, Jordan
University of Jordan Center for Documents and Manuscripts, Amman, Jordan

Online Archival Databases

Department of the National Library Archive. National Library of Jordan. http://www.nl.gov.jo/.
    Abbreviated as NLJ.
Historical Jewish Press. National Library of Israel. https://www.nli.org.il/en/discover
    /newspapers. Abbreviated as NLIH.
Israel State Archives. https://www.archives.gov.il/en/.
"Jrayed" Arabic Newspaper Archive of Ottoman and Mandatory Palestine. National Library of
    Israel. https://web.nli.org.il/sites/nlis/en/jrayed. Abbreviated as NLIJ.
UNESCO Digital Library. https://unesdoc.unesco.org/home.

United Nations Digital Library. Digital Library. https://digitallibrary.un.org/.
U.S. Intelligence and the Middle East. https://primarysources.brillonline.com/browse/us
-intelligence-on-the-middle-east.

Interviews

Anonymous
  Basel S., London, January 22, 2013
  Basel S., London, February 7, 2013
  Iraqi former official, Amman, January 2, 2012
  Jewish woman, Jerusalem, May 5, 2012
  Dr. M., London, February 15, 2013
  Dr. M., London, March 1, 2013
  Y. F., Jerusalem, July 18, 2012
Abu Hanna, Hanna, interview by Hilary Falb and Chana Morgenstern, Haifa, June 7, 2012
Abu-Jaber, Kamel, Amman, June 30, 2013
Abu Manneh, Butrus, Haifa, July 12, 2013
Al-Gharaibeh, ʿAbd al-Karim, Amman, April 17, 2012
Al-Gharaibeh, ʿAbd al-Karim, Amman, April 18, 2012
Hamadan Gattan, Nadia, London, February 16, 2013
Hashisho, Nawal, Amman, April 23, 2012
Khalidi, Tarif, Beirut, January 20, 2012
Kishtainy, Khalid, London, December 12, 2011
Kojaman, Yeheskel, London, January 14, 2013
Kojaman, Yeheskel, London, February 28, 2013
Majid, Kamal, London, March 3, 2013
Muhafaza, Ali, Amman, April 17, 2012
Othman, Ibrahim, Amman, April 16, 2012
al-Qasem, Anis, Amman, April 15, 2012
Rashid, Hosana, Amman, July 5, 2013
Shasha, Alfred, Boston/New York, August 2, 2011
al-Tikriti, Siri, New Orleans, October 12, 2013
Yehuda, Zvi, Or Yehuda, July 24, 2012

Newspapers and Periodicals

Iraq Government Gazette, Baghdad
Al-Jarida al-Rasmiyya [Official Gazette], Amman
Al-Kulliyah, Beirut
Al-Muʿallim al-Jadid, Baghdad
Palestine Government Gazette, Jerusalem
Al-ʿUrwat ul-Wuthqa, Beirut

Government Reports and Syllabi

Egypt, Wizarat al-Ma'arif al-Umumiyya [Ministry of Public Education]. *Manhaj al-Dirasa al-Ibtida'iyya li-Madaris al-Banat* [Elementary school syllabus for girls' schools]. Cairo: Matba'at al-Amiriyya bi-Bulaq, 1935.

Government of Palestine, Department of Education. *Annual Report for the Year 1925, 1925–26, 1926–27, 1927–28, 1928–29, 1929–30, 1930–31, 1931–32, 1932–33, 1933–34, 1934–35, 1935–36, 1936–37, 1937–38, 1939–40, 1940–41, 1941–42, 1942–43, 1943–44* (titles vary). Jerusalem: Government Printing Press.

———. *Education in Palestine General Survey, 1936–1946.* Jerusalem: Government Printing Press, 1946.

———. *Elementary School Syllabus: Revised Edition.* Jerusalem: Government Printing Press, 1925.

Great Britain, Colonial Office. *Report by His Majesty's Government in the United Kingdom of Great Britain and Northern Ireland to the Council of the League of Nations on the Administration of Palestine and Trans-Jordan for the Year 1933.* London: H. M. Printing Office. 1933.

———. *Special Report by His Majesty's Government in the United Kingdom of Great Britain and Northern Ireland to the Council of the League of Nations on the Progress of 'Iraq during the Period 1920–1931.* H.M. Stationery Office, 1931.

Great Britain, Naval Intelligence Division. *Palestine and Transjordan.* Oxford, 1943.

Great Britain Palestine Royal Commission. *Palestine Royal Commission Report.* London: H. M. Stationery Office, 1937.

Hashemite Kingdom of Jordan Ministry of Education. "Teacher Dictionary." http://www.moe .gov.jo/App/teacherDictionary/. Accessed April 2013.

Iraq, Department of Education and the Education Committee of Iraq. "Syllabus of the Primary Course of Study, Government Schools of Iraq." *India Office Records and Private Papers.* London: British Library, 1919.

Iraq, Wizarat al-Ma'arif [Ministry of Education]. *Al-Taqrir al-Sanawi an Sayr al-Ma'arif li-Sanat* [Annual report on educational progress for the year/years] *1928/29, 1929/30, 1930/31–1932/33, 1933/34, 1934/35–1935/36, 1936/37–1937/38, 1938/39, 1939/40–1942/43, 1943/44, 1944/45, 1945/46, 1946/47, 1946/47, 1952/53, 1953/54, 1954/55, 1955/56.* Baghdad: Wizarat al-Ma'arif.

———. *Al-Taqrir al-Sanawi, al-Ihsa al-Tarbawi 1946–47, 1953–54, 1960–61* [Educational statistics, annual report 1960–61]. Baghdad: Wizarat al-Ma'arif.

———. *Manhaj al-Dirasa al-Ibtida'iyya.* [Elementary school syllabus] Baghdad: Wizarat al-Ma'arif, 1931.

Israel Central Bureau of Statistics (Lishka ha-merkazit, li-statistika). "Statistical Abstract of Israel." 64. 2013.

Israel, State of. *Government Yearbook.* Tel Aviv: Israel Yearbook Publications, Israel Publications, 1950–1951.

———. *Israel Yearbook.* Tel Aviv: Israel Yearbook Publications, Israel Publications, 1958, 1960.

Jordan, Al-Mamlaka al-Urduniyya al-Hashimiyya, Wizarat al-Tarbiyya wa-al-Ta'lim, *Al-Taqrir al-Sanawi—Wizarat al-Tarbiyya wa-al-Ta'lim* [The Hashemite Kingdom of Jordan, Annual report—Ministry of Education], *1953/1954, 1955/1956, 1956/1957, 1957/1958, 1958/1959, 1960/1961, 1962/1963.* Amman: Wizarat al-Tarbiyya wa-al-Ta'lim.

Palestine and J. B. Barron. *Palestine. Report and General Abstracts of the Census of 1922. Taken on the 23rd of October, 1922.* Jerusalem: Greek convent Press, 1923.

Palestine and Transjordan Administration Reports, 1918–1948. 16 vols. Slough, UK: Archive Editions, 1995.

References

Abd al-Hadi, Mahdi. *Documents on Jerusalem.* Vol. 2. Jerusalem: PASSIA, Palestinian Academic Society for the Study of International Affairs, 2007.

ʾAbd al-Latif, Dhu al-Kifl. *Mudhakkirati: Qissat kifahi min al-thawra al-Filistiniyya al-Kubra ila al-harb 1948* [My memoirs: The story of my struggle from the great Palestinian revolt to the war of 1948]. Amman: Dar Sindbad lil-Nashr, 2000.

Abdul-Hadi, Muhammed M. "The Place of the Urban Teacher in Modern Jordanian Society." Dissertation, Teachers College, Columbia University, 1958.

Abdul Majid, Hammoudi. "Guides for the Improvement of Teacher Education in Iraq." Dissertation, Teachers College, Columbia University, 1953.

Abidi, Mahmud. "The Arab College, Jerusalem." In *Encyclopaedic Survey of Islamic Culture.* Vol. 3: *Educational Developments in Muslim World,* edited by Mohamed Taher. New Delhi: Anmol Publications, 1997.

Abu Gharbiyah, Bahjat. *Fi Khidam al-Nidal al-ʾArabi al-Filastini: Mudhakkirat al-Munadil Bahjat Abu Gharbiyah, 1916–1949* [In the midst of the Palestinian Arab struggle: The memoirs of the fighter Bahjat Abu Gharbiyah]. Beirut: Muassasat al-Dirasat al-Filastiniyya, 1993.

Abu-Ghazaleh, Adnan Mohammed. *Arab Cultural Nationalism in Palestine during the British Mandate.* Beirut: Institute for Palestine Studies, 1973.

Abu-Manneh, Butrus. "The Christians between Ottomanism and Syrian Nationalism: The Ideas of Butrus Al-Bustani." *International Journal of Middle East Studies* 11, no. 3 (1980): 287–304.

Abu Nowar, Maan. *The Development of Trans-Jordan 1929–1939: A History of the Hashemite Kingdom of Jordan.* Reading, PA: Ithaca Press, 2006.

Adams, Doris G. "Current Population Trends in Iraq." *Middle East Journal* 10, no. 2 (1956): 151–65.

Adely, Fida J. *Gendered Paradoxes: Educating Jordanian Women in Nation, Faith, and Progress.* Chicago: University of Chicago Press, 2012.

Ágoston, Gábor, and Bruce Masters. *Encyclopedia of the Ottoman Empire.* New York: Facts on File, 2008.

Ahmad ʾAbd al-Fattah Tuqan and Ahmad Salim Saʾidan. *Mabadiʾ al-Jabr al-Jazaʾ al-Awwal* [The foundations of algebra part 1]. Vol. 1. Beirut: al-Maktaba al-ʾAsriyya, 1947.

Akrawi, Matta. "Curriculum Construction in the Public Primary Schools of Iraq in the Light of a Study of the Political, Economic, Social, Hygienic and Educational Conditions and Problems of the Country, with Some Reference to the Education of Teachers. A Preliminary Investigation." Dissertation, Teachers College, Columbia University, 1942.

———. *Mashruʾ al-Taʾlim al-Ijbari fi al-ʾIraq* [The project of compulsory education in Iraq]. Baghdad: Wizarat al-Maʾarif, 1937.

Akrawi, Matta, and A. A. El-Koussy. "Recent Trends in Arab Education." *International Review of Education* 17, no. 2 (1971): 181–97.

Ali, Nadje Sadig al. *Iraqi Women: Untold Stories from 1948 to the Present*. London: Zed Books, 2008.

Allaq, A. J. "The Dialogue of Ink, Blood and Water—Higher Education in Iraq, Progress and Problems." In *Higher Education in the Gulf: Problems and Prospects*, edited by Ken E. Shaw. Exeter, UK: University of Exeter Press, 1997.

Allen, Danielle S., and Rob Reich. *Education, Justice, and Democracy*, Chicago: University of Chicago Press, 2013.

Alon, Yoav. *The Making of Jordan: Tribes, Colonialism and the Modern State*. London: I. B. Tauris, 2009.

———. "Tribal Shaykhs and the Limits of British Imperial Rule in Transjordan, 1920–46." *Journal of Imperial and Commonwealth History* 32, no. 1 (2004): 69–92.

———. "The Tribal System in the Face of the State-Formation Process: Mandatory Transjordan, 1921–46." *International Journal of Middle East Studies* 37, no. 2 (2005): 213–40.

A M Qattan Foundation, "Leila Darwish Miqdadi—Al-Qattan (1934–2015)." http://www.qattanfoundation.org/en/members/leila-darwish-miqdadi-al-qattan-1934-2015.

Amara, Muhammad, and Abd el-Rahman Mar`i. *Language Education Policy: The Arab Minority in Israel*. London: Springer, 2011.

`Amayira, Muhammad Hasan. *Al-Tarbiyya wa-al-Ta`lim fi al-Urdun: Mundhu awakhir al-`ahd al-`Uthmani wa-hatta 1997* [Education in Jordan: From the end of the Ottoman era to 1997]. Amman: Dar al-Masira lil-Nashr wa-al-Tawzi` wa-al-Tiba`a, 1999.

American Jewish Committee, David Singer, and Lawrence Grossman. *American Jewish Yearbook 2003*. New York: American Jewish Committee, 2003.

Amin, Mudhaffar Abdullah. "Jama' at Al—Ahali: Its Origin, Ideology, and Role in Iraqi Politics 1932–46." Dissertation, University of Durham, UK, 1980.

`Anabtawi, Wasfi, and Husayn Ghunaym. *Al-Majmal fi al-Tarikh al-`Usur al-Mutawassata Wa al-Haditha* [A summary of medieval and modern history]. Jaffa: al-Matba`a al-`Asriyya, 1943.

`Anabtawi, Wasfi, Husayn Ghunaym, Ahmad Khalifa, and Sa'id Sabbagh. *Al-Qira`a al-Tarikhiyya al-Musawwara* [The illustrated history reader]. Part 1. Haifa: al-Matba`a al-`Asriyya, 1949.

`Anabtawi, Wasfi, and Sa'id Sabbagh. *Al-Jughrafiiyya al-Iqtisadiyya* [Economic geography] Jerusalem (al-Quds): Matba'at al-Aba' al-Faransisiyyin, 1941.

———. *Jughrafiyya al-Sharq al-Adna: wa-Sair Buldan Hud al-Bahr al-Mutawassat wa Gharbi Urubba* [Geography of the Near East and the other countries of the Mediterranean basin and western Europe]. Jaffa: Maktabat al-Tahir Ikhwan, 1943.

———. *Jughrafiiyya Filastin wa-al-Bilad al-`Arabiyya*. [Geography of Palestine and the Arab countries]. Jaffa: Maktabat al-Tahir Ikhwan, 1946.

Anderson, Benedict R. *Imagined Communities: Reflections on the Origin and Spread of Nationalism*. London: Verso, 1991.

———. *The Spectre of Comparisons: Nationalism, Southeast Asia, and the World*. London: Verso, 1998.

Anderson, Betty S. *The American University of Beirut: Arab Nationalism and Liberal Education*. Austin: University of Texas Press, 2011.

———. "The History of the Jordanian National Movement: Its Leaders, Ideologies, Successes and Failures." Dissertation, University of California, Los Angeles, 1997.

———. *Nationalist Voices in Jordan: The Street and the State*. Austin: University of Texas Press, 2005.

———. "Writing the Nation: Textbooks of the Hashemite Kingdom of Jordan." *Comparative Studies of South Asia, Africa and the Middle East* 21, no. 1 (2001): 5–14.

Anderson, Charles W. "From Petition to Confrontation: The Palestinian National Movement and the Rise of Mass Politics, 1929–1939." Dissertation, New York University, 2013.

Anglo-American Committee of Inquiry on Jewish Problems in Palestine and Europe. *A Survey of Palestine*. Jerusalem: Government Printing Press, 1946.

Antonius, George. *The Arab Awakening: The Story of the Arab National Movement*. Beirut: Librairie du Liban: Lebanon Bookshop, 1969.

Apple, Michael W. *Teachers and Texts: A Political Economy of Class and Gender Relations in Education*. New York: Routledge & Kegan Paul, 1986.

Apter, Lauren Elise. "Disorderly Decolonization the White Paper of 1939 and the End of British Rule in Palestine." Dissertation, University of Texas, 2008.

Armytage, W. H. G. "The 1870 Education Act." *British Journal of Educational Studies* 18, no. 2 (1970).

Arnove, Anthony, and Ali Abunimah. *Iraq under Siege: The Deadly Impact of Sanctions and War*. Cambridge, MA: South End Press, 2000.

Arnove, Robert F., and Carlos Alberto Torres. *Comparative Education: The Dialectic of the Global and the Local*. Lanham, MD: Rowman & Littlefield, 2007.

Aruri, Naseer Hasan. *Jordan: A Study in Political Development (1921–1965)*. The Hague: Nijhoff, 1972.

Askari, Ja'far. *A Soldier's Story: From Ottoman Rule to Independent Iraq: The Memoirs of Jafar Pasha Al-Askari (1885–1936)*. London: Arabian, 2003.

Assaad, Ragui. "The Effects of Public Sector Hiring and Compensation Policies on the Egyptian Labor Market." *World Bank Economic Review* 11, no. 1 (1997): 85–118.

Ayalon, Ami. *Reading Palestine: Printing and Literacy, 1900–1948*. Austin: University of Texas Press, 2004.

Ayyub, Dhu al-Nun. *Al-Athar al-Kamila li-Adab Dhi al-Nun Ayyub* [The complete works of the author Dhi (Dhu) al-Nun Ayyub]. Vol. 3. Baghdad: al-Jumhuriyya al-'Iraqiyya, Wizarat al-I'lam, 1977.

———. "A Pillar of the Tower of Babel." In *Arab Stories: East and West*, edited by R. Y. Young and M. J. L. Ebied. Leeds, UK: Leeds University Oriental Society, 1977.

Al-Babatin, Fariq al-'Smal Mu'jam. "Muhammad Naji al-Qishtayni," Mu'assasat Ja'izat 'Abd al-'Aziz Sa'ud al-Babatin lil-Ibda' al-Shi'ri. Accessed April 11, 2015. https://www.almoajam .org/lists/inner/6927.

Badawi, Muhammad Mustafa. *Modern Arabic Literature*. New York: Cambridge University Press, 1992.

Badran, Nabil A. "The Means of Survival: Education and the Palestinian Community, 1948–1967." *Journal of Palestine Studies* 9, no. 4 (1980): 44–74.

Baerlein, Henry, and Abu al-Ala al-Ma'arri. *Abu 'l Ala, the Syrian*. London: J. Murray, 1914.

Bagley, William C. *Classroom Management Its Principles and Technique*. New York: Macmillan, 1907.

Banko, Lauren E. "The Invention of Citizenship in Palestine." In *Routledge Handbook of Global Citizenship Studies*, edited by Engin F. Isin and Peter Nyers. Hoboken, NJ: Taylor and Francis, 2014.

———. *The Invention of Palestinian Citizenship, 1918–1947*. Edinburgh: Edinburgh University Press, 2016.

Barakat, Nora. "Marginal Actors? The Role of Bedouin in the Ottoman Administration of Animals as Property in the District of Salt, 1870–1912." *Journal of the Economic and Social History of the Orient* 58 (2015): 105–34.

Baram, Amatzia. "A Case of Imported Identity: The Modernizing Secular Ruling Elites of Iraq and the Concept of Mesopotamian-Inspired Territorial Nationalism, 1922–1992." *Poetics Today* 15, no. 2 (1994): 279–319.

Baram, Amatzia, Achim Rohde, and Ronen Zeidel. *Iraq Between Occupations: Perspectives from 1920 to the Present*. New York: Palgrave Macmillan, 2010.

Barari, Hazaa el. "Adib Wahbeh. Min Fursan al-Haraka al-Wataniyya" [Adib Wahbeh. One of the knights of the national movement]. *Al-Rai*, August 6, 2012.

Al-Barghouti, Umar al-Salih. *Al-Marahil* [The stages]. Beirut: Al-Muassasat al-ʿArabiyya lil-Dirasat wa-al-Nashr, 2001.

Barkey, Karen. *Bandits and Bureaucrats: The Ottoman Route to State Centralization*. Ithaca, NY: Cornell University Press, 1997.

Baron, Beth. *Egypt as a Woman: Nationalism, Gender, and Politics*. Cairo: American University in Cairo Press, 2005.

Barnes, John Robert. *An Introduction to Religious Foundations in the Ottoman Empire*. Leiden: Brill, 1987.

Bashkin, Orit. "Iraqi Democracy and the Democratic Vision of ʿAbd Al-Fattah Ibrahim." In *Iraq between Occupations: Perspectives from 1920 to the Present*, edited by Amatzia Baram, Achim Rohde, and Ronen Zeidel. New York: Palgrave Macmillan, 2010.

———. *New Babylonians: A History of Jews in Modern Iraq*. Stanford, CA: Stanford University Press, 2012.

———. *The Other Iraq: Pluralism and Culture in Hashemite Iraq*. Stanford, CA: Stanford University Press, 2009.

———. "'Out of Place': Home and Empire in the Works of Mahmud Ahmad Al-Sayyid and Dhu Nun Ayyub." *Comparative Studies of South Asia, Africa and the Middle East* 28, no. 3 (2008): 428–42.

———. "To Educate an Iraqi-Jew." In *World Yearbook of Education 2010: Education and the Arab "World": Political Projects, Struggles, and Geometries of Power*, edited by André Elias Mazawi and Ronald G. Sultana, 163–77. New York: Routledge, 2010.

———. "When Muawiya Entered the Curriculum: Some Comments on the Iraqi Education System in the Interwar Period." *Comparative Education Review* 50, no. 3 (2006): 346–66.

Basten, Carolyn. "A Feminised Profession: Women in the Teaching Profession." *Educational Studies* 23, no. 1 (1997): 55–63.

Batatu, Hanna. *The Old Social Classes and the Revolutionary Movements of Iraq: A Study of Iraq's Old Landed and Commercial Classes and of Its Communists, Baʾthists, and Free Officers*. Princeton, NJ: Princeton University Press, 2004.

Bawalsa, Nadim. "Sakakini Defrocked." *Jerusalem Quarterly* 42 (Summer 2010): 5–25.

Baysan, Ibrahim Vehbi. "State Education Policy in the Ottoman Empire during the Tanzimat Period (1839–1876)." Dissertation, University of Manchester, 2004.

Beinin, Joel. *Workers and Peasants in the Modern Middle East.* Cambridge: Cambridge University Press, 2001.

Bénéï, Véronique. *Schooling Passions: Nation, History, and Language in Contemporary Western India.* Stanford, CA: Stanford University Press, 2008.

Ben-Or, J. L. "Arab Education in Israel." *Journal of Educational Sociology* 27, no. 8 (April 1954): 380–84.

Ben-Porath, Yoram. "Market, Government, and Israel's Muted Baby Boom." *National Bureau of Economic Research Working Paper Series,* no. 1569. 1985.

Bentwich, Joseph Solomon. *Education in Israel.* Philadelphia: Jewish Publication Society of America, 1965.

Berkson, Isaac B. "Jewish Education in Palestine." *Annals of the American Academy of Political and Social Science* 164 (1932): 139–54.

Bernhardsson, Magnus Thorkell. *Reclaiming a Plundered Past: Archaeology and Nation Building in Modern Iraq.* Austin: University of Texas Press, 2005.

Bernstein, Deborah. *Constructing Boundaries: Jewish and Arab Workers in Mandatory Palestine.* Albany: State University of New York Press. 2000.

Bertelsen, Rasmus G. "Private Foreign-Affiliated Universities, the State, and Soft Power: The American University of Beirut and the American University in Cairo." *Foreign Policy Analysis* 8, no. 3 (July 2012): 293–311.

Bhambra, Gurminder K. *Rethinking Modernity: Postcolonialism and the Sociological Imagination.* Basingstoke, UK; Palgrave, 2007.

Bidwell, Robin Leonard. *Dictionary of Modern Arab History: An A to Z of over 2000 Entries from 1798 to the Present Day.* New York: Kegan Paul International, 1998.

Biklen, Sari Knopp. *School Work: Gender and the Cultural Construction of Teaching.* New York: Teachers College Press, 1995

Blake, Corinne. "Training Arab-Ottoman Bureaucrats: Syrian Graduates of the Mülkiye Mektebi, 1890–1920." Dissertation, Princeton University, 1991.

Bosworth, Clifford Edmund. *The Encyclopaedia of Islam.* Vol. 6, fascicules 107–8. Leiden: Brill, 1980.

Bourdieu, Pierre. *The Logic of Practice,* translated by Richard Nice. Stanford, CA: Stanford University Press, 1990.

———. "Physical Space, Social Space and Habitus." Institutt for sosiologi og samfunnsgeografi Universitetet i Oslo. Rapport 10: 1996.

Bouveresse, Jacques. "Rules, Dispositions and the *Habitus*." In *Bourdieu: A Critical Reader,* edited by Richard Shusterman, 45–64. Oxford: Blackwell, 2011.

Bowman, Humphrey Ernest. *Middle-East Window: With an Introduction by Sir Ronald Storrs.* London: Longmans, Green, 1942.

Braham, Randolph L., and United States Office of Education. *Israel, a Modern Education System: A Report Emphasizing Secondary and Teacher Education.* Washington, DC: U.S. Department of Health, Education, and Welfare, Office of Education, 1966.

Brand, Laurie A. "Palestinians in Syria: The Politics of Integration." *Middle East Journal* 424 (1988): 621–37.

Burton, Antoinette. "Introduction: The Unfinished Business of Colonial Modernities." In *Gender, Sexuality and Colonial Modernities*, edited by A. Burton, 1–16. London: Routledge, 1999.

Butti, Rafa'il Faiq. *Rafa'il Butti, Dhakira 'Iraqiyya, 1900–1956* [Rafa'il Butti, Iraqi memory, 1900–1956]. Damascus: al-Mada, 2000.

Büssow, Johann. "Children of the Revolution: Youth in Palestinian Public Life, 1908–14." In *Late Ottoman Palestine: The Period of Young Turk Rule* by Yuval Ben-Bassat and Eyal Ginio, 55–80. London: Tauris, 2011.

Campante, Filipe R., and Davin Chor. "Why Was the Arab World Poised for Revolution? Schooling, Economic Opportunities, and the Arab Spring." *Journal of Economic Perspectives* 26, no. 2 (2012): 167–87.

Carman, Harry J. "England and the Egyptian Problem." *Political Science Quarterly* 36, no. 1 (1921): 51–78.

Çetinsaya, Gökhan. *The Ottoman Administration of Iraq, 1890–1908*. London: Routledge, 2011.

Ceylan, Ebubekir. *The Ottoman Origins of Modern Iraq: Political Reform, Modernization and Development in the Nineteenth Century Middle East*. London: Tauris Academic Studies, 2011.

Chakrabarty, Dipesh. "Legacies of Bandung: Decolonisation and the Politics of Culture." *Economic and Political Weekly* 40, no. 46 (2005): 4812–18.

———. *Provincializing Europe: Postcolonial Thought and Historical Difference*. Princeton, NJ: Princeton University Press, 2008.

Chamberlain, Muriel Evelyn. *Britain and India: The Interaction of Two Peoples*. Hamden, CT: David & Charles; Archon Books, 1974.

Chatterjee, Partha. *Nationalist Thought and the Colonial World: A Derivative Discourse*. Minneapolis: University of Minnesota Press, 1993.

Cheah, Pheng, and Jonathan D. Culler. *Grounds of Comparison: Around the Work of Benedict Anderson*. New York: Routledge, 2003.

Chirol, Valetine. *The Egyptian Problem*. London: Macmillan, 1920.

Choueiri, Youssef M. *Arab Nationalism, a History: Nation and State in the Arab World*. Oxford: Blackwell, 2005.

Cicek, Nazan. "The Role of Mass Education in Nation-Building in the Ottoman Empire and the Turkish Republic, 1870–1839." In *Mass Education and the Limits of State Building, c. 1870–1930*, edited by Laurence Brockliss and Nicola Sheldon, 224–51. Basingstoke, UK: Palgrave Macmillan, 2012.

Clancy-Smith, Julia A. *Rebel and Saint: Muslim Notables, Populist Protest, Colonial Encounters: Algeria and Tunisia, 1800–1904*. Berkeley: University of California Press, 1997.

Clark, Victor. *Compulsory Education in Iraq*. Paris: UNESCO, 1951.

Cleveland, William L. *The Making of an Arab Nationalist: Ottomanism and Arabism in the Life and Thought of Sati' al-Husri*. Princeton, NJ: Princeton University Press, 1971.

Cochran, Judith. *Democracy in the Middle East: The Impact of Religion and Education*. Lanham, MD: Lexington Books, 2011.

———. *Education in Egypt*. London: Croom Helm, 1986.

Cohen, Hayyim J. *The Anti-Jewish Farhud in Baghdad, 1941*. London: Frank Cass, 1966.

Cohen, Hillel. *Army of Shadows: Palestinian Collaboration with Zionism, 1917–1948*. Berkeley: University of California Press, 2009.

Cooper, Frederick. *Colonialism in Question: Theory, Knowledge, History*. Berkeley: University of California Press, 2010.

Cott, Nancy F. "Marriage Crisis and All That Jazz." In *Domestic Tensions, National Anxieties: Global Perspectives on Marriage, Crisis, and Nation*, edited by Kristin Celello and Hanan Kholoussy, 49–61. Oxford: Oxford University Press, 2016.

Cubberley, Ellwood Patterson. *Readings in Public Education in the United States; a Collection of Sources and Readings to Illustrate the History of Educational Practice and Progress in the United States*. Boston: Houghton Mifflin, 1934.

Curtis, Stanley James. *History of Education in Great Britain*, with a foreword by W. R. Niblett. 4th ed. London: University Tutorial Press, 1957.

Dagli, Murat. "The Limits of Ottoman Pragmatism." *History and Theory* 52, no. 2 (2013): 194–213.

Darwazeh, Muhammad ʾIzzat. *Mudhakkirat Muhammad ʾIzzat Darwazeh, 1305 H-1404 H/1887 M-1984 M: Sijill Hafil bi-Masirat al-Haraka al-ʾArabiyya wa-al-Qadiya al-Filastiniyya Khilal Qarn Min Al-Zaman* [The memoirs of Muhammad ʾIzzat Darwazeh, 1305 H-1404 H/ 1887 M-1984: A full record of the march of the Arab movement and the Palestinian cause over a century]. Vol. 1. Beirut: Dar al-Gharb al-Islami, 1993.

———*Mukhtasar Tarikh al-ʾArab wa-al-Islam* [A brief history of the Arabs and Islam]. Egypt: al-Matbaʾa al-salafiyya, 1925.

Davis, Eric. *Memories of State: Politics, History, and Collective Identity in Modern Iraq*. Berkeley: University of California Press, 2005.

Davis, Rochelle. "Commemorating Education: Recollections of the Arab College in Jerusalem, 1918–1948." *Comparative Studies of South Asia, Africa and the Middle East* 23, no. 1–2 (2003): 190–204.

———. *Palestinian Village Histories: Geographies of the Displaced*. Stanford, CA: Stanford University Press, 2011.

Dawisha, Adeed. *Arab Nationalism in the Twentieth Century: From Triumph to Despair*. Princeton, NJ: Princeton University Press, 2003.

———. *Iraq: A Political History from Independence to Occupation*. Princeton, NJ: Princeton University Press, 2009.

Dawn, C. Ernest. "An Arab Nationalist View of World: Politics and History in the Interwar Period: Darwish Al-Miqdadi." In *The Great Powers in the Middle East, 1919–1939*, edited by Uriel Dann, 355–70. New York: Holmes & Meier, 1988.

———. *From Ottomanism to Arabism; Essays on the Origins of Arab Nationalism*. Urbana: University of Illinois Press, 1973.

Degani, Arnon Y. "They Were Prepared: The Palestinian Arab Scout Movement 1920–1948." *British Journal of Middle Eastern Studies* 41, no. 2 (2014): 200–218.

Demichelis, Marco. "From Nahda to Nakba: The Governmental Arab College of Jerusalem and Its Palestinian Historical Heritage in the First Half of the Twentieth Century." *Arab Studies Quarterly* 37, no. 3 (2015): 264–28.

Deringil, Selim. "Legitimacy Structures in the Ottoman State: The Reign of Abdülhamid II (1876–1909)." *International Journal of Middle East Studies* 23, no. 3 (1991): 345–59.

———. "'They Live in a State of Nomadism and Savagery': The Late Ottoman Empire and the Post-Colonial Debate." *Comparative Studies in Society and History: An International Quarterly* 45, no. 2 (2003): 311–42.

Di-Capua, Yoav. *No Exit: Arab Existentialism, Jean-Paul Sartre, and Decolonization.* Chicago: Chicago University Press, 2018.

Diskin, John J. "The 'Genesis' of the Government Educational System in Iraq." Dissertation, University of Pittsburgh, 1971.

Dodge, Bayard. *The American University of Beirut: A Brief History of the University and the Lands Which It Serves.* Beirut: Khayat, 1958.

Dodge, Toby. "Can Iraq Be Saved?" *Survival* 56, no. 5 (2014): 7–20.

———. *Inventing Iraq: The Failure of Nation-Building and a History Denied.* New York: Columbia University Press, 2003.

Doori, Khalid. "The Administration of Education in Iraq." Dissertation, University of Arizona, 1960.

Doumani, Beshara. *Rediscovering Palestine: Merchants and Peasants in Jabal Nablus, 1700–1900.* Berkeley: University of California Press, 1995.

Drudy, Sheelagh. "Gender Balance/Gender Bias: The Teaching Profession and the Impact of Feminisation." *Gender and Education* 20, no. 4 (2008): 309–23.

Educational Inquiry Commission Iraq. *Report of the Educational Inquiry Commission* by Paul Monroe. N.p.: Government Press, 1932.

Efrati, Noga. "The Effendiyya: Where Have All the Women Gone?" *International Journal of Middle East Studies* 43, special issue no. 2 (2011): 375–77.

———. *Women in Iraq: Past Meets Present.* New York: Columbia University Press, 2012.

Eisenman, Robert H. *Islamic Law in Palestine and Israel: A History of the Survival of Tanzimat and Shari'a in the British Mandate and the Jewish State.* Social, Economic and Political Studies of the Middle East, vol. 26. Leiden: Brill, 1978.

El-Ariss, Tarek. *Trials of Arab Modernity: Literary Affects and the New Political.* New York: Fordham University Press, 2013.

Elliot, Matthew. *"Independent Iraq": British Influence from 1941–1958.* London: Tauris, 1994.

Ellis, Catriona. "Education for All: Reassessing the Historiography of Education in Colonial India." *History Compass* 7, no. 2 (2009): 363–75.

Elshakry, Marwa. *Reading Darwin in Arabic, 1860–1950.* Chicago: University of Chicago Press, 2013.

El Shakry, Omnia S. *The Great Social Laboratory: Subjects of Knowledge in Colonial and Postcolonial Egypt.* Stanford, CA: Stanford University Press, 2007.

Emrence, Cem. *Remapping the Ottoman Middle East Modernity, Imperial Bureaucracy and Islam.* London: I. B. Tauris, 2015.

Eppel, Michael. "The Elite, the 'Effendiyya,' and the Growth of Nationalism and Pan-Arabism in Hashemite Iraq, 1921–1958." *International Journal of Middle East Studies* 30, no. 2 (1998): 227–50.

———. "The Fadhil Al-Jamali Government in Iraq, 1953–54." *Journal of Contemporary History* 34, no. 3 (1999): 424–25.

———. *Iraq from Monarchy to Tyranny: From the Hashemites to the Rise of Saddam.* Gainesville: University Press of Florida, 2004.

———. "Note about the Term Effendiyya in the History of the Middle East." *International Journal of Middle East Studies* 41, no. 3 (2009): 535–39.

Etzioni, Amitai. *The Semi-Professions and Their Organization; Teachers, Nurses, Social Workers.* New York: Free Press. 1969

Evered, Emine Önhan. *Empire and Education Under the Ottomans: Politics, Reform and Resistance from the Tanzimat to the Young Turks.* London: Tauris, 2012.

———. "The Politics of the Late Ottoman Education: Accommodating Ethno-Religious Pluralism amid Imperial Disintegration." Dissertation, University of Arizona, 2005.

Fahmy, Khaled. *All the Pasha's Men: Mehmed Ali, His Army and the Making of Modern Egypt.* Cairo: American University in Cairo Press, 2008.

Fanon, Frantz. *Black Skin, White Masks.* New York: Grove Press, 2008.

Farah, Najwa Kawar. *A Continent Called Palestine: One Woman's Story.* London: SPCK, 1996.

Fariz, Husni. *Tarikh Al-`Abbasiyun wa-al-Fatimiyun lil-Soff al-Khamis al-Ibtidayyi* [The history of the Abbasids and the Fatimids for the fifth elementary class]. Amman: Maktabat al-Istiqlal, 1952.

———. *Stories from the Arab World.* London: Longman, 1978.

Farouk-Sluglett, Marion, and Peter Sluglett. "The Historiography of Modern Iraq." *American Historical Review* 96, no. 5 (1991): 1408–21.

———. *Iraq since 1958: From Revolution to Dictatorship.* London: Tauris, 2003.

Faruki, Deena Taji. "In Fear of Palestine: British and Israeli Educational Policy and History Curriculum for Palestinians." Dissertation, University of Washington, 2007.

Feldman, Ilana. *Governing Gaza: Bureaucracy, Authority, and the Work of Rule, 1917–1967.* Durham, NC: Duke University Press, 2008.

Fischbach, Michael R. *State, Society, and Land in Jordan.* Boston: Brill, 2000.

Fischman, Gustavo E. "Persistence and Ruptures: The Feminization of Teaching and Teacher Education in Argentina." *Gender and Education* 19, no. 3 (2007): 353–68.

Fleischmann, Ellen. *The Nation and Its "New" Women: The Palestinian Women's Movement, 1920–1948.* Berkeley: University of California Press, 2003.

Foot, Hugh Baron Caradon. *A Start in Freedom.* New York: Harper & Row, 1964.

Forman, G., and A. Kedar. "From Arab Land to 'Israel Lands': The Legal Dispossession of the Palestinians Displaced by Israel in the Wake of 1948." *Environment and Planning. D, Society & Space* 22, no. 6 (2004): 809–30.

Fortna, Benjamin C. "Education for the Empire: Ottoman State Secondary Schools During the Reign of Sultan Abdulhamid II (1876–1909)." University of Chicago, 1997.

———. *Imperial Classroom: Islam, the State, and Education in the Late Ottoman Empire.* Oxford: Oxford University Press, 2002.

Foucault, Michel, and Paul Rabinow. *The Foucault Reader.* New York: Pantheon Books, 1984.

Franzén, Johan. *Red Star over Iraq: Iraqi Communism before Saddam.* New York: Columbia University Press, 2011.

Frazer, Elizabeth. "Introduction: The Idea of Political Education." *Oxford Review of Education* 25, no. 1/2 (1999): 5–22.

Frisch, Hillel. *Israel's Security and Its Arab Citizens.* New York: Cambridge University Press, 2011.

Fu, Songtao. "Initial Exploration of the Phenomenon of the Feminization of Teachers." *Chinese Education and Society* 33, no. 4 (2000): 40–46.

Fuchs, Eckhardt, and Roldán Vera, Eugenia. *The Transnational in the History of Education.* Cham, Switz.: Springer International, 2019.

Furas, Yoni. *Educating Palestine: Teaching and Learning History under the Mandate.* Oxford: Oxford University Press, 2020.

Galal, Ahmed. *The Paradox of Education and Unemployment in Egypt.* Cairo: Egyptian Center for Economic Studies, 2002.

Galbraith, John S. "No Man's Child: The Campaign in Mesopotamia, 1914–1916." *International History Review* 6, no. 3 (1984): 358–85.

Gellner, Ernest, and John Breuilly. *Nations and Nationalism.* Malden, MA: Blackwell, 2006.

Gershoni, I., and James P. Jankowski. *Confronting Fascism in Egypt: Dictatorship versus Democracy in the 1930s.* Stanford, CA: Stanford University Press, 2010.

———. *Redefining the Egyptian Nation, 1930–1945.* Cambridge Middle East Studies, vol. 2. New York: Cambridge University Press, 1995.

———. *Rethinking Nationalism in the Arab Middle East.* New York: Columbia University Press, 1997.

Gershoni, Israel, Sara Pursley, and Beth Baron. "Editorial Foreword." *International Journal of Middle East Studies* 43, no. 2 (2011): 197–202.

Ghareeb, Edmund, and Beth Dougherty. *Historical Dictionary of Iraq.* Lanham, MD: Scarecrow Press, 2004.

Gibb, Hamilton, Alexander Rosskeen, and Harold Bowen. *Islamic Society and the West: A Study of the Impact of Western Civilization on Moslem Culture in the Near East.* Vol. 1: *Islamic Society in the Eighteenth Century.* London: Oxford University Press, 1957.

Gilbar, Gad G. *Population Dilemmas in the Middle East: Essays in Political Demography and Economy.* London: Frank Cass, 1997.

Goffman, Erving. *Asylums: Essays on the Social Situation of Mental Patients and Other Inmates.* Harmondsworth, UK: Penguin Books, 1970.

Golan-Agnon, Daphna. "Separate but Not Equal." *American Behavioral Scientist* 49, no. 8 (2006): 1075–84.

Graham-Brown, Sarah, and Neil MacDonald. *Education, Repression, Liberation: Palestinians.* London: World University Service, 1984.

Grainger, John D. *The Battle for Palestine 1917.* Warfare in History. Rochester, NY: Boydell Press, 2006.

Gran, Peter. *Beyond Eurocentrism: A New View of Modern World History.* Syracuse, NY: Syracuse University Press, 1996.

Green, Andy. *Education and State Formation: The Rise of Education Systems in England, France and the USA.* London: Palgrave Macmillan, 1990.

Greenberg, Ela. "Between Hardships and Respect: A Collective Biography of Arab Women Teachers in British-Ruled Palestine." *Hawwa* 6, no. 3 (2008): 284–314.

———. "*Majallat Rawdat al-ma ʾarif*: Constructing Identities within a Boys' School Journal in Mandatory Palestine." *British Journal of Middle Eastern Studies* 35, no. 1 (2008): 79–95.

———. *Preparing the Mothers of Tomorrow: Education and Islam in Mandate Palestine.* Austin: University of Texas Press, 2009.

Griffiths, Morwenna. "The Feminization of Teaching and the Practice of Teaching: Threat or Opportunity?" *Educational Theory* 56, no. 4 (2006): 387–405.

Grover, B. L., and S. Grover. *A New Look at Modern Indian History: From 1707 to the Present Day.* New Delhi: S. Chand, 2018.

Guckian, Noel Joseph. "British Relations with Trans-Jordan, 1920–1930." Dissertation, Aberystwyth University, 1985.

Haddad, Heskel M., and Phyllis I. Rosenteur. *Flight from Babylon: Iraq, Iran, Israel, America*. New York: McGraw-Hill, 1986.

Al-Haj ʿIsa and Muhyi al-Din. *Masra ʿ Kulayb* [The death of Kulayb]. Cairo: Tibi ʿa bi-matba ʿat Dar Ihya ʾ al-Kutub al- ʿArabiyya, 1947

———. *Min Ahdath Nakbat Filastin: Usrat Shahid* [From the events of the Palestinian nakba (catastrophe): The family of a martyr]. Damascus: Matba ʿat al-Insha ʾ, 1966.

———. *Min Filastin Wa-ilayha* [From and to Palestine]. Al-Tab ʿat. Halab: Al-Matba ʿa al-Suriyya, 1975.

Al-Haj, Majid. *Education, Empowerment, and Control: The Case of Arabs in Israel*. Albany: State University of New York Press, 1995.

Haj, Samira. *The Making of Iraq, 1900–1963 Capital, Power, and Ideology*. Albany: State University of New York Press, 1997.

Hakim, Selim. *A Critical Assessment of Teaching Materials Used in the First Two Years of English Teaching in Government Schools and in Primary Teacher Training Colleges in Iraq for the Training of Teachers of English: (Post–World War I to 1970)*. London: Institute of Education, University of London, 1984.

Haklai, Oded. *Palestinian Ethnonationalism in Israel*. Philadelphia: University of Pennsylvania Press, 2011.

Halliday, Denis J. "The Impact of the UN Sanctions on the People of Iraq." *Journal of Palestine Studies* 28, no. 2 (1999): 29–37.

Halpern, Ben, and Reinharz, Jehuda. *Zionism and the Creation of a New Society*. New York: Oxford University Press, 1998.

Hamadeh, Najla S. "Wives or Daughters: Structural Differences between Urban and Bedouin Lebanese Co-wives." In *Intimate Selving in Arab Families: Gender, Self and Identity*, edited by Suad Joseph. Syracuse, NY: Syracuse University Press, 1999.

Hamzah, Dyala. *The Making of the Arab Intellectual (1880–1960): Empire, Public Sphere and the Colonial Coordinates of Selfhood*. New York: Routledge, 2012.

Hanioglu, M. Sükrü. *A Brief History of the Late Ottoman Empire*. Princeton, NJ: Princeton University Press, 2008.

———. *The Young Turks in Opposition*. New York: Oxford University Press, 1995.

Hanley, Will. *Identifying with Nationality: Europeans, Ottomans and Egyptians in Alexandria*. New York: Columbia University Press, 2017.

Hanssen, Jens. *Fin De Siècle Beirut: The Making of an Ottoman Provincial Capital*. Oxford: Clarendon Press, 2006.

Harker, Richard K. "On Reproduction, Habitus and Education." *British Journal of Sociology of Education* 5, no. 2 (1984): 117–27.

Harte, John. "Contesting the Past in Mandate Palestine: History Teaching for Palestinian Arabs under British Rule, 1917–1948." Dissertation, University of London, School of Oriental and African Studies, 2009.

Hazri, Tengu Ahmad. "Religious Education and the Challenge of Modernity." *Islam and Civilisational Renewal* 1, no. 4 (April 2010): 713–16.

Hevrah ha-Mizrahit, ha-Yisreelit. *Middle East Record*. Vol. 1. London, 1960.

Higgins, A. Pearce. *The Hague Peace Conferences and Other International Conferences Concerning the Laws and Usages of War. Texts of with Commentaries Section III.: Military Authority over the Territory of the Hostile State. Art. 3, 48, 52.* Cambridge: Cambridge University Press, 1909.

Hilali, ʿAbd al-Razzaq. *Tarikh al-Taʿlim fi al-ʿIraq fi ʿAhd al-Ihtilal al-Baritani, 1914–1921* [The history of education in Iraq during the era of British occupation, 1914–1921]. Baghdad: Matbaʿat al-Maʿarif, 1975.

———. *Tarikh al-Taʿlim fi al-ʿIraq: fi Ahd al-ʿUthmani 1638 M.–1917 M* [The history of education in Iraq: during the Ottoman era 1638–1917]. Baghdad: Saʿdat Wizarat al-Maʿarif ʿala nashr, 1959.

Hilali, ʿAbd al-Razzaq, and Ayif Habib Khalil Ani. *Tarikh al-Taʿlim fi al-ʿIraq fi al-ʿAhd al-Intidab al-Baritani, 1921–1932* [The history of education in Iraq during the era of the British Mandate, 1921–1932]. Baghdad: Wizarat al-Thaqafa wa-al-Iʿlam, Dar al-Shuʾun al-Thaqafiyya al-ʿAmma, "Afaq ʿArabiyya," 2000.

Hindawi, Abdallah Abdelaziz. "Educational Needs and Program Relevancy in Jordan." California Western University, 1969.

Hirsch, Moshe, Deborah Housen-Couriel, and Ruth Lapidoth. *Whither Jerusalem? Proposals and Positions Concerning the Future of Jerusalem.* The Hague: Martinus Nijhoff, 1995.

Hobsbawm, E. J. *Nations and Nationalism since 1780: Programme, Myth, Reality.* Cambridge: Cambridge University Press, 2012.

Hodgkin, E. C. "Lionel Smith on Education in Iraq." *Middle Eastern Studies* 19, no. 2 (1983): 253–60.

Hofman, Amos. "The Politics of National Education: Values and Aims of Israeli History Curricula, 1956–1995." *Journal of Curriculum Studies* 39, no. 4 (2007): 441–70.

Hofman, Amos, Bracha Alpert, and Izhak Schnell. "Education and Social Change: The Case of Israel's State Curriculum." *Curriculum Inquiry* 37, no. 4 (2007): 303–28.

Hourani, Albert. *Arabic Thought in the Liberal Age: 1798–1939.* London: Oxford University Press, 1967.

———. "Ottoman Reforms and the Politics of Notables." In *Beginnings of Modernization in the Middle East: The Nineteenth Century,* edited by Richard L. Chambers and William Roe Polk. Chicago: University of Chicago Press, 1968.

Hughes, Matthew. "Assassination in Jerusalem: Bahjat Abu Gharbiyah and Sami Al-Ansari's Shooting of British Assistant Superintendent Alan Sigrist 12th June 1936." *Jerusalem Quarterly* 44 (Winter 2010): 5–13.

———. *Britain's Pacification of Palestine: The British Army, the Colonial State, and the Arab Revolt, 1936–1939.* Cambridge Military Histories. Cambridge: Cambridge University Press, 2019.

———. "A History of Violence: The Shooting in Jerusalem of British Assistant Police Superintendent Alan Sigrist, 12 June 1936." *Journal of Contemporary History* 45, no. 4 (2010): 725–43.

Hurvitz, Nimrod. "Muhibb Ad-Din Al-Khatib's Semitic Wave Theory and Pan-Arabism." *Middle Eastern Studies* 29, no. 1 (1993): 118–34.

Al-Husri, Abu Khaldun Sati. *Mudhakkirati fi al-ʿIraq 1921–1941* [My memoirs in Iraq 1921–1941].2 vols. Beirut: Dar al-Taliʿa, 1967.

Al-Hussein, Ihsan Muhammad. "Jamʿiyat al-Jawwal: Fasl min tarikh al-qamiyya al-ʿArabiyya, fi al-Iraq" [The Jawwal(rover) society: A chapter from the history of Arab nationalism in Iraq]. *Majallat Kulliyat al-Adab* 33, no. 6 (December 1962): 243–309.

Al Husseini, Jalal. "UNRWA and the Refugees: A Difficult but Lasting Marriage." *Journal of Palestine Studies* 40, no. 1 (2010): 6–26.

Husseini, Rafiq. *Exiled from Jerusalem: The Diaries of Hussein Fakhri Al-Khalidi*. London: Tauris, 2020.

Ibrahim, 'Abd al-Fattah. '*Ala Tariq al-Hind [On the history of India]*. Dimashq: Wizarat al-Thaqafa fi al-Jumhuriya al-'Arabiyya al-Suriyya, 1991.

International Bureau of Education, Unesco. *International Yearbook of Education, 1953*. Vol. 15. Paris: UNESCO International Bureau of Education, 1954.

———. *International Yearbook of Education 1958*. Vol. 20. Paris: UNESCO International Bureau of Education, 1958.

———. *International Yearbook of Education 26, 1964*. Vol. 23. Geneva: UNESCO International Bureau of Education, 1964.

The International Who's Who of the Arab World. London: International Who's Who of the Arab World, 1984.

The Iraq Legal Database. "Nizam Wizarat Al-Ma'arif. 7,7, 1958" [The regulation of the Ministry of Education, 7,7. 1958]. United Nations Development Programme. https://iraqld.hjc.iq /LoadLawBook.aspx?SC=120120016618718.

Ireland, Philip Willard. *Iraq: A Study in Political Development*. New York: Routledge, 2009.

Islamoğlu, Huri. "Islamicate World Histories?" In *A Companion to World History*, 447–63. Chichester, UK: Wiley-Blackwell, 2012.

Ismael, Tareq Y. *The Rise and Fall of the Communist Party of Iraq*. Cambridge: Cambridge University Press, 2008.

Ismael, Tareq Y., and Jacqueline S. Ismael. *Iraq in the Twenty-First Century: Regime Change and the Making of a Failed State*. Durham Modern Middle East and Islamic World Series. London: Routledge. 2015.

Issawi, Charles Philip. *An Economic History of the Middle East and North Africa*. New York: Columbia University Press, 1982.

Issawi, Charles Philip, and Carlos Dabezies. "Population Movements and Population Pressure in Jordan, Lebanon, and Syria." *Milbank Memorial Fund Quarterly* 29, no. 4 (1951): 385–403.

'Izz Al-Din, Yusuf. *Shu'ara' al-'Iraq fi al-Qarn al-'Ashrin* [The poets of Iraq in the twentieth century]. Baghdad: Matba'at As'ad, 1969.

Jabareen, Yousef T. "Law and Education." *American Behavioral Scientist* 49, no. 8 (2006): 1052–74.

Jabr, Yahya, 'Abd al-Rauf, and 'Abd al-Hadi Jawabira. *Mawsu'at 'Ulama Filastin wa-A'yanuha* [Encyclopedia of Palestinian scholars and notables]. Nablus: Jami'at al-Naja al-Wataniyya: Dairat al-Ma'arif al-Filastiniyya, 2010.

Jabra, Jabra Ibrahim. *The First Well: A Bethlehem Boyhood*. Fayetteville: University of Arkansas Press, 1995.

Jacob, Wilson Chacko. *Working Out Egypt: Effendi Masculinity and Subject Formation in Colonial Modernity, 1870–1940*. Durham, NC: Duke University Press, 2011.

al-Jamali, Muhammad Fadil. "Arab Struggle: Experience of Mohammed Fadil Jamali, 1943–1958." Ms., 1974.

———. "The New Iraq: Its Problem of Bedouin Education." Dissertation, Teachers College, Columbia University, 1934.

Jami'at Mutah, and Lajnat Ihya al-Turath. *Madrasat Al-Karak Al-Thanawiyya: Rihlat Al-Miat 'Am* [The secondary school of al-Karak: Journey of a hundred years]. Karak: Jami'at Mutah, Lajnat Ihya al-Turath, 1994.

Jardine, David, and Rahat Naqvi. "Learning Not to Speak in Tongues: Thoughts on 'The Librarian of Basra.'" *Canadian Journal of Education* 31, no. 3 (2008): 639–66.

Jarzmik, Oscar. "'Adjusting to Powerlessness' in Occupied Jerusalem: Theodore 'Teddy' Kollek, the Palestinians and the Organizing Principles of Israeli Municipal Policy, 1967–1987." Dissertation, University of Toronto, 2016.

Johnson, Amy J. *Reconstructing Rural Egypt: Ahmed Hussein and the History of Egyptian Developmen.* Syracuse, NY: Syracuse University Press, 2004.

Jones, Kevin M. *The Dangers of Poetry: Culture, Politics, and Revolution in Iraq.* Stanford, CA: Stanford University Press, 2020.

Joyce, Patrick. "Remaking Liberal Education: Classics and the Public Examination." In *State of Freedom*, 2009.

Kabaha, Mustafá. *The Palestinian Press as Shaper of Public Opinion 1929–39: Writing Up a Storm.* London: Vallentine Mitchell, 2007.

Kadhim, Abbas K. *Reclaiming Iraq: The 1920 Revolution and the Founding of the Modern State.* Austin: University of Texas Press, 2012.

Kadhim, Abdul Hamid. "A Plan for the Reconstruction of Teacher Education in Iraq." Dissertation, Teachers College, Columbia University, 1947.

Kaestle, Carl F., and Eric Foner. *Pillars of the Republic: Common Schools and American Society, 1780–1860.* New York: Hill and Wang, 1983.

Kahati, Yoram. "The Role of Education in the Development of Arab Nationalism in the Fertile Crescent During the 1920s." In *Political Thought and Political History: Studies in Memory of Elie Kedourie*, edited by Elie Kedourie, Gammer M. Kostiner, and Joseph Shemesh Moshe. London: Frank Cass, 2003.

———. "The Role of Some Leading Arab Educators in the Development of the Ideology of Arab Nationalism." Dissertation, University of London, 1992.

Kahlenberg, Caroline. "The Star of David in a Cedar Tree: Jewish Students and Zionism at the American University of Beirut (1908–1948)." *Middle Eastern Studies* 55, no. 4 (2019): 570–89.

Kalekin-Fishman, Devorah. *Ideology, Policy, and Practice Education for Immigrants and Minorities in Israel Today.* Dordrecht: Springer Netherlands, 2004.

Kalisman, Hilary Falb. "Bursary Scholars at the American University of Beirut: Living and Practising Arab Unity." *British Journal of Middle Eastern Studies.* 42, no. 4 (2015): 599–617.

———. "Education Policy in Iraq: Competing Visions of the State." In *State and Society in Iraq: Citizenship under Occupation, Dictatorship and Democratization*, edited by Shamiran Mako, Fadi Dawood, and Benjamin Isakhan, 90–108. New York: Tauris, 2015.

———. "The Little Persian Agent in Palestine: Husayn Ruhi, British Intelligence and World War I." *Jerusalem Quarterly (Institute of Jerusalem Studies)*, no. 66 (2016): 65–74.

———. "Schooling the State: Educators in Iraq, Palestine and Transjordan: c. 1890–c. 1960." Dissertation, University of California, Berkeley, 2015.

Kanafani, Ghassan. *Palestine: The 1936–1939 Revolt.* London: Tricontinental Society, 1980.

Kassab, Elizabeth Suzanne. *Contemporary Arab Thought: Cultural Critique in Comparative Perspective.* New York: Columbia University Press, 2010.

Katul, Salim. *Al- 'Ulum al-Haditha: Khamsa Ajza lil-Sufuf al-Ibtida 'i* [Modern sciences: Five parts for the elementary classes]. Beirut: Matba 'at Sadir Rihani, 1946.

———. *'Ilm Al-Kimya al- 'Amali* [Practical chemistry]. Al-Quds: Matba 'at Bayt al-Quds, 1932.

———. *'Ilm al-Kimya al- 'Amali lil-Sufuf al-Thanawiyya al-Juz '* al-Thani al-Tab 'a al-Thaniyya [The science of practical chemistry for the secondary classes, part 2, second edition]. Al-Quds: al-Matba 'a al-ma 'iyya al-hayya, 1947.

Kayali, Hasan. *Arabs and Young Turks: Ottomanism, Arabism, and Islamism in the Ottoman Empire, 1908–1918.* Berkeley: University of California Press, 1997.

Kedourie, Elie. "The American University of Beirut." *Middle Eastern Studies* 3, no. 1 (1966): 74–90.

———. *Arabic Political Memoirs and Other Studies.* London: Frank Cass, 1974.

———. *In the Anglo-Arab Labyrinth: The Mcmahon-Husayn Correspondence and Its Interpretations, 1914–1939.* Cambridge: Cambridge University Press, 1976.

———. *Nationalism.* Oxford: Blackwell, 1993.

Khaddouri, Rose. "Suggestions for the Improvement of Instruction in the Urban Primary Schools of Iraq." Dissertation, Teachers College, Columbia University, 1951.

Khadduri, Majid. *Independent Iraq, 1932–1958: A Study in Iraqi Politics.* London: Oxford University Press, 1960.

———. *Republican Iraq; a Study in Iraqi Politics since the Revolution of 1958.* London: Oxford University Press, 1969.

Khalaf, Samir. "New England Puritanism and Liberal Education in the Middle East: The American University of Beirut as a Cultural Transplant." In *Cultural Transitions in the Middle East,* edited by Serif Mardin. Leiden: Brill, 1994.

Khalidi, Rashid. *The Iron Cage: The Story of the Palestinian Struggle for Statehood.* Boston: Beacon Press, 2006.

———. *The Origins of Arab Nationalism.* New York: Columbia University Press, 1991.

———. "Ottomanism and Arabism in Syria before 1914: A Reassessment." In *The Origins of Arab Nationalism,* edited by Rashid Khalidi. New York: Columbia University Press, 1991.

———. *Palestinian Identity: The Construction of Modern National Consciousness.* New York: Columbia University Press, 1997.

Khalidi, Walid. *Before Their Diaspora: A Photographic History of the Palestinians, 1876–1948.* Washington, DC: Institute for Palestine Studies, 1984.

———. "Al-Kulliya al- 'Arabiyya fi al-Quds: Khalifiyya, Tarikhiyya wa Natharat Mustaqballiya" [The Arab College in Jerusalem: Historical background and future vision]. *Majallat al-Dirasat al-Filistiniyya* 11, no. 44 (Fall 2000): 136–48.

Khams wa Saba 'un Sana 'ala Ta'sis al-Kulliyya al- 'Arabiyya fi al-Quds [Seventy-five years after the founding of the Arab College in Jerusalem]. Amman: Al-Bank al- 'Arabi, 1995.

Khoury, Dina Rizk. *State and Provincial Society in the Ottoman Empire: Mosul, 1540–1834.* Cambridge: Cambridge University Press, 1997.

———. "Ambiguities of the Modern: The Great War in the Memoirs and Poetry of the Iraqis." In *The World in World Wars: Experiences, Perceptions and Perspectives from Africa and Asia,* edited by Heike Liebau. Leiden: Brill, 2010.

Khulusi, Safa. "Ma 'ruf al-Rusafi in Jerusalem." *Journal of Palestine Studies* 22–23 (2005): 63–68.

Khuri-Makdisi, Ilham. *The Eastern Mediterranean and the Making of Global Radicalism, 1860–1914.* Berkeley: University of California Press, 2010.

Kimmerling, Baruch, and Joel S. Migdal. *The Palestinian People: A History*. Cambridge, MA: Harvard University Press, 2003.

Knudsen, Are. "Widening the Protection Gap: The Politics of Citizenship for Palestinian Refugees in Lebanon, 1948–2008." *Journal of Refugee Studies* 22, no. 1 (2009): 51–73.

Kozma, Liat. *Global Women, Colonial Ports: Prostitution in the Interwar Middle East*. Albany: State University of New York Press, 2017.

———. "Going Transnational: On Mainstreaming Middle East Gender Studies." *International Journal of Middle East Studies*. 48, no. 3 (2016): 574–77.

Krämer, Gudrun. *A History of Palestine: From the Ottoman Conquest to the Founding of the State of Israel*. Princeton, NJ: Princeton University Press, 2011.

Kunz, Josef L. "The United Nations Declaration of Human Rights." *American Journal of International Law* 43, no. 2 (1949): 316–23.

Kupferschmidt, Uri M. *The Supreme Muslim Council: Islam under the British Mandate for Palestine*. Leiden: Brill, 1987.

Lahiri, Shompa. *Indians in Britain: Anglo-Indian Encounters, Race and Identity, 1880–1930*. London: Frank Cass, 2000.

Lamaison, Pierre. "From Rules to Strategies: An Interview with Pierre Bourdieu." *Cultural Anthropology* 1, no. 1 (1986): 110–20.

Lawrence, Jon. "Paternalism, Class and the British Path to Modernity." In *The Peculiarities of Liberal Modernity in Imperial Britain*, edited by Simon Gunn, and James Vernon. Berkeley: Global, Area, and International Archive, University of California Press, 2011.

Lerner, Daniel. *The Passing of Traditional Society: Modernizing the Middle East*. New York: Free Press, 1968.

Lesch, Ann M. "Palestinians in Kuwait." *Journal of Palestine Studies* 20, no. 4 (1991): 42–54.

Lewis, Bernard. *The Arabs in History*. Oxford: Oxford University Press, 1993.

———. *The Emergence of Modern Turkey*. London: Oxford University Press, 2002.

Levy, Joseph M. "Red Propaganda Rife in Palestine: Communists Find a New Sphere of Activity among Men of British Military Garrisons." *New York Times*, April 18, 1930.

Likhovski, Assaf. *Law and Identity in Mandate Palestine*. Chapel Hill: University of North Carolina Press, 2006.

Lloyd, George Ambrose. *Egypt since Cromer*. London: Macmillan, 1933.

Lockman, Zachary. *Comrades and Enemies: Arab and Jewish Workers in Palestine*. Berkeley: University of California Press, 1996.

Lucas, Christopher J. "Arab Illiteracy and the Mass Literacy Campaign in Iraq." *Comparative Education Review* 25, no. 1 (1981): 74–84.

Lukitz, Liora. *Iraq: The Search for National Identity*. London: Routledge, 2006.

Lustick, Ian. *Arabs in the Jewish State: Israel's Control of a National Minority*. Austin: University of Texas Press, 1980.

Lutfiyya, Abdulla M. *Baytin, a Jordanian Village: A Study of Social Institutions and Social Change in a Folk Community*. The Hague: Mouton, 1966.

Lyman, Robert Gerrard Howard. *Iraq 1941: The Battles for Basra, Habbaniya, Fallujah and Baghdad*. Oxford: Osprey, 2005.

Macaulay, Thomas Babington, John Leonard Clive, and Thomas Pinney. *Selected Writings*. Classics of British Historical Literature., Chicago: University of Chicago Press, 1972.

Mack, Edward Clarence. *Public Schools and British Opinion since 1860: The Relationship between Contemporary Ideas and the Evolution of an English Institution*. New York: Columbia University Press, 1941.

Mahasina, Muhammad Husayn, Muhammad Salim Ghathayan Tarawina, Suleiman Dawud Tarawina, Khalil ʿAbd ʿAbd al-ʿAziz Karki, Zayd Ibn Shaakir, and ʿAbd al-Rahman ʿAtiyat. *Madrasat Al-Salt: Sira Wa-Masira* [The school of al-Salt: Biography and career]. Al-Karak: Jamiʿat Muʿta, ʿImadat al-Baʿth al-ʿIlmi wa-al- Dirasat al-ʿUlya, 1997.

Majlis al-Aʿyan al-Urduni. "Al-Majlis Al-Sabiqa" [Previous parliaments]. Jordanian Senate: Hashemite Kingdom of Jordan. Accessed March 20, 2015. http://www.senate.jo/content/%D8%A7%D9%84%D9%85%D8%AC%D8%A7%D9%84%D8%B3-%D8%A7%D9%84%D8%B3%D8%A7%D8%A8%D9%82%D8%A9.

———. "Dawlat Suleiman Al-Nabulsi" [The state of Suleiman al-Nabulsi]. Jordanian Senate: Hashemite Kingdom of Jordan. Accessed March 20, 2015. http://www.senate.jo/en/node/404.

———. "Maʿli Al-Said Dhawqan Hindawi" [His excellency Dhawqan Hindawi]." Jordanian Senate: Hashemite Kingdom of Jordan. Accessed March 20, 2015. http://www.senate.jo/en/node/380.

Makdisi, Ussama. *Artillery of Heaven: American Missionaries and the Failed Conversion of the Middle East*. Ithaca, NY: Cornell University Press, 2008.

———. "Reclaiming the Land of the Bible: Missionaries, Secularism, and Evangelical Modernity." *American Historical Review* 102, no. 3 (1997): 680–713.

Makiya, Kanan. *Republic of Fear: The Politics of Modern Iraq*. Berkeley: University of California Press, 2003.

Al-Marashi, Ibrahim Salama Sammy. *Iraq's Armed Forces: An Analytical History*. London: Routledge, 2009.

Marʿi, Sami Khalil. *Arab Education in Israel*. Contemporary Issues in the Middle East. Syracuse, NY: Syracuse University Press, 1978.

Massad, Joseph Andoni. *Colonial Effects: The Making of National Identity in Jordan*. New York: Columbia University Press, 2001.

Massey, W. T. *How Jerusalem Was Won: Being the Record of Allenby's Campaign in Palestine*. London: Constable, 1919.

Matar, Dina. *What It Means to Be Palestinian: Stories of Palestinian Peoplehood*. London: I. B. Tauris, 2011.

Matossian, Bedross. "Administrating The Non-Muslims and the 'Question Of Jerusalem' after the Young Turk Revolution." In *Late Ottoman Palestine: The Period of Young Turk Rule*, by Yuval Ben-Bassat and Eyal Ginio. London: Tauris, 2011.

Mattar, Philip. *Encyclopedia of the Palestinians*. New York: Facts on File, 2000.

Matthews, Roderic D., and Matta Akrawi. *Education in Arab Countries of the Near East: Egypt, Iraq, Palestine, Transjordan, Syria, Lebanon*. Washington, DC: American Council on Education, 1949.

Matthews, Weldon C. *Confronting an Empire, Constructing a Nation: Arab Nationalists and Popular Politics in Mandate Palestine*. New York: Tauris, 2006.

———. "Pan-Islam or Arab Nationalism? The Meaning of the 1931 Jerusalem Islamic Congress Reconsidered." *International Journal of Middle East Studies* 35, no. 1 (2003): 1–22.

Mayhew, Arthur. *Education in the Colonial Empire*. London: Longmans, Green, 1938.

Mazower, Mark. *Governing the World: The History of an Idea, 1815 to the Present*. New York: Penguin Books, 2013.

McNay, Lois. *Gender and Agency: Reconfiguring the Subject in Feminist and Social Theory*. Malden, MA: Blackwell: 2000.

Medding, Peter Y. *Mapai in Israel*. Cambridge: Cambridge University Press, 1972.

Mekhon Shiloah le-heker ha-Mizrah ha-tikhon, ve-Afrikah (Universitat Tel Aviv). *Middle East Contemporary Survey*. Vol. 10. New York: Holmes & Meier, 1986.

Mendales, Ben. "A House of Cards: The Arab Satellite Lists in Israel, 1949–77." *Israel Affairs* 24, no. 3 (2018): 442–59.

Merkaz le-mehkar ʾal shem Shiloah Reuven. *Middle East Record*. Vol. 2. Jerusalem: Reuven Shiloah Research Center, Israel Program for Scientific Translations, 1961.

Metzer, Jacob. *The Divided Economy of Mandatory Palestine*. Cambridge: Cambridge University Press, 1998.

Meyer, Fernon. *Al-Mabadi ʾal-Fiziya* [Principles of physics], translated by ʾIzz al-Din al-Tanoukhi. Dar al-Salam, Baghdad, 1927.

Migdal, Joel S. *State in Society: Studying How States and Societies Transform and Constitute One Another*. Cambridge: Cambridge University Press, 2010.

Miller, Ylana N. "From Village to Nation: Government and Society in Rural Palestine, 1920–1948." University of California, Berkeley, 1975.

———. *Government and Society in Rural Palestine, 1920–1948*. Austin: University of Texas Press, 1985.

Mitchell, Timothy. *Colonising Egypt*. Berkeley: University of California Press, 1988.

———. *Rule of Experts: Egypt, Techno-Politics, Modernity*. Berkeley: University of California Press, 2012.

———. "Society, Economy and the State Effect." In *The Anthropology of the State: A Reader*, edited by Aradhana Sharma, and Akhil Gupta. Malden, MA: Blackwell, 2010

Moed, Kamal. "Educator in the Service of the Homeland: Khalil Al-Sakakini's Conflicted Identities." *Jerusalem Quarterly*, no. 59 (2014): 68.

Mohl, Sophia Berger. *History of the Israel (Palestine) Association of University Women*. Jerusalem: International Federation of University Women, 1950.

Mokyr, Joel. *The Oxford Encyclopedia of Economic History*. Oxford: Oxford University Press, 2003.

Moreh, Shmuel, and Zvi Yehuda. *Al-Farhud: The 1941 Pogrom in Iraq*. Jerusalem: Vidal Sassoon International Center for the Study of Antisemitism, Babylonian Jewry Heritage Center, Hebrew University Magnes Press, 2010.

Moubayed, Sami M. *Steel & Silk: Men and Women Who Shaped Syria 1900–2000*. Seattle, WA: Cune, 2006.

Mufti, Malik. *Sovereign Creations: Pan-Arabism and Political Order in Syria and Iraq*. Ithaca, NY: Cornell University Press, 1996.

Musawi, Muhsin Jasim. "Dhu Al-Nun Ayyub." In *Essays in Arabic Literary Biography*, edited by Roger Allen. Wiesbaden: Harrassowitz Verlag, 2009.

———. *Reading Iraq: Culture and Power in Conflict*. London: I. B. Tauris, 2006.

Mushtaq, Talib. *Awraq Ayyami* [Pages from my life]. Beirut: Dar al-Taliʾa lil Tibaʾa wa-al-Nashr, 1968.

Nadan, Amos. *The Palestinian Peasant Economy under the Mandate: A Story of Colonial Bungling.* Cambridge, MA: Center for Middle Eastern Studies, Harvard University Press, 2006.

Nakhleh, Emile A. "The Anatomy of Violence: Theoretical Reflections on Palestinian Resistance." *Middle East Journal* 25, no. 2 (1971): 180–200.

Nardi, Noah. "Zionism and Education in Palestine." Dissertation, Teachers College, Columbia University, 1934.

———. *Zionism and Education in Palestine.* New York: AMS Press, 1972.

Nashabeh, Hisham. "Al-Kulliya al-'Arabiyya fi al-Quds" [The Arab College in Jerusalem]. In *Dirasat Filastiniyya: Majmu'at Abhath Wudi'at Takriman lil-Duktur Qustantin Zurayk*, ed. Hisham Nashabeh. Studia Palaestina: Studies in Honour of Constantine K. Zurayk. Beirut: Mu'assasat al-Dirasat al-Filastiniyya, 1988.

Nassar, Gertrude, Bea Wagner, and Joanne Nicgorski. *My Life in Palestine: Memoirs of Gertrude Nassar, 1888–1976.* Valders, WI: Journal Press, 1978.

Nassar, Maha. *Brothers Apart: Palestinian Citizens of Israel and the Arab World.* Stanford, CA: Stanford University Press, 2017.

Norris, Jacob. *Land of Progress: Palestine in the Age of Colonial Development, 1905–1948.* Oxford: Oxford University Press, 2013.

Odeh, Sadiq 'Ibrahim. "The Arab College in Jerusalem 1918–1948: Recollections." *Jerusalem Quarterly* 3, no. 1 (Summer 2000): 48–58.

Office of the Cultural Attaché, Embassy of Iraq. *Education in Iraq.* Washington, DC: Office of the Cultural Attaché, Embassy of Iraq, 1957.

Okkenhaug, Inger Marie. "'She Loves Books & Ideas, & Strides Along in Low Shoes Like an Englishwoman': British Models and Graduates from the Anglican Girls' Secondary Schools in Palestine, 1918–48." *Islam and Christian-Muslim Relations* 13, no. 4 (2002): 461–79.

Oldenburg, Veena Talwar. *The Making of Colonial Lucknow, 1856–1877.* Princeton, NJ: Princeton University Press, 1984.

Al-Omari, Aieman Ahmad. "Total Quality Management in Public and Private Jordanian Universities: A Comparative Study." In *Towards an Arab Higher Education Space: International Challenges and Societal Responsibilities: Arab Regional Conference on Higher Education, Cairo, May 31–June 2, 2010: Proceedings*, UNESCO Regional Bureau for Education in the Arab States, and Bechir Lamine, 373–88. Beirut: UNESCO, 2010.

Owen, Roger, and Şevket Pamuk, *A History of Middle East Economies in the Twentieth Century.* London: Tauris, 1998.

Palestinian Academic Society for the Study of International Affairs. "Abdul Hadi, Awni (1889–1970)." Accessed April 15, 2015. http://www.passia.org/palestine_facts/personalities/alpha_a.htm.

———. "'Anabtawi, Wasfi (1903–1984)." Accessed April 17, 2014. http://www.passia.org/palestine_facts/personalities/alpha_a.htm.

———. "Al-Husseini, Abdul Qader 1907–1948)." Accessed April 17, 2014. http://www.passia.org/palestine_facts/personalities/alpha_h.htm.

———. "Dr. Khalil Totah (1886–1955)." Accessed April 17, 2014. http://www.passia.org/images/personalities/totah-khalil/khalil-text.htm.

———. "Zu'aiter, Akram (1909–1996), Palestine Personalities." Accessed April 17, 2014. http://www.passia.org/palestine_facts/personalities/alpha_z.htm.

Pedersen, Susan. *The Guardians: The League of Nations and the Crisis of Empire*. Oxford: Oxford University Press, 2015.

Penrose, Stephen B. L. *That They May Have Life: The Story of the American University of Beirut, 1866–1941*. New York: Trustees of the American University of Beirut, 1941.

Picaudou, Nadine, "The Historiography of the 1948 Wars." Accessed March 20, 2015. http://www.massviolence.org/The-Historiography-of-the-1948-War.

Plascov, Avi. *The Palestinian Refugees in Jordan 1948–1957*. London: Frank Cass, 1981.

Pool, David. "From Elite to Class: The Transformation of Iraqi Leadership, 1920–1939." *International Journal of Middle East Studies* 12, no. 3 (1980): 331–50.

Porath, Yehoshua. *The Emergence of the Palestinian Arab National Movement*. Vol. 2. London: Frank Cass, 1977.

———. *In Search of Arab Unity, 1930–1945*. London: Frank Cass, 1986.

Provence, Michael. *The Great Syrian Revolt and the Rise of Arab Nationalism*. Austin: University of Texas Press, 2005.

———. *The Last Ottoman Generation and the Making of the Modern Middle East*. Cambridge: Cambridge University Press, 2017.

———. "Late Ottoman State Education." In *Religion, Ethnicity and Contested Nationhood in the Former Ottoman Space*, edited by Jørgen S. Nielsen. Leiden: Brill, 2012.

Pursley, Sara. "Building the Nation through the Production of Difference." In *Writing the Modern History of Iraq: Historiographical and Political Challenges*, edited by Jordi Tejel Gorgas and Riccardo Bocco. London: World Scientific, 2012.

———. "Education for Real Life: Pragmatist Pedagogies and American Interwar Expansion in Iraq." In *The Routledge Handbook of the History of the Middle East Mandates*, edited by Cyrus Schayegh and Andrew Arsan. Routledge History Handbooks. London: Routledge, 2015.

———. *Familiar Futures: Time, Selfhood, and Sovereignty in Iraq*. Stanford Studies in Middle Eastern and Islamic Societies and Cultures. Stanford, CA: Stanford University Press, 2018.

———. "The Stage of Adolescence: Anticolonial Time, Youth Insurgency, and the Marriage Crisis in Hashimite Iraq." *History of the Present* 3, no. 2 (2013): 160–97.

Qasim, ʿAbd al-Karim. "Speech by Major General ʿAbd Al-Karim Qasim, Iraqi Prime Minister and Commander in Chief of the Armed Forces. Delivered at the Congress of Arab Lawyers," November 26, 1958. In *The Arab States and the Arab League; a Documentary Record*, edited by Muhammad Khalil, League of Arab States. Beirut: Khayats, 1962.

Qasimi, Zafir. *Maktab ʿAnbar: Suwar wa-dhikrayat min hayatina al-thaqafiyya wa-al-siyasiyya wa-al-ijtima ʿiyya* [Maktab ʿAnbar: Pictures and memories from our cultural, political and social life]. Beirut: al-Matbaʿa al-Kathulikiyya, 1964.

Qato, Mezna. "A Primer for a New Terrain: Palestinian Schooling in Jordan, 1950." *Journal of Palestine Studies* 48, no. 1 (2018): 16–32.

Qaysi, Mahir. "Youth Education in Iraq and Egypt, 1920–1980: A Contribution to Comparative Education within the Arab Region, 1920–1980." Catholic University of Leuven, Belgium, 1983.

Al-Qazzaz, Ayad. "Power Elite in Iraq—1920–1958: A Study of the Cabinet." *MUWO The Muslim World* 61, no. 4 (1971): 267–83.

Al-Qishtayni, Muhammad Naji. *Min ʿUyun al-Shiʿr: Mukhtarat* [From the eyes of poetry: An anthology]. Baghdad: Dar al-Jumhuriyya, 1968.

Radwan, Abd Allah, Sadik I. Odeh, and Mustafa Wahbi al-Tall. *Arar, the Poet and Lover of Jordan.* Amman: Greater Amman Municipality, 1999.

Ranjan, Rakesh Kumar, and Prakash C. Jain. "The Decline of Educational System in Iraq." *Journal of Peace Studies* 16, no. 1–2 (January–June 2009). http://www.icpsnet.org/pdf /1251368150.pdf.

Rashdan, ʾAbdullah Zahi, and Omar Ahmad Mohammad Hamshari. *Nizam al-Tarbiyya wa-al-Taʿlim fi al-Urdun, 1921–2002* [The education system in Jordan, 1921–2002]. Amman: Dar Safa lil-Nashr wa-al-Tawziʿ, 2002.

Al-Rashoud, Talal. "Modern Education and Arab Nationalism in Kuwait, 1911–1961." Dissertation, University of London, School of Oriental and African Studies, 2017.

Reeder, David. "The Reconstruction of Secondary Education in England, 1869–1920." In *The Rise of the Modern Educational System: Structural Change and Social Reproduction, 1870–1920,* edited by Detlef K. Müller, Fritz Ringer, and Brian Simon. Cambridge: Cambridge University Press, 1989.

Reich, Bernard. *Political Leaders of the Contemporary Middle East and North Africa: A Biographical Dictionary.* New York: Greenwood Press, 1990.

Rejwan, Nissim. *The Last Jews in Baghdad: Remembering a Lost Homeland.* Austin: University of Texas Press, 2004.

Renton, James. "Changing Languages of Empire and the Orient: Britain and the Invention of the Middle East, 1917–1918." *Historical Journal* 50, no. 3 (September 2007): 645–57.

Ricks, Thomas M., and Khalil Totah. *Turbulent Times in Palestine: The Diaries of Khalil Totah, 1886–1955.* Jerusalem: Institute for Palestine Studies; PASSIA, 2009.

Riley, F. B. "Education in a Backward Country." *Phi Delta Kappan* 7, no. 4 (1925): 1–5.

Robinson, Shira. *Citizen Strangers: Palestinians and the Birth of Israel's Liberal Settler State.* Stanford, CA: Stanford University Press, 2013.

Rogan, Eugene L. *Frontiers of the State in the Late Ottoman Empire: Transjordan, 1850–1921.* Cambridge: Cambridge University Press, 1999.

———"The Political Significance of an Ottoman Education: Maktab ʾAnbar Revisited." In *From the Syrian Land to the States of Syria and Lebanon,* ed. Thomas Philipp and Christoph Schumann, 77–94. Beirut: Orient Institute, 2004.

Rogan, Eugene L., and Avi Shlaim. *The War for Palestine: Rewriting the History of 1948.* New York: Cambridge University Press, 2001.

Rogan, Eugene L. and Tariq Tell. *Village, Steppe and State: The Social Origins of Modern Jordan.* London: British Academic Press, 1994.

Rouhana, Nadim. "The Political Transformation of the Palestinians in Israel: From Acquiescence to Challenge." *Journal of Palestine Studies* 18, no. 3 (1989): 38–59.

Rousso-Schindler, Steven Neil. "Israeli and Palestinian National Narratives: National and Individual Constructions, Social Suffering Narratives, and Everyday Performances." Dissertation, University of Southern California, 2007.

Rugh, A. Douglas. "Issues and Trends in Arab Teacher Education." *Journal of Teacher Education* 7, no. 4 (1956): 316–22.

Ruhi, Ali. "Obituary: Husayn Ruhi." *The Bahá'í World: an International Record* 13, no. B (1960): 938–39.

Al-Rusafi, Ma'ruf and 'Abd al-Hamid Rashudi. *Al-Rasa'il al-Mutabadala bayna al-Rusafi wa-Mu'asirihi* [Letters exchanged between Al-Rusafi and his contemporaries]. Beirut: al-Mu'assasa al-'Arabiyya lil-Dirasat wa-al-Nashr, 1994.

Rush, A. de L., and Jane Priestland. *Records of Iraq, 1914–1966*. 15 vols. Slough, UK: Archive Editions, 2001.

Russell, Mona L. "Competing, Overlapping, and Contradictory Agendas: Egyptian Education under British Occupation, 1882–1922." *Comparative Studies of South Asia, Africa and the Middle East* 21, no. 1 (2005): 50–60.

Ryzova, Lucie. *The Age of the Efendiyya: Passages to Modernity in National-Colonial Egypt*. Oxford: Oxford University Press, 2014.

Sa'di, Ahmad H., and Lila Abu-Lughod. *Nakba: Palestine, 1948, and the Claims of Memory*. New York: Columbia University Press, 2007.

Said, Edward W. "Afterword: The Consequences of 1948." In *The War for Palestine: Rewriting the History of 1948*, edited by Eugene L. Rogan and Avi Shlaim. New York: Cambridge University Press, 2001.

———. *Culture and Imperialism*. New York: Knopf, 1993.

Sakakini, Hala. *Jerusalem and I: A Personal Record*. Amman: Economic Press, 1990.

Al-Sakakini, Khalil. *Dalil al-Awal lil-Jadid al-Awal fi al-Afaba* [The first guide to the new, the first in the alphabet]. Jerusalem: Mutba'at Bayt al-Muqaddis, 1934.

———. "Khalil al-Sakakini's Ottoman Prison Diaries: Damascus (1917–1918)," translated by Jennifer Peterson. *Jerusalem Quarterly*, no. 2 (January 2004): 7–23.

———. "Such Am I, O World." In *Anthology of Modern Palestinian Literature*, edited by Salma Khadra Jayyusi, 672. New York: Columbia University Press, 1992.

———. *Yawmiyyat Khalil al-Sakakini: Yawmiyyat, Rasail wa-Taammulat. Al-Kitab al-Thalith. Ikhtibar al-Intidab wa-As'ilat al-Huwiyya, 1919–1922* [The diaries of Khalil al-Sakakini: diaries, letters and reflections.The third book: Testing the mandate and identity questions]. Vol. 3, edited by Akram Musallam. Ramallah: Markaz Khalil al-Sakakini al-Thaqafi: Mu'assasat al-Dirasat al-Muqaddasiya, 2004.

———. *Yawmiyyat Khalil Al-Sakakini: Yawmiyyat, Rasail Wa-Taammulat. al-Kitab al-Thani l-Nahda al-Urthudhuksiyya, al-Harb al-'Uzma, al-Nafy ila Dimashq, 1914–1918* [The diaries of Khalil al-Sakakini: Diaries, letters and reflections. The second book: Orthodox renaissance, World War I, exile to Damascus]. Vol. 2, edited by Akram Musallam. Ramallah: Markaz Khalil al-Sakakini al-Thaqafi: Mu'assasat al-Dirasat al-Muqaddasiyya, 2003.

Samha, M. "The Impact of Migratory Flows on Population Changes in Jordan: A Middle Eastern Case Study." *International Migration* 28, no. 2 (1990): 215–28.

Samiuddin, Abida. *Administrative Development in the Arab World: A Case Study of Iraq*. Delhi: Mittal, 1985.

Samuel, Edwin. *A Lifetime in Jerusalem: The Memoirs of the Second Viscount Samuel*. London: Vallentine, Mitchell, 1970.

Sasson, Victor. *Memoirs of a Baghdad Childhood*. Bloomington, IN: Iuniverse, 2011.

Sassoon, Joseph. *Economic Policy in Iraq, 1932–1950*. London: Frank Cass, 1987.

Satia, Priya. "Developing Iraq: Britain, India and the Redemption of Empire and Technology in the First World War." *Past and Present* 197, no. 1 (2007): 211–55.

Sawalha, Jacky. *Voices: The Pioneering Spirit of Women in Jordan*. Amman: Jordan Ahli Bank, 2012.

Sawdayee, Maurice M. "The Impact of Western European Education on the Jewish Millet of Baghdad, 1860–1950." Dissertation, New York University, 1981.

Sayigh, Yusuf ʿAbd Allah and Rosemary Sayigh. *Yusif Sayigh: Arab Economist and Palestinian Patriot: A Fractured Life Story*. Cairo: American University in Cairo Press, 2015.

Schayegh, Cyrus. *The Middle East and the Making of the Modern World*. Cambridge, MA: Harvard University Press, 2017.

Schleifer, Abdullah. "Izz Al-Din Al-Qassam: Preacher and Mujahid." In *Struggle and Survival in the Modern Middle East*, edited by Edmund Yaghoubian and David N. Burke, 137–51. Berkeley: University of California Press, 2006.

Schneider, Suzanne. *Mandatory Separation: Religion, Education, and Mass Politics in Palestine*. Stanford, CA: Stanford University Press, 2018.

Schumann, Christoph. "The Generation of Broad Expectations: Nationalism, Education, and Autobiography in Syria and Lebanon, 1930–1958." In *The Making of the Arab Intellectual: Empire, Public Sphere and the Colonial Coordinates of Selfhood*, edited by Dyala Hamzah. New York: Taylor & Francis, 2012.

Segev, Tom. *One Palestine, Complete: Jews and Arabs under the British Mandate*, translated by Haim Watzman. New York: Metropolitan Books, 2000.

Seikaly, Sherene. *Men of Capital: Scarcity and Economy in Mandate Palestine*. Stanford, CA: Stanford University Press, 2015.

Al-Seqal, Lufti, and Khalil Hindawi. *Al-Mukhatar fi al-Qiraʾa wa al-Inshaʾ wa al-Muta laʾa wa al-Istithahar* [Selections in reading, composition, perusal, and recitation]. Damascus: Jamʿiya al-ʿIlmiyya al-Suriyya lil-Maʿlumatiya, 1949.

Seth, Sanjay. *Subject Lessons: The Western Education of Colonial India*. Durham, NC: Duke University Press, 2007.

Seton, C. R. W., and Transjordan. *Legislation of Transjordan, 1918–1930: Translated from the Arabic, Including the Laws, Public Notices, Proclamations, Regulations, Etc*. London: For the govt. of Transjordan by the Crown agents for the Colonies, 1931.

Shah, Hemant. *The Production of Modernization: Daniel Lerner, Mass Media, and the Passing of Traditional Society*. Philadelphia: Temple University Press, 2011.

Shahid, Serene. *Jerusalem Memories*. Beirut: Naufal, 1999.

Sharabi, Hisham. "Crisis of the Intelligentsia in the Middle East." *Muslim World* 47, no. 3 (1957): 189.

———. *Embers and Ashes: Memoirs of an Arab Intellectual*. Northampton, MA: Olive Branch Press, 2008.

Sharkey, Heather J. *Living with Colonialism: Nationalism and Culture in the Anglo-Egyptian Sudan*. Berkeley: University of California Press, 2003.

Shawkat, Sami. "The Profession of Death." In *Arab Nationalism, an Anthology*, edited by Sylvia Kedourie. Berkeley: University of California Press, 1962.

Shemesh, Moshe. *The Palestinian National Revival In the Shadow of the Leadership Crisis, 1937–1967*. Bloomington: Indiana University Press, 2018.

Shepherd, Naomi. *Ploughing Sand: British Rule in Palestine, 1917–1948*. New Brunswick, NJ: Rutgers University Press, 2000.

Shusterman, Richard. *Bourdieu: A Critical Reader*. Oxford: Blackwell, 2011.

Silverfarb, Daniel. *Britain's Informal Empire in the Middle East a Case Study of Iraq, 1929–1941*. New York: Oxford University Press, 1986.

Simon, Reeva S. "The Imposition of Nationalism on a Non-Nation State: The Case of Iraq During the Interwar Period, 1921–1941." In *Rethinking Nationalism in the Arab Middle East*, edited by James P. Jankowski and Israel Gershoni. New York: Columbia University Press, 1997.

———. *Iraq between the Two World Wars: The Militarist Origins of Tyranny*. New York: Columbia University Press, 2004.

———. "The Teaching of History in Iraq before the Rashid Ali Coup of 1941." *Middle Eastern Studies* 22, no. 1 (1986): 37–51.

Sirignano, Rosanna. "Mother and Child in Palestine: the Artas material in Hilma Granqvist's Nachlass at the Palestine Exploration Fund." In *Studi Interculturali*, 159–81. Trieste: Mediterránea, Centro di Studi Interculturali, 2013.

Skelton, Christine, Becky Francis, and Lisa. Smulyan. *The Sage Handbook of Gender and Education*. Thousand Oaks, CA: Sage, 2006.

Sluglett, Peter. *Britain in Iraq: Contriving King and Country*. Library of Middle East History, vol. 12. London: Tauris, 2007.

———. "The Iraqi Communist Party 1934–1979." In *The Middle East Online Series 2: Iraq 1914–1974*. Reading, PA: Thomson Learning EMEA, 2006.

———. "The Urban Bourgeoisie and the Colonial State: The Iraqi and Syrian Middle Classes between the Two World Wars." In *The Role of the State in West Asia*, edited by Annika Utas Bo Rabo. Istanbul: Swedish Research Institute in Istanbul, 2005.

Smith, Anthony D. *Nationalism and Modernism: A Critical Survey of Recent Theories of Nations and Nationalism*. London: Routledge, 2008.

Snobar, Ibrahim Mahmud. *Tadhakkurat Ibrahim Snobar* [The recollections of Ibrahim Snobar], edited by Ali Jarbawi and Lubna ʿAbd al-Hadi. Bir Zayt: Markaz Dirasat wa-Tawthiq al-Mujtamaʿ al-Filastini, Jamiʿat Bir Zayt, 1992.

Somekh, Sasson. *Baghdad, Yesterday: The Making of an Arab Jew*. Jerusalem: Ibis Editions, 2007.

Somel, Selçuk Aksin. *The Modernization of Public Education in the Ottoman Empire, 1839–1908: Islamization, Autocracy, and Discipline*. The Ottoman Empire and Its Heritage, vol. 22. Leiden: Brill, 2001.

Sousa, Ahmed. *Hayati fi Nisf Qarn* [My life in half a century]. Al-Tabʿa. Baghdad: Dar al-Shuʾun al-Thaqafiyya al-ʿAmma, 1986.

Soysal, Yasemin Nuhoglu, and David Strang, "Construction of the First Mass Education Systems in Nineteenth-Century Europe." *Sociology of Education* 62, no. 4 (1989): 277–88.

Spencer, Sarah. *Migrants, Refugees and the Boundaries of Citizenship*. London: Institute for Public Policy Research, 1995.

Starrett, Gregory. *Putting Islam to Work: Education, Politics, and Religious Transformation in Egypt*. Berkeley: University of California Press, 2010.

Staudt, Ida Donges. *Contemporary Issues in the Middle East: Living in Romantic Baghdad: An American Memoir of Teaching and Travel in Iraq, 1924–1947*. Syracuse, NY: Syracuse University Press, 2012.

Stone, Lawrence. "Prosopography." *Daedalus* 100, no. 1 (1971): 46–79.

Storrs, Ronald. *Orientations*. London: Nicholson & Watson, 1943.

Sulaiman, Halid A. *Palestine and Modern Arab Poetry*. London: Zed, 1984.

Susser, Asher. *On Both Banks of the Jordan: A Political Biography of Wasfi Al-Tall*. Portland, OR: Frank Cass, 1994.

Swedenburg, Ted. *Memories of Revolt: The 1936–1939 Rebellion and the Palestinian National Past*. Minneapolis: University of Minnesota Press, 1995.

———. "The Role of the Palestinian Peasantry in the Great Revolt (1936–9)." In *The Israel/Palestine Question*, edited by Ilan Pappé, 129–67. London: Routledge, 1999.

Swirski, Shlomo. *Politics and Education in Israel Comparisons with the United States*. New York: Garland, 1999.

Szyliowicz, Joseph S. *Education and Modernization in the Middle East*. Ithaca, NY: Cornell University Press, 1973.

Takriti, Shakir ʿAli. *Mudhakkirati wa-dhikrayati–hadhihi* [My diary and my memories-these]. Baghdad: Dar al-Shuʾun al-Thaqafiyya al-ʿAmma "Afaq ʿArabiyya," 1997.

Tal, Lawrence. "Britain and the Jordan Crisis of 1958." *Middle Eastern Studies* 31, no. 1 (1995): 39–57.

Talhami, Ghada Hashem. *Palestinian Refugees: Pawns to Political Actors*. New York: Nova Science, 2003.

———. *Syria and the Palestinians: The Clash of Nationalisms*. Gainesville: University Press of Florida, 2001.

Al-Tall, Ahmad Yousef. *Education in Jordan: Being a Survey of the Political, Economic and Social Conditions Affecting the Development of the System of Education in Jordan 1921–1977*. Islamabad: National Book Foundation, 1979.

Al-Tall, Mustafa Wahbi, and Mahmud Mutlaq. *Mustafa's Journey: Verse of Arar, Poet of Jordan*. Irbid: Yarmouk University, 1988.

Al-Tall, Mustafa Wahbi, Ziyad Saleh al-Zouʿabi, and Ussama Hassan ʿAaish. *Watha'iq Mustafa Wahbi al-Tall (ʿArar) 1899–1949 al-Majlad al-Awwal* [The documents of Mustafa Wahbi al-Tall (ʿArar) 1899–1941 the first volume]. Yarmouk: Jamiʿat al-Yarmouk, 2012.

Al-Tall, Wasfi. *Kitabat fi al-Qadaya al-ʿArabiyya* [Writings on the Arab cause]. Amman: Wizarat al-Thaqafa, 2010.

Tamari, Salim. "The Great War and the Erasure of Palestine's Ottoman Past." In *Transformed Landscapes: Essays on Palestine and the Middle East in Honour of Walid Khalidi*, edited by Camille Mansour and Leila Tarazi Fawaz, 105–37. Cairo: American University in Cairo Press, 2009.

———. "Jerusalem's Ottoman Modernity: The Times and Lives of Wasif Jawhariyyeh." *Jerusalem Quarterly File*, no. 9 (2000): 5–27.

———. *Mountain against the Sea: Essays on Palestinian Society and Culture*. Berkeley: University of California Press, 2008.

———. "The Short Life of Private Ihsan: Jerusalem 1915." *Jerusalem Quarterly*, no. 30 (Spring 2007): 26–58.

Al-Tamimi, Rafiq. *Tarikh al-ʿAsr al-Hadir* [History of the current era]. Jaffa: al-Maktaba al-ʿAsriyya, 1946.

Tarbush, Mohammad A. *The Role of the Military in Politics: A Case Study of Iraq to 1941*. London: Kegan Paul International, 1982.

Tauber, Eliezer. *The Emergence of the Arab Movements*. Hoboken, NJ: Taylor and Francis, 2013.

Tell, Tariq. *The Social and Economic Origins of Monarchy in Jordan*. Middle East Today. New York: Palgrave Macmillan, 2013.

Thompson, Elizabeth F. *Colonial Citizens: Republican Rights, Paternal Privilege, and Gender in French Syria and Lebanon*. New York: Columbia University Press, 2000.

———. *Justice Interrupted: The Struggle for Constitutional Government in the Middle East*. Cambridge, MA: Harvard University Press, 2013.

———. "The 1948 Wathba Revisited: Comrade Fahd and the Mass Appeal of Iraqi Communism." *International Journal of Contemporary Iraqi Studies* 12, no. 2 (2018): 127–45.

Tibawi, Abdul Latif. *Arab Education in Mandatory Palestine: A Study of Three Decades of British Administration*. London: Luzac, 1956.

———. "Educational Policy and Arab Nationalism in Mandatory Palestine." *Die Welt des Islams* 4, no. 1 (1955): 15–29.

———. *English-Speaking Orientalists: A Critique of Their Approach to Islam and Arab Nationalism*. Geneva: Islamic Centre, 1965.

———. *Islamic Education: Its Traditions and Modernization into the Arab National Systems*. London: Luzac, 1972.

———. *A Modern History of Syria, Including Lebanon and Palestine*. New York: St. Martin's Press, 1969.

———. "Primary Education and Social Change in Underdeveloped Areas (Some of the Lessons of Mandatory Palestine)." *International Review of Education* 4, no. 4 (1958): 503–9.

———. "Religion and Educational Administration in Palestine of the British Mandate." *Die Welt des Islams* 3, no. 1 (1954): 1–14.

"Tibawi Trust Award." University of London (School of Oriental and African Studies). Accessed April 13, 2015. https://www.soas.ac.uk/registry/scholarships/tibawi-trust-award.html.

Tignor, Robert L. "The 'Indianization' of the Egyptian Administration under British Rule." *American Historical Review* 68, no. 3 (1963).

Totah, Khalil. "The Contribution of the Arabs to Education." Teachers College, Columbia University, 1926.

———. "Education in Palestine." *Annals of the American Academy of Political and Social Science* 164 (1932): 155–66.

Tramontini, Leslie. "Poetry in the Service of Nation Building? Political Commitment and Self-Assertion." In *Writing the Modern History of Iraq: Historiographical and Political Challenges*, edited by Jordi Tejel, 459–74. Singapore: World Scientific Publishing, 2012.

Tripp, Charles. *A History of Iraq*. Cambridge: Cambridge University Press, 2002.

Troch, Pieter. *Nationalism and Yugoslavia: Education, Yugoslavism and the Balkans before World War II*. London: Tauris, 2015.

Trouvé-Finding, Susan. "Teaching as a Woman's Job." *History of Education (Tavistock)* 34, no. 5 (2005): 483–96.

ʿUbaydat, Mahmud. *Al-Mujahid al-ʿAqid Mahmud al-Musa al-ʿUbaydat: batal maʿarik al-Quds al-qadima wa-farisuha, 1914–1988* [The warrior colonel Mahmud al-Musa al-ʿUbaydat: Hero of the battles of the old city of Jerusalem, and its knight]. Amman: N.p., 1999.

UNESCO. *World Survey of Education* 3, no. 3. Paris: UNESCO, 1961.

United Nations, Department of Economic and Affairs Social. *Growth of the World's Urban and Rural Population, 1920–2000*. New York: United Nations, 1969.

United Nations, Relief Works Agency for Palestine Refugees in the Near East. *Report of the Commissioner-General of the United Nations Relief and Works Agency for Palestine Refugees in the Near East*. 1957.

United Nations. "The United Nations and the Human Person: Universal Declaration of Human Rights." Accessed May 14, 2015. http://www.un.org/en/documents/udhr/.

Universal House of, Justice. *The Bahá'í World: An International Record*. Vol. 13: *1954–1963*. Haifa, Israel: Universal House of Justice, 1971.

University of Baghdad, "Maruf al Rusafi Foundation Ceremony of Al-Tifayidh School—1928." https://commons.wikimedia.org/wiki/File:Maruf_al_Rusafi_foundation_ceremony_of_Al-Tifayidh_School_-_1928.jpg.

Uzri, ʿAbd al-Karim. *Tarikh fi Dhikrayat al-ʿIraq, 1930–1958* [A history of Iraq in memories, 1930–1958]. Beirut: Markaz al-Abjadiyya lil-Saff al-Taswiri, 1982.

Vinogradov, Amal. "The 1920 Revolt in Iraq Reconsidered:The Role of Tribes in National Politics." *International Journal of Middle East Studies* 3, no. 2 (1972): 123–39.

Wagner, Heather Lehr. *Iraq*. New York: Chelsea House, 2009.

Watenpaugh, Keith David. *Being Modern in the Middle East: Revolution, Nationalism, Colonialism, and the Arab Middle Class*. Princeton, NJ: Princeton University Press, 2006.

Whidden, James. *Monarchy and Modernity in Egypt: Politics, Islam and Neo-Colonialism between the Wars*. London: I. B. Tauris, 2013.

Whitehead, Clive. *Colonial Educators: The British Indian and Colonial Education Service 1858–1983*. London: Tauris, 2003.

———. "The Nestor of British Colonial Education: A Portrait of Arthur Mayhew Cie, Cmg (1818–1948)." *Journal of Educational Administration and History* 29, no. 1 (1997): 51–76.

Wickham, Carrie Rosefsky. *Mobilizing Islam: Religion, Activism, and Political Change in Egypt*. New York: Columbia University Press, 2003.

Wien, Peter. *Iraqi Arab Nationalism: Authoritarian, Totalitarian, and Pro-Fascist Inclinations, 1932–1941*. London: Routledge, 2006.

———. "The Long and Intricate Funeral of Yasin Al-Hashimi: Pan-Arabism, Civil Religion, and Popular Nationalism in Damascus 1937." *International Journal of Middle East Studies* 43, no. 2 (2011): 271–92.

———. "Watan and Rujula: The Emergence of a New Model of Youth in Interwar Iraq." In *Youth and Youth Culture in the Contemporary Middle East*, edited by Jørgen Simonsen Bæk. Proceedings of the Danish Institute in Damascus 3. Aarhus: Aarhus University Press, 2005.

Wilson, Mary C. *King Abdullah, Britain, and the Making of Jordan*. Cambridge: Cambridge University Press, 1987.

Wolf, Judith L. "Selected Aspects in the Development of Public Education in Palestine 1920–1946." University Microfilms International, 1981.

Woodsmall, Ruth. *Moslem Women Enter a New World*. New York: AMS Press, 1975.

Yasin, Mohammed Hussain. "Education for All Iraqi Youth: Reorganization of Secondary Education in Iraq." Dissertation, Teachers College, Columbia University, 1947.

Yousif, Bassam. *Human Development in Iraq: 1950–1990*. London: Routledge, 2012.

Yusuf, Abdulqadir Mohammad. "The British Educational Policy in the Arab Public Schools of Palestine during the Mandate." Dissertation, Indiana University, 1956.

Zaki, Saniha Amin, and Ellen Jawdat. *Memoir of an Iraqi Woman Doctor*. N.p.: CreateSpace, 2014.

Ziadeh, Nicola. "Journeys in Palestine during the British Colonial Period." *Jerusalem Quarterly*, no. 51 (2012): 65–74.

Ziadeh, Nicola, and A. Jarrah Nuri. *Hawla al-ʾAlam fi 76 ʾAman: Rihlat Muthaqqaf Shami fi Asiya wa-Urubba wa-al-Shamal al-Ifriqi 1916–1992* [Around the World in 76 Years: The journeys of a Levantine intellectual in Asia, Europe, and North Africa]. Beirut: al-Muassasat al-ʾArabiyya lil-Dirasat wa-al-Nasr, 2007.

Zuʾaytir, Akram. *Min Mudhakkirat Akram Zuʾaytir: Bawakir al-Nidal: 1909–1935* [From the memoirs of Akram Zuʾaytir: the beginning of the struggle: 1909–1935]. Beirut: al-Muassasat al-ʾArabiyyat lil-Dirasat wa-al-Nashr, 1994.

Zuʾaytir, Akram, and Bayan Nuwayhid Hut. *Wathaʾiq al-Haraka al-Wataniyya al-Filastiniyya, 1918–1939: Min Awraq Akram Zuʾaytir* [Documents of the Palestinian national movement, 1918–1939: From the papers of Akram Zuʾaytir]. Beirut: Muʾassasat al-Dirasat al-Filastiniyya, 1984.

Zuʿaytir, Akram, and Darwish al-Miqdadi. *Tarikhuna bi-Uslub Qisasi* [Our history in stories]. Beirut: Dar al-Katib al-ʾArabi, 1979.

INDEX

Italicized page numbers indicate illustrations.
For Arabic surnames, initial hyphenated articles (al-) are disregarded in alphabetization.

interwar era, 54–183; education during (*see*
education, interwar and mandate-era);
habitus in, 98–139; politics in, 9, 161–64;
and self-determination, 9–10, 99. *See also*
mandates, British/mandate era; *specific
topics, e.g.,* nationalism; transnationalism
Iran, 13, 171
Iraq, 1–5, 7–10, 13–14, 18–19, 65, 218–20, 222–23;
Anglo-Iraqi Treaties, 134, 211, 222; Anglo-
Iraqi War, 10, 129, 171; Arab nationalism
in, 151, 176, 189, 205; AUB graduates employed by, 114; Communist Party in (ICP),
163–64, 200–201, 210–13; coup in, 175, 212;
education in (*see* Iraq, education in *as
separate entry, below*); *effendiyya* in, 101;
and gender differentiation, 156; Hashemite monarchy (and its overthrow) in, 10,
123, 150, 171, 175–79, 183, 188, 201–2, 212;
independent government of, 18, 185–86,
188; intellectuals in, 93, 149; interwar,
130–31, 140, 144; and Iraqi unity, 78, 142;
July revolution in, 176; League of Nations,
admittance to, 150, *152*; mandate for, 1,
100, 149; nationalism in, 13–14, 137; and
oil revenue, 187, 194, 223; Ottoman-era, 44;
pan-Arabism in, 127, 154, 158–60, 175–78,
201; peasants in, 182; poets of, 18n43, 101–2,
122–24, 137n128; politics in, 41, 134, 211;
prime ministers of, 3, 173; republic of, 172,
188–89, 212; sanctions against, 223; and
sovereignty, 100, 108n28. *See also* Baghdad; Basra; Baʾathism; Mosul; Qasim,
Abdul-Karim; *specific topics, e.g.,* American University of Beirut: alumni of
Iraq, education in, 1–10, 100, *188–189*, 194–95,
197, 219–20, 222–23; Bir Idhren, school in,
68–69; government school teachers in,
75–79, 155; and inspections, 204–5; and
literacy, 182–83, 223; mandate Department of
Education and, 65, 74–75, 90, 145–46, 159;
mandate-era, 10, 51, 63–69; al-Markaziyya
School in, 63, 102, 134, 137; and Ministry
of Education, Iraqi, 74, 88, 107, 115, 120,
128, 130–31, 134, 137n128, 149, 151, 153,

159–60, 184, 189, 206–7, 217; and noncitizen
teachers, 1, 100, 120–21, 201–2; Sharqat,
village school at, 68–69; and teachers'
colleges, 105; and teachers/educators,
75–79, 158, 161, 207; and teachers' unions,
184, 210–13; Teaching Service Law of 1951,
200; Al-Tifayidh School in, *123*; women
teachers in, 78–79, 121, 210; Zakho School
in, 67–68; and Zuʾaytirʾ as teacher, 1, 147.
See also collective action by educators;
textbooks: as transnational; *specific topics,
e.g.,* educator politicians
Iraqi authors, 128
Iraqi Communist Party, 163–64, 200–201,
210–13
Iraqi Teachers Association, 184, 210–13
Iraq Petroleum Company, 114
Irbid, Jordan, 45–46, 48, 51, 88, 199, 221
irredentism, 13
ʾIsa, Muhieddin Haj, 82, 90–93
ISIS (al-Dawla al-Islamiyya fi al-ʾIraq wa
al-Sham), 13
Islam, 13, 21, 28–34, 36–38, 44–45, 54–55,
90–91; and Arab-Islamic history/culture,
117, 125–26, 129n102, 132–33, 154; and
Christian school attendance, 77; and
katatib, 29–30, 33–34, 38; and Muslim
girls'/women's schooling, 62, 70, 85–87,
108–13; and Muslim unity, 178; and
Muslim women teachers, 86, 108–13; and
Ottomanism, 52; and Sharia courts,
91n137; Shiʾite, 30, 65, 77–78, 90, 137, 159;
Sunni, 29, 41, 45, 76–78. *See also* Qurʾan
Islamic Girls School in Jerusalem, 86–87
Islamism, 13, 51, 143
Israel, 2, 5, 9, 14, 18–19, 186, 188–92, 214–16,
218; Jewish citizens of, 180–81, 214; Pales-
tinian citizens of, 14, 180–81, 191–92; and
pan-Arabism, 180–81. *See also* Balfour
Declaration; Haifa; Jerusalem; Palestine;
Palestinians, Arab; Zionism
Israel, education in, 188–92, 202, 214–16,
223–24; council on Arab education in, 215;
and the education law of 1953, 190–91;

CPSIA information can be obtained
at www.ICGtesting.com
Printed in the USA
JSHW030828050822
28608JS00001BA/1